# THE OLD CATHOLIC MOVEMENT,
## ITS ORIGINS AND HISTORY

# THE
# OLD CATHOLIC MOVEMENT

## Its Origins and History

*By the Rev.*
## C.B. Moss, D.D.

*Second Edition*

the apocryphile press
BERKELEY, CA
www.apocryphile.org

apocryphile press
BERKELEY, CA


Apocryphile Press
1700 Shattuck Ave #81
Berkeley, CA 94709
www.apocryphile.org

Cover is a woodcut of Archbishop Dominique-Marie Varlet, artist
unknown.

For sale in the USA only. Sales prohibited in the UK.
Printed in the United States of America

ISBN 0-9764025-9-9

DEDICATED TO THE MEMORY OF
FRANCIS KENNINCK
18TH ARCHBISHOP OF UTRECHT

# PREFACE TO FIRST EDITION

My first knowledge of the Old Catholic Churches came through my finding Dr. J. M. Neale's *History of the So-called Jansenist Church of Holland* in the Union Library at Oxford when I was an undergraduate. The book fascinated me, and I could hardly put it down.

My first personal contact with the Old Catholics was during a visit to Bishop Prins when I was in the Netherlands in October 1913. I was present at all the Old Catholic Congresses between the wars, from Berne in 1925 to Zürich in 1938.

The Old Catholic Movement cannot be understood unless it is recognized as the heir of Gallicanism, of Febronianism, and in some respects of Port Royal. It is for this reason that I have begun the story with the Conciliar movement, which culminated in the Councils of Constance and Basle.

It appears to me that Gallicanism, in all its forms, has been proved both by history and logic to be a failure. The papal claims cannot be permanently combined with Gallicanism, either as a constitutional and decentralizing movement, or as a privileged position for particular churches. The Vatican Council was the inevitable outcome of the system by which the Roman communion had been governed ever since Trent. Thenceforward " Old Catholicism " was for Latin Christians the only alternative to Ultramontanism.

It is impossible to acknowledge all the help which I have received through many years in writing this book.

But I must especially thank the Very Rev. A. S. Duncan-Jones, Dean of Chichester, who lent me some scarce books which are original sources for the history of the Church of Utrecht; the late Rev. Prof. van Riel, who corrected the Dutch chapters for me; the Rev. Hugo Flury, who did the same for the Swiss chapters, and supplied me with many books on the history and constitution of

the Swiss movement; Miss Ruth Clark (an American, quite
unknown to me), who presented me with a copy of her valuable
book on Port Royal; the Rev. W. G. Warwick, who gave me an
important German book; Canon G. V. Jourdan, of Trinity
College, Dublin, and the present Archbishop of Utrecht, Mgr.
Andreas Rinkel.

C. B. Moss.

# TABLE OF CONTENTS

# CHAPTER I

# THE DEVELOPMENT OF THE PAPAL CLAIMS

THE Old Catholic Churches are a group of self-governing national churches, united by their acceptance of the Declaration of Utrecht (1889) as their dogmatic basis; for this reason their members sometimes refer to them as the Churches of the Union of Utrecht. They are made up of three different groups: (1) the Old Catholic Church of Holland, which retains its organic continuity with the medieval see of Utrecht, and which was separated finally from Rome by the consecration of Archbishop Steenoven (1724); (2) the Old Catholic Churches of Germany, Switzerland, Austria and Czecho-Slovakia, for the most part German-speaking, which were formed in consequence of the revolt against the Vatican Council (1870); (3) the Old Catholic movements which sprang up later in Slavonic nations, the Czechs, the Yugo-Slavs, and the Poles in Europe and America.

There are now seven Old Catholic Churches: those of Holland, Germany, Switzerland, Austria, Czecho-Slovakia, and Yugo-Slavia, and the "Polish National Catholic Church", the headquarters of which is in America.[1]

The Old Catholic Movement is a revolt against the claims of the Papacy, but within Latin Christendom. Its position must be distinguished from that of the Eastern churches, which have never been either Latin or subject to the Papacy; from that of the Anglican churches, which were once both Latin and Papalist, but have ceased to be either, and have established in the English-speaking world a third form of Catholic Christianity, neither Latin nor Eastern; and from that of Evangelical Christianity, in all its forms, which lays emphasis rather on the personal experience of the individual than on his membership in the visible Church. The Old Catholic Movement, on the other hand, is the heir of the anti-papal movements within Latin Christendom. I shall begin, therefore, with a short sketch of the development of the claims of the Papacy, and an account of the various forms which the opposition to them within the Latin

[1] *Ekklesia*, No. 11, *Die Altkatholische Kirche*, pp. 4–10.

ecclesiastical system took; for otherwise the reader would not be able to envisage the background by which the origin of the Old Catholic Movement must be explained.

The claims of the Papacy, upon which its gigantic power and influence have been, and still are, based, may be distinguished as follows:

(1) The primacy of Christendom: the see of Rome ranks first among all the bishoprics. This is sometimes called the " primacy of honour ".

(2) Supremacy, sometimes called the "primacy of jurisdiction ". These two claims must be carefully distinguished, though a primacy often has a tendency to become a supremacy. The Archbishop of Canterbury has the primacy, by general consent, among all Anglican bishops; but he has no jurisdiction outside his own province and certain missionary dioceses, therefore no supremacy. Under a system of primogeniture, primacy is the right of the eldest brother; but the right of a father over his children is a supremacy.

(3) The claim that communion with (and therefore, because of (2), obedience to) the Roman Pontiff is necessary to salvation.

(4) The claim that the Pope, when he speaks *ex cathedra* on faith or morals, as pastor and teacher of all Christians, possesses " that infallibility with which the Divine Redeemer willed that His Church should be furnished in the definition of doctrine on faith and morals " (Vatican Council).

(5) The claim that the Pope has full and supreme power of jurisdiction (not merely the duty of inspection and direction) over all churches and all members of the Church, corporately and individually.

These five claims are based on Divine right: it is this claim to Divine right which is the source both of the strength of the Papacy and the persistent opposition to it. A strong case, at some periods an overwhelming case, can be made out for the Papacy on grounds of expediency alone; but a Papacy which should base its claims on expediency would not be the actual Papacy. If the Divine right on which the papal claims are based is untrue, or even uncertain, the claims themselves, and the whole gigantic structure based upon them, are indefensible.

Two other papal claims, though of great historical importance, are of a different character.

(6) The claim to patriarchal jurisdiction over the whole

" western " part of the Church. The division of the Church (within the Roman Empire) into five patriarchates is due to the political conditions of the fifth century, and has no meaning in the modern world. The four venerable patriarchates of the East are now reduced to small dimensions, and the other patriarchates which have in modern times been established in the East (those of Russia, Yugo-Slavia, and Roumania) are really national churches. In the Roman Communion to-day the title of " patriarch " is a mere honour conferred on the occupants of certain Sees (Lisbon, Venice, Goa), or else it is the title of the heads of those churches of the Eastern rites which Rome has set up in opposition to the ancient Eastern churches (the Maronite Church is the one instance of such a church without any " opposite number " outside the Roman Communion). The original patriarchate of Rome was confined to the " suburbicarian dioceses "—that is, central and southern Italy with Sicily, Sardinia, and Corsica: it included neither Milan nor Carthage, still less Gaul, Spain, or Britain. There were many churches which did not belong to any patriarchate: as Cyprus, and later Georgia, in the East, Milan (which did not submit to Rome till 1059), and many others in the West. The division into five patriarchates was made by the Council of Chalcedon (451), and the enlargement of a patriarchate required the decision of a general council. But no general council ever enlarged the Roman patriarchate. The patriarchal jurisdiction of Rome, therefore, was, strictly speaking, limited to central and southern Italy and the islands. It was extended later to the whole of Latin Christendom, but that extension was part of the development of the Papacy. Those who reject the developed papal claims have no reason for regarding themselves as bound by the patriarchal jurisdiction of Rome outside its original limits. If the former are usurped, so is the latter.[1]

(7) The claim to temporal power. This took two forms, which must not be confused. The medieval Popes claimed that the emperors and all other lords in Christendom held their dominions as a grant from the Pope; this claim was based on the text, " Lord, here are two swords " (St. Luke 22. 38), which. were interpreted as the spiritual and temporal authority, which were both given to St. Peter; also on the legendary " Donation of Constantine " to Pope Sylvester, and on the fact that Charles

[1] E. Denny, *Papalism*, section 1201 ff.

the Great received his crown from the Pope (800). This claim carried with it the claim to depose kings, exercised for the last time against Elizabeth of England in 1570, which was one of the chief causes of the English Reformation. But in modern times the Papacy has tacitly dropped these claims (though the Syllabus was believed by many to be a revival of them, see Chapter XIV).

The other form of the claim to temporal power is the claim to the possession of certain territories in Italy, originally bestowed on the Pope by Pepin,[1] King of the Franks, in 754,[2] and taken away by the Kingdom of Italy in 1870. Recently the Pope has surrendered his claim to these territories, all but the small area of the Vatican City, by the Concordat with Italy in 1931.

But the position of the Pope as a temporal Italian prince was for centuries closely connected with opposition to his spiritual claims. " The Papal States were a veritable body of death to the true spiritual life of the greatest institution in human history." [3]

Belief in the Divine right of the Papacy must be distinguished from a belief that the Papacy was providentially ordered, with which it has sometimes been confused. All who believe in the Divine government of human affairs may frankly admit that the Papacy was necessary for the development of the Church, and indeed of European civilization, at a particular period; but this is not the same thing as to believe that the Papacy was designed by our Lord to be a permanent and necessary part of His religion. If the Papacy was merely " by Divine Providence ", it may have been intended for a particular period, or a particular region, and its ultimate disappearance, as an institution no longer needed, may be equally " by Divine Providence " .

The belief in the Divine origin of the Papacy and of the rights attributed to it is based upon three passages in the Gospels.

(1) " Thou art Peter, and upon this rock I will build My Church: and the gates of Hades shall not prevail against it. And I will give unto thee the keys of the kingdom of heaven: and whatsoever shall be bound on earth shall be bound in heaven: and whatsoever thou shalt loose on earth shall be loosed in heaven " (St. Matt. 16. 18–19).

---

[1] Pepin was induced to make this grant by the forged "Donation of Constantine".
[2] M. Deanesley, *History of the Medieval Church*, p. 65; Janus (Döllinger), *The Pope and the Council*, p. 133.
[3] A. L. Smith, *Church and State in the Middle Ages*, p. 192.

(2) " Simon, Simon, behold, Satan asked to have you that he might sift you as wheat: but I have prayed for thee, that thy faith fail not: and do thou, when once thou hast turned again, strengthen thy brethren " (St. Luke 22. 31).

(3) The threefold charge to St. Peter, " Feed My lambs "; " tend My sheep "; " feed My sheep " (St. John 21. 15–17).

The method of proof-texts is unsatisfactory: as we shall see, the theory based on these passages is contrary to the general teaching of the Gospels.  But even if the proof-text method be accepted, these passages do not prove the theory which is based upon them.

If that theory is to be accepted, the following three points must be certain.  (It is not enough that they should be merely probable: they must be sufficiently certain to be regarded as historic facts which cannot reasonably be denied.)

(1) Christ gave to St. Peter all the rights which the Popes in later times have claimed as theirs by Divine right; and St. Peter exercised all these rights in the apostolic Church for the rest of his life.

(2) St. Peter became Bishop of Rome, in the sense of a territorial bishop.

(3) St. Peter left all these rights to the Bishops of Rome, who were his only successors.

If any one of these points is proved to be untrue, or even uncertain, the whole theory that the papal claims are of Divine right falls to the ground.

Of the three passages which are regarded as the charter of the Papacy, the second and third may be dealt with briefly. No one reading these two passages without any knowledge of the history or the claims of the Papacy, or even without a strong bias in favour of the papal claims, would ever suppose that they referred to anything but St. Peter's denial: the one being a prophecy of his repentance, and the other his public restoration. And this is, in fact, the interpretation given by the Fathers, without exception: for instance, by St. John Chrysostom, Homily 82. on St. Matthew; St. Ambrose, *On the Psalms*, 43. 41, where the passage in St. Luke is treated as a prophecy of St. Peter's denial and repentance, without any reference to any permanent office bestowed upon him. The quotations from the Fathers which are sometimes put forward as supporting their interpretation of this passage are derived from the Pseudo-

Isidorian Decretals and other spurious writings. The earliest genuine case of this interpretation of the passage is found in a letter of Pope Agatho to the Third Council of Constantinople, A.D. 680.[1]

The passage in St. John 21. 15 was interpreted by St. Ambrose and St. Augustine, St. Gregory Nazianzen and St. Cyril of Alexandria, as the "healing of the triple denial". Others, such as St. Basil and St. John Chrysostom, regard it as a charge to St. Peter as the typical bishop; his successors, in their view, are not the bishops of Rome only, but all bishops. There seems to be no patristic support for the later Roman interpretation of this passage.[2]

So the whole weight of the claims of the Papacy to Divine right rests on one passage, the famous "Thou art Peter", etc. This passage occurs only in St. Matthew, and its historical character is not altogether certain. For most modern scholars are agreed that the First Gospel is later than the Second, and is largely based upon it, and that the passages which occur in the First Gospel only are the least trustworthy stratum in the Synoptic Gospels. Now, the incident here recorded appears in a shorter form in St. Mark 8. 27, and St. Luke 9. 8, which omits the section beginning, "And I say unto thee that thou art Peter". If, as early tradition relates, St. Mark was the interpreter of St. Peter, and if this passage was, as is claimed, of supreme dogmatic importance, it is strange that St. Peter, if he was the teacher of the whole Church in a special sense, as is claimed, should not have taken care that it should appear in the Gospel which was written under his direction; on the other hand, the expression "bind and loose" could not have been understood by the Gentiles for whom St. Mark wrote. It is to be observed that this is the only passage in which our Lord is stated to have explicitly foretold the building of His Church; but I do not think that this is necessarily a sound argument against its historical character.

If we assume that this saying is historical (as I am quite ready to do), it by no means follows that it has anything to do with the Papacy. The Fathers held five different opinions as to the meaning of the passage. Seventeen Fathers held that the rock referred to was St. Peter; eight, that it was the Apostles, whom St. Peter represented; forty-four, that it was the faith which

[1] E. Denny, 146-157.          [2] Denny, 131-141.

St. Peter had confessed (with these are reckoned the Liturgy of St. James, and the Collect for the Vigil of St. Peter and St. Paul in the Roman Missal); sixteen, that the rock was Christ; and Origen and others, that it was the whole body of the faithful.[1] Some of the Fathers, as St. Ambrose, St. Augustine, and St. Cyril of Alexandria, gave different interpretations in different places. But the earliest germ of the theory that this passage refers to the rights claimed by the Bishops of Rome appears in a letter from Pope Siricius to Bishop Himerius of Tarragona, written in 385. St. Leo, the great fifth-century Pope, took up the idea, and it became generally accepted in Latin Christendom. But for more than three centuries it was quite unknown. The power of the keys, as Origen, St. Ambrose, the Venerable Bede, and many other Fathers taught, was given to all the Apostles (St. Matt. 18. 18), not to St. Peter only.[2]

Nor is there any evidence that St. Peter occupied any such position in the Church as is claimed by the Popes. Our Lord firmly refused to give any of His Apostles a position superior to the others, though they more than once disputed which should be the greatest. The power of binding and loosing was given to all the Apostles (St. Matt. 18. 18); they were to sit on twelve thrones, judging the twelve tribes of Israel (St. Matt. 19. 28, St. Luke 22. 30). According to the Fourth Gospel (which, even if we do not accept it as historical, represents what was universally believed at the end of the first century), the representative of the ascended Christ, the teacher of His disciples when He was gone, the true Vicar of Christ, was not any human being, but the Divine Paraclete (St. John 16. 13). However, St. Cyprian, St. Basil, and other Fathers call all bishops " Vicars of Christ ".[3]

After the Ascension, St. Peter appears as the leader and spokesman of the Apostles, as he had also done during our Lord's ministry. " Go tell His disciples and Peter," said the Angel at the tomb (St. Mark 16. 7). In the earlier chapters of the Acts the primacy of St. Peter is very clear. In any assembly or society there must be one leader, and in the earliest days of the Church that leader was unquestionably St. Peter. But there is no evidence that he had a supremacy, still less that he was infallible or had control over all Christians corporately and individually. On the contrary, " when the apostles which were at Jerusalem heard that Samaria had received the word of God,

---

[1] Denny, 52 ff.      [2] Denny, 114-130.      [3] Denny, 38.

they sent unto them Peter and John " (Acts 8. 14). When the apostles and elders at Jerusalem heard of the baptism of Cornelius, St. Peter had to explain his action to them. Clearly St. Peter was not the master of the Church. When the question whether Gentile Christians were to be circumcised came up for settlement, St. Peter was not asked for his infallible decision; but a council was called, and St. Peter was not even in the chair (attempts to show that he was have failed). St. Paul tells the Corinthians, " I reckon that I am not a whit behind the very chiefest apostles" (2. Cor. 11. 5; 12. 11); he resists St. Peter to the face, " because he stood condemned " (Gal. 2. 11). But if St. Peter had no supremacy or infallibility himself, he could not pass them on to his successors. If we accept the interpretation of St. Matt. 16. 18, that St. Peter is the rock, he is so as being the first in order of the foundations of the Church (cf. Rev. 21. 14), but in that capacity he could have no successors.

The universal tradition that St. Peter went to Rome and was martyred there is probably correct; but there is hardly any contemporary evidence for his visit. The reference to " Babylon " in 1 St. Pet. 5. 13 is usually supposed to refer to Rome, but some scholars deny that St. Peter wrote this epistle. Apart from this, the evidence for St. Peter's presence at Rome consists mainly of four passages: an allusion in St. Clement's Epistle to the Corinthians, ch. 5 (A.D. 96, unless, with Edmundson, we place this letter in A.D. 70); another in St. Ignatius (Epistle to the Romans 4.), who says, " I do not command you like Peter and Paul "; and definite statements by Dionysius of Corinth (165),[1] and St. Irenæus (185).[2] All these couple St. Peter with St. Paul as the two organizers of the Church at Rome. There is also some evidence from archæology. But while we may accept, with Salmon, Gore, Denny, and other anti-papal writers, the tradition that St. Peter visited Rome and was martyred there, and that he and St. Paul together were the joint-founders of the Roman Church, it does not follow that St. Peter was Bishop of Rome in the later sense. This is not stated by any writer earlier than Hippolytus in his lost *Chronicon* quoted by Eusebius, and by St. Jerome, who is the earliest extant authority for the later legend that St. Peter was Bishop of Rome for twenty-five years. The tradition of the second century was that Linus

[1] Eusebius, *Ecclesiastical History*, ii. 25.
[2] Irenæus, *Against Heresies*, iii. 1.

was the first Bishop of Rome, and was consecrated by St. Peter and St. Paul together, as is clearly stated by St. Irenæus, who lived for a considerable period at Rome.[1] Dionysius of Corinth also ascribes the planting of the Roman Church to St. Peter and St. Paul. It seems incredible that St. Peter was or had been at Rome when St. Paul wrote his Epistle to the Romans. Bishop Lightfoot says, " If silence can ever be regarded as decisive, its verdict must be accepted in this case." [2] The assumption that when St. Paul said " lest I should build on another man's foundation " (Rom. 15. 20), he meant that the Roman Church was another man's foundation, and that man St. Peter, is mere speculation.

The evidence shows, then, that St. Peter, though he probably visited Rome and was martyred there, was never Bishop of Rome; indeed, it is doubtful whether diocesan bishops existed so early, except at Jerusalem. But it is essential to the papal claims to show that St. Peter was Bishop of Rome, not merely that he happened to be there when the persecution of Nero broke out.

Lastly, the theory that the Roman bishops were successors of St. Peter in an unique sense, and derived their primacy, as well as all the other rights which have been based upon it, from St. Peter, belongs to a much later period. The earlier Fathers held that all bishops were the successors of St. Peter; and when St. Cyprian,[3] St. Jerome,[4] St. Augustine,[5] and others speak of the chair of Peter, they mean, not the Roman see, but the episcopal office.

We find, then, that not one of the three points, every one of which must be certain if the papal claim to Divine right is to be accepted, is even probable. The selection from the evidence which I have given above is only a very small part of the whole. The Papacy has no claim to Divine right: it is a purely human institution. As such, it was for many centuries a beneficent and even necessary institution; but, like other human institutions, it may outlive its usefulness.

The primacy of the Roman see goes back to the earliest times: and it has never been repudiated by any part of the Church, even by those which have rejected most strongly the papal supremacy and the Divine origin of the primacy. It

---

[1] Irenæus, iii. 23; cf. Denny, 475.
[2] Bishop Lightfoot, *St. Clément of Rome*, vol. ii, p. 91.
[3] Denny, 544-573.          [4] Denny, 586-597.
[5] Denny, 598-651.

was inevitable that the church which possessed the tombs of
St. Peter and St. Paul, and was situated in the capital of the
Empire, should have a primacy of honour.  But before the fourth
century it had nothing more.  The famous passage in St. Irenæus,
which is extant only in a Latin translation, " Ad hanc ecclesiam
propter potentiorem principalitatem necesse est omnem convenire ecclesiam, hoc est, eos qui sunt undique fideles, in qua
semper ab his, qui sunt undique, conservata est ea quae est ab
apostolis traditio ", is quoted, as by the Vatican Council, to
show that St. Irenæus held that the sovereignty of the Roman
Church compelled all other local churches to agree with it.  But
the words " convenire ad hanc ecclesiam " mean, not " agree
with this Church ", but " resort to this Church ", as F. W.
Puller has shown,[1] and his interpretation is to some extent supported by Roman Catholic scholars such as Funk.  Others,
referred to by Puller, are Thomasius, Waterworth, and even
Bishop Bonner.[2]  Dr. T. W. Jalland in his Bampton Lectures
accepts the common Roman interpretation, but does not answer
Puller's criticism.

Other incidents sometimes mentioned as proving the supremacy
of the Bishop of Rome, such as Victor's excommunication of the
Asiatic sees,[3] and the Emperor Aurelian's decision that the
property of the see of Antioch should belong to the bishop recognized by the bishops of Rome and Italy,[4] so far from proving
the existence of the supremacy, prove that it was then unknown.

The reign of Constantine marks a turning-point in the history
of the Roman see, as of the whole Church.  Constantine changed
Christianity from a persecuted to a privileged religion; and he
transferred the capital of the Empire from Rome to Constantinople.  The Bishop of Rome no longer held a position of danger,
but one of great worldly importance: " make me Bishop of
Rome ", said the pagan official Prætextatus to Pope Damasus,
" and I will turn Christian." [5]  The Roman Emperors no longer
lived at Rome, after 476 not even in Italy; and the Popes
inherited much of their authority and responsibility.  Under
Theodosius (379–95) it became illegal to hold any religion other
than orthodox Christianity.  Church and State were no longer

---

[1] F. W. Puller, *The Primitive Saints and the See of Rome*, pp. 19–35;  Denny,
494–525;  B. J. Kidd, *Roman Primacy*, p. 15.
[2] For Funk's interpretation, see Denny, 1233.
[3] Denny, 532.                                    [4] Denny, 1264–1265.
[5] W. Bright, *The Age of the Fathers*, vol. i, p. 363.

separate societies; the medieval synthesis of Church and Empire had begun. The authority of the Roman see was greatly increased by its steadfast orthodoxy during the Christological conflicts of the fourth and fifth centuries, and by the need for some universally recognized centre of authority during the barbarian invasions, when all civilized institutions in Western Europe were falling to pieces. Thus the original primacy passed gradually into a supremacy.

The appellate jurisdiction (that is, the right to be appealed to) of the Bishop of Rome had previously been confined to the *suburbicarian* provinces (central and southern Italy and the islands); the Council of Sardica, 343, gave the Bishop of Rome the right to judge accusations against bishops only; this canon was afterwards quoted, by mistake, as a canon of Nicæa. This right was extended to the whole western Empire, first by Valentinian I, between 367 and 372,[1] by his son Gratian in 382, and with greatly increased powers by Valentinian III in 445.[2] The latter rescript was issued when St. Leo was Pope, and it was his ability and pertinacity that led to the great increase of the papal powers and claims at this period. It was not very long before the jurisdiction originally bestowed by the Emperor was claimed as belonging to the Pope as successor of St. Peter. This claim was more fully developed by St. Gregory the Great (590–604), who was assisted by the conditions of his age; but his jurisdiction did not extend to the Celtic churches, which were outside the Empire, nor to any of the Eastern churches.

During the whole of this period there was rivalry between the sees of Old Rome and New Rome (Constantinople). On the theological issues Rome was almost invariably right, though we may speculate whether a less intransigent attitude towards Monophysitism on the part of St. Leo might not have prevented the Egyptian schism, and perhaps even saved the eastern provinces from the Arab conquest. In the Church-State which the Roman, or rather Byzantine, Empire had now become, Rome stood for the principle of the independence of the spiritual authority of the Church from civil interference; Constantinople, for the consecration of the whole of life, including civil government. Thus, while the Papal theologians ultimately came to hold that all authority, even in·civil matters, is derived from the Pope, the Byzantine theologians held that the Emperor derived his

---

[1] F. W. Puller, p. 144.                    [2] Denny, 206.

authority direct from God and was supreme, as Sovereign of the Christian Empire, over all persons and causes within his dominions—the same claim which Henry VIII and his successors made for the Kings of England.

There does not appear to be any evidence that anyone in this period believed the Pope to be infallible. Pope Liberius, in 357, signed an Arian formula, and even condemned St. Athanasius.[1] Zosimus seems to have coquetted with Pelagianism.[2] Vigilius vacillated in the controversy of the Three Chapters, showing by his conduct that the theory of papal infallibility was unknown to him, as it was to the Fifth General Council which condemned the Three Chapters.[3] The history of the province of Aquileia, which refused to accept the condemnation of the Three Chapters, and remained in schism, with a patriarch of its own, for 150 years[4] (a relic of this independence still survives in the title of Patriarch of Venice), shows that the theory that communion with Rome is essential to salvation was not then known. On many occasions Constantinople was out of communion with Rome: whether she was right or wrong in the reason for the schism, it is clear that she did not regard communion with the Roman see as necessary to membership of the Catholic Church. The case of Pope Honorius, condemned as a heretic by the Sixth General Council, and by all his Roman successors down to the eleventh century (Liber Diurnus Pontificum Romanorum), shows still more plainly that the theory of papal infallibility was at that time unknown.[5]

The next stage in the development of the papal claims is the ninth century. Just before it began, Pope Leo III had crowned Charles the Great, and set up the Roman Empire of the Germans in opposition to the Roman Empire of the Byzantine Greeks; from this event was derived the later claim that the Pope was the feudal superior of the Emperor. At some period between 829 and 853 appeared the series of forged papal letters known as the Pseudo-Isidorian Decretals. A decretal is an official letter from the Pope to a bishop; the earliest known genuine decretal was written by Siricius to Himerius of Tarragona in 385. About 853 a long series of decretals, attributed to

[1] Denny, 758–769. That Liberius was not under constraint is proved by his own statement under oath to Valens and Ursacius, *Ep. Liberii in S. Hilar. Fragm.*, vol. iv, S.6.
[2] Denny, 770–781.       [3] Denny, 934–968.
[4] H. St. L. B. Moss, *Birth of the Middle Ages*, p. 116.
[5] Denny, 782–799.

the Roman bishops from St. Clement in 95 to Melchiades in 314, was produced by someone in France who pretended that they had been collected by St. Isidore, a well-known Spanish bishop of the previous century. It has long been universally agreed that all these documents are forgeries. But they were accepted as genuine by Pope Nicholas I (though he must have known that no such decretals existed in the Roman archives), and used by him against Hincmar of Rheims and against the Greek churches. Moreover, these decretals, having become generally accepted as genuine, were used as sources by the codifiers of Western Canon Law. Before their spuriousness was recognized, they had done their work by impressing both law and public opinion with the belief that the papal supremacy dated from the earliest times.[1] It was at this period that the pallium, formerly given to leading bishops as a mark of honour, came to be regarded as the necessary means of conveying juris-diction to an archbishop.[2] It was at this period, too, that the dispute broke out between Nicholas I of Rome and Photius I of Constantinople, which was the forerunner of the final breach of communion in 1054.

The great increase of papal power which took place in the eleventh century under the influence of Hildebrand (Pope Gregory VII) was, as far as spiritual authority was concerned, rather the making effective what already existed in theory than the setting up of new rights. The protests against papal usurpa-tions, which from the thirteenth century onwards became stronger and stronger, were protests against temporal, not spiritual, claims. The great period of the medieval Papacy, which began with Gregory VII, ended with Boniface VIII, who had explicitly laid down that " it is necessary to the eternal salvation of every human being that he should be subject to the Roman Pontiff ", and whose death, due to the ill-treatment he had received, led to the flight of his successor to Avignon. From this time the secularizing and corruption of the Papacy proceeded apace. Because the whole administration of the Church was now centred in the papal court, where the vested interests of the officials prevented any reforms, men began to wonder whether there was any way of escaping from a sovereignty whose Divine right no one in Latin Christendom disputed, but whose practical consequences were so disastrous.

[1] Denny, 228-242.          [2] Denny, 1288 ff.

# CHAPTER II

# THE CONCILIAR MOVEMENT

THE end of the fourteenth century was a period when revolutionary ideas were widespread, and when great social changes were threatened. The medieval synthesis of Church and Empire, now 1,000 years old, was beginning to show signs of wear. One hundred and fifty years before, the Popes had won their great victory over the Emperors by destroying the House of Hohenstaufen; and the taxes which they had raised for the purpose had created in the minds of the English, hitherto the most devoted subjects of Rome, a dislike of papal interference which continues to this day. The Papacy was now confronted, not by a single Empire, but by a group of national states. From 1308 to 1378 the Popes lived at Avignon, and the Papacy was an appanage of France, and thereby lost the respect of Europe. The return of the Pope to Rome in 1378, under the influence of St. Catherine of Siena, was followed by the Great Schism of the West. For forty years there were two rival Popes, for the latter part of the period three. Each claimed to be the only true Pope, and excommunicated all who adhered to his rivals. Not only did different kingdoms take different sides, but every diocese and every monastery contained an Urbanist and a Clementine party. While the Papacy was becoming more and more discredited, strange new forms were arising. In 1354 the Black Death had decimated Europe and destroyed the economic basis of feudalism; risings of the peasants were taking place—the rebellion of Wat Tyler in England and the Jacqueries in France, to be followed in the next century by the Hussite Wars in Bohemia—and they could find support in the violent attacks of Wiclif on the whole order of society, both ecclesiastical and civil. Even thinkers who had supported the Emperor Ludwig of Bavaria against the Pope, William of Ockham and Marsilius of Padua, had gone very far in their opposition to the ordinary medieval doctrine of the Papacy. William of Ockham taught that the Pope was subject to the judgment both of the Emperor and of a General Council; and that none of the three was free from liability to error.[1] Marsilius of Padua went farther: he rejected the claim of the Pope to represent St. Peter, and denied to any authority short of the General Council (which he placed above the Pope) the right to excommunicate; yet even the General Council, in his opinion, could not decide on the truth of all things.[2] It has been said that Marsilius in some ways antici-pated the theories, not only of the Reformation, but even of the French Revolution: he believed in religious toleration, repre-sentative government, and the sovereignty of the people.[3]

At that period the University of Paris was the greatest theo-logical school in Europe; for the Italian universities were devoted to law and medicine rather than to theology.[4] There arose in the University of Paris a group of divines who came to the con-clusion that the only way to put an end to the schism was to appeal to a general council. The leaders of this group were Jean Gerson and Pierre d'Ailly: they were the founders of the Gallican party, which was more or less dominant among the French clergy for nearly five centuries.

Councils of bishops had been held in every age of the Church. In earlier days general councils had been summoned by Emperors.[5] But the medieval "general councils", held after the breach with Constantinople, had been summoned by Popes, who had, by the later development of Canon Law, the sole right to summon and to preside at them, personally or by deputy. Hence general councils had been instruments of papal policy rather than means to control the Pope. National councils of bishops had often been summoned by the earlier Frankish kings, and had even resisted papal orders, as in the dispute between Hincmar of Rheims and Pope Nicolas I (863); at the Council of Rheims in 995 the French bishops had threatened to become independent, like the Greeks. But there were no recent cases of conciliar opposition to the Pope, still less of conciliar supremacy. The theory of Gerson and d'Ailly had its roots in history, but it was contrary to the recent development of the Church, and of the Canon Law: nor had it any strong popular backing. What gave the scholars of Paris their chance was the crying scandal of the

[1] M. Creighton, *History of the Papacy*, vol. i, p. 41.
[2] Elliott Binns, *Decline and Fall of the Medieval Papacy*, p. 131. Creighton, vol. i, pp. 42–46. [3] J. N. Figgis, in *Our Place in Christendom*, p. 78.
[4] H. Rashdall, *History of Medieval Universities*.
[5] cf. Article 21, "General Councils may not (non possunt) be gathered together without the commandment and will of princes."

schism, which everyone in Europe deplored, but no one was able to bring to an end.

The first efforts of Gerson and d'Ailly, backed by the University of which d'Ailly was Chancellor (he afterwards became Archbishop of Cambrai, and was succeeded as Chancellor by Gerson), were suppressed by the Government, which supported the French claimant to the Papacy, Clement VII. However, in 1394 the University was allowed to consult how to end the schism, and decided to urge both Popes to resign. Clement VII was so angry at this suggestion that he fell into an apoplectic fit and died; and the cardinals of Avignon elected Benedict XIII as his successor. The King of France then summoned an extraordinary assembly, representing all the estates of the realm, at Paris, to discuss the proposals of the University; and it was decided to invite both Popes to resign. But though the embassy to Benedict XIII included the King's own brother and two uncles, the Pope received it with such furious discourtesy that on July 27, 1398, the French Church withdrew its obedience from him, without submitting to his rival, and its decree was registered by the Parlement of Paris.[1] Appeals to the Pope were to be treated as if the papal see were vacant: they were to be heard by the Metropolitan, and in the last resort by the Provincial Council.[2] Thus the French Church was for the moment as free from the Pope as she had been in the time of the Merovingian kings. Unfortunately, the civil government seized the opportunity of extending its powers of interference with the exercise of patronage and with the spiritual courts. There were always two kinds of "Gallicanism": episcopal Gallicanism, which was the assertion of the ancient constitutional rights of the bishops assembled in council, whether national or general, against the despotic authority claimed by the Popes; and royal Gallicanism, which was the claim of the civil power, first to be free from, and then to interfere with and to dominate, the spiritual authority of both Pope and bishops. Whatever power was wrested from the Pope was immediately annexed by the Crown, and one of its claims was the right to appoint to bishoprics, to the prejudice of the ancient right of the chapters to elect their bishops. This was the great weakness of Gallicanism all through its history. The clergy became so dissatisfied with the encroach-

---

[1] The French "Parlements" were judicial bodies, composed of lawyers: not Parliaments in the English sense.
[2] W. H. Jervis, *History of the Gallican Church to the Revolution*, vol. i, pp. 83–86.

ments of the Crown that in 1403 obedience to Benedict XIII was renewed, on conditions which the Pope accepted, and then broke without scruple. In 1408 obedience was again withdrawn, and careful arrangements were made for the administration of the Church until the proposed council should meet.[1]

The lawfulness of this council was doubted, on the ground that, by Canon Law, only the Pope could summon a general council; and neither of the rival Popes could do this, since the purpose of the council was to decide between them. If, again, the cardinals took upon themselves to summon the council, it was doubtful which set of cardinals was lawfully appointed. To these doubts Gerson answered with his treatise *On the Removability of the Pope*, in which he argued that the Church, like every other society, had the power to remove an untrustworthy or incapable chief officer, and to replace him by another: thus carrying the discussion out of the region of law into that of political theory.[2]

The council, summoned by the two Colleges of Cardinals, met at Pisa in 1409. Unfortunately it only succeeded in making matters worse. It declared both Popes deposed, and elected Alexander V, a Greek from Crete, in their place. He survived barely a year, and was succeeded by that strangest of Popes, Baldassare Cossa, the ex-condottiere, who took the name of John XXIII. Neither of the other Popes recognized his deposition, and there were now three rival Popes instead of two.

Through the efforts of Gerson and d'Ailly, a fresh council assembled at Constance, on November 5, 1414. Its membership, unlike that of earlier councils, was not confined to bishops: abbots and other notable persons sat in it. The council, at the suggestion of Robert Hallam, Bishop of Salisbury, decided that voting should be by nations; this prevented the bishops of Italy, where dioceses have always been many and small, from outvoting those of England, France, and Germany. Pope John XXIII consented to preside, but when he found that the council was determined that he should cease to be Pope, he escaped from Constance. He was brought back, and formally deposed. He retired to Florence, and died there; his tomb, on which he is robed as a bishop, not as a Pope, may still be seen in the Baptistery. Of the other two Popes, Gregory XII, the successor of Urban, resigned, and Benedict XIII, the successor of Clement,

---

[1] Jervis, vol. i, p. 86; Creighton, vol. i, p. 196.
[2] Jervis, vol. i, pp. 89–90.

was deposed.. He did not accept his deposition, but his adherents soon became so few as to be negligible. The council, in its fourth and fifth sessions, laid down, in spite of the opposition of the Italian nation, that " this holy Synod of Constance, being a General Council lawfully assembled in the name of the Holy Ghost, and representing the Church militant, has received immediately from Jesus Christ a power to which all persons of whatever rank and dignity, not excepting the Pope himself, are bound to submit in those matters which concern the faith, the extirpation of the existing schism, and the reformation of the Church in head and members ".[1]

Moreover, it decreed that it could not be transferred to another place, or dissolved, without its own consent; and that another general council should be held in five years, and others at regular intervals. These decrees, passed through the influence of Gerson, are the high-water mark of the Gallican theory of the Church. The Council of Constance was the last council in which Western Christendom spoke with a united voice (for Basle and Florence were rival councils, the Lateran Council of 1517 was composed only of Italian bishops, and before Trent assembled the Reformation had broken Western Christendom in pieces). And the Council of Constance declared explicitly that a general council is above the Pope, and can judge or even depose him.

Nevertheless, in spite of this great triumph for the University of Paris and its divines, the Council of Constance committed two fatal mistakes.

The purpose of the council was to end the schism and to reform the Church. When the three rivals had been disposed of, the bishops were anxious to crown their work by the election of a Pope, and to return home. The reform of the Church would be a long and thorny business. There were great vested interests in the way. Surely this could be left to the next council, which was to meet in five years. So the unique opportunity was let slip. The Fathers of Constance took no steps to reform the Church, or to impose real checks on the Pope's power. They established no permanent self-government for the national churches. But they elected Oddo Colonna Pope, as Martin V, and he and his successors took care that the opportunity of reforming the Church and setting limits to the growth of the Papal claims should never recur.[2] From that day the Reformation became inevitable.

[1] Jervis, vol. i, p. 91.          [2] Creighton, vol. ii, pp. 99 ff.

The other mistake the council made was its treatment of John Huss. The great Czech reformer had come to Constance, with a safe-conduct given him by the Emperor Sigismund, to be tried on a charge of heresy. He refused to submit unreservedly to the decision of the council, and to withdraw his statements unless they could be proved by Scripture and reason to be false. This sealed his fate. All parties agreed that no promise to a heretic need be kept, and Huss was burned at the stake.

The result was not only the devastation of Germany by the ghastly Hussite Wars, but the discrediting (for future genera-tions, not for its own) of all that the council stood for. Huss was not a forerunner of Luther: he was a Catholic priest whose main interest was the moral reform of the clergy. The Czech Old Catholics to-day look back to him as a precursor of their move-ment. When he appealed to Scripture and reason in defence of his teaching, he met with the same refusal to meet him in argu-ment, the same demand for unreserved submission, from the Gallican council, as he would have received from a Pope; indeed, the council was forced, by the very fact that it was a reforming council, to deal severely with more extreme reformers, in order to reassure public opinion as to the limits of its pro-gramme. But the burning of Huss shows that the Gallican party was not equal to the task of reforming the Church.

The next council, assembled first at Pavia and then at Siena in 1423, was quickly dissolved. In 1431 the Council of Basle was opened. The main business before it was the reconciliation of the Czechs. After the burning of Huss and his disciple Jerome of Prague by the Council of Constance, Bohemia had broken out into rebellion, at once national and religious. Huss had been not only a religious reformer, but also the champion of the Czechs against German culture; and the whole Czech nation rallied in support of the cause which drew its inspiration from him. Crusades were preached against the Hussites, but the crusading armies were defeated again and again, and the Hussites devas-tated all the neighbouring German countries. So the Council of Basle, when force had failed, consented to negotiate with the heretics. A startling light is thrown on the moral condition of the Church by the orders given by the council that prostitutes were to be removed from the streets of Basle, for fear the pre-judices of the heretical ambassadors might be shocked.[1]

[1] Creighton, vol. ii, p. 236.

The moderate Hussites, known as Calixtines (" Chalicers ") or Utraquists (" Bothists ") because they insisted that all should be allowed to receive Communion in both kinds, persuaded the council to agree to four articles, known as the Compactata. These were: (1) Those who wished might receive Communion in both kinds; (2) free preaching of the Word of God; (3) reduction of the clergy to apostolic poverty; (4) severe repression of open sins. Agreement with the council on these terms broke the Hussite party in two: for the extreme section, the Taborites (from their stronghold Tabor), who had been the backbone of the rebellion, would not accept the terms. They were, however, overthrown in battle by the Utraquists in 1434. On the other hand, the Compacts were never accepted by the Papacy; they were formally annulled by Pope Pius II in 1460, but remained law in Bohemia until 1567, by which time most of the Utraquists had attached themselves to the Lutheran Reformation.

Apart from this partial success, the Council of Basle accomplished little. It quarrelled with Pope Eugenius IV, who held a rival council at Florence: it went so far as to depose him, and elect Felix V, the last anti-pope, in his place. But it was not supported by any of the great European nations. After lingering on till 1449, it came to an end, discredited and futile. Meanwhile Charles VII of France had seized the opportunity of winning independent rights for the French Church. In 1438 he assembled a great National Assembly at Bourges, which issued a decree called the Pragmatic Sanction. This document was registered by the Parlement of Paris on July 13, 1439, and so became part of the statute law of France. It recognized the decrees of Constance and Basle on the supremacy of general councils and on the time and manner of convening them. It also reserved for the chapters of cathedrals, collegiate churches, and monasteries their ancient rights of election; abolished annates and various other papal dues and encroachments; and forbade the Pope to interfere in ecclesiastical law-suits until they had reached the final court of appeal.[1] The Popes protested strongly against the Pragmatic Sanction: Pius II denounced it, but was reminded that it rested on the decrees of Constance and Basle, which his predecessors had recognized. It was revoked by Louis XI (but the revocation was not certainly legal), re-established by Louis XII, and finally abolished by the Concordat of

[1] Jervis, vol. i, pp. 97-100.

Bologna (1516), by which the King and the Pope came to an agreement at the expense of the rights of the clergy, and which was confirmed by the Council of the Lateran, which also declared that the Pope is above councils, and alone has the right to summon, transfer, and dissolve them.

However, the Pragmatic Sanction had little significance for the well-being of Western Christendom as a whole; France fought for its own privileges only. From this time Gallicanism became more and more the assertion of special privileges for the French Church and the French Crown, not an attempt to change the papal supremacy over all western Europe into a constitutional monarchy. The Conciliar Movement failed; the Church remained unreformed. The result was revolution, in the person of Martin Luther.

The fundamental weaknesses of Gallicanism were its dependence on the civil power, its purely aristocratic and academic character, and its acceptance of the supremacy and Divine right of the Pope, behind all which was the absence of any great spiritual or moral principle. It had its origin in a university, in the researches of learned men: there was no tradition of independence behind it. Historically, the supremacy of general councils over the Pope was sound; but the precedents were remote, and the advantages, once the schism was healed, were not obvious. Nobody was prepared to die for the constitutional rights of the bishops, especially as it was far from certain that their desire for reform, except so far as it might increase their own power, was sincere. The great obstacle to the administrative reform of the Church (doctrinal reform was not yet demanded, except in Bohemia) was the enormous vested interests which the centralized Papacy had created at Rome. The Popes would not, and indeed could not, disturb these vested interests. The object of the conciliar party was to make the Pope a constitutional monarch, so that he could be forced to reform the Church. But to transform an autocrat into a constitutional monarch is almost impossible without the monarch's consent, especially when not only the monarch himself and his partisans, but also his opponents, believe firmly in his Divine right. The supremacy of the Pope, and the Divine gift to St. Peter upon which it was supposed to be founded, were not disputed by anyone. (At this period the real nature of the Pseudo-Isidorian Decretals was still unknown.) The Popes were determined to use every means at their disposal to maintain and increase their power: they had no interest in the reform of the Church, and they had behind them the whole Italian people, which profited by the abuses. They had on their side tradition, canon law, and the power that monarchy always has over men's imaginations, which was especially strong in the Middle Ages, and was not diminished by the Renaissance. To oppose the papal autocracy with success, the Gallicans should at least have been able to show that the Pope's supremacy was usurped, and his claim to Divine right founded on a lie. But this, on their own principles, they could not do. Moreover, the general council was not a suitable instrument for their purpose. The original general councils were extraordinary assemblies, summoned to deal with a particular crisis, such as the outbreak of a heresy. The ordinary government of the Church was in early times conducted by provincial councils, not by general ones. The scheme proposed at Constance, by which a general council was to assemble every ten years, was expensive and unworkable; during the intervals between the councils the Pope controlled the machinery of government, and used his power to prevent the assembling of a council. The only way out would have been to free the national churches of England, France, Germany, and Spain from the papal jurisdiction, and to leave the Pope with only a primacy of honour over a union of free self-governing churches. But this was too great a breach with tradition to occur to anyone. Besides, it would probably have led to the subjection of each national church to its own king, as happened in England under Henry VIII. Christendom was not ready for such a solution; in the fifteenth century no one could imagine the Church without a Pope (even though the Orthodox Eastern Church was there as a model). From first to last, Gallicanism failed to go far enough in its opposition to the Papacy. The word of freedom was not spoken until the Convocations of Canterbury and York, in 1533, declared that " the Bishop of Rome has not by Scripture any greater jurisdiction in this kingdom of England than any other foreign prelate ". (Luther and many other individuals had said much more, but the declaration quoted is the first of the kind made by a provincial or national synod).[1]

---

[1] The Riksdag of Vesterås (1528) was an assembly of the Swedish nation, not a synod.

# CHAPTER III

## JESUITS AND GALLICANS

WHEN we pass from the age of Gerson and Huss to the age of Pascal and Bossuet we pass from one world to another: from the age of Gothic to the age of Baroque; from the medieval state with its Assembly of Estates and its complex liberties and franchises, to the state in which despotism is becoming more and more supreme, the Great Leviathan of Hobbes; from Europe united in one religion, to Europe permanently divided by the Reformation and the Counter-Reformation.

The Reformation, both English and Continental, is outside the scope of this book; but the Counter-Reformation is the background against which the whole history of modern resistance to the Papacy must be viewed. Roman Catholicism, as distinct from the Catholicism of medieval Europe, is based upon, and limited by, the Counter-Reformation. Two great new factors have entered into the life of Latin Christendom, which were not there before: the decrees of the Council of Trent, and the Society of Jesus.[1]

The rapid spread of the Reformation, and the secession of half Europe from the Roman obedience, forced Pope Paul III to summon the long-demanded General Council. It did not meet till 1545, because of the war between France and the Empire. By that time the Reformation had gone so far that a reconciliation had become impossible, and the Society of Jesus, which was utterly opposed to any concessions, had become strong enough to have a considerable, if not decisive, influence on the council. It is difficult to maintain either that the Council of Trent was a free council, or that it represented the whole even of Western Christendom. The Papal legates, who presided, prevented the words " representing the universal Church " from being added to the title of the council, on the ground that these words implied the superiority of the council to the Pope. They claimed for themselves the right to confirm or veto all that was done by the council. They arranged that none but

[1] B. J. Kidd, *Counter-Reformation*, p. 10.

bishops and generals of orders should have the right to vote, since in the ancient councils only bishops had been full members (though at Constance and Basle abbots and others had voted). They abolished the practice of voting by nations, so that the Italian bishops were in an enormous majority; and the Italian bishops had all taken an oath of allegiance to the Pope, and were also dependent on him for pensions and prospects. Absent bishops, moreover, had no right to vote by proxy; but many bishops north of the Alps dared not be long away from their dioceses, lest they should be overrun by the Reformation. Of the five nations which had voted separately at Constance, England was not represented at all, and France very inadequately.

The council had before it two classes of business: doctrinal definition, and administrative reform. The first doctrinal decision that it made was the most important: the decree that Scripture and Tradition were equal sources of necessary dogma. This point was carried by Cardinal Reginald Pole, afterwards Archbishop of Canterbury under Mary (he did not represent the Church of England, but was present as a Cardinal of the Roman Church); it made, as it was meant to make, the breach between Rome and the Reformation in all its forms, Anglican as well as Lutheran and Calvinist, permanent.[1] The Fathers had taught that all necessary doctrine was found in Scripture: the office of Tradition was to interpret Scripture, and such tradition must come down from the Apostles. But it was necessary to the maintenance of the papal system that Tradition should be made equal to Scripture; for many dogmas of that system were neither scriptural nor apostolic, and could only be defended on the ground of Tradition. The Pope, having alone the power to decide what is true tradition, can add new dogmas to the ancient Faith (having first prepared the ground for their reception); and there is no limit to the novelties which may by this means be added to the Catholic Faith. Thus the Tridentine decree making Tradition equal to Scripture is essential to the papal system, and is the great barrier between Roman and non-Roman Christendom. The other doctrinal definitions of Trent hardened into irreformable dogmas many medieval doctrines, such as Purgatory; and on certain subjects, such as the Eucharistic Sacrifice, made use of language which modern scholarship has found more and more difficult to accept. Some extreme forms

[1] Kidd, pp. 59-60.

of teaching were rejected, and in some departments valuable statements were made, particularly about sin and grace. The council did not commit itself to any statement on the Infallibility of the Pope, or the Immaculate Conception of the Blessed Virgin Mary. Both these questions were even then highly controversial, and no unanimity could have been reached.

The administrative reforms of Trent were far-reaching. Many of the abuses which had led to the Reformation were abolished or strongly discouraged, such as plurality, non-residence of bishops, and the sale of indulgences. Seminaries for training the clergy were to be established in every diocese. But the method used was not decentralization, but greater centralization. All the decisions of the council were submitted to the Pope for his confirmation. The Creed of Pope Pius IV, which sums up the faith as taught by the council, includes the words " I recognize the holy catholic apostolic and Roman church as the mother and mistress of all churches, and I promise and swear true obedience to the Roman Pontiff, the successor of blessed Peter prince of the Apostles, and vicar of Jesus Christ ". Not without reason did Philip II of Spain complain that his bishops went to Trent bishops and came back parish priests.

The Council of Trent had provided the dogmatic basis for the reformed Roman Communion, and laid down the methods by which it was to be defended and taught. The work was carried out by means of a great spiritual revival: the agents of which were the new religious orders, and above all the Jesuits. This great order was founded by Ignatius Loyola, a Spanish knight, with the purpose of forming a kind of army for propagating the Faith, to be at the absolute disposal of the Pope, to whom each member took a special vow of obedience. It is almost impossible to exaggerate the zeal, the ability, or the success of the Jesuits, both in promoting the Counter-Reformation in Europe, and in preaching the Faith to the heathen. One of their methods was to obtain control of schools and colleges, and to give the best education possible. Another was to win personal influence over kings and nobles. Thus they turned the school, the pulpit, and the palace, which had done so much to propagate the Reformation, into weapons against it.

The Jesuits were the champions of the most extreme claims of the Papacy. They held that the Church was a *societas perfecta*, a society wholly distinct from the State (they were the first clearly to reject the medieval synthesis), and completely controlled in all its parts by the Pope. They repudiated the medieval conception of the " community of communities " (which, according to Dr. J. N. Figgis, is the natural formation of human society, and the necessary condition of human freedom),[1] and denied that any authority within the Church could exist which was not derived from the supreme authority. They therefore tried to destroy all remains of episcopal or national independence of Rome. This was, as we shall see, the fundamental cause of their quarrel with the Archbishop and Chapter of Utrecht, which was the beginning of the Old Catholic movement.

Moreover, they maintained the papal claim to complete control in the region of faith as well as in that of government. As far back as the *Dictatus Papæ*, a book of maxims drawn up for the use of Pope Gregory VII, we find the statement that the Roman see never has erred and never will err. St. Thomas Aquinas (died 1274) did not formally teach that the Pope was infallible, but only that the authority of the Universal Church resided principally in the Supreme Pontiff. (St. Thomas did not know that the patristic passages upon which he relied were not genuine.) As early as 1300 Arnald of Villanova wrote, " Which of the faithful does not know, when Chaldeans (*i.e.*, Moslems) and barbarians are not ignorant of it, that the Roman Pontiff is a second Christ on the earth ?" [2] At the Lateran Council of 1517 one bishop called the Pope " a second God upon the earth ". On the other hand, Pope Hadrian VI (1522–24) taught, not only before, but after he became Pope, that a Pope may err, not only in his private, but also in his official capacity.

The Jesuits made the doctrine of Papal Infallibility the cornerstone of their system, which was worked out in detail by Bellarmine (1542–1621); and it became the main issue between the two chief parties in the Roman Communion, the " Ultramontanes ", who accepted it, and the " Gallicans ", who denied it. But the difference must not be exaggerated. Both parties believed that the Church possesses " oracular " infallibility— that is, that the Church, when making formal definitions on faith and morals, is preserved by God from the possibility of error. They differed only as to the *organ* of infallibility. The Ultramontanes held that the Pope is infallible, and that a true general

---

[1] J. N. Figgis, *Churches in the Modern State*, p. 42.
[2] Mirbt, *Quellen zur Geschichte des Papsttums und der Rom. Katholizismus*, p. 211.

council—that is, one whose decrees have been confirmed by the Pope—is also infallible. The Gallicans held that a true general council, whose decrees have been confirmed by the Pope, is infallible, but not the Pope by himself. This doctrine of oracular infallibility does not appear to have any basis in the New Testament; for St. Matt. 16. 18, and St. John 16. 13, give it no real support; and it has been finally shattered by the unanswerable logic of Dr. Salmon.[1] That " the gates of Hades shall not prevail " against the Church appears to mean that she will never entirely fail to be the means of salvation, not that she is immune from making mistakes. The Orthodox Eastern Communion teaches, indeed, that the Church is ἀσφαλής, which should perhaps be translated " indefectible "; but Orthodox divines are not agreed whether it is the Church represented by her bishops assembled in council (which does not differ much from the Gallican doctrine),[2] or the whole Church, clergy and laity together, which possesses this gift, so that no council is œcumenical which has not been ratified by the whole body of the faithful.[3] The latter is a view which Dr. Salmon did not take into consideration.

In addition to their belief in despotic government, which was characteristic of the period, though carried out by no one so consistently as by the Jesuits, and their infallibilism, which was characteristic of the whole Roman Communion (and, transferred from the Church to the Bible, of most Protestants), the Jesuits had a special mark of their own: their teaching on moral theology. It was in the period of the Counter-Reformation that both moral and ascetic theology were more fully developed than they had ever been before. Compulsory confession to a priest, which had been imposed on all the faithful since 1215, made it important to settle the question in what circumstances the priest was justified in refusing absolution. The Jesuits, anxious not to " quench the smoking flax ", but to make approach to the sacraments as easy as possible, devised the theory of " Probabilism "—that is, that a penitent who has chosen the less safe of two possible courses, even though more probable opinions can be alleged on the other side, may be absolved if the course he has chosen is

[1] G. Salmon, *Infallibility of the Church*, passim.
[2] F. Gavin, *Greek Orthodox Thought*, p. 255, ref. to Androutsos, Δογματική, p. 290.
[3] Stefan Zankov, *Das Orthodoxe Christentum des Ostens*, pp. 84–85, following Khomiakov and Florensky (translation by Donald A. Lowrie, *The Eastern Orthodox Church*, pp. 94–95).

supported by the probable opinion of a single doctor of the Church [1] (Bartholomew à Medina, 1528–1581). This theory led to serious moral laxity: the Jesuits were accused of letting the sinner remain in his sin, and yet receive the sacraments, in order to retain their influence over him. It was a strong temptation, when they were fighting desperately against what they believed to be soul-destroying heresy, to let off lightly powerful persons who would support the Roman Catholic cause if too high a moral standard was not required of them. The influence of the Jesuits was predominant at Rome, except for short intervals, from their foundation in 1540 to their suppression in 1773. (With the later history of the Society after its revival we are not now concerned.)

The Inquisition, Roman or Spanish, is no part of our subject. But something must be said of one of the most effective instruments of the Papacy—the Index of Prohibited Books. At that period the Press was rigidly controlled by the government in all countries, including England. But the Roman Communion is the only part of Christendom which has compiled a list of books which the faithful are forbidden to read. The origin of the Index of Prohibited Books was due to Cardinal Caraffa, afterwards Pope Paul IV.[2] We shall see what difficulties were produced by this practice of prohibiting theological works by authority. When the power of the central government of the Church had become so great, those who could control it were tempted to make use of it for party purposes, to suppress by force any rival party. For no school of thought can exist in the Roman Communion if the Pope and his advisers have determined to destroy it; and the reason for that determination has not always been a pure desire for the preservation of revealed truth: while men are men, we cannot expect that it should be.

The Counter-Reformation, largely under Jesuit influence, is a special development of Christianity, far more orderly and efficient than medieval Catholicism, but narrower, more southern, and for good and evil more clear-cut. The mysterious beauty of Byzantine and Gothic Christianity has departed; in its place we find that the mysteries of God are reduced to rigid formulæ which may not be criticized, and from which both dignity and liberty have largely disappeared.

[1] K. E. Kirk, *Some Principles of Moral Theology*, p. 196.
[2] Kidd, p. 47.

During the Wars of Religion in France, the University of Paris, the traditional stronghold of Gallicanism, was long under the influence of the Catholic League, the extreme party in alliance with Spain. When Henri IV had restored peace to the distracted nation, the older Gallican tradition began to regain its place in the University. In 1594, on account of an attempt to murder Henri IV, the Jesuits were expelled from France. Nine years later Henri IV allowed them to come back, and made Father Coton, a Jesuit, his own confessor. After the King's death in 1610 the power of the Society increased rapidly. In 1611 they proposed to make a demonstration, by means of a public lecture, before the young King, Louis XIII, and his court, the subject of which was the following three articles:

(1) The Pope is infallible in judging on faith and morals.
(2) In no case whatever is a council superior to the Pope.
(3) It belongs to the Pope to determine doubtful questions, and to confirm or disallow the decisions of councils.

The Syndic of the University, Edmond Richer, vetoed this lecture, on the ground that these articles were contrary to the decrees of Constance; and at the request of the President of the Parlement of Paris, Nicolas de Verdun, issued a small treatise, *De Ecclesiastica et Politica Potestate*, setting forth the Gallican position. He asserted that ecclesiastical jurisdiction belonged to the whole Church, and that the authority of the Pope, as its ministerial head, was not over the Church as a whole, but over particular churches taken singly; that only the whole Church was infallible, and that every bishop, including the Pope, was liable to error; that the Pope had no right to enact canons, but only to interpret and execute them, nor could he impose any article of doctrine or discipline on the Church without its consent; and that the Church had no temporal jurisdiction. Every kind of influence was used to crush Richer, but the University supported him. The Jesuits were forbidden, by a decree of the University, to interfere with education in Paris; and they had to close their college. Further, they were ordered to sign a statement containing four articles:—

(1) That a general council is superior to the Pope.
(2) That the Pope has no jurisdiction over the temporal power of sovereigns, and cannot deprive them of it by excommunication.

(3) That a priest who learns in the confessional of a conspiracy against the State is bound to reveal it to the civil
magistrate.

(4) That all ecclesiastics are subjects of the King and
answerable to his government.

They refused to sign this statement, but after some negotiation
agreed to assent in general to the Gallican liberties. But as
they did it without the consent of their General at Rome, their
assent meant nothing. Richer, however, was deprived of his
post in the University by letters-patent from the Regent, and had
to retire into private life. He was pursued even there by his
enemies, and was induced by Father Joseph, the agent of Richelieu, to submit his work to the Roman see, as " the infallible
judge of truth ".[1]

This incident is a good example of the state of parties in the
French Church at this period. The University of Paris was the
stronghold of Gallicanism, which was an assertion, partly of the
rights of the French clergy against the Pope, partly of those of
the civil government against the ecclesiastical. The lawyers in
the Parlement of Paris supported the University, on national
grounds. The Crown was under the influence of the Jesuits;
the bishops, appointed by the Crown and confirmed by the
Pope, could not be trusted to maintain their own rights against
either. At the States-General of 1614 (the last one held before
1789), the Third Estate, the representatives of the Commoners,
refused, in spite of pressure put on them, to allow the decrees
of Trent to be accepted as part of the civil law of France. The
clergy in their Assembly accepted those decrees, but they were
never at any time accepted by the civil authority.[2] On the
other hand, when Antonio de Dominis, Archbishop of Spalato
(now Split) in Dalmatia, wrote his De Republica Ecclesiastica, in
which he entirely repudiated the Papal supremacy, his book
was condemned by a majority of the Theological Faculty at
Paris, though a strong minority protested.[3] This shows how far
some Gallicans were ready to go; for de Dominis wrote from
an Anglican rather than a Gallican standpoint. He had taken
refuge in England, where James I made him Dean of Windsor,
and where in 1617 he assisted at the consecration of Montaigne,
Bishop of Lincoln, afterwards Archbishop of York, and one of the

[1] W. H. Jervis, Gallican Church, vol. i, pp. 266-274.
[2] Jervis, vol. i, pp. 277-282.          [3] Jervis, vol. i, p. 288.

consecrators of Archbishop Laud, from whom all the modern Anglican lines of episcopal succession are derived. De Dominis, whose original name was Gospodovitch, was a Slav, and the Croatian Old Catholics have a great respect for him, not perhaps altogether deserved; for he lacked stability, and afterwards returned to the Roman Communion. He died in the prison of the Inquisition at Rome, and his dead body was publicly burned.[1]

In 1618 the Jesuit college at Paris was opened again by order of the Crown, then completely under the influence of Cardinal Richelieu. In the latter part of Richelieu's rule, however, his relations with Rome were not so good, because he supported, for political reasons, the Protestant side in the Thirty Years War. In 1640 persistent rumours arose that Richelieu was about to break off relations with Rome:[2] and a priest named Charles Hersent wrote, under the pseudonym of " Optatus Gallus ", a book strongly protesting against the scheme of setting up a French patriarchate, which, he said, would reduce the Church of France to the condition of the schismatical Church of England. This book was ordered by the Parlement of Paris to be burnt by the hangman (their favourite way of treating theologically objectionable books), and Richelieu arranged that a Jesuit named Rabardeau should publish a reply, in which he argued that the appointment of a patriarch by a national church was not a schismatical act, and that the consent of the Pope was not necessary. At the same time Pierre de Marca, one of the most learned French theologians, published, at the request of Richelieu, an important work called *De Condordantia Sacerdotii et Imperii*, in defence of the Gallican liberties. But when he was nominated for the bishopric of Couserans in 1642, the Pope refused to confirm the appointment, and he had to modify his position in order to get his bishopric. The right of veto on appointments to bishoprics, secured by the medieval Papacy, but abolished, except for certain specified reasons, by the Pragmatic Sanction in France (1438–1516), is an extremely powerful weapon against any resistance to the papal policy. But the power of the King was quite as dangerous as the power of the Pope. Gaston, Duke of Orleans, brother of Louis XIII and heir to the throne, had married Marguerite of Lorraine without the King's consent. Louis XIII declared that by the ancient

[1] Ollard and Crosse, *Dictionary of English Church History*, s.v. Reunion.
[2] Jervis, vol. i, p. 349.

custom of France, the marriage of a prince of the Blood Royal without the King's consent was invalid. Both the lawyers and the clergy supported this contention, in opposition to the Pope. It seems clear that on this point the Gallicans were wrong. The " custom of France " might alter the legal consequences of a marriage (our own Royal Marriages Act, passed in 1772 and still in force, has similar consequences), but it could not affect the sacramental character of the marriage, since " consensus facit matrimonium ". At length a compromise was agreed upon. Louis XIII consented to recognize his brother's marriage, on certain political conditions.[1]

There was one French priest who, when the rest of the nation supported the King and the Cardinal in this unpleasant affair, declared openly that he would rather have killed ten men than consent to the ruin of one of the sacraments of the Church. This fearless priest was Jean du Verger de Hauranne, Abbot of St. Cyran, the founder of the " Jansenist " party. Cardinal Richelieu never forgave him.

<hr>

[1] Jervis, vol. i, pp. 359-361.

# CHAPTER IV

# PORT ROYAL

WE now come to the great controversy which distracted the French Church for more than a century, and which was the immediate cause of the schism between Rome and Utrecht: the controversy on Grace.

There have always been two opposite tendencies in Christianity: the tendency to exalt the sovereignty of God, and the tendency to exalt the free will of man. In the New Testament St. Paul is the representative of the former, St. James of the latter; the former, carried to its extreme point, results in the doctrine of Calvin, the latter in the doctrine of Pelagius. In what was called the Jansenist controversy, the Jesuits were the defenders of free will and " sufficient grace "; the " Jansenists " of Divine sovereignty and " efficacious grace ".

The name " Jansenist " was a term of abuse, which was no more accepted by the party to which it was applied than the term " Puseyite " was accepted by the Tractarians, with whom the school of Port Royal had much in common. They called themselves the defenders of the doctrine of St. Augustine. I shall use the unavoidable term " Jansenist " without prejudice, for the followers of St. Cyran, Arnauld, and Quesnel. I do not intend to deal with the technical theological issues, more than is necessary to set forth the origins of the Old Catholic movement.

The rigid doctrine of St. Augustine, once predominant in Latin Christendom, though never accepted among the Greeks, had declined in popularity during the Middle Ages. The system of St. Thomas Aquinas, held by the Dominicans, was much less rigid. But strict Augustinianism was always taught at Louvain. In 1567, Baius, a professor at Louvain, had accused the Jesuits of Pelagianism, but his teaching had been condemned by Pope Pius V. In 1588, Luis Molina, a Spanish Jesuit, published a book *On Grace and Free-Will*, the teaching of which was regarded by Baronius and many other divines as Pelagian.[1] The Jesuits,

[1] W. H. Jervis, *Gallican Church*, vol. i, pp. 381-385; J. M. Neale, *History of the Church of Holland*, p. 8.

while never formally committing themselves to Molina's teaching, would not allow him to be condemned.

The founder of " Jansenism " was Jean du Vergier de Hauranne, commonly called M. de St. Cyran, because he was Abbot of St. Cyran, in the diocese of Poitiers. He was born at Bayonne in 1581, and was educated at Louvain and Paris. Here he formed a lifelong friendship with Cornelius Jansen, a young Fleming. Both were enthusiastic students of St. Augustine, whose writings they regarded as ranking next to Scripture. Jansen became a professor of theology at Louvain, and ultimately Bishop of Ypres; he died in 1638, six months after his consecration. His famous book, the *Augustinus*, was only published after his death. He had worked at it for twenty years, and is said to have read the whole works of St. Augustine twenty times. It was still in manuscript when he died of the plague. The Jesuits discovered, through the treachery of one of the printers, that the book was in course of publication, and appealed to Rome to get it stopped; for after the condemnation of Baius, Popes Paul V and Urban VIII had forbidden the publication of books on this subject. However, the book was published in 1640,[1] and soon afterwards a reprint appeared in Paris. The Jesuits at once attacked it in a series of theses. In 1642 Pope Urban VIII, by the Bull " In Eminenti ", condemned both the *Augustinus* and the theses written against it; but this Bull was not accepted by the University of Paris, and had no binding effect in France; nor was it accepted in the Spanish Netherlands.[2] Meanwhile St. Cyran had in 1636 become the director of the famous nunnery of Port Royal, and had formed the design of making it the centre of a movement which should oppose the dominant teaching of the Jesuits in doctrine, morals, and devotion.[3] The tragic story of Port Royal can be told here only in the barest outline. It was a Cistercian convent, founded in 1204, but its influence began when Jacqueline Marie Arnauld, better known as Mère Angélique, became its abbess in 1602, at the age of eleven, having been given this office, as was common at that time, as a means of providing for her. At that time there were only eleven nuns in the convent, of whom three were imbeciles. In 1609 the young Abbess, having been converted by the Lenten sermons of a Capuchin friar, enforced the rules of the convent strictly, and

---

[1] Neale, p. 11.    [2] Neale, p. 13; Jervis, vol. i, pp. 386–388.
[3] Jervis, vol. i, p. 374.

forbade her own parents to come within the grille. This day, known as the Journée du Guichet (day of the Convent Wicket), September 25, 1609, was the beginning of the reform, which soon spread to other convents. Mère Angélique placed herself under the direction of St. François de Sales, whose influence was one of the causes of the holiness and piety of Port Royal. On one occasion St. François, speaking of the corruptions of the Roman Court, said to Mère Angélique, " It is the duty of Œcumenical Councils to reform the head and members: they are above the Pope. . . . I know this, but prudence forbids my speaking of it, for I can hope for no results if I did speak. We must weep and pray in secret that God will put His hand to what man cannot, and we should humble ourselves to the ecclesiastical powers under whom He has placed us, and beseech Him that He would convert and humble them by the might of His Spirit." [1]

Port Royal was closely connected with the Arnauld family. Mère Angélique was one of twenty children; at one time her widowed mother and four of her five sisters were nuns at Port Royal together. Of her brothers, Robert, the eldest (M. d'Andilly), retired to Port Royal after a distinguished career, and lived there as a *solitaire* or hermit. Henri, Bishop of Angers, was one of the four bishops who refused in 1665 to sign the " Formulary " against Jansenism, and Antoine, " Le Grand Docteur ", succeeded St. Cyran as leader of the party. Four nephews were *solitaires*, and four nieces, one of whom was the second Mère Angélique, were members of the community.

In 1626 Mère Angélique decided to move the community to Paris, partly for reasons of health, and partly in order to escape from the jurisdiction of the Abbot of Citeaux into that of the Archbishop of Paris;[2] the old convent near Pontoise remained as the home of the *solitaires*. Placed thus in the capital, Port Royal extended its influence enormously. Its story is part of the history, not only of French religion, but also of French politics and French literature. People of all classes were converted to living Christianity through Port Royal; from the Duchesse de Longueville and her brother, the Prince de Conti, who were members of the royal House of Bourbon, to the crowd of gardeners, shoemakers, and other poor people who shared in the religious life of the house.

The Queen of Poland was an intimate friend of Mère

[1] E. Romanes, *Story of Port Royal*, p. 36.  [2] Romanes, p. 54.

Angélique's: Queen Henrietta Maria of England was once invited to stay at Port Royal de Paris, and her son, Charles II, during his exile, received much help from the convent.[1] During the persecution Mère Angélique complained that she had been accused of intriguing with Cromwell, " cet horrible monstre, parricide de son Roi ";[2] and her brother Antoine remarked, " They have not been ashamed to carry to the ears of the Queen Mother that I had a close understanding with Cromwell: I am expecting that one of these days they will announce that I have had one with the Grand Vizier, and that we are thinking of retiring to Hungary, to be under the protection of the Sultan of Turkey! "[3]   It was through Ludovic Stuart d'Aubigny, who had at one time been connected with Port Royal, that Charles II, soon after the Restoration, began a negotiation with Rome in which he proposed, first, the establishment of a Roman Catholic Bishop of Dunkirk (at that time in the possession of England), with jurisdiction over all Roman Catholics in England, and second, the submission of the Churches of England, Scotland, and Ireland to Rome, on conditions which included a clause against Jansenism, but also Gallican restrictions of the Papal authority to which Rome would never have consented.[4]

The influence of Port Royal on French literature was no less great. Pascal was one of the leaders of the Jansenist party. Racine's aunt was Abbess of Port Royal, and he himself was brought up there; so was Tillemont, the great Church historian. St. Cyran had been a friend of Mère Angélique's since 1620, and he became director of Port Royal in 1636. He was one of the greatest of spiritual guides, and it was his influence that gave Port Royal its peculiar stamp. He was a man of fearless independence of mind, combined with profound spirituality and insight into human character. There was a severity about him, derived from his great master, St. Augustine, which we also find in Dr. Pusey, whose favourite Father St. Augustine was. St. Cyran's ideas were broad and deep, but were very different from those which had become predominant in the Roman Communion. He came first into prominence by means of an anonymous work called Petrus Aurelius. On the marriage of Henrietta Maria to King Charles I, Richard Smith was appointed by

[1] Ruth Clark, Strangers and Sojourners at Port Royal, pp. 41-42, 46.
[2] Antoine Arnauld, Lettres, vol. ii, p. 455; see Clark, p. 46.
[3] Antoine Arnauld, Œuvres, vol. i, p. 301; see Clark, loc. cit.
[4] Lord Acton, Historical Essays, p. 95.

Urban VIII his Vicar-Apostolic in England, with the title of Bishop of Chalcedon. Smith proceeded to restrain the powers of members of religious orders, and came into sharp conflict with the Jesuits. Edward Knott and John Floyd, two English Jesuits, published books minimizing the authority of diocesan bishops. Among the propositions which they maintained were the following: " It is utterly false, and of dangerous consequence, to say that there must be a bishop in each particular church ". " Bishops are necessary for the sole purpose of ordaining priests and deacons." " Members of the regular orders belong to the hierarchy absolutely, and not in this or that sense." " The superiors of religious houses, since they are properly the ordinaries and pastors of their own communities, are in that respect more truly members of the hierarchy than a bishop who is only deputed to act as such in one particular place." " Catholics who have received the chrism in baptism are perfect Christians in the sense of the Fathers, even though they have not been confirmed by the bishop."

The effect of this teaching will be seen when we come to the dispute between the Jesuits and the see of Utrecht. It was completely in accordance with the Jesuit conception of the Church as a single centralized monarchy, in which the bishops were merely representatives of the Pope.[1] *Petrus Aurelius* was an attack upon these novel doctrines, so contrary to the teaching of the Fathers, and was warmly welcomed by the Assembly of the Clergy and by the University of Paris. It was never openly acknowledged by St. Cyran as his work, but there is no doubt that he either wrote or inspired it. Cardinal Richelieu perceived the greatness of St. Cyran, and offered him, first the post of principal chaplain to Queen Henrietta Maria, and then the bishopric of Clermont. St. Cyran refused both. He felt no vocation to the episcopate: he was completely without personal ambition. Richelieu could not understand a man of this kind. He resented St. Cyran's opposition to himself on the question of the marriage of the Duke of Orleans,[2] and also on the question of the necessity of contrition. Richelieu, in a catechism which he had written for his diocese of Luçon, had taught, in accordance with the usual Roman doctrine, that " attrition ", or sorrow caused by fear of consequences, is

[1] Jervis, vol. i, pp. 365–367; Clark, pp. 10–12; Neale, p. 7.
[2] Jervis, vol. i, p. 359; see above, p. 32.

enough for true penitence and for sacramental absolution. St. Cyran denied this, holding that " contrition "—sorrow caused by the love of God—is necessary for penitence and absolution.[1] This dispute became one of the principal issues between the Jesuits and the Jansenists. St. Cyran was falsely accused of not believing in the necessity of the sacrament of penance, on the ground that, since forgiveness always follows complete contrition, if absolution cannot be given without contrition it is really unnecessary. Richelieu had another grievance against St. Cyran. He was known to be a friend of Jansen, who had written a book called *Mars Gallicus*, complaining of Richelieu's policy of alliance with the German Protestants. The book greatly pleased Philip IV of Spain, so that he gave Jansen the bishopric of Ypres, but it annoyed Richelieu exceedingly.[2]

For all these reasons, Richelieu, who could not endure any opposition to his will, had St. Cyran arrested and imprisoned at Vincennes. To the protests made by powerful friends of St. Cyran, including the Prince de Condé and St. Vincent de Paul, Richelieu replied, " This man is more dangerous than six armies. If Luther and Calvin had been placed in durance in good time, so as to stop their public preaching, all Germany and all France would now be Catholic." [3]

St. Cyran remained in prison till Richelieu's death in 1642. He might have been released if he would have withdrawn his teaching on the necessity of contrition, but he was the last man to surrender his principles in order to escape from prison. However, his influence became all the greater on account of his imprisonment. Among those who visited him in prison, and under his influence threw up all worldly prospects and joined the band of *solitaires* at Port Royal des Champs, were Antoine Arnauld, the youngest brother of Mère Angélique, then a theological student, and his nephew, Charles Henri Arnauld (M. de Luzanci).

St. Cyran was regarded by everyone at Vincennes and the neighbourhood as a saint. General de Wert, a German prisoner of war, who had seen a spiteful play produced by Richelieu to annoy the Queen, Anne of Austria, at which several bishops had been present, remarked that what surprised him most was to see that in Christian France bishops were to be seen at such a

---

[1] Jervis, vol. i, pp. 370–372; Romanes, p. 94.
[2] Jervis, vol. i, p. 371.        [3] Jervis, vol. i, p. 372.

play, and saints in prison.[1]   Cardinal Richelieu died on December 4, 1642, and St. Cyran was at once released.   But he survived only ten months, and died on October 11, 1643.

St. Cyran was a great educationalist.   The school for boys at Port Royal began with his own two nephews, and among those who were educated there during the fifteen years that it lasted were Racine the poet, and Tillemont the Church historian.   St. Cyran's ideas were in some respects in advance of his time; for instance, corporal punishment was very sparingly used, and only for very grave faults.   The first consideration was the souls of the boys, and above all the preservation of baptismal innocence. But there was nothing of the hot-house about Port Royal: the young boys were not taken to Mass very frequently during the week.   The masters were to have the boys continually in their prayers, and to suit themselves to the minds of individual boys when correcting their faults.   For this reason there were not to be too many boys in the school.   The atmosphere was to be that of a home, while the example of the self-surrendered life of the neighbouring convent was to be ever in view.   Greek and Latin were taught through French: Greek had at that time almost ceased to be taught in French schools.   The best-known book written for the school was the Port Royal Logic, which was influenced by the philosophy of the contemporary Descartes, not based on the traditional philosophy of the Schoolmen.   The authors of this book were Antoine Arnauld and his friend Nicole.[2]

What were the special doctrines of the Port Royalists, for which they were so constantly accused of heresy?

They were not in any sense Protestants.   Their doctrine of the Church and Sacraments was the same as that of other Roman Catholics.   They even accepted the Infallibility of the Pope, with certain limitations, as we shall see: so that they were not in all respects even Gallicans.   But they based their doctrine of grace wholly on St. Augustine.   Now, St. Augustine held many opinions which the Church as a whole has not accepted, and his influence over Latin theology had been getting weaker for centuries.   The Jansenists, however, argued that as St. Augustine had been recognized as a Doctor of the Church, it could not be unlawful to believe what he believed: "If you condemn us," they said, "you condemn St. Augustine".   But they found (as

[1] Romanes, p. 119.                    [2] Romanes, pp. 170–178.

the Tractarians were to find later, when they appealed to the Caroline Divines) that a doctrine is one thing in an ancient and venerated doctor of the Church, and quite another when it appears with a controversial emphasis in a modern author.[1]

As to discipline, their principal difference from the rest of the Roman Communion was their view that contrition is necessary for absolution. (This was later the subject of the *Amor Pœnitens* of Archbishop van Neercassel, which brought upon the see of Utrecht the first accusation of Jansenism.) While this may appear an obvious truth, it raised great practical difficulties. France was a Roman Catholic country, where confession was compulsory for all but the hated and more and more restricted Huguenots. No one could, for instance, be given either Holy Communion or Christian burial, who had not received absolution from a priest. But great numbers of those who came to confession were obviously not contrite. King Louis XIII declared openly that he could not love God and, therefore, could not feel contrition. Still less, at a later period, could Louis XIV, with his train of mistresses, be regarded as contrite; but to excommunicate the greatest sovereign in Europe, which involved, on Ultramontane principles, the release of his subjects from their obligation to obey him, was not to be thought of. Elizabeth of England had been excommunicated; what had been the result? Where Christianity is the religion of a whole nation, still more where it is enforced by legal penalties, as it was, in one form or another, in every European country at that period, some compromise between the pure Gospel and the world is inevitable. St. Cyran and his friends wanted Christianity without compromise, but it is a question whether they had fully realized what the consequences would be. Certainly the rulers of the Roman Communion (and probably those of any other communion) were not prepared for any such thing.

The Jansenists were also accused of forbidding frequent Communion to the laity: a primitive practice, unknown in medieval Christianity, which the Jesuits had introduced. The truth behind this accusation was, that St. Cyran and his followers regarded the Holy Eucharist with the greatest possible awe, and discouraged approach to it without careful preparation. Their manifesto on this subject was *La Fréquente Communion*, by Antoine Arnauld, published in 1643, just before St. Cyran's death. The origin of the book was this. The Princesse de

---

[1] R. W. Church, *History of the Oxford Movement*, p. 305.

Guémenée, a lady of the Court who had been converted from an irregular life by St. Cyran, was invited by her friend the Marquise de Sablé to accompany her to a ball on the day on which she had made her Communion. The Princess, by St. Cyran's directions, refused to go. In the discussion between them, Madame de Sablé produced a letter from her confessor, a Jesuit, in which he had written, "The more one is destitute of grace, the more one ought boldly to approach Jesus Christ in the Eucharist; the more full we are of self-love and worldliness, the more often we ought to communicate." The letter came into the hands of Antoine Arnauld, and he determined to refute it.[1] Arnauld's position was, that not everybody was fit to communicate every week: that those who had committed mortal sin should be advised to abstain for a time from communicating, in order to prepare themselves for Communion by acts of penitence. He was inclined to demand a standard of conduct so lofty that it might well frighten the penitent. He said that he did not know which was the worse sin, to communicate without sufficient preparation, or to abstain from communicating through neglecting the task of preparing oneself. Following his master St. Augustine, he taught, like Bishop Gore and the best Anglican divines, that the effect of Communion is the permanent presence of Christ in the soul, not, as most Romanists hold, that the presence is only temporary.

Arnauld's book was a "best-seller". It caused a greater sensation in Paris than any religious book since the *Vie Dévote* of St. François de Sales. It was received with enthusiasm by the University of Paris and by many of the bishops, and with indignation by the Jesuits, who could not find words violent enough to express their hatred of it. They persuaded Cardinal Mazarin, who was then the ruler of France, and whose influence over the Queen-Mother, Anne of Austria, was supreme, to have a royal order sent to Arnauld to go to Rome and submit his book to the Pope. But his friends told him that this order was illegal, and that if he went he would probably find himself in the dungeons of the Inquisition. The University and the Parlement of Paris protested so strongly that Anne of Austria withdrew her order. All the same, Arnauld thought it wise to conceal himself, and he did not again appear in public till the "Peace of the Church" in 1668.

[1] Jervis, vol. i, p. 394; Romanes, p. 178.

In order to counteract the complaints of the Jesuits at Rome, the Archbishop of Sens and other bishops wrote a letter in defence of Arnauld to Pope Urban VIII, to which was added a declaration by Arnauld himself, submitting his book unreservedly to the judgment of the Pope, the Archbishop of Paris, and the Theological Faculty of the University. After a delay of three years (1644–7), the Inquisition reported that there was nothing worthy of censure in Arnauld's teaching; and Pope Innocent X assured Bourgeois, Arnauld's agent, in a private audience, that nothing since his accession had given him so much pleasure as this decision. But, to compensate the Jesuits for their defeat, the Pope condemned as heretical a statement in the preface of the book, that St. Peter and St. Paul were the two leaders of the Church, who made but one. ("Les deux chefs de l'Eglise, qui n'en font qu'un.") This phrase had been inserted by M. Barcos, a nephew of St. Cyran. It was of course historically true, but it was a fact which the Pope did not wish to have emphasized, since his authority rested on his claim to be the successor of St. Peter only; and he feared a reference to the design once attributed to Richelieu, to set up a French patriarchate with independent rights derived from St. Paul.[1]

The Jansenists differed from the Jesuits as much in the character of their devotion as they did in doctrine and discipline. The differences between Christians are quite as much devotional as dogmatic; there is much truth in the Greek view that orthodoxy means not only "right opinion", but also "right glory" ($\mathring{o}\rho\theta\eta$ $\delta\acute{o}\xi a$), the right way of worshipping God. The devotion of Port Royal was based on the New Testament, the private study of which was encouraged; and it was extremely stern and severe. There were no great austerities, but there was tremendous emphasis on sin and the need of penitence. The weakness of the system was the want of joy. Jansenist devotion was Puritan in its rigour. There have always been two views of the relation of the Christian to the world. He may accept all that is good in the philosophy, literature, art, and amusement of the world, and try to consecrate it to the glory of God; or he may renounce it all, and confine his thoughts and actions wholly to the things of the spirit. Both methods are needed: some souls are called to one, others to the other. The method of Port Royal was the method of renouncing all; and it was needed in an age

[1] Jervis, vol. i, pp. 396–399.

and country where the Church and the world had become so much mingled together. But it was in sharp contrast to the method practised by the Jesuits. The Jesuit, of course, had to make the most complete surrender of himself to the Society, and no missionaries have ever been more heroic than some of the French Jesuits. But their devotion was not so much based on Scripture as on the lives of the saints; and there is in the popular lives of some Jesuit saints, such as St. Aloysius Gonzaga and St. Stanislas Kotska, as also in the cult of the Sacred Heart, begun a little later than this period by Margaret Mary Alacoque, and encouraged everywhere by the Jesuits, a sentimental element which is as remote as possible from the severity of Port Royal. Whatever may have been the faults of St. Cyran, Arnauld, and their friends, they were at any rate *men*: men who valued obedience highly, but conscience more highly still.

In estimating the reasons for the violence of the opposition to Jansenism, we must remember the ideals which the Jesuits had set before them. Half Europe had been lost to what they believed to be the only true Church, and they had worked out a method, in many countries a very successful method, of winning it back. In order to carry through their task to the end, they needed the whole strength of Latin Christendom behind them. They certainly would not have had it if the Jansenists had been successful. It is easy for a great religious order, especially when its discipline is as strict as that of the Jesuits, to identify its own cause with the cause of God, and to attribute what is really jealousy and party spirit to zeal for the Catholic Faith. Moreover, there were fundamental principles at stake. The Jesuits, following St. Ignatius Loyola, their founder, believed in blind obedience as the first of virtues. The Jansenists, while thoroughly loyal to the Pope, as well as to the King, were independent thinkers. Only a very enlightened despot will tolerate independence of thought in his subjects: Louis XIV always suspected some political conspiracy behind the independence of Port Royal.[1] As we shall see, the persecution of Jansenism was due in the first place to the French Government rather than to the Pope. It is impossible to avoid the suspicion that the high moral standard expected by Port Royal of its converts was a perpetual reproach to the Court, and that it was partly for this reason that Louis XIV said, " If people go to Port

[1] Romanes, p. 287.

Royal, they cannot come to Marly ". It was unfortunate that the Jansenists, who had themselves no political interests, should have had friends who were connected with the rebellion of the Fronde.

The real struggle between the rival parties began when Nicolas Cornet, Syndic of the Faculty of Theology in the University of Paris, asked the Faculty to decide as to the orthodoxy of seven propositions, which were afterwards reduced to five. He did this, he said, because new opinions which he believed to be false were arising in the University; one of the holders of these opinions had ignored the corrections which Cornet had made in his thesis for a degree. These Five Propositions, which were to play so important a part in the schism between Rome and Utrecht, were as follows : [1]—

(1) Aliqua Dei præcepta hominibus justis volentibus et conantibus, secundum præsentes quas habent vires, sunt impossibilia : deest quoque iis gratia qua possibilia fiant.

(Some commandments of God are impossible to righteous persons even desiring and endeavouring to keep them, according to the strength which they then possess : and such grace is lacking to them as would render them possible.)

(2) Interiori gratiæ in statu naturæ lapsæ nunquam resistitur.

(In the state of fallen nature internal grace is never resisted.)

(3) Ad merendum et demerendum in statu naturæ lapsæ non requiritur in homine libertas a necessitate, sed sufficit libertas a coactione.

(In order to merit and demerit in the state of fallen nature, freedom from necessity is not required of man, but it is enough that there be freedom from constraint.)

(4) Semipelagiani admittebant prævenientis gratiæ interioris necessitatem ad singulos actus, etiam ad initium fidei : et in hoc erant hæretici, quod vellent eam gratiam talem esse cui posset humana voluntas resistere vel obtemperare.

(The Semi-Pelagians admitted the necessity of internal prevenient grace for each separate act, and even for the

[1] Jervis, vol. i, pp. 401 ff.

beginning of faith: their heresy consisted in this, that they considered that grace to be such as the will of man might either resist or obey.)

(5) Semipelagianorum error est dicere Christum pro omnibus omnino hominibus mortuum esse aut sanguinem fudisse.

(It is a Semi-Pelagian error to say that Christ died or shed His blood for all men absolutely.) [1]

Cornet did not attribute these propositions to any author by name. But Antoine Arnauld at once produced a reply, in which he said that these propositions had never been taught by anyone, and that it was contrary to the rule of the Faculty for anonymous propositions to be discussed. The question was dropped in the University, but eighty-five French bishops appealed to the Pope to condemn the Five Propositions; on the other hand, ten bishops, headed by the Archbishop of Sens, wrote to the Pope pointing out that such questions, according to the custom of the French Church, must be brought before the French bishops before being referred to Rome. The Pope appointed a commission, which discussed the question in his presence. The representatives of the Jansenists submitted to the commission a statement drawn up by Antoine Arnauld, placing side by side three possible explanations of the Five Propositions, one orthodox and two heretical. But it did not convince the commission, which by a majority of nine to four reported that the propositions ought to be condemned. (One of the minority was Father Luke Wadding, an Irishman, who, according to the Jesuit Rapin, was the first to declare that the fifth proposition was not in the *Augustinus*.) [2] On June 8, 1653, the Pope issued the Bull " Cum occasione ", in which he formally condemned the Five Propositions as heretical. But though he declared that the controversy had arisen about five of the opinions of Cornelius Jansen, Bishop of Ypres, he did not actually say, though he implied, that the Five Propositions were to be found in his book.

The Bull was accepted by a council of thirty bishops at Paris, summoned by royal edict for the purpose by the Theological Faculty of Paris (the Sorbonne), by the University of Louvain, the centre of Jansenist theology, and by the Archbishop of

[1] Text and translation from W. H. Jervis, *Gallican Church*, vol. i, p. 402.
[2] Clark, p. 202.

Utrecht, Jacobus de la Torre, and his clergy, most of whom had Jansenist sympathies. The rebellion of the Fronde, with which the Jansenists were wrongly supposed to be connected, had just been suppressed, and Jansenist influence was therefore politically weak. But Antoine Arnauld now changed his tactics. Accepting the condemnation of the Five Propositions as just, he claimed that they had never been taught by Jansen, and were not to be found in the *Augustinus*; and this remained to the end the position for which the Jansenists fought.[1]

The French bishops appointed a committee to decide whether the Five Propositions were really to be found in the *Augustinus*. The committee reported that they were, that the teaching of St. Augustine was to be understood in the light of the decrees of Trent, and that Baius (condemned by Pope Pius V in 1567) and Jansen had both misinterpreted him. (Observe the effect of belief in the infallibility of Trent. It is an outrage on the history of theological opinion that men should be forced to interpret St. Augustine in the light of the teaching of a council more than 1000 years later, which was opposing the ultra-Augustinianism of the Reformation.)

The report was sent to the Pope, who replied that he had certainly intended to condemn the doctrine of Jansen, as contained in the *Augustinus*, and that he also condemned the treatises of Arnauld in defence of Jansen. On receiving this letter, Cardinal Mazarin, who was governing France during the minority of King Louis XIV, persuaded the bishops not only to accept the Pope's letter, but to require all persons holding public office in the Church to sign it, together with the Bull " Cum occasione ", on pain of being treated as heretics.

The Duc de Liancourt, one of the friends of Port Royal, on making his confession at the church of St. Sulpice, was refused absolution unless he would promise to remove his daughter from the school at Port Royal, where she was being educated, and to send away two Jansenist priests who were staying in his house. He left the church without absolution, and told the story to his friends.[2] Antoine Arnauld thereupon wrote two treatises, *Letter to a Person of Condition*, and *Letter to a Duke and Peer of France* (the Duc de Luynes), in defence of the whole Jansenist position. He sent the *Letter to a Duke and Peer* to Pope Alexander VII, declaring

---

[1] Jervis, vol. i, p. 417; Neale, pp. 19–21.
[2] Romanes, p. 236; Jervis, vol. i, p. 421.

at the same time his unqualified submission. His opponents at once brought the *Letter to a Duke and Peer* before the Theological Faculty of Paris, accusing Arnauld of maintaining that the Five Propositions were not to be found in the *Augustinus*, and that St. Peter was lacking in that grace without which we can do nothing, on the occasion on which he fell into sin, which was said to be a re-assertion of the first of the condemned propositions. At the end of the furious debate which followed persons were allowed to vote who had no statutory right to do so. Arnauld was condemned, and expelled from the Theological Faculty, and it was laid down that in future all candidates for theological degrees were to sign their names to the censure.

It was at this moment, when the Jansenist party seemed to be finally defeated, that the most famous book published by the party appeared, a book which was sufficient by itself to make the controversy immortal, and which brought the issue out from the technical subtleties of the theologians to the understanding of the educated laity: the *Provincial Letters* of Blaise Pascal. The *Provincial Letters* was a scathing exposure of the whole doctrinal and moral system of the Jesuits, and especially of the theory of Probabilism and of the lax morals which it encouraged. The book was not fair to the Jesuits (such a book written in such circumstances was not likely to be), but it has never been adequately answered. The Society of Jesus has never completely recovered from the discredit caused by the *Provincial Letters*. It was translated into English as early as 1657, with the title *Les Provinciales, or the Mysterie of Jesuitism*.[1] Though censured both by the Pope and by the University of Paris, it continued to exercise enormous influence on lay opinion, and to win popular support for Jansenism.

Meanwhile the persecution of Port Royal had begun. In 1648 Mère Angélique and some of the nuns had returned from Port Royal de Paris, which was now too small for the community, to Port Royal des Champs, which had been drained and made more habitable by the *solitaires*. On March 20, 1656, the school for boys was broken up, and the *solitaires* were dispersed. Mère Angélique and her prioress were examined by a magistrate, but nothing could be found to their discredit.[2] Then suddenly the tide turned. The convent had been given a reliquary said to contain one of the thorns of our Lord's crown. Marguérite Perier, the niece of

[1] Clark, p. 101.    [2] Romanes, pp. 250–253.

Pascal, who was being educated at Port Royal, had a serious abscess in her eye. The Holy Thorn was applied to it, and it was immediately cured. No one could deny that the cure was genuine: it was attested by four doctors; the Queen-Mother sent her own surgeon, who confirmed their verdict. The girl herself lived till 1733, and believed till her death that she had been the subject of a miracle.[1]

A tremendous revulsion took place. It was popularly believed, not merely that the cure was a miracle, but that it showed the Divine approval of the Jansenist party. The *solitaires* were allowed to return, and the persecution ceased for a time.

Meanwhile the Assembly of the French clergy decided to draw up a formulary against the errors of Jansenism, to be signed by all ecclesiastics and members of religious orders. It was drafted by Pierre de Marca, Archbishop of Toulouse, the Gallican author of *De Concordantia Sacerdotii et Imperii*, and submitted to Pope Alexander VII, who replied with the Bull " Ad Sacram ", declaring that the Five Propositions were condemned in the sense of Jansen. Accordingly, the Formulary was issued in the following terms: " I, the undersigned, do submit sincerely to the constitution of Pope Innocent X, of May 31, 1653, according to its true meaning, which has been determined by the constitution of our Holy Father Pope Alexander VII, of October 16, 1656. I acknowledge myself bound in conscience to obey these constitutions, and I condemn with heart and mouth the doctrine of the Five Propositions of Cornelius Jansen, contained in his book entitled *Augustinus*, which has been condemned by two Popes, and by the bishops: the said doctrine being not that of St. Augustine, but a misinterpretation of it by Jansen, contrary to the meaning of that great doctor." [2]

This " Formulary " was the cause of all the trouble that followed, for the Jansenists could not sign it without asserting that Jansen's book did contain the Five Propositions. But the bishops did not enforce it, and it remained a dead letter for three years. If the Formulary was to be enforced, on pain of excommunication, it would be treated as a matter of faith. But had the Pope the right to impose a new dogma on the faithful, without the assent of a general council? On Gallican principles, certainly not. This was the point where Gallicanism, which

---

[1] Neale, p. 27; Romanes, pp. 254–256.
[2] Jervis, vol. i, pp. 445 ff.

was a constitutional opposition, and Jansenism, which was a doctrinal opposition, began to converge.

On March 9, 1661, Cardinal Mazarin died, and the young King took the government of France into his own hands. Now, Louis XIV had been educated by the Jesuits, and they were in his confidence all his life; their despotic principles, and perhaps also the laxity of their discipline in morals, suited him exactly. He regarded Jansenism as rebellion against his authority, both civil and ecclesiastical, and was determined to root it out of his kingdom. Accordingly, he insisted that subscription to the Formulary should be enforced by all the bishops.

The Archbishop of Paris, Cardinal de Retz, was in exile because of the part he had taken in the rebellion of the Fronde. His Grand-Vicars, who were in charge of the diocese, issued the Formulary to be signed in an altered form, saying that the only point on which submission was required was the heretical character of the Five Propositions. In this form the nuns of Port Royal were ordered to sign it. They did so unwillingly, as they were not learned in the points at issue (Mère Angélique was dying at the time, and she passed away on August 6, 1661). But the Grand-Vicars were severely reprimanded by the King, and, when they appealed to Rome, by the Pope; and the nuns were ordered to sign the Formulary in its original form. After much discussion, and many prayers, they consented to sign the following statement: " We, the Abbess, Prioress, and nuns of Port Royal, in consideration of our ignorance concerning what is beyond our province, both as regards our sex and our religious profession, feel that all we can do is to testify to the purity of our faith and to declare willingly by our signatures that . . . we willingly agree to all that His Holiness (Alexander VII) and Pope Innocent have declared, and we reject every error which they have rejected." [1]

This was not enough: they were ordered simply to sign the Formulary without qualification. About this time Cardinal de Retz resigned his see, and the new archbishop, Hardouin de Péréfixe, was ordered by the King to insist on obedience. The nuns refused to sign, and they were excommunicated. M. Singlin, a wise and saintly priest who had been their director since the death of St. Cyran, was banished to Brittany. The *solitaires* were finally dispersed. The abbess, and Mère Agnes Arnauld,

[1] Romanes, p. 303.

formerly abbess, and sister of Mère Angélique, with ten other nuns, were removed to other convents. Those who remained were given a new abbess, who was a convert from Protestantism and an ardent Ultramontane; she had belonged to St. François de Sales' Order of the Visitation, and several of her nuns came with her. Life at Port Royal de Paris in these conditions was not happy. At Port Royal des Champs, though there were no intruders, all the nuns were excommunicated.

Meanwhile four bishops—Pavillon of Alet, Henri Arnauld of Angers (brother of Mère Angélique and Antoine Arnauld), de Buzanval of Beauvais, and de Caulet of Pamiers—protested against the enforcement of the Formulary, and issued instructions to their dioceses that there is no infallible judge as to truths not revealed, and, therefore, that the Pope might be mistaken in asserting that certain propositions were contained in a certain book. The King and the Pope could not agree on the method of prosecuting these bishops; for Louis XIV, though determined to crush Jansenism, was also determined to maintain the Gallican liberties, because they included important privileges for the King of France. The Ultramontanes held that the Pope was the sole judge of bishops, while the Gallicans claimed that a bishop could only be tried, in the first instance, before the metropolitan and his suffragans. Louis XIV was not on good terms with the Pope; and before they could come to an agreement the Pope died, May 20, 1667. He was succeeded by Clement IX, who was anxious for peace. With great difficulty negotiations between the Jansenist leaders and the Pope were begun. At last it was agreed that the bishops, without withdrawing their previous instructions, should sign the Formulary afresh, and cause it to be signed by their clergy, giving such explanations as they might wish to their diocesan synods, which explanations were to be deposited at the diocesan registries, but not published. These bishops then sent a letter of explanation and submission to the Pope, which was drawn up by Antoine Arnauld. The Pope declared himself satisfied, and the King assented, and issued an order forbidding all controversy on the subject. The excommunication was removed from Port Royal; Antoine Arnauld came out of concealment and was presented to the King. The " Peace of the Church " was ratified by the Pope on January 19, 1669.[1]

[1] Jervis, vol. i, pp. 454-476.

Pascal had died on August 19, 1662. He had come to differ from the other Jansenists: whereas they distinguished between the " droit " on which the Pope was infallible and the " fait " on which he was not, Pascal perceived that this distinction could not be permanently maintained, and rejected papal infallibility altogether.[1]

[1] Jervis, vol. i, p. 443.

# CHAPTER V

# THE BULL "UNIGENITUS"

SAINTE-BEUVE observes that if, in the first years of the "Peace of the Church", the nuns at Port Royal had been told that these were the last days of prosperity that they would enjoy, and that their decline was at hand, they would not have believed it.[1] Everything seemed to be going well. But the compromise by which the Jansenists signed the Formulary, satisfying their consciences by unpublished qualifications, was too fragile to be permanent. Neither the Jansenists themselves, nor their adversaries the Jesuits, nor the French people, nor the Papacy, were fitted by temperament to maintain a compromise of this kind, or perhaps of any kind, permanently.

But though Clement IX, to whom the peace was due, died on December 9, 1669, a few months after it had been arranged,[2] the controversy and the persecution ceased for about ten years. The Arnauld family was restored to favour at Court. M. de Pomponne (Simon Arnauld), who was French Ambassador in Sweden, was recalled and made Secretary of State; his father, M. d'Andilly, the brother of Mère Angélique and of Antoine Arnauld, who had been for many years a hermit at Port Royal, went to Court, and was received by the King;[3] Antoine himself appeared in public, after years of concealment, and devoted himself, with the assistance of his friend Nicole, to a controversial book against the Calvinistic view of the Eucharist, in order to show that he and his friends had no sympathy with Calvinism, as their enemies alleged.[4]

M. de Saci, the director of Mme. de Longueville, who had been in the Bastille for two years, was released, and was even presented at Court by the Archbishop of Paris.[5]

The Duchesse de Longueville, a princess of the Blood Royal,

[1] C. A. Sainte-Beuve, *Port Royal*, book v, ch. 9 (vol. v, p. 1).
[2] W. H. Jervis, *Gallican Church to the Revolution*, vol. i, p. 476.
[3] Sainte-Beuve, *Port Royal*, vol. v, p. 8.
[4] J. M. Neale, *Church of Holland*, p. 32.
[5] E. Romanes, *Story of Port Royal*, p. 372.

and sister of the great Condé, who had lived a life of amorous adventure in the French Court, and had been the moving spirit of the rebellion of the Fronde, had been converted at Port Royal in 1661. She had played an important part in bringing about the " Peace of the Church ", and she now settled down in a small house near Port Royal des Champs. As long as she lived, her influence with her cousin, King Louis XIV, protected Port Royal and its friends from persecution. She died on April 15, 1679.[1]

Meanwhile the King had quarrelled with the Pope over the " droit de régale "—the ancient right of the Kings of France, in certain dioceses, to exercise the patronage of the bishop during the vacancy of the see, without any institution to the care of souls being required of his presentee. This right appears to have arisen from the position of bishops under the feudal system : Henri IV had in 1606 promised not to extend it to any dioceses where it had not been customary before. The question had long been in dispute between the clergy and the lawyers, and on February 10, 1673, Louis XIV declared that he possessed the " droit de régale " in all archbishoprics and bishoprics in his kingdom, except those which had been expressly exempted in return for certain cessions or exchanges. Most of the bishops submitted to the royal claim, but Nicolas Pavillon, Bishop of Alet, and François de Caulet, Bishop of Pamiers, both of whom had been among the bishops who refused to accept the " Formulary of Alexander VII ", declined to submit, and appealed to Pope Innocent XI. Pavillon died in 1677. Caulet was deprived of all his possessions by the King, and died soon afterwards, in 1680.[2]

In the dispute which followed, the Jesuits, contrary to all their principles and traditions, supported the King, while the Jansenists were on the side of the Pope. Louis XIV was all his life devoted to the Jesuits, and his confessor belonged to the Society. Innocent XI hated Louis XIV personally, admired the Jansenists for their courage and high moral principles, and was determined not to allow any infringement of what the Popes, ever since Hildebrand, had held to be the rights of the Church.

In 1682 the Assembly of the French clergy issued the celebrated declaration known as the Four Gallican Articles. It was

[1] Romanes, p. 391 ; C. Beard, *Port Royal*, vol. ii, p. 324.
[2] Jervis, *op. cit.*, vol. ii, pp. 25–29.

drawn up by Jacques Benigne Bossuet, Bishop of Meaux, the most famous divine and preacher in France. Gilbert de Choiseul, Bishop of Tournai in French Flanders, had been associated with him in the task, but they could not agree on one very important point. Choiseul maintained that not only particular Popes, but also the Roman see itself, were capable of falling into heresy. Bossuet denied this: he held that the Roman see was indefectible, but not infallible; particular Popes might err, but the Papacy could not fall permanently into error. Choiseul therefore resigned his share in the task of drawing up the declaration, and Bossuet is alone responsible for it. Bossuet, though the best-known champion of Gallicanism, was quite a moderate Gallican, and an enthusiastic defender of the Papacy within Gallican limits, especially in his controversies with Protestants; for the reconciliation to Rome of Protestants, especially French Protestants, was one of the chief aims of his life. It was he who took part with Leibnitz in the last attempt to bring back the Lutherans of Germany to the Roman Communion. The time was favourable to such an enterprise; for the wars of religion, with the passions they had aroused, were over, and the difference of outlook among the Lutherans caused, first by Pietism and then by the Enlightenment (*Aufklärung*), had not yet begun. But when Leibnitz found that so moderate a Romanist as Bossuet regarded the decrees of Trent as irreformable, and insisted on their acceptance without criticism, he broke off the discussion.[1]

We must not exaggerate the difference between the Gallicans and the Ultramontanes. Both accepted the papal claims based on the alleged succession to St. Peter, and the decrees of Trent in which those claims are asserted. The Gallican Articles were drawn up in as moderate language as possible, and were, in any case, only an expression of opinion, not a declaration of faith.

They were enforced in France, but the French did not seek to persuade other Roman Catholics to accept them: they were regarded as privileges of the French Church and nation, rather than universal truths.[2]

The text of the Four Gallican Articles is as follows:—

(1) St. Peter and his successors, vicars of Christ, and likewise the Church herself, have received from God power in things

---

[1] C. J. Jordan, *Reunion of the Churches*, pp. 167–176.
[2] Some Gallicans believed them to be universal truths, but they were not so treated in practice, and Roman Catholics in other countries were not interested.

spiritual and pertaining to salvation, but not in things temporal and civil, inasmuch as the Lord says, " My Kingdom is not of this world "; and again, " Render unto Cæsar the things which are Cæsar's, and unto God the things which are God's ". The Apostolic precept also holds, " Let every soul be subject unto the higher powers ", etc. Consequently kings and rulers are not by the law of God subject to any ecclesiastical power, nor to the keys of the Church, with respect to their temporal government. Their subjects cannot be released from obeying them, nor absolved from the oath of allegiance; and this maxim, necessary to public tranquillity, and not less advantageous to the Church than to the State, is to be strictly maintained, as conformable to the word of God, the tradition of the Fathers, and the example of the Saints.

(2) The plenitude of power in things spiritual, which resides in the Apostolic See and the successors of St. Peter, is such that at the same time the decrees of the Œcumenical Council of Constance, in its 4th and 5th sessions, approved as they are by the Holy See and by the practice of the whole Church, remain in full force and perpetual obligation; and the Gallican Church does not approve the opinion of those who depreciate the said decrees, as being of doubtful authority, insufficiently approved, or restricted in their application to a time of schism.

(3) Hence the exercise of the Apostolic authority must be regulated by the canons enacted by the Spirit of God and consecrated by the reverence of the whole world. The ancient rules, customs, and institutions received by the realm and Church of France remain likewise inviolable; and it is for the honour and glory of the Apostolic See that such enactments, confirmed by the consent of the said see and of the churches, should be observed without deviation.

(4) The Pope has the principal place in deciding questions of faith, and his decrees extend to every church and to all churches; but nevertheless his judgment is not irreversible until confirmed by the consent of the Church.[1]

The Assembly of the French clergy, numbering sixty-eight persons, which was summoned because of the dispute over the " droit de régale " (for this was the occasion of the publication of the Articles), passed the Four Articles unanimously; and the King ordered the Parlement of Paris to register them (so as to

[1] Jervis, vol. ii, p. 50.

make them part of the law of the land), and the bishops to enforce them everywhere in France.[1] Antoine Arnauld, who had retired to Brussels in 1677, supported the Gallican Articles, and as he was in favour at Rome because he supported the Papal side in the dispute about the " droit de régale ", tried to persuade the Pope not to condemn them. The Pope, however, objected to the Articles so strongly that he refused to confirm the appointment to a bishopric of anyone who had been a member of the Assembly which passed them. Louis XIV appealed to the future General Council, and occupied Avignon, which was Papal territory. The struggle continued until 1691, when a new Pope, Innocent XII, consented to a reconciliation. The bishops-elect, who had not received Papal confirmation, and therefore could not be consecrated, had to send, as individuals, a letter to the Pope, which had been agreed to beforehand by the French and Roman Courts, and which was drawn up in such a way that the Pope could regard it as a repudiation of the teaching of the Gallican Articles, while the French King and bishops could regard it merely as an expression of regret that the Assembly had displeased the Pope. The essential part of it ran thus: " Prostrate at the feet of your Holiness, we confess and declare that we are profoundly and beyond all words distressed by those acts of the aforesaid Assembly which have given such serious offence to your Holiness and your predecessors. Accordingly, whatever may have been deemed to be decreed in that Assembly concerning the power of the Church and the pontifical authority, we hold as not decreed, and declare that it ought to be so regarded. Moreover we regard as not synodically determined that which may have been taken to be so determined by that Assembly to the prejudice of the rights of the churches." [2]

Making all allowances for the conventions of a sycophantic age, we see from this humiliating and servile form of address how far the Gallican bishops were, even at the highest point of Gallicanism, from claiming any kind of equality between themselves and the Pope. However, this letter was only sent by the bishops-elect as individuals, not by the whole Assembly, still less by the French Episcopate. Louis XIV withdrew his order enforcing the Gallican decrees; but he maintained the right of all Frenchmen to hold them as matters of private opinion, and

[1] Jervis, vol. ii, p. 51.          [2] Jervis, vol. ii, p. 77.

this right continued until the Ultramontane reaction which followed the French Revolution.

The Assembly which issued the Four Articles also settled the question of the "droit de régale" by a compromise. The extension of this right to all French dioceses was accepted by the Assembly, but the King undertook to apply to the bishop for canonical institution for the priest whom he should appoint, wherever the right should be used. The compromise was condemned by Innocent XI in his anger at the issue of the Four Articles; but it remained in force none the less.

It was during the period of the struggle with Rome that Louis XIV, under the influence of Madame de Maintenon, his morganatic wife, revoked the Edict of Nantes, and thereby deprived the French Protestants of all civil rights, and even of the right to escape from France. This measure was supported by Ultramontanes, Gallicans, and Jansenists alike: Antoine Arnauld defended it on the ground of the fatal letter in which St. Augustine had approved of the persecution of the Donatists by the imperial Government. Only Pope Innocent XI privately disapproved of it because it led to insincere conversions, and perhaps also because it was the work of Louis XIV. Nevertheless, he ordered it to be celebrated by a Te Deum and public rejoicings.[1]

The English Revolution, of which the Revocation of the Edict of Nantes was one of the contributory causes (by showing the English people what the English Church might expect if James II were allowed to carry out his policy to its probable conclusion), took place during this dispute between Louis XIV and the Pope. James II was, of course, closely allied with Louis XIV, who was his first cousin, and it was for this reason that the Pope gave his support to William of Orange at the time of the Battle of the Boyne.

The Four Articles were attacked by Ultramontane theologians in various countries, among others by the Primate of Hungary, by the General of the Jesuits, and most bitterly of all by Roccaberti, Archbishop of Valencia, in Spain. In reply, Bossuet composed his great treatise, *Defensio Declarationis Cleri Gallicani* (Defence of the Declaration of the French Clergy). It was finished in 1685, but not published, for fear of breaking the peace between France and the Papacy; revised and consider-

[1] Jervis, vol. ii, pp. 66—68; Arnauld, *Lettres*, 537, 538, 541.

ably altered in 1696–9, and bequeathed by the author to his nephew, the Bishop of Troyes, with instructions to entrust it to no one but the King himself; and at last published in 1745, forty years after the author's death. It was never condemned at Rome, because the Pope did not wish to revive the controversy; and it remains the classical defence of the Gallican position.[1]

Meanwhile the persecution of Port Royal had broken out again. As early as 1676, the Bishop of Angers (Henri Arnauld, brother of Antoine) had unwisely raised the question of *droit* and *fait*, and had provoked the King to issue an edict from his camp declaring that the concessions of 1669 were only for the benefit of weak consciences. But, as I have mentioned above, on April 15, 1679 the Duchesse de Longueville died. After her stormy youth she had been a true penitent for twenty years, through the influence of Mère Angélique and M. Singlin of Port Royal. Her example had been followed by her brother, the Prince de Conti, and his wife, who was a niece of Cardinal Mazarin. Conti was governor of Languedoc, and was under the guidance of the saintly Bishop of Alet, Nicolas Pavillon (one of the four bishops who refused to sign the Formulary, and one of the two who repudiated the " droit de régale "), who bade him, instead of retiring from the world, as he wished to do, devote his wealth, his influence, and his position as Governor to helping the miserable peasants of the provinces ravaged by the civil war of the Fronde, carried on by Conti and his friends.[2]

Whatever mistakes Port Royal may have made, this at least must be put down to its credit, that it brought to genuine and lifelong penitence so many members of that most difficult class to convert, the high nobility of France, trained from birth to regard themselves as superior to the rest of mankind, and encouraged by only too many of their spiritual advisers to think that such important persons as they were had a licence to sin.

It was the influence of Madame de Longueville which had protected Port Royal so long: as soon as she was dead, the persecution began again. The truth was, that Louis XIV was jealous, as Richelieu had been before him. He could not bear the thought that there were subjects of his who cared nothing for his favour, whose strict morality was a reproach to his own,

---

[1] Jervis, vol. ii, pp. 56–59.
[2] Romanes, *Story of Port Royal*, pp. 402–406; Beard, vol. ii, pp. 291—295.

and who had attracted many of his nobles, of both sexes, from his brilliant court to their convent.[1]

The King at once forbade Antoine Arnauld to hold any gatherings in his lodgings, since the conferences which he had attended at Madame de Longueville's house did not meet with the royal approval. Louis XIV had now a fresh grievance against him; not only was he the recognized leader of the Jansenist party, which the King's Jesuit advisers, as well as his own jealous inclinations, were always urging him to suppress, but he was a determined opponent of the King's claim to the " droit de régale ". An address which had been sent in 1677 to Pope Innocent XI by the Bishops of Arras and St. Pons, attacking the maxims of certain casuists as dangerous to morality, and which had been written with the assistance of Nicole, was another cause of complaint against him; though he personally had nothing to do with it. Perceiving that he would never be safe or free in France, Arnauld retired to Mons, and spent the remaining fifteen years of his life in voluntary exile. From 1681 to 1689 he lived at Veen in the United Provinces. Archbishop van Neercassel of Utrecht (see Chapter VI) was an intimate friend of his. But he had to leave Dutch territory because of his attack on William of Orange for his conduct in dethroning James II, his father-in-law (see Appendix B).[2]

On May 6, 1679, the Archbishop of Paris, François de Harlai, an able but harsh and ambitious prelate whose personal morals were bad, closed the school for girls at Port Royal (the school for boys had been closed in 1661), sent away the priests and *solitaires*, and soon afterwards forbade the profession of any more novices. The abbess at this time was the second Mère Angélique Arnauld, who had been elected the year before; she was the niece of the first Mère Angélique and of Antoine Arnauld, the daughter of M. d'Andilly, and the sister of M. de Pomponne, the Secretary of State. She continued to be abbess until her death in 1684. The *solitaires* of Port Royal, to whom the King had a special and unreasonable objection, retired to Pomponne. The abbey of St. Cyran was suppressed altogether; Lancelot, a well-known member of the party, who was a monk there, retired to Quimperlé in Brittany (see Appendix). About the same time M. de Pomponne was dismissed from his office. Sainte-Beuve

[1] Sainte-Beuve, *Port Royal*, vol. v, p. 199.
[2] Jervis, vol. ii, p. 20; Romanes, p. 432.

thinks that his dismissal had nothing to do with Port Royal, but was due to incompetence, and quotes a letter of the King's to this effect,[1] but it is not certain that Louis was sincere, especially as Pomponne was restored to the ministry in 1691. Antoine Arnauld, though now an old man, did not cease from controversy. He attacked, at the request of Bossuet, the speculations of Malebranche, which were afterwards condemned at Rome; and denounced the theory of the Jesuit Meunier, that a sin against the law of reason, if committed by one who has no knowledge of God, or even has at the moment no thought of God, is " philosophical sin ", and does not offend God or deserve everlasting punishment. In revenge for this attack the Jesuits got the Pope to condemn a number of propositions quoted from Arnauld's book on Frequent Communion, which had been examined and declared harmless forty years before. They went further: in 1691 they forged letters in Arnauld's name to a young and ignorant priest at Douai, called de Ligny, inviting him to sign a thesis maintaining an extreme form of Jansenism. De Ligny fell into the trap, and was then offered by the pretended Arnauld non-existent preferment in a southern diocese. Arnauld, then nearly eighty years old, protested against this attempt to discredit him, which is known as the " Fourberie de Douai ", but he could obtain no redress. He died at Brussels on August 8, 1694, and was buried in St. Catherine's Church there. Cardinal D'Aguirre, addressing the Consistory at Rome, said that Arnauld had done no less honour to France than Clement and Origen to Egypt or St. Jerome to Dalmatia; and that the place which he himself occupied in the sacred College was at first intended for Arnauld, who would have occupied it with greater merit and success than he did.[2]

In 1695 Archbishop de Harlai died, and was succeeded in the archbishopric of Paris by Louis Antoine de Noailles. The Jansenists had reason to believe that the new archbishop was favourable to them, for he had, when Bishop of Châlons, formally sanctioned the *Moral Reflexions on the New Testament*, written by Paschasius Quesnel and originally published in 1671. Quesnel, who was of Scottish descent, was born at Paris in 1634, and was educated by the Congregation of the Oratory. (This was the community founded by St. Philip Neri, to which Newman and Faber afterwards belonged.) He had become a member of the

[1] Sainte-Beuve, vol. v, p. 199.          [2] Jervis, vol. ii, p. 88.

Oratory, but left it in 1684, because he would not sign a repudiation of Jansenism imposed by the community on its members. Soon afterwards he joined Arnauld at Veen, ministered to him on his death-bed, and after his death was generally regarded as his successor, " the Elisha of the Jansenist Elijah ".[1] His book, which had been originally published with the approval of Felix Vialant, Bishop of Châlons, appeared in an enlarged edition in 1693, with a laudatory preface by Bishop de Noailles.

The new archbishop had hardly taken possession of his see, when the publication of the *Exposition de la Foi Catholique touchant la Grâce et la Predestination* (Exposition of the Catholic Faith on grace and predestination), a posthumous work by the Abbé de Barcos, nephew of St. Cyran, raised loud demands that he should condemn it. This he proceeded to do, in a manifesto partly written for him by Bossuet. Whereupon an anonymous writer, who is said to have been a Jesuit named Doucin,[2] produced a pamphlet showing that the teaching of Quesnel's book, for which Noailles, as Bishop of Châlons, had written a preface, was the same as that of Barcos' book which, as Archbishop of Paris, he had condemned. The Archbishop had the pamphlet (known as the *Problème Ecclesiastique*) publicly burnt, and got Bossuet to write a reply, which took the form of a defence of the *Reflexions Morales* of Quesnel: interesting when the subsequent fate of that book is remembered! But the *Avertissement* of Bossuet was only published much later, in Holland.[3] The result of all this was that Noailles got a reputation for sympathy with Jansenism which clung to him for the rest of his life. He was an irresolute man, who had been appointed mainly for his noble birth; his personal character was above reproach, but he had neither the knowledge nor the judgment needed for an Archbishop of Paris at a period when great ecclesiastical, and even political, disturbances were caused by subtle theological differences.

In 1702, M. Eustace, confessor to the nuns of Port Royal, who was not a good theologian, unwisely stirred up again the whole controversy by publishing a work called the *Cas de Conscience*, on the question whether a priest might give absolution to a penitent who, while condemning the Five Propositions, did

---

[1] Jervis, vol. ii, p. 91.
[2] Jervis attributes it to Thierry de Viaixnes, a well-known Jansenist, but the researches of M. le Roy have shown that Viaixnes denied all knowledge of it: See J. H. Lupton, *Archbishop Wake and the Prospect of Union*, p. 27.
[3] Jervis, vol. ii, p. 95; Neale, *Church of Holland*, p. 35.

not believe that they were to be found in the *Augustinus* of Jansen, or that the Pope was infallible in matters of historic fact, but who (the penitent) was willing to observe " a respectful silence " on the question.[1] The book caused much alarm, because it received the approval of forty doctors of divinity in the University of Paris. Bossuet went into the whole question again, and his researches confirmed him in the conclusion that the Five Propositions were to be found in the *Augustinus*. Noailles, who had been made a Cardinal in 1700, on Bossuet's advice persuaded thirty-five of the forty doctors to recant; the remaining five were sent into exile by *letteres de cachet*. But very diverse opinions were held among the French bishops. On July 17, 1705, Pope Clement XI issued the Bull " Vineam Domini Sabaoth ", requiring universal submission to the Formulary of Alexander VII in express terms, and thereby annulling the compromise of 1669.[2] This Bull led to the final destruction of Port Royal. The remnant of the nuns was ordered to accept it; but they refused to do so without the additional clause "sans dérogera ce qui s'est fait à notre égard à la paix de l'Église sous le pape Clement IX " (without prejudice to what was done on our behalf at the Peace of the Church under Pope Clement IX). According to Saint-Simon this would have satisfied Rome; but the King of France was inexorable: Cardinal de Noailles was compelled, against his will, to take action. He admitted to a friend that even if the nuns had been willing to submit, the King had long been determined to destroy Port Royal.[3] In 1706 the King prohibited the abbess from receiving any more novices. In the next year the whole revenue of Port Royal des Champs was given to Port Royal de Paris (which had been completely separated from the original Port Royal in 1669). This reduced the nuns to complete destitution. The last abbess, Mère Elizabeth de Boulard, who had succeeded Mère Agnes de Racine, the aunt of the great tragic poet, had died on April 20, 1706, and they had been forbidden to elect any successor to her; they were led by the Prioress, Louise de Mesnil, who had been appointed by the abbess on her death-bed. On November 18, 1707, Cardinal de Noailles excommunicated the nuns for refusing

---

[1] Sainte-Beuve, vol. vi, p. 169; Jervis, vol. ii, p. 169. Eustace was also opposed to the favourite Jesuit doctrine of the Immaculate Conception of the Blessed Virgin.
[2] Jervis, vol. ii, p. 177.
[3] Jervis, vol. ii, p. 187; *Histoire de Port Royal*, vol. iii, p. 150.

to submit to the Bull "Vineam Domini"; their saving clause was pronounced "illusory, evading the law, and injurious to the Holy See". They appealed to the Archbishop of Lyons, as Primate of France, but in vain. In March 1708, at the King's request, Clement XI definitely suppressed Port Royal des Champs. Various acts of resistance postponed the final catastrophe till the next year. In August 1709 the Abbess of Port Royal de Paris came and took formal possession of the buildings; but the prioress and nuns refused to accept her as abbess. On October 24 M. d'Argenson, a lieutenant of police, arrived with 300 soldiers, and took possession. The nuns, all aged women, were removed to different convents in various parts of France, where they were treated as prisoners and refused the Sacraments. The convent was razed to the ground, and the very bodies of the dead were removed from the churchyard;[1] those of the Arnauld family were claimed by M. de Pomponne, who buried them in a chapel on his estate, but many of the others were thrown into one pit in the cemetery of St. Lambert.[2] At last the hatred of Louis XIV and the Jesuits for Port Royal was satisfied.

In all this Cardinal de Noailles had been the unwilling agent of the King and the Pope. He made a pilgrimage to the site of Port Royal, accompanied only by his secretary, and throwing himself on the ground, cried to Heaven for mercy. It was with difficulty that the secretary, who had always advised him against the destruction of Port Royal, could bring him back to Paris.[3]

Sainte-Beuve observes that the fate which Louis XIV inflicted on the bodies of the nuns of Port Royal befell his own body, with those of all his house, in the French Revolution.[4]

In 1709 Michel Le Tellier, the Provincial of the French Jesuits, became confessor to the King. He was a narrow-minded and fanatical Norman peasant, who hated Cardinal de Noailles personally, detested his supposed sympathy with Jansenism, and determined to bring discredit on him by attacking Quesnel's *Moral Reflexions on the New Testament*, to which Noailles, as Bishop of Châlons, had given his approval. The book had already been condemned at Rome, through the influence of Cardinal Fabroni, who had been offended by a remark by Cardinal de Noailles which he had applied to himself: Noailles had spoken of "the enemy sowing tares", and Fabroni chose to consider that he

---

[1] Some of them were devoured by dogs.   [2] Jervis, vol. ii, p. 192.
[3] Jervis, vol. ii, p. 193.   [4] Sainte-Beuve, *Port Royal*, vol. vi, p. 239.

himself was meant.[1] But the condemnation had never been accepted in France. The book was widely used there. Père la Chaise, the King's former confessor, himself a Jesuit, had it always by him for his own edification.

Two bishops, De Lescure of Luçon and Champflour of La Rochelle, issued, in July 1710, a denunciation of the *Moral Reflexions* (Saint Simon says that they acted under the influence of Le Tellier, but this is doubtful). The book was advertised by handbills in Paris; and some of these were placed on the gates of the archbishop's palace. Lescure and Champflour had each a nephew who was a student at the Seminary of St. Sulpice: the archbishop, hastily assuming that these students had fastened the bills on his gate, had them both sent down. The bishops, their uncles, made a strong protest; but the Chapter of Notre Dame, the clergy of the diocese, and the Theological Faculty of the University gave their support to the archbishop, who proceeded to publish an order condemning the work of the two bishops, and even accusing it of Jansenism. The King was much annoyed; but at this moment the archbishop obtained proof, through a private letter which fell into his hands, that Le Tellier had formed a plot to induce the bishops to denounce Noailles to the King and to force him to take action against the *Moral Reflexions*. There was a storm of indignation, and Noailles wrote to Madame de Maintenon, " What hope is there of his Majesty's salvation, so long as he entrusts himself to a confessor who, far from recommending virtue by his example, is false to the first principles of truth and sincerity, having offered to declare upon oath that he had no concern in what has passed, though he was the principal author of it, as is proved by the papers which have come to light? " However, the old King could not bring himself to dismiss his confessor, or break his life-long alliance with the Jesuits.

Cardinal de Noailles now felt it his duty to inhibit most of the Jesuits in Paris for teaching false doctrine and stirring up rebellion against himself. It was at this moment that Louis XIV, under the influence of Le Tellier, asked the Pope for a Bull distinctly specifying and condemning the errors in the *Moral Reflexions*. Accordingly, a " congregation " or commission of sixteen theologians, five of whom were cardinals, was appointed by the Pope to report on the book. The only member of the

[1] Jervis, vol. ii, p. 183.

commission who understood French, Le Drou, was sent to Liège on a special mission through the influence of Cardinal Fabroni; and they had to use a Latin translation, said by some to have been misleading. But they examined it with great care for eighteen months. Meanwhile Cardinal de Noailles issued a defence of his own attitude, denying that he had ever been a Jansenist, except as a follower of St. Augustine and St. Thomas Aquinas, and pointing out that the *Moral Reflexions* had been defended by Bossuet.

The result of the inquiry into the character of the *Moral Reflexions* was the Bull " Unigenitus ", dated September 8th, 1713. This was the famous Bull which nearly broke the Roman Communion in two, distracted the French Church for three-quarters of a century, and was one of the contributing causes of the French Revolution. The Bull "Unigenitus" now took the place of the Five Propositions and the Formulary of Alexander VII, which declared them to be Jansen's, as the test of blind obedience to the papal decrees, which was all along the real point at issue.

The Bull condemned 101 propositions, taken out of the *Moral Reflexions on the New Testament* by Quesnel, as false, captious, ill-sounding, offensive to pious ears, scandalous, pernicious, temerarious, injurious to the Church and her practice, and also to the temporal powers, seditious, impious, blasphemous, suspected of heresy already condemned, and renewing divers heresies, principally those contained in the Five Propositions of Jansen, taken in the sense in which they were condemned.[1]

The 101 propositions were not all condemned with equal severity: only twelve were asserted to be actually heretical. Pope Clement XI, who is said to have used the condemned book for his own edification, told M. Amelot, the envoy of the French Government, that he had been told that the Bull would be unanimously accepted, and that he would never have issued it if he had known what trouble it would cause. He added that the real reason why 101 propositions had been condemned was that Le Tellier had told Louis XIV, that more than 100 propositions in the book deserved censure, and that the Pope had therefore been forced by the Jesuits to condemn at least 101, so as to justify Le Tellier.[2]

---

[1] Denzinger, *Enchiridion Symbolorum*, 1451 ; Jervis, vol. ii, p. 213.
[2] Jervis, vol. ii, p. 266; Saint-Simon, *Memoirs*, vol. viii, p. 246.

The following propositions are specimens of the teaching condemned by the Bull " Unigenitus " (the full text of the condemned propositions will be found in Appendix A to this chapter).

*Proposition* 1.  What else remains in a soul which has lost God and His grace, except sin and its consequences, a proud poverty, and idle indigence—that is, a general inability to work, to pray and to perform any good work? (St. John 15. 5, St. Matt. 9. 26, 2 Cor. 3. 5).  Condemned as heretical.

*Proposition* 2.  "The grace of Jesus Christ, the efficacious principle of every kind of good, is necessary for every good action. Without it we not only do nothing, but we can do nothing" (St. John 6. 44, Phil. 2. 13).  As it stands, heretical; from the context, suspected of heresy.

*Proposition* 3.  " In vain Thou commandest, O Lord, if Thou dost not give that which Thou commandest " (Ps. 127. 1. Council of Orange, Canon 9: " Every time that we do any good thing, it is God who acts in us and with us, to the end that we may do it ").  Ill-sounding and offensive to pious ears.

*Proposition* 25.  " God enlightens and heals the soul as well as the body by His will alone; He commands, and is obeyed " (St. John 5. 21; Jer. 31. 18).  Suspected of heresy.

*Proposition* 28.  " The first grace which God grants the sinner is the pardon of his sins " (St. Augustine, *Tractat.* 3 in S. Johannem, section 8; S. Fulgentius, *De Remissione Peccatorum* 5). Suspected of heresy.

*Proposition* 50.  " It is in vain that we cry to God, My Father, if it is not the spirit of love that cries " (St. Augustine, Sermon 71 on St. Matthew).  Pernicious in practice and offensive to pious ears.

*Proposition* 54.  " It is love alone that speaks to God, it is love alone that God hears " (1 Cor. 13. 1; St. Augustine on Psalm 119).  Scandalous, temerarious, impious, and erroneous.

*Proposition* 58.  " There is neither God nor religion, where love is not."

*Proposition* 71.  " Man may dispense, for his preservation, with a law which God made for his benefit" (St. Matt. 12. 3; 1 Sam. 21. 6; 1 Macc. 2. 41).  Scandalous and pernicious in practice.

*Proposition* 74.  "The Church, or the whole Christ, has the Incarnate Word as Head, and all the saints as members " (1 Cor. 12. 27; Eph. 1. 22).

*Proposition* 78.  " Man is separated from the chosen people, whose type was the Jewish people and whose head is Jesus Christ, as much by not living according to the Gospel, as by not believing the Gospel."

*Proposition* 79. "It is useful and necessary, at every time, at every place, and for every kind of person, to study and appreciate the spirit, piety, and mysteries of the Holy Scriptures" (1 Cor. 14. 5).

*Proposition* 80. "The obscurity of the word of God is no reason why the laity should be dispensed from reading it" (St. John Chrysostom, Sermon 3, on Lazarus). Dubious.

*Proposition* 84. "To take away the New Testament from the hands of Christians, or to keep it closed from them, by taking away from them the means of understanding it, is to gag for them the mouth of Christ."

*Proposition* 90. "The Church has authority to excommunicate that she may exercise it through the chief pastors, with the consent, at any rate presumed, of the whole body."

*Proposition* 91. "The fear of an unjust excommunication ought never to prevent us from doing our duty: we never depart from the Church even when we appear to be expelled from her by the wickedness of men when we are attached to God, Jesus Christ, and the Church herself by love."[1] It was the condemnation of this proposition that horrified Saint-Simon.

To sum up, the chief doctrines condemned by this Bull were that Divine Grace is irresistible (which St. Augustine undoubtedly taught), that prayer is useless without love, that immorality separates from God no less than unorthodoxy, that all the faithful ought to study the New Testament, and that the Church's excommunication, if unjust, is not to be feared.

The Bull was registered at Paris, both by the University and by the Parlement, through pressure from the King, who sent a number of recalcitrant members of the University to the Bastille. But it at once aroused a storm of protest and criticism, which was headed by Cardinal de Noailles and eight other bishops; they were the Archbishop of Tours and the Bishops of Verdun, Laon, Châlons, Senez (Soanen, of whom more hereafter), Boulogne, St. Malo, and Bayonne. The Bishop of Laon afterwards withdrew.[2]

---

[1] Denzinger, *op. cit.*, 1351–1451; Jervis, vol. ii, pp. 213–215; Neale, pp. 42–45.

[2] Jervis, vol. ii, p. 219; Neale, p. 46.

There were two objections to the Bull " Unigenitus ": the Jansenist objection, that its teaching was false, being contrary to Holy Scripture and to the teaching of the Fathers; and the Gallican objection, that the Pope had no right to impose any doctrine on the French Church against the will of the French bishops, without the assent of a General Council. Dr. Neale quotes at length the Abbé Rohrbacher's unconvincing defence of the Bull. Fénélon, who was himself in favour of it, wrote thus to Père Daubenton: " People exclaim on all sides that the Pope has condemned St. Augustine, St. Paul and even Jesus Christ. They declare that the constitution (the Bull) is Pelagian, and that it only serves to demonstrate the fallibility of Rome." [1]

Saint-Simon says that the Bull " has made so many martyrs, depopulated our schools, introduced ignorance, fanaticism, and misrule, rewarded vice, thrown the whole community into the greatest confusion, and established the most arbitrary and barbarous inquisition: evils which have doubled in the last thirty years."

While the controversy was at its height, on September 1, 1715, Louis XIV died, after a reign of seventy-two years (the longest in modern European history). On his death-bed he said to Cardinals de Rohan and de Bissy (the former was Bishop of Strasbourg, the latter was Bossuet's successor at Meaux), in the presence of Madame de Maintenon, his wife, and Le Tellier, his confessor, " I am not learned enough to understand the questions which disturb the Church; I have simply followed your advice." The two cardinals answered by praising all that he had done. He wished to see Cardinal de Noailles and be reconciled with him, but Le Tellier would not admit Noailles unless he would first accept the " Unigenitus "; and the King died without seeing him. It was said that just before he died he was admitted to full membership of the Society of Jesus, which was regarded as a kind of passport to Heaven.[2] (Saint-Simon, however, does not believe this.)

The King's death changed the whole situation. The new King, Louis XV (his predecessor's great-grandson), was a child, and the Regent, Philip Duke of Orleans, was indifferent to both religion and morals. He at once formed an alliance with the Gallican party, in order to prevent an alleged plot to deprive

---

[1] Jervis, vol. ii, p. 218; Correspondence de Fénélon, vol. iv, p. 263.
[2] Jervis, vol. ii, p. 228.

him of the Regency, in which he believed some of the leading courtiers to be implicated. He appointed Cardinal de Noailles head of the department of government dealing with Church affairs, "the Council of Conscience". By this means he hoped to have the support of the large section of the nation, whose sympathies were ardently Gallican. He tried to induce the Pope to explain or modify the Bull, but in vain. However, the opposition to it grew stronger and stronger: four bishops—De la Broux of Mirepoix, Soanen of Senez, Colbert of Montpellier, and Delangle of Boulogne—drew up a formal appeal to the future General Council against the Bull "Unigenitus", and against any measures which the Pope might take against them in consequence of their appeal. At the same time they declared that they did not intend to speak, or even to think, anything contrary to the teaching of the Church or to the authority of the see of Rome.[1]

On March 5, 1717, the Theological Faculty of Paris, by an overwhelming majority, concurred with the appeal of the four bishops, thus withdrawing its former assent to the Bull, which Louis XIV had forced upon it.

But there were two great weaknesses in the apparently triumphant cause. One was the timidity of Cardinal de Noailles, who, instead of putting himself at the head of the opposition to the "Unigenitus" by joining the appellants, kept the appeal which he had written locked up. The other was the fact that the Regent, to whom religious questions were of no interest, thought it wise to hold the balance even between the two parties, and sent the four bishops who had signed the appeal back to their dioceses. The whole country became divided into two parties, the Acceptants or "Constitutionnaires", who accepted the Bull, and the Appellants, who rejected it and appealed to the future General Council. The former was supported by most of the bishops (who had, of course, been appointed by Louis XIV); the latter by the Theological Faculty of Paris, the lawyers headed by the Parlement of Paris, and the great majority of the nation.

The Pope refused to confirm the twelve candidates for bishoprics nominated by the Regent, whereupon the Regent set up a commission to inquire into the possibility of appointing bishops without Papal confirmation. (There was a recent precedent for this: when Portugal had gained its independence from Spain, in

[1] Jervis, vol. ii, p. 235.

1640, the Pope had at first refused to confirm Portuguese candidates for the episcopate, and canonists had declared that they
might be consecrated without his confirmation; which would
have been done, if he had not yielded.) [1]

The Pope, on hearing of the Regent's design, was so much
alarmed that he confirmed the appointments at once, in such
haste that the courier who brought the necessary documents to
Paris died of fatigue! [2]

Since all attempts to induce the Appellants to accept the
Bull had failed, the Pope, by his Bull " Pastoralis Officii ",
August 28, 1718, excommunicated them.  Upon this, Cardinal
de Noailles published his appeal to the General Council, which
hitherto he had kept secret; the four bishops renewed their
appeal, and twelve others joined them; so did the University
of Paris, the Chapters of Notre Dame and many other cathedrals,
several religious communities, and many priests, numbering in
all over 2000.

Cardinal de Noailles did not forget the surviving nuns of
Port Royal.  Only six were left; five at Malnoue, one at Etrées.
The Cardinal wrote to the latter, promising to receive her back
into communion, in public, as an act of penitence for the destruction of Port Royal.  But the nun, Madame de Valais, in order
to spare his feelings, insisted on fixing the hour at 4 a.m.[3]

It was at this moment when the French Church seemed to be
torn asunder by a schism, and many of the leading bishops had
been excommunicated by the Pope, that the famous negotiation
took place between the Archbishop of Canterbury, Dr. William
Wake, and one of the Paris theologians, Dr. Louis du Pin, with
the object of bringing about reunion between the English and
French Churches.

Archbishop Wake had in 1682 been appointed chaplain to
Lord Preston, the English Ambassador in Paris, and had spent
six years there, at the time of the controversy over the Four
Gallican Articles.  He was well known in France, and had
written an answer to Bossuet's *Variations of Protestantism*, showing
that Roman Catholics also had their variations.  William Beauvoir, who held the same post as chaplain to the English Ambassador in Paris thirty-five years later, began in 1717 to correspond with Archbishop Wake about French ecclesiastical affairs.

[1] *Second Apology of the Bishop of Babylon*, chap. xi, p. 304.
[2] Jervis, vol. ii, p. 239.          [3] Neale, p. 50.

On February 11, 1718, Du Pin wrote to Beauvoir expressing an ardent desire for the reunion of the English and French Churches. Beauvoir sent the letter to Archbishop Wake, who sent a cautious reply, stating the principle on which he would promote reunion. "The Church of England," he wrote, "as a national Church has all that power within herself over her own members which is necessary to enable her to settle her own doctrine, government, and discipline, according to the will of Christ and the edification of her members. We have no concern for other Christian Churches more than that of charity, and to keep up the unity of the Catholic Church in the Communion of Saints. The Church of France, if it would once in good earnest throw off the Pope's pretensions, has the same right and independence. She may establish a different worship, discipline, etc., and in some points continue to differ from us in doctrine too, and yet maintain a true communion with us, so long as there is nothing in either her worship or ours to hinder the members of each Church from communicating with the other, as they have opportunity. . . . To frame a common confession of faith, or liturgie, or discipline, for both Churches, is a project never to be accomplished. But to settle each so that the other shall declare it to be a sound part of the Catholic Church, and communicate with each other as such. . . this may easily be done without much difficulty by them abroad, and I make no doubt but the best and wisest of our Church would be ready to give all due encouragement to it." [1]

The resemblance between this and the Agreement of Bonn, 200 years later, is remarkable.

Some letters then passed between the Archbishop and Du Pin. On March 28, 1718, Piers de Girardin, a doctor of the University of Paris who claimed to be related to the "Geraldines" or Fitzgeralds of Ireland, addressed the Theological Faculty on reunion with the Church of England. He claimed that it would be easier to reconcile the English than the Greeks, and that the dispute between France and Rome might assist that work, as the dispute between St. Paul and St. Barnabas resulted in the spread of the Gospel. Still he compared the English Church to a branch torn from the tree, a comparison of which Archbishop Wake can hardly have approved.[2]

[1] J. H. Lupton, *Archbishop Wake and the Prospect of Reunion*, p. 50.
[2] Lupton, p. 53.

The address was well received, and its author sent a copy of it to Archbishop Wake, who, however, was not at all hopeful of success. Du Pin sent to the Archbishop a " Commonitorium ", or proposed scheme for reunion. No copy of this document is known to exist (there may be one at the Vatican), and we depend for our knowledge of it on a summary made by Dr. Archibald Maclaine. It appears to have been a commentary on the Thirty-Nine Articles, somewhat similar to the well-known one by Sancta Clara, or Newman's *Tract* 90. I need not summarize his views at length, since the Articles are no longer regarded as a basis for agreement with other communions; but his comments on Articles 6 and 20, which played so important a part in the Bonn Conference of 1931, are worth recording. On Article 6 he says, " This we will gladly admit, provided tradition be not excluded, which does not exhibit new articles of faith, but confirms and explains what is contained in Holy Scripture, and fortifies with new safeguards against those who are other-wise minded; so that there is no statement of new things, but of old things in a new way." (An admirable statement, but how it is consistent with the creed of Pius IV is not explained.)

On Article 20 Du Pin agrees that the Church may not (*non licet ecclesiæ*) ordain anything contrary to God's word written, but adds that it must be assumed that the Church will never do this in matters which overthrow the substance of the faith (*quæ fidei substantiam evertant*).

On Article 21 he says that the general councils, received by the Universal Church, cannot err: which, as was pointed out by Pusey, amounts to saying that no general council, received by the Universal Church, has erred. He appears to have accepted the validity of Anglican ordinations, for Wake had sent him, through Beauvoir, a full account of the Anglican succession; and he was also satisfied with the method of appointing bishops in England, as being similar to that used in Charlemagne's time (of course appointment by Prime Ministers who need not be members of the Church was a development later than Wake's time). As to transubstantiation, he is willing to omit all mention of the word, and merely says, " The bread and wine are really changed into the Body and Blood of Christ; which last are truly and really received by all, though none but the faithful partake of any benefit from them." On the crucial question of the Papacy, he denies all temporal and all immediate spiritual jurisdiction to the Pope; whose rights he confines to a Primacy, and to the duty of seeing that the true faith is maintained and the canons everywhere observed: the Primacy does not give the Pope a higher grade among bishops.[1]

On August 30, 1718, the archbishop, having received the " Commonitorium " from Beauvoir, writes to the latter very frankly. He says that he will never comply with the " Commonitorium ", and that he cannot treat with the French theologians as Archbishop of Canterbury, but only as a private divine. He insists on the dignity of his own office: " I do not think my character at all inferior to that of an Archbishop of Paris; on the contrary, without lessening the authority and dignity of the Church of England, I must say that it is in some respects superior. If the Cardinal were in earnest for such a union, it would not be below him to treat with me himself about it. I should then have a sufficient ground to consult with my Brethren and to ask his Majestie's leave to correspond with him concerning it. . . . I am a friend to peace, but more to Truth, and they may depend upon it I shall always account our Church to stand upon an equal foot with their theirs; and that we are no more to receive laws from them than we desire to impose any upon them.[2]

" The Church of England is free, is orthodox, she has a plenary authority within herself. She has no need to recur to others to direct her what to believe or what to do. . . . If they mean to deal with us, they must lay down this for a foundation, that we are to deal with one another on equal terms. . . . For myself, as Archbishop of Canterbury, I have more power, larger privileges, and a greater authority, than any of their Archbishops; from which, by the grace of God, I will not depart, no, not for the sake of union with them." [3]

(This appears to be correct. Even before the Reformation, the Archbishop of Canterbury, who was on one occasion called by a Pope "Alterius orbis Papa ",[4,5] had a more imposing position than his fellow Primates, the Archbishops of Lyons, Toledo and Mainz (which perhaps was partly due to the influence of Theodore the Greek of Tarsus); it had been raised by the

---

[1] Lupton, pp. 107–116.    [2] cf. Agreement of Bonn.
[3] Lupton, pp. 57–59.    [4] St. Anselm by Pope Urban II in 1098.
[5] W. R. W. Stephens, *History of the English Church* 1066–1272, p. 108.

rejection of papal supremacy, though Canterbury was not then, as it is now, the centre of a world-wide communion.)

A few days later Girardin wrote to the archbishop. Cardinal de Noailles had been told about the correspondence, and sent his hearty thanks to Archbishop Wake. Girardin sent a list of " things indifferent ", among which he includes images, communion in one kind, and the elevation of the Host.[1]

It was at this point that Cardinal de Noailles and the opponents of the " Unigenitus " were formally excommunicated by the Pope; and Wake wrote more hopefully in consequence; for he was well aware that a complete breach with Rome was a necessary condition of union with Canterbury. His letter to Du Pin contained an account of the making of bishops in the Church of England; and he urged both Du Pin and Girardin to reject any authority of the Pope but " a primacy of place and honour, and that merely by ecclesiastical authority ". He quotes in support of the Anglican position on this assertion the letter of Firmilian to St. Cyprian attacking the Roman attitude towards those who rebaptized heretics.[2]

Du Pin and Girardin were greatly pleased, and Wake's letter to Du Pin was shown to Cardinal de Noailles and to the Procureur-General. The existence of the correspondence became known in Paris, and on November 14 (O.S.), 1718, the English chapel at Paris was crowded with visitors, anxious to see what the Anglican service was like; Beauvoir preached a sermon in French. On November 18 Archbishop Wake wrote to Beauvoir, suggesting that the most helpful scheme was, to agree in the independence of national churches, and as far as possible in doctrine; to arrange that no one should be admitted to communion in one church who had been excommunicated in the other; and to purge out of the services whatever might prevent either from communicating with the other. He says that there was nothing in the Anglican Liturgy which the French objected to, except the " Black Rubric ", nor anything objectionable to the English Church in the French Liturgy, except what was admitted to be indifferent (probably communion in one kind, and the elevation of the Host).

Du Pin, in his reply, claims that the liberties of the French Church were not special privileges, but the rights of all churches from ancient times. (In spite of his opinion, which is of course

[1] Lupton, p. 61.                    [2] Lupton, pp. 66-73.

historically correct, they were not treated as such, and no other churches in the Roman Communion claimed them but those of France and Holland.)

Wake now wrote to Beauvoir that the Anglican treatment of the Pope was more sincere and respectful than the Gallican: " for to own a power and yet keep a reserve to obey that power only so far and in such cases as we make ourselves judges of, is a greater affront, than honestly to confess that we deny the power, and for that reason refuse to obey it ". He is satisfied that " most of our high-church bishops and clergy would readily come into such a design ", but he does not care to confide in them.[1]

The Dutch chaplain in Paris confused the issue by some indiscreet action; the notion that the religion of the Dutch Reformed Church was the same as that of the English Church was then widespread, and is not even yet quite dead in some quarters. (Two hundred years later some Dutch Old Catholic laymen were doubtful about reunion with the English Church for this reason.)

On January 23 (O.S.) Wake wrote to Beauvoir, that though he accounted all temporal grandeur as nothing, and feared it had rather hurt than helped the Church, yet the French would be more likely " to return to the truth of Christianity, and leave the corruptions of Rome ", if they could do so without giving up their authority or their revenues, and " be still as great, but much better bishops ".[2]

He adds, that Anglican and Gallican theologians alike allow the Pope a primacy of order: " they would have thought it necessary to hold communion with him, and allow him a little canonical authority, as long as he will leave them to prescribe the bounds of it: we fairly say we know of no authority he has in our realm. But for actual submission to him, they as little mind it as we do."

But now the French Government intervened, on the complaint of Cardinals de Rohan and de Bissi. Guards were placed outside the English chapel at Paris to prevent French visitors from attending it (which was not surprising, for many were joining the English Church), and on February 10 Du Pin's papers were seized, by order of the Regent. Father Lafitean, a Jesuit, was present when these papers were brought to the Palais Royal.

[1] Lupton, p. 82.                    [2] Lupton, pp. 86-87.

He called the correspondence between Archbishop Wake and Du Pin " the most abominable plot that a Catholic teacher could have contrived in religious affairs " ; and accused Du Pin of asserting that it was possible, without altering the integrity of dogma, " to abolish auricular confession, speak no longer of transubstantiation . . . annul the vows of monks and nuns, allow priests to marry, curtail fasting and abstinence in Lent, and do without the Pope ".[1] (This account is no doubt an exaggeration, for there is no other evidence for some of his charges against Du Pin.)

On June 6, 1719, Du Pin, who had been failing for some months, died ; and soon afterwards, as we shall see, the vacillating Noailles became reconciled with Rome, and the opportunity of reunion with Canterbury passed away.

It is tempting, but useless, to speculate on what might have happened if the English and French Churches had been reunited in consequence of a schism in France over the Bull " Unigenitus ". Jervis is probably right in thinking that the decrees of Trent would have been an insuperable obstacle if formal negotiations had been reached,[2] though it is remarkable that Du Pin never mentions Trent ; evidently he had gone far beyond Bossuet. We do not know how the proposal would have been received in England, although there was one savage attack on Wake by Archdeacon Blackburn. This was the very time of the suppression of Convocation and the Bangorian Controversy ; it is hard to see how the English Church, with Convocation suppressed, could have done anything, or to believe that any Gallican would have accepted Hoadly, with his extreme opinions on the Church and Sacraments, as a Catholic bishop, or that healthy reunion could have taken place under the joint patronage of Robert Walpole and Philip, Duke of Orleans!

Cardinal de Noailles had not the resolution needed by the leader of a rebellion. He resigned his seat on the Council of Conscience in 1719. The Government gave its support to the " Acceptants ", and Guillaume Dubois, an agent of the Regent, and a man of great intelligence, but of the worst character, was made Archbishop of Cambrai, Cardinal, and in 1722 Prime Minister. He hated Noailles, who had, with good reason, refused to ordain him, and he exercised all the powers of the Government against the Appellants. In 1720 Noailles declared

[1] Lupton, p. 88.          [2] Jervis, vol. ii, p. 437.

himself willing to sign a declaration, adopted by the government, making the Bull " Unigenitus " a law of the State, with explanatory comments. In 1728, just before his death, he accepted the Bull unconditionally, and in 1730 the Theological Faculty of Paris, the backbone of the opposition, accepted it too; those who refused were struck off the roll. The supporters of the Bull were now triumphant. Only two of the original four appellant bishops remained. Colbert of Montpellier was left alone till his death in 1738. But Jean Soanen of Senez, a small mountain diocese in Provence, issued in 1726 a Pastoral Instruction to his diocese, in which, at the age of eighty, he reviewed his whole position in the controversy. He regretted that he had ever signed the Formulary of 1665, withdrew his adhesion to the Bull " Vineam Domini Sabaoth ", blamed himself for prohibiting, against his real convictions, the *Moral Reflexions*, and promised never to accept the " Unigenitus ". Soanen was deprived of his see by the Provincial Synod of Embrun, which on various canonical grounds he refused to recognize, and was banished to the abbey of Chaise Dieu in Auvergne, where he remained imprisoned till his death in 1740, at the age of ninety-five.[1]

Paschasius Quesnel, the author of the book which had caused all the trouble, had long since taken refuge in Holland, and had died there, December 2, 1719.

The later history of French Jansenism does not concern us. On the religious side it degenerated into fanaticism and superstition; on the political side it became closely connected with the resistance of the lawyers to absolute monarchy which was one of the causes of the French Revolution. Anyone might be refused the sacraments if he would not sign the " Unigenitus ". From 1733 onwards there were many cases of this form of persecution, which was often applied to the dying; if they would not accept the condemnation of the 101 propositions, they were refused the last sacraments and Christian burial. It was the intolerant spirit of which this is typical that first led Voltaire and Diderot to open their campaign against the Christian religion.

The most prominent of the later opponents of the " Unigenitus " among the bishops were de Caylus of Auxerre and Fitzjames of Soissons. The latter was a son of the Marshal Duke of Berwick, and illegitimate grandson of James II of England by Arabella

[1] Jervis, vol. ii, pp. 261–265, 297.

Churchill, sister of the great Duke of Marlborough. He accepted the " Unigenitus " himself, but supported those who refused to do so. In 1744, when Louis XV was dangerously ill, Bishop Fitzjames refused him the last sacraments till he should have dismissed his mistress, the Duchesse de Châteauroux, and made a declaration of penitence in the presence of his family. The King did it, but on his recovery he recalled his mistress, and dismissed Fitzjames to his diocese. Whenever Louis XV came to his palace at Compiègne, which was in the diocese of Soissons, the bishop always wrote to him warning him of his sins and of the inevitable result of continuing to lead an immoral life, but without result. Fitzjames died in 1765.[1]

Another member of the party was Charles Coffin the hymn-writer, who was President of the Collège de Beauvais at Paris, and who in 1749 was compelled to die without the last sacraments, because he would not accept the " Unigenitus ". The case caused much excitement, for Coffin's nephew was a leading member of the Parlement de Paris, and was active in his uncle's cause, but in vain.[2]    (Eight of Coffin's hymns from the revised Paris Breviary appear in the *English Hymnal*, eight in the *Irish Church Hymnal*, and twenty in *Hymns Ancient and Modern*; perhaps the best known are " On Jordan's bank the Baptist's cry " and " As now the sun's declining rays ".)

What are we to think of the great controversy which has been sketched?

It is clear that the main issue was the infallibility of the Pope, and his right to blind obedience, which seems to have been accepted by all Roman Catholics outside France and the Low Countries. As Charles Beard says, " The whole power of the Society of Jesus leagued itself with the absolute authority of the French monarchy, to destroy an insignificant convent of Cistercian nuns, who, submitting themselves to the Holy See in every article of faith, refused to declare that five condemned propositions were contained in a book, which they had never read, and which was written in a language they did not understand ".[3]

As early as 1654, the Anglican divine, Isaac Barrow, asked why the Pope did not give the references for the Five Propositions

---

[1] Jervis, vol. ii, pp. 300–302.     [2] Jervis, vol. ii, pp. 310–311.
[3] Charles Beard, *Port Royal*, vol. i, p. 22.

if they were really to be found in the *Augustinus*: a question
which has never been answered. Again, the whole force of the
Papacy was exerted to enforce the universal repudiation, on pain
of excommunication, of a book which had been twenty years
published, had been defended by the greatest divine of the
age, and had been condemned in order to satisfy the vengeance
of a King's confessor, a man proved to be a liar and a plotter,
against the archbishop of his master's capital city. But the Pope
had said that the Five Propositions were to be found in Jansen;
the Pope had said that the *Moral Reflexions* was a heretical book;
and all his successors were bound to insist on blind obedience to
his word. A papal pronouncement, however hasty, however
partisan, however unreasonable, might not be criticized. The
Jansenists were one-sided, though not more so than their
opponents; their veneration for St. Augustine was exaggerated,
and their rigour at times too strict for human nature. But they
certainly produced saints and converted sinners; they received
the devotion of such men as Pascal, Tillemont, and Racine;
they represented, at their best, an aspect of Christianity which is
always needed, and never more so than in that age and country.
But the Counter-Reformation had turned Latin Christendom
into a Renaissance autocracy. A dictator, especially one who
claims to be infallible, cannot withdraw or concede anything
which affects his authority. The Roman Communion, which
claimed, as it still claims, to be the whole of the Christian Church,
had no room for St. Cyran and the Arnaulds, Pascal and Quesnel,
Pavillon and Soanen, though every one of them accepted without question all its dogmas, including the Petrine claims of the
Papacy, and the decrees of Trent. The reason for this is clear.
The Counter-Reformation had centralized all power in the
Papacy; the Society of Jesus was the means by which this was
brought about, and it could no more permit the existence of
rival parties or rival outlooks than the Communist party can
permit them in Soviet Russia. Neither the early nor the medieval
Church was totalitarian, nor is any non-Roman part of Christendom to-day; but Trent has made the Roman Communion
totalitarian, and Ultramontanism is the inevitable consequence
of Trent. There is no middle way between accepting Ultramontanism and rejecting the Papal claims completely, as incompatible with the liberty necessary to the Christian religion.

APPENDIX A.—THE 101 PROPOSITIONS, TAKEN FROM THE "MORAL
REFLEXIONS ON THE NEW TESTAMENT" BY PASCHASIUS
QUESNEL, CONDEMNED BY THE BULL "UNIGENITUS"

1. Quid aliud remanet animae, quae Deum atque ipsius gratiam
amisit, nisi peccatum et peccati consecutiones, superba paupertas
et segnis indigentia, hoc est generalis impotentia ad laborem, ad
orationem et ad omne opus bonum?

2. Jesu Christi gratia, principium efficax boni cujuscumque
generis, necessaria est ad omne opus bonum: absque illa, non
solum nihil fit, sed nec fieri potest.

3. In vanum, Domine, praecipis, si tu ipse non das quod
praecipis.

4. Ita, Domine, omnia possibilia sunt ei, cui omnia possibilia
facis, eadem operando in illo.

5. Quando Deus non emollit cor per interiorem unctionem
gratiae suae, exhortationes et gratiae exteriores non inserviunt
nisi ad illud magis obdurandum.

6. Discrimen inter foedus Judaicum et Christianum est, quod
in illo Deus exigit fugam peccati et implementum legis a pecca-
tore, relinquendo illum in sua impotentia; in isto vero Deus
peccatori dat, quod jubet, illum sua gratia purificando.

7. Quae utilitas pro homine in veteri foedere, in quo Deus
illum reliquit ejus propriae infirmitati, imponendo ipsi suam
legem? Quae vero felicitas non est admitti ad foedus, in quo
Deus nobis donat, quod petit a nobis?

8. Nos non pertinemus ad novum foedus, nisi in quantum
participes sumus ipsius novae gratiae, quae operatur in nobis
id, quod Deus nobis praecipit.

9. Gratia Christi est gratia suprema, sine qua confiteri Christum
nunquam possumus, et cum qua nunquam illum abnegamus.

10. Gratia est operatio manus omnipotentis Dei, quam nihil
impedire potest aut retardare.

11. Gratia non est aliud, quam voluntas omnipotentis Dei
jubentis et facientis, quod jubet.

12. Quando Deus vult salvare animam, quocumque tempore,
quocumque loco, effectus indubitabilis sequitur voluntatem Dei.

13. Quando Deus vult animam salvam facere, et eam tangit
interiori gratiae suae manu, nulla voluntas humana ei resistit.

14. Quantumcumque remotus a salute sit peccator obstinatus,
quando Jesus se ei videndum exhibet lumine salutari suae gratiae,

oportet ut se dedat, accurrat, sese humiliet et adoret Salvatorem suum.

15. Quando Deus mandatum suum et suam aeternam locutionem comitatur unctione sui Spiritus et interiori vi gratiae suae, operatur illam in corde obedientiam, quam petit.

16. Nullae sunt illecebrae, quae non cedunt illecebris gratiae: quia nihil resistit omnipotenti.

17. Gratia est vox illa Patris, quae homines interius docet, ac eos venire facit ad Jesum Christum: quicumque ad eum non venit, postquam audivit vocem exteriorem Filii, nullatenus est doctus a Patre.

18. Semen verbi, quod manus Dei irrigat, semper affert fructum suum.

19. Dei gratia nihil aliud est, quam ejus omnipotens voluntas: haec est idea, quam Deus ipse nobis tradit in omnibus suis Scripturis.

20. Vera gratiae idea est, quod Deus vult sibi a nobis obediri, et obeditur: imperat et omnia fiunt: loquitur tanquam Dominus, et omnia sibi submissa sunt.

21. Gratia Jesu Christi est gratia fortis, potens, suprema, invincibilis, utpote quae est operatio voluntatis omnipotentis, sequela et imitatio operationis Dei incarnantis et resuscitantis Filium suum.

22. Concordia omnipotentis operationis Dei in corde hominis cum libero ipsius voluntatis consensu demonstratur illico nobis in Incarnatione, veluti fonte atque architypo omnium aliarum operationum misericordiae et gratiae, quae omnes ita gratuitae atque ita dependentes a Deo sunt, sicut ipsa originalis operatio.

23. Deus ipse nobis ideam tradidit omnipotentis operationis suae gratiae, eam significans per illam, quae creaturas e nihilo producit et mortuis reddit vitam.

24. Justa idea, quam centurio habet de omnipotentia Dei et Jesu Christi in sanandis corporibus solo motu suae voluntatis, est imago ideae, quae haberi debet de omnipotentia suae gratiae in sanandis animabus a cupiditate.

25. Deus illuminat animam et eam sanat aeque ac corpus sola sua voluntate; jubet, et ipsi obtemperatur.

26. Nullae dantur gratiae, nisi per fidem.

27. Fides est prima gratia et fons omnium aliarum.

28. Prima gratia, quam Deus concedit peccatori, est peccatorum remissio.

29. Extra Ecclesiam nulla conceditur gratia.

30. Omnes, quos Deus vult salvare per Christum, salvantur infallibiliter.

31. Desideria Christi semper habent suum effectum: pacem intimo cordium infert, quando eis illam optat.

32. Jesus Christus se morti tradidit ad liberandum pro semper suo sanguine primogenitos, id est electos, de manu angeli exterminatoris.

33. Proh! quantum oportet bonis terrenis et sibimetipsi renuntiasse, ad hoc, ut quis fiduciam habeat sibi, ut ita dicam, appropriandi Christum Jesum, ejus amorem, mortem, et mysteria! ut facit sanctus Paulus, dicens: Qui dilexit me, et tradidit semetipsum pro me. (Gal. 2. 20.)

34. Gratia Adami non producebat nisi merita humana.

35. Gratia Adami est sequela creationis, et est debita naturae, sanae et integrae.

36. Differentia essentialis inter gratiam Adami et status innocentiae ac gratiam christianam est, quod primam unusquisque in propria persona recepisset, ista vero non recipitur, nisi in persona Jesu Christi resuscitati, cui nos uniti sumus.

37. Gratia Adami, sanctificando illum in semetipso erat illi proportionata: gratia christiana, nos sanctificando in Jesu Christo, est omnipotens et digna Filio Dei.

38. Peccator non est liber, nisi ad malum, sine gratia Liberatoris.

39. Voluntas, quam gratia non praevenit, nihil habet luminis, nisi ad aberrandum, ardoris, nisi ad se praecipitandum, virium, nisi ad se vulnerandum: est capax omnis mali et incapax ad omne bonum.

40. Sine gratia nihil amare possumus, nisi ad nostram condemnationem.

41. Omnis cognitio Dei, etiam naturalis, etiam in philosophis ethnicis, non potest venire nisi a Deo: et sine gratia non producit nisi praesumptionem, vanitatem, et oppositionem ad ipsum Deum loco affectuum adorationis, gratitudinis, et amoris.

42. Sola gratia Christi reddit hominem aptum ad sacrificium fidei: sine hoc nihil nisi impuritas, nihil nisi indignitas.

43. Primus effectus gratiae baptismalis est facere, ut moriamur peccato, adeo ut spiritus, cor, sensus, non habeant plus vitae pro peccato, quam homo mortuus habet pro rebus mundi.

44. Non sunt nisi duo amores, unde volitiones et actiones

omnes nostrae nascuntur: amor Dei, qui omnia agit propter Deum, quemque Deus remuneratur, et amor, quo nos ipsos ac mundum diligimus, qui, quod ad Deum referendum est, non refert et propter hoc ipsum fit malus.

45. Amore Dei in corde peccatorum non amplius regnante, necesse est, ut in eo carnalis regnet cupiditas omnesque actiones ejus corrumpat.

46. Cupiditas aut caritas usum sensuum bonum vel malum faciunt.

47. Obedientia legis profluere debet ex fonte, et hic fons est caritas. Quando Dei amor est illius principium interius, et Dei gloria ejus finis, tunc purum est, quod apparet exterius: alioquin non est nisi hypocrisis aut falsa justitia.

48. Quid aliud esse possumus, nisi tenebrae, nisi aberratio, et nisi peccatum, sine fidei lumine, sine Christo et sine caritate?

49. Ut nullum peccatum est sine amore nostri, ita nullum est opus bonum sine amore Dei.

50. Frustra clamamus ad Deum, " Pater mi ", si spiritus caritatis non est ille, qui clamat.

51. Fides justificat, quando operatur, sed ipsa non operatur nisi per caritatem.

52. Omnia alia salutis media continentur in fide tanquam in suo germine et semine: sed haec fides non est absque amore et fiducia.

53. Sola caritas christiano modo facit (actiones christianas) per relationem ad Deum et Jesum Christum.

54. Sola caritas est, quae Deo loquitur: eam solam Deus audit.

55. Deus non coronat nisi caritatem: qui currit ex alio impulsu et ex alio motivo, in vanum currit.

56. Deus non remunerat nisi caritatem: quoniam caritas sola Deum honorat.

57. Totum deest peccatori, quando ei deest spes: et non est spes in Deo, ubi non est amor Dei.

58. Nec Deus est nec religio, ubi non est caritas.

59. Oratio impiorum est novum peccatum: et quod Deus illis concedit, est novum in eos judicium.

60. Si solus supplicii timor animat poenitentiam, quo haec est magis violenta, eo magis ducit ad desperationem.

61. Timor nonnisi manum cohibet, cor autem tamdiu peccato adducitur, quamdiu ab amore justitiae non ducitur.

62. Qui a malo non abstinet nisi timore poenae, illud committit in corde suo, et jam est reus coram Deo.

63. Baptizatus adhuc est sub lege sicut Judaeus, si legem non adimpleat, aut adimpleat ex solo timore.

64. Sub maledicto legis nunquam fit bonum: quia peccatur sive faciendo malum, sive illud nonnisi ob timorem evitando.

65. Moyses, prophetae, sacerdotes, et doctores legis mortui sunt absque eo, quod ullum Deo dederint filium, cum non effecerint nisi mancipia per timorem.

66. Qui vult Deo appopinquare, nec debet ad ipsum venire cum brutalibus passionibus, neque adduci per instinctum naturalem aut per timorem sicut bestiae, sed per fidem et per amorem, sicut filii.

67. Timor servilis non sibi repraesentat Deum nisi ut dominum durum, imperiosum, injustum, intractabilem.

68. Dei bonitas abbreviavit viam salutis, claudendo totum in fide et precibus.

69. Fides, usus, augmentum et praemium fidei, totum est donum purae liberalitatis Dei.

70. Nunquam Deus. affligit innocentes: et afflictiones semper serviunt vel ad puniendum peccatum vel ad purificandum peccatorem.

71. Homo ob sui conservationem potest sese dispensare ab ea lege, quam Deus condidit propter ejus utilitatem.

72. Nota ecclesiae christianae est, quod sit catholica, comprehendens et omnes angelos caeli, et omnes electos et justos terrae et omnium saeculorum.

73. Quid est ecclesia, nisi coetus filiorum Deo, manentium in ejus sinu, adoptatorum in Christo, subsistentium in ejus persona, redemptorum ejus sanguine, viventium ejus spiritu, agentium per ejus gratiam, et expectantium gratiam futuri saeculi?

74. Ecclesia, sive integer Christus, incarnatum Verbum habet ut caput, omnes vere Sanctos ut mcmbra.

75. Ecclesia est unus solus homo compositus ex plurimis membris, quorum Christus est caput, vita, subsistentia et persona: unus solus Christus compositus ex pluribus Sanctis, quorum est sanctificator.

76. Nihil spatiosius ecclesia Dei: quia omnes electi et justi omnium saeculorum illam componunt.

77. Qui non ducit vitam dignam filio Dei et membro Christi, cessat interius habere Deum pro patre et Christum pro capite.

78. Separatur quis a populo electo, cujus figura fuit populus Judaicus et caput est Jesus Christus, tam non vivendo secundum Evangelium, quam non credendo Evangelio.

79. Utile et necessarium est omni tempore, omni loco et omni personarum generi, studere ac cognoscere spiritum, pietatem, et mysteria sacrae Scripturae.

80. Lectio sacrae Scripturae est pro omnibus.

81. Obscuritas sancta verbi Dei non est laicis ratio dispensandi se ipsos ab ejus lectione.

82. Dies Dominicus a Christianis debet sanctificari lectionibus pietatis et super omnia sanctarum Scripturarum. Damnosum est, velle Christianum ab hac lectione retrahere.

83. Est illusio sibi persuadere, quod notitia mysteriorum religionis non debeat communicari feminis lectione sacrorum librorum. Non ex feminarum simplicitate sed ex superba virorum scientia ortus est Scripturarum abusus et natae sunt haereses.

84. Abripere e Christianorum manibus novum Testamentum seu eis illud clausum tenere, auferendo eis modum illud intelligendi, est illis Christi os obturare.

85. Interdicere Christianis lectionem sacrae Scripturae, praesertim Evangelii, est interdicere usum luminis filiis lucis et facere, ut patiantur speciem quandam excommunicationis.

86. Eripere simplici populo hoc solatium jungendi vocem suam voci totius ecclesiae, est usus contrarius praxi apostolicae et intentioni Dei.

87. Modus plenus sapientia, lumine, et caritate est dare animabus tempus portandi cum humilitate et sententiendi statum peccati, petendi spiritum poenitentiae et contritionis, et incipiendi ad minus satisfacere justitiae Dei, antequam reconcilientur.

88. Ignoramus, quid sit peccatum et vera poenitentia, quando volumus statim restitui possessioni bonorum illorum, quibus nos peccatum spoliavit, et detrectamus separationis istius ferre confusionem.

89. Quartusdecimus gradus conversionis peccatoris est, quod, cum sit jam reconciliatus, habet jus assistendi sacrificio ecclesiae.

90. Ecclesia auctoritatem excommunicandi habet, ut eam exerceat per primos pastores de consensu saltem praesumpto totius corporis.

91. Excommunicationis injustae metus nunquam debet nos impedire ab implendo debito nostro; nunquam eximus ab

ecclesia, etiam quando hominum nequitia videmur ab ea expulsi, quando Deo, Jesu Christo, atque ipsi ecclesiae per caritatem affixi sumus.

92. Pati potius in pace excommunicationem et anathema injustum, quam prodere veritatem, est imitari sanctum Paulum; tantum abest, ut sit erigere se contra auctoritatem aut scindere unitatem.

93. Jesus quandoque sanat vulnera, quae praeceps primorum pastorum festinatio infligit sine ipsius mandato, Jesus restituit, quod ipsi inconsiderato zelo rescindunt.

94. Nihil pejorem de ecclesia opinionem ingerit ejus inimicis, quam videre illic dominatum exerceri supra fidem fidelium, et foveri divisiones propter res, quae nec fidem laedunt nec mores.

95. Veritates eo devenerunt, ut sint lingua quasi peregrina plerisque Christianis, et modus eas praedicandi est veluti idioma incognitum; adeo remotus est a simplicitate Apostolorum, et supra communem captum fidelium; neque satis advertitur, quod hic defectus sit unum ex signis maxime sensibilibus senectutis ecclesiae et irae Dei in filios suos.

96. Deus permittat, ut omnes potestates sint contrariae praedicatoribus veritatis, ut ejus victoria attribui non possit nisi divinae gratiae.

97. Nimis saepe contingit, membra illa, quae magis sancta ac magis stricte unita ecclesiae sunt, respici atque tractari tanquam indigna, ut sint in ecclesia, vel tanquam ab ea separata; sed *justus vivit ex fide*, et non ex opinione hominum. (Rom. 1. 17.)

98. Status persecutionis et poenarum, quas quis tolerat tanquam haereticus, flagitiosus, et impius, ultima plerumque probatio est et maxime meritoria, utpote quae facit hominem magis conformem Jesu Christo.

99. Pervicacia, praeventio, obstinatio in nolendo aut aliquid examinare aut agnoscere, se fuisse deceptum, mutant quotidie quoad multos in odorem mortis id, quod Deus in sua ecclesia posuit, ut in ea esset odor vitae, verbi gratia bonos libros, instructiones, sancta exempla, etc.

100. Tempus deplorabile, quo creditur honorari Deus persequendo veritatem ejusque discipulos! Tempus hoc advenit. . . . Haberi et tractari a religionis ministris tanquam impium et indignum omni commercio cum Deo, tanquam membrum putridum, capax corrumpendi omnia in societate sanctorum, est hominibus piis morte corporis mors terribilior. Frustra quis sibi

blanditur de suarum intentionum puritate et zelo quodam religionis, persequendo flamma ferroque viros probos, si propria
passione est excaecatus aut abreptus aliena, propterea quod nihil
vult examinare. Frequenter credimus sacrificare Deo impium,
et sacrificamus diabolo Dei servum.

101. Nihil spiritui Dei et doctrinae Jesu Christi magis opponitur,
quam communia facere juramenta in ecclesia; quia hoc est
multiplicare occasiones pejerandi, laqueos tendere infirmis et
idiotis, et efficere, ut nomen et veritas Dei aliquando deserviant
consilio impiorum.

### Appendix B.—Jansenism and the British Isles

Miss Ruth Clark (*Strangers and Sojourners at Port Royal*, C.U.P.,
1932), whose learning is equalled only by her industry, has
ransacked the immense literature of Jansenism for connexions
with the British Isles. Many instances of the interest taken in
the controversy on this side of the English Channel, and of connexions between leading Jansenists and British subjects, of the
Anglican as well as of the Roman Communion, have already
been mentioned, but a few more may be of interest.

Florence Conry, titular Archbishop of Tuam, who was consecrated in 1609, but was never able to visit his diocese, was a
friend of Jansen and a devoted admirer of St. Augustine. He
wrote a book in defence of the most repellent of St. Augustine's
opinions, the damnation of unbaptized infants (*De Poena Parvu-
lorum post hanc vitam*), and another, the *Pilgrim to Jericho*, which was
published after his death by St. Cyran.[1] But on the whole there
was not much Jansenism among the Irish Roman Catholics: at
Paris the Irish students in the University got into trouble more
than once for rebelling against the Gallican teaching of the
University authorities.[2] Anglican exiles living on the Continent
during the usurpation of Cromwell, such as Archbishop Bramhall
of Armagh and Bishop Morley of Winchester, knew something of
the Jansenist controversy; Morley used it as an argument against
Baxter, that the Church of England would do better to win
over moderate Papists, such as the Jansenists, from Rome than
to try to reconcile the Presbyterians and Congregationalists
by making concessions to Calvinism.[3] Archbishop Leighton of

---

[1] Ruth Clark, *Strangers and Sojourners at Port Royal*, pp. 2–5, 207.
[2] Clark, pp. 189 ff.          [3] Clark, p. 135.

Glasgow was much influenced by the Jansenists and the *Spiritual Letters* of St. Cyran, the *Frequent Communion* of Arnauld, the *Constitutions* of the Monastery of Port Royal, and other Jansenist books were in his library.[1] Bishop Ken, according to his biographer, Dean Plumptre, may have been influenced by Bishop Pavillon, whose *Synodal Statutes of the Diocese of Alet* were in his library, along with the works of Jansen, St. Cyran's *Spiritual Letters*, and the *Provincial Letters* of Pascal. Jeremy Taylor, Bishop of Dromore, highly commended Arnauld's *Frequent Communion*.[2] The emphasis laid by Quesnel on Bible-reading in the mother tongue aroused much sympathy among Anglican divines. When, in 1680, Robert Boyle proposed to have the Bible translated into Irish, he suggested to the Bishop of Meath, Dr. Henry Jones, that the preface to the *Mons New Testament*, written at Port Royal, might well be prefixed to it, in order to recommend the translation to Irish Roman Catholics. However, they were unable to use the preface as it stood, on account of its remarks about some of the Reformers, and had to be content with quoting from it.[3]

Antoine Arnauld was devoted to King James II, whom he had probably known during the King's exile in his youth, and when James was driven from his throne, Arnauld, then seventy-seven years old, wrote a violent attack on William of Orange, whom he called the "new Absalom, the new Herod, the new Nero, the new Cromwell". He was living in Holland at the time, and he had to flee to the Spanish Netherlands. Even there he was not safe, since Spain was allied with Holland, and France, of course, was closed to him.[4] King James II, on his way to Ireland for the campaign of the Boyne, stopped one night at an abbey at Quimperlé in Brittany, and Claude Lancelot, one of the best known and most attractive of the "gentlemen of Port Royal", who had been banished to Quimperlé, was placed next to the King.[5] A few years later, September 1, 1693, James II, while hunting, arrived by accident at Port Royal, where he visited the church and had some talk with the Abbess. There was Jansenist influence in his court at St. Germain, and after his death his son's tutor, Dr. Betham, was accused of Jansenism and ultimately dismissed.[6]

[1] Clark, pp. 136–137.    [2] Clark, pp. 138–139.
[3] Clark, pp. 146–147.    [4] Clark, pp. 223–224.
[5] Clark, p. 225.    [6] Clark, pp. 226–228.

The Bull "Unigenitus" aroused more interest in England than the Five Propositions, which could be understood only by theologians, whereas the propositions condemned by the "Unigenitus" raised the question of the right of the laity to read the Bible in their own tongue. As early as 1706 there was actually a rumour that Quesnel was going over to the Church of England and seeking employment from the Archbishop of Canterbury.[1] John Wesley wrote of the Bull as "that abominable Bull 'Unigenitus', which destroys the very foundations of Christianity" and had put an end to all attempts "to bring about a reconciliation between the Protestant and Romish Churches". He possessed all the works of Quesnel, and chose his *Commentary on the Gospels* as one of the books to be studied in his school at Kingswood. The Bull "Unigenitus" was translated into English, together with the entire works of Quesnel, by Richard Russell, a non-juring clergyman, between 1719 and 1725; the book was reprinted as late as 1790, and influenced Bishop Horne of Norwich, who adopted the author's methods in his *Commentary on the Psalms*.[2] Even Lord Chesterfield advised his son to make himself acquainted with the subject of Port Royal.[3] Hannah More was a great admirer of the writers of Port Royal, and made a collection of their works; we find her defending them against no less a person than Dr. Johnson, who was angry because she quoted Boileau's epigram that the Jesuits had lengthened the Creed and shortened the Ten Commandments. She also persuaded her friends to study Port Royal. Bishop Barrington of Llandaff, under her influence, tried in vain to get hold of a History of Port Royal; and Mrs. Schimmelpenninck, to whom Hannah More lent some of her books, became an enthusiast too, and with the help of Grégoire, the "Constitutional" bishop, collected 400 rare books on Port Royal, which are now at Sion College.[4]

[1] Clark, p. 257.
[2] Clark, p. 262. Russell expurgated the book, omitting whatever he considered to be "Romish error". His work was republished in 3 volumes in 1830, with a preface by Daniel Wilson, Vicar of Islington.
[3] Clark, p. 264.                    [4] Clark, pp. 265–275.

# CHAPTER VI

# THE CHURCH OF UTRECHT BEFORE THE SCHISM

IT was not in France, but in the Netherlands, that the movement of which Port Royal had been the spiritual centre was to find a permanent home. Its supporters possessed in the Netherlands two great advantages which did not exist in France. One was the right of the Chapter of Utrecht to elect its own archbishop— a right which the French chapters had lost when the Pragmatic Sanction of Bourges was abolished in 1516. The other was the benevolent neutrality of the civil government, which, being of the " Reformed " religion, was not under the influence of the Court of Rome. By the eighteenth century the Dutch authorities had accepted the principle of toleration for all religions,[1] and they very much preferred that their Roman Catholic subjects should have bishops of Dutch birth, elected by a Dutch chapter, rather than that they should be under the spiritual guidance of Jesuits and other missionaries appointed by the Congregation de Propaganda Fide at Rome.[2]

The bishopric of Utrecht, which until the sixteenth century had been the only bishopric in what is now Dutch territory, was founded by St. Willibrord, an English missionary bishop from Yorkshire. After having been educated, like all the most learned men of that period, in Ireland, he was consecrated at Rome by Pope Sergius I in 696, and given the pallium of an archbishop. Pepin, Mayor of the Palace to the Merovingian dynasty, gave Willibrord the fortress of Utrecht on the Rhine, which has ever since been the ecclesiastical capital of the Northern Netherlands. After fifty years' missionary work among the pagan Frisians, St. Willibrord died, and was buried at his favourite monastery, Echternach in Luxemburg, where his relics are still shown. His feast is kept on November 7. He was succeeded by his friend St. Boniface, born at Crediton in Devonshire, who had given his

---

[1] Dupac de Bellegarde, *Histoire Abregée de l'Église Metropolitaine D'Utrecht*, p. 329.
[2] Bellegarde, p. 330 (*Reply of the Dutch Government to the Doge of Venice*), April 20, 1725.

life to the conversion of the Germans and the organization of the Church in Germany. He had been Archbishop of Mainz, which continued until the French Revolution to be the primatial see of Germany. In the last year of his life St. Boniface resigned his archbishopric and retired to do pioneer missionary work in Frisia, where he suffered martyrdom, June 5, 754. His body, and the book he was reading when he met his death—the *De Bono Mortis* (On the advantage of death) by St. Ambrose—were carried to Fulda, near Frankfurt-on-the-Main, where they still remain.[1] After this the claim of the see of Cologne to jurisdiction over Utrecht was recognized by the Pope, and Utrecht remained a simple bishopric in the province of Cologne until 1559.

In the eleventh century the Bishops of Utrecht became temporal princes, charged with the duty of defending the frontier of the empire against the Northmen and other invaders. They gave their support to the imperial cause against the claims of Pope Gregory VII.[2] In 1145 the right of electing the Bishop was taken away from the people because of their turbulence, and was confined to the Chapter of Utrecht, which consisted of the members of the chapters of the Cathedral of St. Martin and St. Saviour's Church; it was afterwards extended to include the chapters of three other collegiate churches.[3]

The history of the see was marked during the fourteenth and fifteenth centuries by several deplorable disputes between rival candidates, which often led to civil wars. Bishop Philip of Burgundy, who reigned from 1517 to 1524, obtained from Pope Leo X a Bull giving to him and his successors, and to the clergy and laity of the diocese, the privilege of freedom from the claim of the Popes to " evoke " local causes to be heard at Rome; any attempt to evoke any church case from Utrecht was to be null and void. (This Bull was later of great importance in the defence of the see against the Jesuits.)[4]

Philip's successor, Henry of Bavaria, was driven from Utrecht by the partisans of the Duke of Gelderland; and in 1528, four years after his election, he had not yet been consecrated. With the consent of his chapter, and of the nobles of the province,

---

[1] G. F. Browne, *Boniface and his Companions* (1910), p. 31.
[2] Bellegarde, p. 8.
[3] J. M. Neale, *History of the So-Called Jansenist Church of Holland*, p. 64.
[4] Neale, p. 72.

he surrendered his temporal sovereignty to the Emperor Charles V on condition that the Emperor should restore him to his see. From this time the Bishops of Utrecht ceased to be prince-bishops.

During the fifteenth century Utrecht had been remarkable for the society known as " The Brothers of the Common Life ", which was founded by Gerard the Great (Geert Groote), who died in 1378, for the purpose of teaching the young, sending out preachers, and recommending the study of Holy Scripture. It was not a monastic order, but a voluntary association, the members of which did not take vows. The parent house was at Deventer; the most famous member was Thomas à Kempis, usually regarded as the author of the *Imitation of Christ*, who spent most of his life at Mount St. Agnes, near Zwolle. The Brothers of the Common Life laid great emphasis on the study of Scripture; they tried to have a translation of it made into Dutch, and they were particular about using the best manuscripts available. Among their pupils were Johann Wessel Gansfort, who had considerable influence over Luther,[2] and Erasmus, who was educated in one of their schools.[3] The type of piety encouraged by the Brothers of the Common Life persisted in the Netherlands, and was one of the causes of opposition to the very different type of piety encouraged by the Jesuits. Thomas à Kempis says, " Before all arts, learn to read and understand the Holy Scriptures "; but the Bull " Unigenitus ", as we have seen, condemned the opinion that the laity are bound to read the Bible. Another pupil of the Brothers of the Common Life was Pope Hadrian VI, who was born at Utrecht (where his house is still shown), was educated either at Deventer or Zwolle, became tutor to the Emperor Charles V, and in 1522 was elected Pope. He was the last non-Italian Pope, and is celebrated for having given as his private opinion that the Pope is not infallible.

In the sixteenth century, the Netherlands, like the rest of Germany, England, and indeed nearly all Northern Europe, had far too few bishoprics. The remoteness and the secular duties of the bishops were one reason why the Reformers did not value episcopacy.[4] Philip II of Spain, on succeeding to the

[1] Bellegarde, p. 30; Neale, p. 72.
[2] S. Kettlewell, *Thomas à Kempis* (1885), p. 355; but compare E. F. Jacob, *Essays in the Conciliar Epoch*, p. 132 (1943).
[3] Neale, p. 99. They were too orthodox for Erasmus (Jacob, p. 135).
[4] T. M. Parker, in *The Apostolic Church*, ed. K. E. Kirk, p. 385.

hereditary possessions of his father Charles V, decided to re-organize the Church throughout the Netherlands, and in 1559, when the war with France was over, persuaded the Pope to set up a number of new provinces and dioceses. Utrecht became an archbishopric, with the five new sees of Haarlem, Deventer, Groningen, Leeuwarden and Middelburg under it; [1] they were endowed out of the revenues of wealthy abbeys, on the suggestion of Cardinal Granvelle, President of the Council of State at Brussels. But this necessary reform came too late, and only precipitated the revolution. The provinces of the Netherlands were full of men who had learned from Erasmus to study the Bible and to adopt a critical attitude towards the abuses of the Church. The Reformation therefore found fruitful soil there. Luther, indeed, does not appear to have exercised much influence: it was the extremer forms of the Reformation that spread through the Netherlands. Charles V did what he could to suppress heresy; but there was something in the character of the burghers of the Netherland cities which was attracted by the austerity and the independence of Calvinism, and it spread rapidly after 1550.[2] The seventeen provinces, which were only united because they had been inherited by one sovereign, were beginning to develop a national consciousness. They had their common language (except the French-speaking districts in the south), they had their States-General at Brussels, they had the same interests. The difference between Holland and the Flemish part of Belgium which we see to-day was not in the first place due to a difference of religion or of culture, but simply to the fact that the Spaniards recaptured the southern provinces, but were unable, for geographical reasons, to recapture the northern ones. There was at first a " reformed " movement in Flanders and Brabant, as strong as in Holland and Zealand; there was all along, as there is to-day, a very large Roman Catholic minority in Holland (in early days a majority), but consisting largely of villagers.[3] Holland has never been a Protestant country in the same sense as the Scandinavian countries.

Charles V had been born in the Netherlands, and spoke the language. Philip II was by birth and character a Spaniard who had not the least sympathy with his subjects in the Netherlands.

[1] Bellegarde, p. 33.
[2] P. Geyl, *Revolt of the Netherlands* (1932), p. 58.
[3] Geyl, pp. 64, 258, etc.

His main object in setting up the new bishoprics was to have a better organization for suppressing heresy; and the Spanish Inquisition was introduced in 1565. National hatred of the Spaniard, combined with an independent attitude towards religion, as hateful as it was unintelligible to the Spanish King and his ministers, and with a determination to maintain the ancient privileges of provinces and cities, which the King was equally determined to destroy in the interests of autocracy, led to the Dutch War of Independence (1568–1648), carried on by both sides with horrible atrocity; it became a religious war in which both sides had great numbers of martyrs. The most celebrated martyrs on the Catholic side were the nineteen Martyrs of Gorcum (eleven Capuchins, four members of other orders, and four secular priests), whose festival is still observed by the Church of Utrecht on July 9.[1] Finally the seven northern provinces—Holland, Zealand, Utrecht, Gelderland, Overyssel, Friesland, and Groningen—became a republic, and adopted the Reformed religion.[2] Their independence was recognized by Spain by the Treaty of Westphalia, 1648.

Meanwhile the new bishops took possession of their sees. Frederick Schenk, Baron von Teutenburg, was consecrated in 1560, as the first Archbishop of Utrecht since St. Willibrord and the fifty-seventh occupant of the see. His suffragans were Nicolas Nieuwland, Bishop of Haarlem, who had been coadjutor to the last Bishop of Utrecht; John Mahusius, Bishop of Deventer; John Knyff, Bishop of Groningen; Cunerus Petersen, Bishop of Leeuwarden (the first bishop, Dirutius, was appointed to Bruges before he had been consecrated); and Nicolas de Castro or Verburg, Bishop of Middelburg.

On October 12, 1565, Archbishop Schenk held a provincial synod, which accepted the decrees of the Council of Trent, on faith, the Sacraments, and morals; the chapter protested against interference with its rights and privileges, but the Synod rejected its protest.[3]

The Revolution began in 1565;[4] it was at first a movement for the defence of the rights of the provinces, " with no other design but to preserve the Catholic religion in its purity " (William the Silent),[5] but the most ardent and successful of its promoters

---

[1] Bellegarde, pp. 48–55. Neale tells the story in *Lent Legends* (S.P.C.K., 1905).
[2] Reformed rather than Protestant, because it was Calvinist, not Lutheran.
[3] Bellegarde, p. 35.        [4] Geyl, p. 85.        [5] Bellegarde, p. 42.

were Calvinists, who, whenever a city fell into their hands, stripped the churches of their ornaments and handed them over to the Reformed ministers, while the practice of the Roman Catholic religion was prohibited, in spite of all guarantees to the contrary. The change was effected at Haarlem on May 29 (Corpus Christi), 1578, when the congregation assembled in the cathedral was attacked by the garrison, and the bishop had to flee for his life.[1]

According to the terms of the Union of Utrecht, January 23, 1579 (from which date the independence of the Dutch Republic is reckoned), the rights and privileges of the Roman Catholic religion were guaranteed, but on June 14, 1580, the practice of that religion was forbidden by the magistrates of Utrecht,[2] and the cathedral of St. Martin was taken from the archbishop and his chapter. In truth the Prince of Orange and the Government were unable to control the extremists.

On August 25, 1580, Archbishop Schenk died, and the see remained vacant till 1602. The Bishop of Haarlem, Godfrey de Mierlo, a Dominican who had succeeded Nieuwland in 1569, took refuge at Bonn, and died there in 1587; he had no successor till 1742. John Mahusius, Bishop of Deventer, was succeeded by Ægidius van den Berge (de Monte) in 1570; both were Franciscans. Van den Berge died at Zwolle, May 26, 1577. He had no successor till 1758. Philip II did indeed nominate Gisbert Coeverinck as Bishop of Deventer in 1590, but he was never consecrated, as there was no money to pay even his fees to the Pope.

Cunerus Petersen, Bishop of Leeuwarden, founded a cathedral chapter there, but it did not survive his death in 1580, at Cologne. He had no successors. John Knyff, Bishop of Groningen, who was not so violently opposed as the others, died in his cathedral city in 1576. He had no successors: for John de Bruherzen, Dean of Utrecht, who was appointed to succeed him, was elected Archbishop of Utrecht, though never consecrated; and Arnold Nylen, who was then appointed, had to flee to Brussels, and died there in 1603, without having been consecrated. Nicolas Verburg, the first Bishop of Middelburg, died there in 1573, and was succeeded by John van Styren, who, though consecrated, was never able to live in his diocese, and died at Louvain in 1594. Thus the six

---

[1] Geyl, p. 171; Neale, p. 112, calls it a massacre.
[2] Neale, p. 113.

sees of the ecclesiastical province of Utrecht were now all left vacant.[1]

The diocesan organization, however, continued, especially at Utrecht and Haarlem. Although Roman Catholic services were forbidden, a large proportion of the people was still Roman Catholic. It was the duty of the cathedral chapter to appoint " Grand-Vicars " or Vicars-General to administer the diocese during the vacancy of the see, according to the directions of the Council of Trent; but at Utrecht the Dean of the cathedral was by statute Vicar-General *ex-officio*. John de Bruherzen, Dean of Utrecht, therefore became Grand-Vicar on the death of Archbishop Schenk; he was elected archbishop, but the election was never confirmed by the Pope;[2] he had been banished from the country, because he had refused, as President of the Council of Utrecht, to invite William the Silent to the city; and he died at Cologne in 1600. He was succeeded as Vicar-General in 1583 by Sasbold Vosmeer, Dean of St. Mary's Church, The Hague, who was also, in 1592, appointed by the Pope Vicar-Apostolic (a post not to be confused with that of Vicar-General[3]) for the whole of the United Provinces. The Chapter of Haarlem also continued to administer that diocese; the Chapter of Deventer, removed to Oldenzaal in 1591, continued until 1665.

It was in 1592 that the Jesuits first entered the country; and the difference between their policy and that of Vosmeer and the national clergy, which ultimately led to the schism, began at once. The Roman Catholics of Holland had their own diocesan organization; the chapters had the right to elect bishops and present them to the Pope for confirmation. They regarded the Pope as their lawful superior, but held that he was bound to respect their canonical rights. A parallel may be drawn, perhaps, between their attitude towards their ecclesiastical and their civil ruler. They recognized the King of Spain as their sovereign, but held that he was bound to respect the privileges of the provinces; they regarded the Pope also as a constitutional sovereign, bound to respect the canonical rights of local churches. But neither King nor Pope would recognize these limitations. Both were convinced believers in the Renais-

---

[1] Bellegarde, pp. 35–41.                [2] Bellegarde, p. 39.
[3] A Vicar-Apostolic is the representative of the Pope, and is ordinarily, though not necessarily, a bishop. A Vicar-General is the representative of the chapter to govern the diocese while the see is vacant.

sance ideal of absolute monarchy; both demanded blind obedience to their edicts. The Jesuits were the new papal militia,
vowed to absolute obedience to their General. Their conception of the Church, as we have seen, left no room for local rights,
or for diocesan organization. Their policy was to abolish the
hierarchy and the dioceses, and to secure that the Roman Catholic
mission in the Netherlands should be controlled entirely by the
Congregation *de Propaganda Fide* at Rome—that is, in practice,
by themselves.

With this object, the Jesuits did their utmost, from the moment
of their arrival in the country, to prevent the bishoprics from
being filled. They held that the bishop who was needed for
ordination and confirmation should be only a vicar-apostolic
appointed by the Pope and removable at his direction; not a
diocesan bishop with canonical rights of his own and power to
hinder the designs of their Society.

The chapters, on the other hand, and the majority of the
clergy and people, while perfectly loyal to the Pope, did not
want to be directly controlled from Rome. They valued their
ancient rights, and were determined to maintain them; they
detested what they regarded as the moral laxity of the Jesuits,
and they thought that their countrymen were more likely to
return to the Church if the ancient constitution and the ancient
type of piety were retained, and the bishops were elected by their
clergy, than if the Church were entirely administered by Jesuits,
whose moral teaching and exotic piety were alike repugnant to
the Dutch. Moreover, the Jesuits, who were believed to be in
favour of political assassination, were particularly odious to the
government.

This was the real cause of the dispute, which began more than
forty years before the publication of Jansen's *Augustinus*.

The accusation of Jansenism was brought against the Chapter
of Utrecht much later, on the principle of " Give a dog a bad
name and hang him ". But from first to last the real issue was
the rights of the chapters; and, behind it, the claim of the
Papacy to unlimited obedience.

As early as 1598 the Jesuits successfully prevented the appointment of Vosmeer to the see of Haarlem. In 1602 he went to
Rome to protest against the intrusion of the Jesuits on the rights
of the secular clergy, and to ask for the appointment of an archbishop. The Archduke Albert, who had married the daughter

of Philip II, and to whom the sovereignty of the Netherlands had
been left by the King's will (Philip died in 1598), believed (mis-
takenly) that he had the right to nominate the Archbishop of
Utrecht under an edict of Charles V; he nominated Vosmeer,
who was also elected archbishop by the chapter,[1] and, much
against his will, was consecrated at Rome, September 22, 1602,
with the title of Archbishop of Philippi (in order not to offend
the Dutch Government), but with the condition that he might
assume his real title of Archbishop of Utrecht when circumstances should permit.  The evidence that he was indeed Archbishop of Utrecht is given at length by Neale, *History of the
Church of Holland*, Appendix 2.  The following are some examples
of it.  On January 11, 1603, the archbishop wrote to his brother,
Tilman Vosmeer (who had been suggested for the see of Haarlem) :
" The Pope wished to promote me by a foreign title: but he
gave me the people of St. Willibrord, that I may be truly called
Archbishop of Holland, Zealand, and Utrecht ".  In 1609 he
wrote to Gravius, his agent at Rome, that the Archduke had
nominated him as Archbishop of Utrecht, but the Pope, in giving
him the title of Archbishop of Philippi, had said to him, " You
may change your title as soon as your Archduke pleases ".
(From the standpoint of the Roman Catholic clergy, the Archduke was the lawful sovereign of the whole of the Netherlands,
and the Dutch Government mere " insurgents ".)  In 1613
Vosmeer told Gravius that his title of Philippi referred, not to
Philippi in Macedonia, but to King Philip!

He was banished by the government for having sought and
accepted nomination to the archbishopric of Utrecht from the
Archduke Albert: which was naturally regarded as high treason
by the Republic.  (Dr. Neale thinks he was denounced to the
government by the Jesuits themselves, p. 122.)  Moreover, the
Jesuits ordinarily addressed him as Archbishop of Utrecht—
*e.g.*, Louis Makeblyd, August 6, 1611, Gerard Contonnel, September 18, 1613.  He himself used the title regularly, often in
the form Archiepiscopus Ultrajectensis et Philippensis.  Besides
his " ordinary " jurisdiction as archbishop, he had his special
jurisdiction, as vicar-apostolic of the Pope; these two separate
forms of authority are carefully distinguished in his official
documents.[2]

[1] *Seconde Apologie de l'Evêque de Babilone*, Preface, p. vi.
[2] Neale, pp. 393–395.

Having been banished from the United Provinces, Vosmeer had to govern his diocese from abroad, first from the Spanish Netherlands, later from Cologne, though he visited it when he could, at the risk of his life. He had continually to struggle against the intrusion of the Jesuits and the mendicant orders; he once wrote to his brother, " The inconvenience caused by the Protestants is less than the trouble due to the Jesuits ".[1] There were only eight Jesuits in the country in 1609, but in that year the republic agreed to a truce with Spain for twelve years, and the Jesuits were able to enter the country more easily. By every means in their power they encouraged the clergy and people to ignore the authority of the archbishop, with the object of increasing the power and wealth of their own order: they complained to the Internuncios at Brussels that the archbishop was hindering their work; but, as Vosmeer's correspondence shows, they left the really laborious and dangerous work of ministering in the villages to the parish priests. On December 16, 1609, the archbishop formally inhibited the Jesuits and the mendicant orders from the administration of the Sacraments and from preaching, and forbade the people to have recourse to them. The Jesuits complained to the Pope, who deprived Vosmeer of his vicariate-apostolic, but the archbishop made a complete defence of himself, and the Pope gave way.[2]

Archbishop Vosmeer died on May 3, 1614, and was buried in the Franciscan church at Cologne. The Chapters of Utrecht and Haarlem had already recommended that Philip Rovenius, Dean of Oldenzaal, should be consecrated as his coadjutor. Rovenius was unwilling, and the Chapter of Utrecht recommended Henry Vorden; but the Chapter of Haarlem insisted on having Rovenius, and the dispute was decided in favour of Rovenius by Jacobus Jansonius, then President of Hadrian VI College at Louvain. Rovenius was elected by the clergy immediately after the death of Vosmeer[3] and was consecrated Archbishop of Utrecht, November 8, 1620, at Voorst near Brussels, by the Papal Nuncio. He had already been vicar-apostolic for six years.

In 1583 there had been about 600 priests in the United Provinces. By 1614 the number was reduced to 170. But from that time the number, both of priests and people, began to

---

[1] Neale, p. 124.
[2] Bellegarde, p. 96; Neale, p. 130.
[3] *Seconde Apologie de l'Evêque de Babilone*, Preface, p. vii.

increase. In 1663 there were 383 parishes in the six dioceses.[1] The cause of the increase seems to have been the cessation of the persecution after the truce with Spain had been agreed to.

The new archbishop had the same titles as his predecessor, but since the sovereignty of the Netherlands (according to the legitimist view) had reverted, on the death of the Archduke Albert, to Philip III of Spain, the clergy asked Cornelius Jansen, who was going to Madrid on other business, to request the King formally to confirm the election of Rovenius as Archbishop of Utrecht. It does not appear that the King ever did so; but on March 10, 1640, Rovenius was banished by the magistrates of Utrecht for having taken the title of Archbishop of Utrecht.[2] Until then he had lived at Utrecht, in secret, in the house of Mademoiselle de Duivenvoorde, a lady of noble birth who had bound herself by a vow of chastity; and he had at least one narrow escape from the officers of the burgomaster. Rovenius continued his predecessor's struggle against the intrigues of the Jesuits: he even had to go to Rome to get his rights over the Jesuits and other orders confirmed. They were compelled to sign an agreement promising obedience, but they did not keep the promise.[3]

The principal work of Archbishop Rovenius was the reconstitution of the Chapter of Utrecht. The canonries had never been suppressed, but most of the members were now Calvinists; the chapter still had its estates, and held regular meetings. In 1622 the Government of Utrecht ordered that only Calvinists should be presented in future. Archbishop Rovenius then chose nine of the few priests remaining in the chapters, added to them two others whom he had intended to present shortly to canonries in the months when he had the right of patronage, and constituted this body the " Vicariate " of the Chapter of Utrecht, with all the ecclesiastical rights of the old chapter.[4] This reorganization, which was completed on June 9, 1633, was necessary if the chapter, as a Roman Catholic institution, was not to come to an end. No protest was raised at the time; most of the canons, who were priests but had not been selected by Rovenius, had left the country to avoid persecution. The nominations made by the reorganized chapter were accepted by Rome, down to the death of Archbishop Codde in 1710; and the chapter itself was

[1] Neale, p. 190.                    [2] Bellegarde, p. 118.
[3] Bellegarde, p. 125.               [4] Bellegarde, pp. 130–134; Neale, p. 143.

recognized expressly, on many occasions, by Papal Nuncios.[1] After this, Rovenius and his successors ceased to use their right of appointing members of the legal chapter, which had ceased to have any significance for them.

Another important achievement of Rovenius' episcopate was the foundation of the " Klopjes " or " Knocking Sisters ", who, wearing ordinary dress and living in their own homes, did the work of teaching and nursing among the persecuted Roman Catholics in the villages. In 1639 they were forbidden by the government to teach children; but after 1667 the laws against them fell into disuse. The last of them died in 1853. They were called " Knocking Sisters " because they went from house to house to summon the people to church.[2]

At the same period churches were built in the towns, hidden behind the houses, and so arranged that if the alarm were given during a service, all traces of the use to which the building was being put could be removed within two minutes, and the place made to look like an ale-house. One such church, preserved as a museum, is still to be seen at Amsterdam.

In 1641 Rovenius, with nine of his priests, gave their approval to the *Augustinus* of Cornelius Jansen.[3] It seems that he also made certain liturgical changes; he transferred the feast of St. Boniface from June 5 to July 5, so that it should never coincide with Corpus Christi, and he forbade the use of music between the consecration and the communion of the people. During his episcopate, in spite of the persecution, the number of Roman Catholics increased from 200,000 to 300,000. In 1647, Jacobus de la Torre was elected by the Chapters of Utrecht and Haarlem to be his coadjutor, and consecrated with the title of Archbishop of Ephesus; but he was shortly afterwards banished, and went to live at Antwerp.[4]

When Rovenius died in 1651, de la Torre succeeded him. He was a weak man, and was induced by the Jesuits to sign a document, known as the " Concessiones Ephesinae " (because his title was Archbishop of Ephesus), which allowed them to increase their missions, although they had done their best to hinder his appointment. He was out of his mind for some time before his death, and had a coadjutor, Zacharias de Metz (appointed by the Pope, though last on the list sent in by the

[1] Neale, pp. 396–397.    [2] Bellegarde, p. 144.
[3] Neale, p. 150.    [4] Neale, p. 153; Bellegarde, p. 150.

chapter), whose hasty temper caused much trouble, but who died two months before the archbishop. Johannes van Neercassel was elected to succeed Metz, and, as coadjutor, had the right to succeed on the diocesan's death, but when the archbishop died on September 16, 1661, Baldwin Catz was appointed archbishop and vicar-apostolic by the Pope, with Neercassel as his coadjutor. They were consecrated together at Cologne on September 8, 1662, Catz as Archbishop of Philippi, and Neercassel as Bishop of Castoria. But Catz soon became imbecile, and died on May 18, 1663, when Neercassel came into possession of the archbishopric.[1]

Archbishop van Neercassel was the last and greatest of the Archbishops of Utrecht who died in full communion with Rome. He succeeded in solving an important problem of marriage for the whole Roman Communion. The Council of Trent, in order to prevent secret marriages, had decreed that no marriage should be recognized as valid without the presence of a priest. This was interpreted as meaning that all Protestant marriages were invalid; that a married person, on joining the Roman Communion, must leave his or her spouse until they should be remarried; and that if the other spouse refused to repeat the marriage the Roman Catholic spouse might then marry any other person. Archbishop van Neercassel, on the other hand, taught that marriages between persons not in communion with Rome were by natural law valid and indissoluble; and that if such persons afterwards joined the Roman Communion, their previous marriage only required the Church's blessing to make it sacramental. This view was accepted by the Roman Penitentiary in 1671, and was made the law of the Church by Pope Benedict XIV in 1741.[2]

Archbishop van Neercassel continued to suffer from the attacks of the Jesuits, who boasted that they would drive the secular clergy out of Holland, and were always trying to discredit him by accusing him of false doctrine. In 1670 he found it necessary to go to Rome to defend himself, taking with him letters of recommendation from the French Ambassador at The Hague, M. de Pomponne (Simon Arnauld, brother of Antoine), the Princesse de Conti (a niece of Cardinal Mazarin), the Grand Duke of Tuscany, and Christina, the former Queen of Sweden.

---

[1] Neale, p. 160.
[2] Neale, pp. 162–163; Bellegarde, pp. 180–185.

He was completely successful, and obtained from the Congregation *De Propaganda Fide* two decrees in his favour.[1] He at once returned to Holland. During his stay in Rome he was much ridiculed for his simplicity of life, because he had only one servant with him. During his journey to Holland he took every opportunity of preaching, especially in the diocese of Münster, where great crowds assembled everywhere to hear him;[2] the Prince-Bishop, who could not preach himself, was delighted to find a bishop who could.

In 1648 Spain had recognized the independence of the Dutch Republic, so that the Dutch Roman Catholics no longer felt bound to regard the King of Spain as their real sovereign, and no longer felt obliged to risk being accused of high treason by seeking his confirmation for Church appointments. On the other hand, the war with France caused some difficulty. In 1672, when the French occupied Utrecht, the cathedral was restored to the Roman Catholics; and when they retired, the archbishop thought it wise to take refuge at Huissen in the duchy of Cleves, where he founded a diocesan seminary.[3]

Some of the French Jansenists took refuge in Holland at this period: in particular, Antoine Arnauld, who was an intimate friend of Archbishop Van Neercassel, wrote, during his retirement at Huissen, a book called *Amor Poenitens*, defending the thesis of Arnauld, that contrition, founded on the love of God, is necessary to penitence and salvation, and that attrition, or sorrow due to punishment, is not enough. This book was attacked with great violence by the Jesuits, but it was formally sanctioned by thirty French bishops, and received the commendation of Pope Innocent XI, who remarked, " The book is a good one, and the author is a saint ". Under Alexander VIII a decree was published forbidding the distribution of the book " until corrected "; but it was never formally condemned, and the author published in 1685 a new and corrected edition.[4]

In 1685 the Revocation of the Edict of Nantes, and the arrival in Holland of crowds of Huguenot refugees from France, led to the last persecution of Roman Catholics; but it was not very severe, because the Roman Catholics gave liberally to the funds raised for the support of the French exiles.[5]

---

[1] Bellegarde, pp. 171–185.  [2] Neale, p. 168.
[3] Bellegarde, p. 175.  [4] Bellegarde, pp. 178–180.
[5] Bellegarde, p. 191.

On June 6, 1686, the archbishop died of fever at Zwolle, while visiting the eastern part of his jurisdiction.[1] According to Bellegarde, the episcopate of Neercassel was the golden age of the Church of Utrecht: the persecution was just severe enough to keep the Church pure, the priests were united, obedient, and devoted to their work, and the number of adherents steadily increased. Out of two millions in the territory of the United Provinces, 330,000 were Roman Catholics.[2] (In England at that time the number of Roman Catholics was only 30,000.)

About this time the jurisdiction of Utrecht was extended in a curious way. In 1652 the Duke of Schleswig gave the island of Noordstrand, on the west coast of his duchy, to a colony of Dutchmen, who built dykes to protect it from the inroads of the sea. The clergy of the colony were Oratorians from Malines, who were under the jurisdiction of Utrecht. In 1681 the Oratorians were withdrawn, and the Archbishop of Utrecht sent secular priests in their place. In 1702 the schism in Holland led to a schism at Noordstrand, but, as in Holland, the government protected the independent party. In 1826 a compromise was made between the two parties: there is now both an Old Catholic and a Roman Catholic parish, and the former is under the Old Catholic Bishop in Germany, but the church land belongs to the Chapter of Utrecht.[3]

[1] Neale, p. 195.                    [2] Bellegarde, p. 208.
[3] Letter to the author from Professor C. G. van Riel of Amsterdam. Bellegarde, p. 172, gives a rather different account.

# CHAPTER VII

## THE BREACH WITH ROME

On the death of Archbishop van Neercassel, the Chapters of Utrecht and Haarlem unanimously elected Hugo Francis van Heussen as his successor; Peter Codde and John Lindeborn were appointed vicars-general to administer the diocese during the vacancy of the see.[1]

Heussen was the favourite disciple of Neercassel, who called him his "Timothy", and he had already, in 1682, been elected coadjutor-bishop. To prevent his consecration, the Jesuits had denounced a treatise on indulgences, which he had written in 1681, as heretical. This book was still being examined by the Holy Office at Rome when he was elected by the chapters to succeed Neercassel. The result of this attack was the condemnation of the book, on May 15, 1687, but this decree was found to be full of mistakes, and the Pope suppressed it.[2] However, the chapters saw that there would be difficulty in getting the election of Heussen confirmed at Rome, so they sent in three alternative names, of which that of Peter Codde was the first. All four, however, were accused of Jansenism, and of supporting the Four Gallican Articles, by the other side. On September 29 the Congregation *de Propaganda Fide* rejected Heussen, and decided that in future the Church in the civil provinces of Utrecht, Holland, Zealand, and Gelderland should be placed under Bassery, the Vicar-Apostolic of Hertogenbosch (Bois-le-duc), and in other provinces under a vicar-apostolic to be chosen by the nuncio at Cologne and the internuncio at Brussels.[3] This arrangement, which would have brought the ancient dioceses to an end, was prevented by Cardinal Howard (uncle of the Duke of Norfolk), who had been a friend of Archbishop van Neercassel, and who used his influence as agent of King James II (this was a year before the English Revolution) to persuade the Pope to reject the decision of the cardinals.[4]

[1] Bellegarde, p. 196; Neale, p. 198.
[2] Bellegarde, p. 198; Neale, p. 199.
[3] Bellegarde, p. 199.
[4] Neale, p. 201; Ruth Clark, *Strangers and Sojourners*, p. 158.

Various other proposals were made, but in the end Peter Codde was chosen, Heussen being rejected solely on account of his book on indulgences. Heussen was profoundly thankful that he had not been made archbishop; he had now leisure to write two large historical works, *Batavia Sacra* and *History of the Bishoprics of the United Netherlands*, upon which his fame chiefly rests.

Peter Codde was born at Amsterdam, November 27, 1648, and educated at Louvain, where he joined the Congregation of the Oratory. He lived for some time in devout retirement in the Oratorian houses at Paris and Orleans.[1] Archbishop van Neercassel called him back to the Netherlands, and in 1683 put him in charge of the most important parish at Utrecht. Codde had published a Dutch translation of Bossuet's *Exposition of the Catholic Faith*, and he was also a celebrated preacher. He was consecrated at Brussels by the Archbishop of Malines and the Bishops of Antwerp and Namur, on Septuagesima Sunday, February 6, 1689, with the title of Archbishop of Sebaste. Before the consecration, the internuncio, De Via, asked him to sign a document condemning Jansenist beliefs: this was the " Formulary " (see Chapter IV, above), though Codde did not know it. He replied that he had not studied the Jansenist controversy, and that he must consult his friends before signing such a document. The internuncio said that it was of no importance, and changed the conversation.[2] However, Archbishop Codde's work was continually interrupted by the complaints made by the Jesuits at Rome that he was a Jansenist and a Gallican. As early as 1691 the worry caused by these complaints, together with overwork, threw him into a serious illness, of which he nearly died. Pope Innocent XII appointed a commission to inquire into these charges, and presided over it himself. The archbishop was unanimously and unconditionally acquitted.[3]

However, the attacks continued, and in 1699 the cardinals secretly decided to get rid of Codde, and to appoint Theodore de Cock in his place. This priest had been sent to Rome by the chapters in 1688 to defend their interests; but since then personal ambition had led him to change sides. The archbishop was invited to come to Rome for the Jubilee of 1700. He did not want to go, but decided that it was less dangerous to go than to stay. Before he went, rejecting the suggestion of

---

[1] Bellegarde, p. 207.     [2] Neale, p. 205; Bellegarde, p. 216.
[3] Bellegarde, p. 218; Neale, p. 208.

the internuncio at Brussels that he should appoint Theodore de Cock as his deputy during his absence, he appointed four " Pro-Vicars " to take charge of his province: Catz and Heussen for Utrecht, Deventer, and Middelburg; Groenhout and Swaen for Haarlem, Leeuwarden, and Groningen.[1] This shows that the six sees, though all but Utrecht had been vacant for over a century, were regarded as still in existence.

On his arrival at Rome the archbishop found that Innocent XII was dead, and that Cardinal Albani, who was entirely devoted to the opposite party, had succeeded as Clement XI. Codde was well received, but fresh accusations were brought against him and his clergy. A protest in support of the archbishop was signed by 300 of his priests, headed by the four pro-vicars, and sent to Rome; among those who signed it were Steenoven and Van der Croon, who afterwards became Archbishops of Utrecht themselves. These 300 constituted the majority of the priests in the six dioceses, of whom there were altogether 470, 340 secular and 130 regular.[2] The commission appointed to decide the truth of the charges against Codde was equally divided (December 1701); nevertheless, in the following May Theodore de Cock was appointed Pro-Vicar-Apostolic of the United Provinces, in the place of Peter Codde, deposed. No mention was made of any reason for the deposition; the brief was not published at Rome, and Codde only heard of it by letters from his friends in the Netherlands. The commission appointed to try the case had not yet issued its report. Even the Ultramontane canonist, Hyacinth de Archangelis, issued a formal opinion that a vicar-apostolic with the rights of an ordinary, as Codde undoubtedly was, could not be arbitrarily deposed. Precisely how this event occurred will probably never be known, for all the members of the commission were ordered to be silent, on pain of excommunication.[3]

The Chapters of Utrecht and Haarlem unanimously decided not to recognize the authority of De Cock, on the ground that the Pope had no canonical right to deprive even a vicar-apostolic, still less an archbishop, without trial and condemnation. From this point begins the schism between the two parties in the Dutch Roman Catholic Church. In some places the adherents of the archbishop and the chapters and those of De

[1] Neale, p. 209.                              [2] Bellegarde, p. 211.
[3] Bellegarde, p. 224; Neale, p. 212.

Cock ceased to communicate with one another; there were popular disturbances; and the Dutch Government, having summoned Van Erkel, one of the leaders of the archbishop's party, to explain the position, issued a decree forbidding Theodore de Cock to exercise any jurisdiction over the Roman Catholics in its dominions.

It is clear that at this point the question at issue was not doctrinal, but the demand for blind obedience. According to the canons, bishops could only be deposed after a proper trial and condemnation, with full opportunity to defend themselves. But to the Jesuits and their pupils the Pope was an absolute monarch, and any rights or privileges interfering with his will were intolerable.

The Counter-Reformation, of which the Jesuits were the chief agents, had practically put the Roman Communion under martial law.

Meanwhile the archbishop found himself in a difficult position at Rome. The Jesuits announced in the Netherlands that he was in the hands of the Inquisition, and would be imprisoned for life, beheaded, or burned. In reality, he was not interfered with; but the Italian clergy could not understand his lack of personal ambition, or his refusal to sign what he called " equivocal documents ", even to further his own cause. However, the Dutch Government, urged on by his three nephews, who were among the burgomasters of Amsterdam, commanded him to return within three months, and warned the Court of Rome that if he were prevented from coming the Jesuits would be banished from the country and De Cock confined to his own house.[1] De Cock accordingly begged the Pope to allow Codde to return, and on April 12, 1703, the archbishop left Rome with special passports from the Emperor and the Republic of Venice, and with permission from the General of the Dominicans to celebrate Mass in every house of that order. After travelling by Vienna and Dresden, in order to avoid the war then raging in Europe, he arrived in the Netherlands on June 27. He had four priests with him, one of whom was Cornelius Steenoven, afterwards his successor.

De Cock, who had rashly accused the government of being bribed by the secular clergy, was banished, and fled to Rome, where he was given a canonry in the Basilica of St. Lawrence.

[1] Bellegarde, p. 237; Neale, p. 217.

The Chapter of Haarlem was in a different position from the Chapter of Utrecht: the archbishop was not their diocesan; his authority over them was that of a metropolitan. To make sure that they were right in rejecting the authority of Theodore de Cock as Vicar-Apostolic, they consulted Van Espen, the great canonist of Louvain. His formal answer, the *Motivum Juris pro Capitulo Cathedrali Haarlemiensi*, laid down that the authority of a vicar-apostolic could not override the right of the chapter to govern the diocese during the vacancy of the see (which in the case of Haarlem had been vacant since 1587), but that in any case the authority of even a diocesan bishop reverted to the chapter if he were exiled, just as it would if he died; therefore, whatever authority De Cock had possessed had ceased when he was exiled.[1]

As this was the first time that Van Espen came forward openly in defence of the rights of the chapters, this seems to be the place to give a short account of that great man, upon whose work not only the independence of Utrecht, but also the Febronian movement in Germany was so largely founded.[2] Zegers Bernard van Espen was the son of John van Espen and Elizabeth Zegers. He was born at Louvain, July 9, 1646, and was educated at the school of the Oratorian Fathers (who were, all through this period, opposed to the party of the Jesuits) and at the University of Louvain. From his earliest boyhood he had a reputation for innocence of life and devotion to study. He took his M.A. in 1665, became Licentiate in Law, 1670, and Doctor of Civil and Canon Law, October 22, 1675. He was chosen by Archbishop de Berghes of Malines to go with him to Rome, but for some reason the journey never took place. He was ordained priest on May 27, 1673, and, being weary of scholastic theology, determined to devote his life to the study of Church History and Canon Law, of which the former had been much neglected at Louvain, and the latter required drastic reconstruction. In 1674 he was given the " Lectureship of Six Weeks ", which carried with it a canonry in St. Peter's Collegiate Church, and this, with the exception of a canonry of Aire in Artois, which he held from 1672 to 1675, was the only preferment which he ever received. In 1677 he joined the staff of the College of the Pope (so called from the Dutch Pope Hadrian VI, who had been its founder), then the best-known college in the University:[3] Van Vianen, its

---

[1] Neale, p. 219. [2] See E. Kemp in *Theology*, Aug.–Sept., 1946.
[3] Cornelius Jansen had been President of it forty years earlier.

president, and Huyghens, who succeeded him, were Van Espen's intimate friends. The college had so good a reputation that Archbishop de Berghes gave Vianen the charge of all its candidates for ordination. At this college Van Espen lived quietly for the greater part of his life, and became the leading canonist of his age, consulted by eminent persons throughout Europe. Perceiving that the usual books on Canon Law were full of corruptions because of the inclusion of false decretals designed to support the autocratic power of the Pope, he made a critical investigation of the sources of Canon Law—Holy Scripture, the canons of the Councils, and the genuine decretals of the Popes— and based on it his *Jus ecclesiasticum universum*, published in 1700, to which he added a supplement in 1729. It was because of his determination to discover what was really canonical without regard to vested interests that he was the object of prolonged and violent opposition; but he never resented it, and was always ready to place his knowledge at the service not only of his friends, but also of his enemies.

His practice was to be in chapel every day at 5 a.m. and to spend two hours in prayer and meditation, after which he would either say Mass himself or serve the Mass of one of his colleagues. He also set apart for devotion the period from 2.30 to 3. When he conducted the annual retreat for the theological students, the other students begged that they might be allowed to come too, and their request was granted.[1]

Among his works were an attack on excessive exemptions from episcopal jurisdiction (1688), a copy of which was sent by Antoine Arnauld to Vaucel, his agent at Rome;[2] and a treatise on the worship of saints, relics, and images (1692), in which, while maintaining the doctrine of the Council of Trent on this subject, he attacked such abuses as the following:—

(*a*) The opinion that if the Foolish Virgins in the parable had addressed their petition not to Our Lord, but to His Mother, saying, "Lady, Lady, open to us", they would have been admitted!

(*b*) The opinion that whereas Our Lord is the fountain of justice, His Mother is the fountain of mercy.

(*c*) The story of the suicide who was restored to life by the Blessed Virgin because he had often used her rosary.

[1] Bellegarde, *Vie de M. van Espen*, book i, art. i (1767).
[2] Bellegarde, *Vie*, pp. 68 ff.

An attempt was made to get this treatise condemned at Rome, but without success.[1]

This was the man who, contrary to all his worldly interests, became the great defender of the canonical rights of the clergy of Utrecht and Haarlem, most of whom he knew personally, because they had been educated at Louvain. He maintained that there was no question of faith or dogma in dispute, but only questions of ecclesiastical jurisdiction; a point on which no one had a better right to speak than he had.[2]

Though De Cock had been banished, his party remained; and Archbishop Codde found his flock divided by a schism. He had been deprived, unjustly and uncanonically, of his powers as Vicar-Apostolic of the Pope, but he was still Archbishop of Utrecht. He had before him three possible courses:—

(i) To submit to the decision of Rome, and retire into private life. But this would have been to desert his friends and to surrender the rights, and even the existence, of his see.

(ii) To continue to exercise his authority as archbishop, while appealing against his suspension as vicar-apostolic. (As archbishop he had diocesan jurisdiction in Utrecht, and metropolitan jurisdiction in the other dioceses; as vicar-apostolic he had diocesan jurisdiction wherever there was no bishop or chapter.) This was the course which Van Espen advised him to follow. It would have led to an immediate breach with Rome: but this was in any case inevitable.

(iii) To retire from the exercise of his office, while protesting against his suspension. This was the course advised by Quesnel, and this he did, because he was afraid of hurting the consciences of simple people if he continued to resist the Pope.

As the archbishop had retired, his jurisdiction reverted to the chapters, and they appointed the four Pro-Vicars as Vicars-General of the See of Utrecht. However, the internuncio at Brussels had received orders, even before the archbishop's return, to declare Jacob Catz, the first of the four Pro-Vicars, to be excommunicated. In consequence, a protest was issued, April 1, 1703, and was signed by more than 150 priests, which shows the strength of the party of the chapters at that time.[3]

Meanwhile, the government, anxious to restore peace, banished Van Beest and Van Wyck, two of the archpriests appointed by

---

[1] Bellegarde, *Vie*, book iii, ch. iii, Art. i.        [2] Bellegarde, *Vie*, pp. 523 ff.
[3] Bellegarde, *Histoire Abregée*, p. 249.

De Cock, and threatened to take more serious measures, beginning with the banishment of all Jesuits; for they were convinced that it was Père La Chaise, the Jesuit confessor of Louis XIV, who was the origin of the trouble. The Jesuits were much alarmed, and tried to put pressure on the government by means of the ambassador of the Emperor, but in vain. Bussi, the internuncio at Brussels, went to The Hague, and finding that there was no hope that De Cock would be allowed to return, recommended the appointment of a new vicar-apostolic. Gerard Potcamp, the parish priest of Lingen, and a friend and supporter of the archbishop, unwillingly accepted the post, November 11, 1705. He was recognized by Archbishop Codde (though without any withdrawal of his protest against his suspension), by the Chapter of Utrecht, whose rights he entirely accepted, and by the government. But he died a month later, December 16, 1705.

The Chapter of Utrecht appointed Catz and Van Heussen Vicars-General, since the see was vacant through the resignation of Archbishop Codde. They begged the internuncio to appoint a new vicar-apostolic from candidates nominated by themselves, but he refused.

At this point the Pope arbitrarily transferred the government of the Church in the Dutch Republic from Bussi, the internuncio at Brussels, to Piazza, the nuncio at Cologne.[1] Piazza announced his appointment to the Grand Vicars; they answered that they could not recognize his immediate jurisdiction over themselves, to the prejudice of the rights of the chapters, but offered to have the point at issue decided by the Church courts. The result was that Van Heussen was forbidden, on pain of excommunication, to exercise any jurisdiction; he replied that such a prohibition was uncanonical, and that the chapters could not recognize it.

Piazza was made a cardinal, and Bussi was transferred from Brussels to Cologne. He proceeded, without consulting either the chapters or the Dutch Government, to appoint Adam Daemen as vicar-apostolic, and to consecrate him, Christmas Day, 1707, with the title of Archbishop of Adrianople. Daemen was a canon of Cologne, born at Amsterdam of foreign parents. The chapter refused to accept him as archbishop, considering his character unsuitable (for he had received 15,000 ducats for

---

[1] Bellegarde, p. 256; Neale, p. 225, gives a different account.

his vote in the Chapter of Cologne); the government forbade him to enter the country, because he had illegally accepted consecration without its permission, and Holland and West Friesland banished all the Jesuits.

The controversy now grew hotter; the priests who supported the chapters were all summoned to be tried at Cologne, but the government forbade them to leave the country. Bussi then excommunicated all who refused to recognize Daemen, declared the appointments recently made by the chapters invalid, and poured in fresh priests of the Jesuit party, who took possession of the parishes. The Chapter of Haarlem, weary of strife, passed a resolution that it would in future perform no capitular act. The Chapter of Utrecht was left to carry on the struggle alone.

Daemen, seeing that he would never be allowed to enter Dutch territory, resigned in 1710. In the same year, on December 18, Archbishop Codde died, after a long and painful illness. He was condemned by the Roman Inquisition after his death for his refusal to sign the Formulary of Alexander VII, which had been presented to him on his deathbed, and he was declared unworthy of the prayers of the faithful, and of Christian burial. It was too late, for he had already been buried beside Gerard Potcamp in the church at Warmond.[1]

At this point I must define clearly the difference between the Chapter of Utrecht and the Jesuits, who were now in control of the papal policy. The Chapter of Utrecht maintained that the province and diocese of Utrecht, with all their ancient and canonical rights and privileges, were still in existence; that the Vicariate instituted by Archbishop Rovenius was the ancient Chapter of Utrecht, and possessed all the rights of the chapter, including the right to elect the Archbishop of Utrecht; and that the later archbishops, from Vosmeer to Codde, were not only Vicars-Apostolic of the Roman See, but also Archbishops of Utrecht, the canonical successors of St. Willibrord. The Jesuits and their party held, as Rome holds to this day, that the Province of Utrecht and all its dioceses, as well as the ancient Chapter of Utrecht, had ceased to exist at the time of the Reformation[2] and that the Roman Catholic Church in the Dutch Republic was a mere mission, governed by a vicar-apostolic who was

---

[1] Bellegarde, p. 267.
[2] This theory began with Papenbrecht (see p. 127); before him the theory was that the dioceses came to an end with the Spanish sovereignty in 1648.

appointed and removed by the Pope at his discretion, and subject to the Congregation *de Propaganda Fide*, where the Jesuits were then all-powerful.

Behind this constitutional issue lay a profound difference in political philosophy. The Chapter of Utrecht, like other Gallicans, held that the Church was a community of communities, in which each diocese, province, and national church had its own rights and privileges; the Pope was monarch, but his monarchy was limited by the canons and by the rights of local churches.

The Jesuits, on the other hand, held that the Church was a centralized despotic kingdom, in which the local churches were mere departments, and the bishops and other officers simply the local representatives of the papal authority. It was a new conception, closely akin to the despotism in civil affairs which at that period was steadily increasing in most European countries; [1] but it was also the natural consequence of the development of the Papacy for many centuries.

It is significant that the only country where it was successfully resisted, though at the cost of schism, was the Dutch Republic, the one great European Power which owed its origin to the Reformation, and the earliest instance of a modern constitutional State.

There were other differences as well. It is true that the charge of doctrinal heterodoxy brought against the party of the chapters was false; their continual protest that they taught all the dogmas that the Roman Church taught was sincere, and it was true. But they denied the right of the Pope to enforce new doctrines without the assent of a General Council; and they were unwilling to assent to statements of fact which they did not believe, simply because they were told to do so. It was for this reason that they refused persistently to sign the Formulary of Alexander VII and the Bull " Unigenitus ". It must be added that most of them had been trained at Louvain, and were in close contact with the French Jansenist party, the leaders of which, such as Arnauld and Quesnel, had taken refuge in the Netherlands.

There were also devotional and ethical differences. We are learning to-day that different types of piety mark the divisions of Christendom quite as much as differences of doctrine. There was a great difference between the austere piety of the Dutch

[1] J. N. Figgis, *Churches in the Modern State*, pp. 147–150.

secular clergy, derived from the Brethren of the Common Life,
and the new sentimental cults which the Jesuits were teaching
everywhere, such as devotion to the Sacred Heart and the
Immaculate Conception. How far these devotions were sometimes pushed is shown by an instance of slightly later date. In
1740, strips of paper, on which praises of the Immaculate Conception were written, were being sold in Naples, to be dissolved
in water and given to hens, that they might lay more eggs!
This descent to Central African superstition was sanctioned by
St. Alfonso Liguori (created a Doctor of the Church by Pope
Pius IX) when he swallowed one of these strips during a serious
illness.[1] It was never condemned by Rome, though acceptance
of the condemnation of Quesnel's 101 propositions was enforced
on all Roman Catholics as necessary to salvation.

The two parties in the Dutch Roman Catholic Church were
There was also a difference between the Dutch secular clergy
and the Jesuits about ethics. The former were strongly opposed
to the Jesuit system of casuistry, especially to the doctrine that
sorrow based on fear, not on love, is sufficient for repentance and
absolution. They held that the Jesuits encouraged sin by giving
absolution too easily.

The Chapter of Utrecht was therefore fighting, not merely for
its own constitutional rights, but also for the right of local churches
to reject novelties contrary to truth and common sense, and
unsuited to the temperament of their people.

The Dutch Government, being Calvinist, had no direct interest
in the dispute, except the maintenance of order; but it naturally
preferred that its Roman Catholic subjects should be governed
by a Dutch archbishop, elected by Dutchmen, rather than
by a vicar-apostolic appointed by the Pope's representative at
Brussels or Cologne. It was fortunate that the religious dispute
was not affected, as in France, by the ever-changing diplomatic
relations between the Government and the Vatican.

The two parties in the Dutch Roman Catholic Church were
now out of communion with each other. The schism had begun
when the Pope arbitrarily deposed Codde, and appointed De
Cock in his place. It had been confirmed when Bussi, the
internuncio, in 1707 excommunicated the Vicars-General and
all who adhered to them. Every effort was made to fill the
parishes with Ultramontane priests, a concentrated attack was
made on the " Béguinages " at Amsterdam and Haarlem, and

[1] F. Nielsen, *History of the Papacy in the Nineteenth Century*, vol. i, p. 104.

the congregations were taught that it was worse to attend a
" Jansenist " service than a Protestant one, that " Jansenist "
baptism no more conveyed remission of sins than circumcision,
and that persons married by " Jansenist " priests were living in
sin.[1] This last instruction, which was formally issued by the
nuncio at Cologne, January 13, 1711, was contrary to the law
of the land, where marriages performed by Roman Catholic
priests, including those who adhered to the Chapter of Utrecht,
were recognized as valid for civil purposes.[2]

An attempt was made at reconciliation, but Cornelius Steenoven
and William Dalenoort, the representatives of the chapter, found
when they reached Cologne that they were required to submit to
Daemen as vicar-apostolic, to deny the existence of the chapters,
and to sign the Formulary of Alexander VII. The first they
were ready to do, as soon as the Dutch Government should
allow it, with the condition that the chapter should retain its
ancient right to elect the archbishop; the second they rejected
absolutely, and the third, after some hesitation, they rejected
also.[3] The question of the Five Propositions was only beginning
to be understood by the Dutch clergy, and Heussen published a defence of the rejection of the " Formulary ". On
May 18, 1712, Jacob Catz, the Dean of Utrecht, died, and was
succeeded by Hugh van Heussen, the other Vicar-General.
Cornelius Stakenberg became Vicar-General in place of Catz.
In the same year Bussi was made a cardinal and recalled to Rome,
and the government of the Ultramontane section of the Dutch
Church was transferred back to the internuncio at Brussels, an
Italian named Santini.[4]

The chapter was now finding great difficulty in getting fresh
priests. No ordinations had been held in Holland since Archbishop Codde's departure for Rome in 1703; their opponents
could easily introduce priests from other countries, but the
chapter had no means of filling vacant parishes, and their party
was in danger of dying out. They had to get their candidates
ordained on letters dimissory to foreign bishops, and it was
difficult to get any bishop to run the risk of ordaining men whom
Rome regarded as schismatics. In 1714 an Irish Carmelite
priest named Marison visited Heussen. Filled with pity for
the plight of the Church of Utrecht, he approached Bishop

[1] Bellegarde, p. 278.          [2] Bellegarde, p. 273.
[3] Bellegarde, p. 274.          [4] Bellegarde, p. 280.

Giffard, the Roman Vicar-Apostolic in London, who sympathized, but did not venture to do anything. Marison then went to Ireland, and persuaded Bishop Fagan, Roman Catholic Bishop of Meath, to ordain some candidates on letters dimissory from Heussen.[1] The first three were ordained in the spring of 1715; the letter of orders of one of them, John Libon, is given in full by Miss Clark.[2] Later Bishop Fagan would only ordain such candidates on condition that they accepted the Formulary of Alexander VII, with the following qualifications: " nimirum sensum ab auctore intentum esse sensum verborum ut jacent, vel sonant; et extractas ex libro Jansenii, vel esse in libro Jansenii, non cadere sub juramento, sed tantum supponi ". The utmost secrecy was observed, and Fagan was much alarmed because the young men had informed others, contrary to his orders. Twelve priests were ordained by Fagan at different times, including Hieronymus de Bock, afterwards Bishop of Haarlem, and Peter Meindaerts, afterwards Archbishop of Utrecht, who, on landing in Ireland in the late summer of 1716, after a very rough voyage, was arrested as a Jacobite spy, and only escaped by proving to the officer, who had been at Louvain, that he was a member of that university, by his knowledge of its customs.[3] A year later Fagan wrote to Heussen, saying that letters had come ordering an investigation, and begging him to let him know whether there was any danger of discovery. Dupac de Bellegarde tells a story which Miss Clark dismisses as a mere rumour, that Fagan, having become Archbishop of Dublin, was ordered to find out who had ordained priests for the Chapter of Utrecht, whereupon he assembled his suffragans, asked each of them whether he had done this, and wrote to Rome, saying that he had made inquiries and found that none of the bishops had performed any such ordinations![4] (It certainly seems odd that the Archbishop of Dublin, who was not Primate, could assemble all the Irish (Roman Catholic) bishops; especially as Meath was not even in his province.)

The nuncio at Cologne was furious when he heard of the ordinations (though he did not find out either who had been ordained, or who had ordained them), and summoned before

[1] Neale, p. 235.
[2] Ruth Clark, *Strangers and Sojourners at Port Royal*, p. 274.
[3] Clark, p. 213.
[4] Neale, p. 236; Clark, p. 214; Bellegarde, p. 292.

him fourteen persons whom he thought had been ordained; but in reality some of them were married, and one or two were apparently Protestants![1] Finding that he was making himself ridiculous by these proceedings, as well as annoying the government, the nuncio made John van Bylevelt, a parish priest at The Hague, his deputy for this purpose, and on October 2, 1717, appointed him vicar-apostolic. But when Bylevelt instituted priests to take the places of those who had been appointed by the chapter, riots ensued at Amsterdam, Hilversum, and other places; whereupon the States of Holland, Zealand, West Friesland, and later Utrecht banished him from their territory, fined him 2000 florins, and forbade their subjects to recognize his jurisdiction. He retired to Arnhem in the province of Gelderland, and governed those who recognized him from there.[2] He was the last vicar-apostolic in Holland for 100 years.

In 1715 some French Jansenists who had taken refuge in Holland invited the theological faculties of Paris and Louvain to answer the following three questions:

(1) Has the Church of Utrecht been reduced to the status of a mere mission?

(2) Has the Chapter of Utrecht survived?

(3) Does the vicariate set up by Rovenius represent the ancient chapter?

The answer given by Van Espen and four other doctors of Louvain was " No " to the first question, and " Yes " to the others. It was dated May 25, 1717. Soon afterwards 102 doctors of theology at Paris and the whole faculty of law associated themselves with this answer, giving additional reasons for it.

Supported by these answers from the Universities, three French bishops—Soanen of Senez, Lorraine of Bayeux, and Caumartin of Blois—declared themselves willing to ordain priests for the Chapter of Utrecht. Soanen ordained four in 1718, one of whom was Barchman Wuytiers, afterwards Archbishop of Utrecht,[3] and others later. Lorraine ordained three in 1720–1721, the first of whom was ordained at Paris, with the formal permission of Cardinal de Noailles; and Caumartin also ordained some.

Early in 1719 Hugo van Heussen, the Dean of Utrecht, drew up a formal appeal to the future General Council against the

---

[1] Bellegarde, p. 293.        [2] Neale, p. 237.        [3] Neale, p. 238.

injustice with which the Church of Utrecht had been treated, and against the Bull " Unigenitus ". This appeal was published on May 9 with the signatures of the eight members of the chapter, forty-three other priests of the diocese of Utrecht, twenty-two from Haarlem, and two from Leeuwarden. The long vacancy of the see and the difficulty of resisting the unceasing propaganda of the opposite party had reduced the 300 who had supported Archbishop Codde to seventy-five. Heussen himself had died on February 14. But the following sentences were added to the appeal, after the signatures: " Nor must the name of Hugo van Heussen, at the time Dean of the Chapter and Vicar-General, the see being vacant, and the principal promoter of the appeal, be separated from the other signatures. Seized with a mortal disease, and finding himself near death, he made a brief declaration, as befitted a dying man, in this form. If the Chapter of the Metropolitical Church shall appeal from the Constitution of Clement XI, which begins with the word Unigenitus, to the future Council, I affirm that I, Vicar of the said Chapter, and Dean, adhere to that appeal. Hugo van Heussen, Leiden, February 11, 1719." He died three days later.

The appeal began with a long quotation from the similar appeal of the University of Paris; criticized the unfairness of condemning a French book (Quesnel's *Moral Reflexions on the New Testament*) in a bad Latin translation, without consulting the original; complained that Quesnel had been treated more harshly than Luther or Wiclif; quoted the statement of Pope Hadrian VI that Popes could err, even in matters touching the faith, and that several Popes had been heretics; and described the special injuries suffered by the Church of Utrecht. It was sent to the University of Paris, and to the four " appellant " bishops in France.

But now at last, by unexpected means, a way was found to fill the long-vacant archbishopric.

Dominique Marie Varlet was a devoted missionary priest who had been since 1712 in charge of the French missions in " Louisiana ", the name then given to the vast region beyond the Alleghany Mountains, from Lake Superior to the Gulf of Mexico: in fact, the region now known as the " Middle West ", but then inhabited only by Indian tribes. He had come to Quebec to report to his bishop on the state of his mission, and was about to go back there with three young priests from the seminary at

Quebec, when he received orders from Rome, dated September 17, 1718, to go to Persia as coadjutor to the Bishop of Babylon. Accordingly he sailed for France, and on arriving at Paris, received instructions to get himself consecrated as soon as possible, and to go to Persia at once: the consecration was to be private, and he was to travel incognito. He was consecrated with the title of Bishop of Ascalon, in the chapel of the Seminary of the Foreign Missions at Paris, where he was staying, on Quinqua-gesima Sunday, February 19, 1719, by the former Bishop of Condom, assisted by the Coadjutor-Bishop of Quebec and the Bishop of Clermont. On the same day he received news of the death of the Bishop of Babylon, which had taken place at Ispahan on November 20, 1717, so that he was no longer coadjutor, but Bishop of Babylon. As it was impossible to travel through Turkey, he was compelled to go through Russia, and he took the opportunity of travelling under the protection of the new French Consul at Shiraz. He left Paris on March 18, without having received any further instructions from Rome. He spent one night at Brussels, where he did not call on the internuncio (as was the usual custom), because he was incognito, and sailed from Antwerp for Lübeck and Petersburg. But when they were already at sea, the consul decided to land at Amsterdam, where they arrived on April 2. They had to wait there for ten or twelve days, which included Holy Week and Easter. Now, foreign priests were not allowed to say Mass in Holland without special permission from the government, for which the Bishop of Babylon could not apply, because he was incognito. One of the parish priests, Jacob Krys, asked him to stay with him, and told him that he could say Mass safely in his house, because he had influence with the magistrates. Accordingly he stayed with Krys. His host, and other priests who heard that the bishop was there, begged him to confirm a large number of candidates who had never had an opportunity of being confirmed; for no bishop had been there since the departure of Archbishop Codde eighteen years before. The bishop consented to confirm 604 orphans and other poor children, who could not go to other countries to be confirmed. Having done this, he sailed imme-diately for Russia. After a rough voyage through the Baltic Sea, he arrived at Moscow on July 10; sailed down the Volga, crossed the Caspian Sea, and arrived in Persia on October 9. His residence was at Schamaké, in the province of Shirwan (now

Shemakh near Baku in the Soviet Republic of Azerbaijan), where he at once began to establish friendly relations with the Armenian Uniats and their Patriarch Isaiah (who clearly hoped that France would somehow deliver them from their Moslem rulers). On March 26, 1720, a Jesuit, Father Bachou, called on him, and handed him a paper, which he found to be a formal suspension from his office, sent by the Bishop of Ispahan by order of the Congregation *de Propaganda Fide*. The reasons given for his suspension were:

(1) that he had not called on the nuncio at Paris and given his adhesion to the Bull " Unigenitus ";

(2) that he had not called on the internuncio at Brussels and obtained permission to perform episcopal functions in the Netherlands, and yet had performed episcopal functions there, to the scandal of Catholics.[1]

After careful consideration and prayer, the bishop decided that he would never be able to carry on his work, because he would not be supplied with money from home, and because the refusal of the Jesuits and Capuchins in his diocese to recognize his authority would make his work impossible.[2] He therefore returned to Europe, and settled at Amsterdam; he felt that he would have more time for study there than in France, his native country. He at once did all he could to get the suspension withdrawn. He pointed out that having just come from Canada, he knew nothing about the question of the " Unigenitus "; that he had been ordered to live as privately as possible, therefore he did not call on anyone; that it was at that time illegal for any French subject to sign the " Unigenitus " (and indeed the order from Rome on the subject had not reached Paris before he left); and that as he had been invited to give confirmation by the representatives of the Chapter of Utrecht, who had jurisdiction there during the vacancy of the see, he had not hesitated to do so. Moreover, the form of his suspension, and the manner in which it had been served on him, were both highly irregular; nor was it in accordance with the canons that a diocesan bishop should be arbitrarily suspended, without trial or opportunity of defence.

Pope Clement XI, the author of the " Unigenitus ", died in 1721, and the bishop's friends at the Paris Seminary thought

---

[1] *Apologie de l'Evêque de Babilone*, Preface, pp. v—x.
[2] *Ibid.*, p. 5.

that he might get better terms from the new Pope if he went back to France. Accordingly he went to Paris, and then to the house of Bishop Caylus at Auxerre. He obtained an opinion on his case from M. Gibert, a well-known French canonist, that the suspension was null and void, and that he might well have ignored it completely: this opinion was supported by several theologians at Paris and Louvain. Van Espen in particular declared that there was no case in all antiquity of such extraordinary treatment of a bishop. But when Bishop Varlet told his agent at Rome that he would never in any case accept the " Unigenitus ", apologize for having given confirmation at Amsterdam, or resign his see, the agent answered that in that case all his appeals were quite useless.[1]

After this he returned to Holland, settled down at Amsterdam, and set to work on an elaborate defence of his action and of the nullity of his suspension.

Meanwhile the Chapter of Utrecht had decided to provide themselves with an archbishop, if possible. Twice they begged Pope Innocent XIII to allow the election and consecration; but he did not even answer their letters. They obtained from Van Espen and two other doctors of Louvain an opinion proving that they had the right, in the special circumstances, to elect their archbishop and get him consecrated without the consent of the Pope. There were recent precedents both in France and Portugal.[2] Moreover, in case of necessity one bishop alone might consecrate. This opinion was signed by nineteen doctors of the theological faculty of Paris (the Sorbonne), and others from Nantes, Rheims and Padua. Van Espen with two other doctors of Louvain had already given their agreement in their *Dissertation on the Miserable Condition of the Church of Utrecht*.

The chapter, having obtained the permission of the government, met at The Hague, April 27, 1723, and after a Mass of the Holy Ghost, elected, with all the canonical forms, Cornelius Steenoven, Canon and Vicar-General, to be Archbishop of Utrecht. Steenoven had been educated at Rome, and had taken the degree of Doctor of Divinity there; he had also been at Rome with Archbishop Codde, as we have seen. He was elected as the candidate likely to be least obnoxious to Rome.[3] Both the chapter and the archbishop-elect asked the Pope to permit the consecration, but they received no answer. Mean-

---

[1] Bellegarde, p. 303.    [2] Neale, p. 248.    [3] Bellegarde, p. 315.

while Van Erkel, the Dean of Utrecht, had written some popular tracts on the right of a national church to have a bishop of its own, and these were widely circulated. On March 9, 1724, the chapter sent a circular letter to all Roman Catholic bishops on the sufferings of their church. At this moment Pope Innocent XIII died, and the cardinals, fearing that his successor might be more lenient, issued a violent attack on the chapter, while the internuncio wrote a letter to all the Roman Catholics in the Dutch Republic, in the same sense. The chapter appealed to all chapters everywhere, and to eleven universities. They wrote to the new Pope, Benedict XIII, but in vain. They asked the neighbouring bishops, and the Jansenist bishops in France, to consecrate Steenoven. Three French bishops certainly, and eight others probably, were in favour of the consecration, but did not venture to carry it out. Three bishops in the Austrian Netherlands, those of Antwerp, Arras, and St. Omer, were almost persuaded to act, but not quite. The Bishop of Antwerp, to show that consecration by a single bishop was lawful without a papal dispensation, consecrated his brother Bishop of Rhodes *in partibus* without any assistance: a strange way of showing sympathy!

The chapter then entreated the Bishop of Babylon to consecrate Steenoven. " What will be your praise in the Catholic Church," they wrote, " if you raise up a church that has almost fallen, a church which God has perhaps preserved free from certain new bondages and scandals, that when He shall renew His signs, and shall do wondrously, it may minister to the execution of His counsels." [1]

The Bishop of Babylon consented. Permission was obtained from the government for the first consecration of an Archbishop of Utrecht under that title, and in Dutch territory, since the Reformation. On October 15, 1724, the 19th Sunday after Trinity, at 6 a.m. (in order that the parish priests might be free for their duties later on), the Bishop of Babylon, in his private chapel at Amsterdam, in the presence of the whole chapter, consecrated Cornelius van Steenoven to be the seventh Archbishop of Utrecht and canonical successor of St. Willibrord.[2] The deed was done: the Church of Utrecht, though as yet she did not know it, had begun her career as a church independent of the see of Rome.

[1] Neale, p. 256.                    [2] Bellegarde, p. 319.

CHAPTER VIII

## THE FIRST YEARS OF INDEPENDENCE

As soon as the news of the consecration of Archbishop Steenoven became known, he received letters of congratulation from friends in France, as well as from the Austrian Netherlands (for what is now Belgium had been transferred from Spain to Austria in 1713) and Holland itself. The Bishops of Auxerre, Bayeux, Mâcon, Montpellier, Pamiers, and Senez, all of them prominent in the struggle against the Bull " Unigenitus ", congratulated him themselves; the Bishops of Bayonne, Castres, Dax, Lombez, Luçon, Rhodes, and Tarbes did so by deputy. One friend, Chassaigne, wrote, " If the consecrator had never performed any other episcopal act than this, I should regard him as the first bishop in the Church ".; another, Ruth D'Ans, writing from Brussels, told the archbishop that he might justly call himself Archbishop of Utrecht by the grace of God, for what other grace could have overcome the obstacles which had opposed the happy consummation of so great a work? [1]

The new archbishop at once wrote to Pope Benedict XIII and to the chief Roman Catholic bishops everywhere, to inform them of his consecration. He also published a manifesto addressed to the whole Church, explaining the principles on which he and his clergy had acted, and with it a formal appeal to the future General Council, confirming the appeal of May 9, 1719.[2]

On February 21, 1725, the Pope issued a brief, declaring the election of Steenoven null and void, and his consecration " illicit and execrable ", forbidding the Roman Catholics in the United Provinces to recognize him as their archbishop or to have any dealings with him, especially in matters of religion, and pronouncing the severest censures on the Bishop of Babylon and his assistants (one of whom, Jacob Krys, the priest with whom Bishop Varlet had stayed on his first visit to Amsterdam, had died only a fortnight after the consecration). Surprise was caused by the Pope's accusation of false doctrine against the

[1] Neale, *Church of Holland*, p. 257.
[2] Bellegarde, *Histoire Abrégée*, p. 319.

124

Church of Utrecht, an accusation which was indignantly repudiated.[1]

When the brief reached Holland, Steenoven was already seriously ill. After making a solemn declaration of his belief in the Catholic Faith, including the prerogatives of the Roman See, and appealing for himself and his flock to the future General Council, he died, April 3, 1725.[2]

On May 15, Cornelius John Barchman Wuytiers, a priest of noble family who had been one of those ordained by Bishop Soanen of Senez, was elected unanimously by the Chapter of Utrecht to fill the vacant see. He had been educated at the Oratorian school at Huissen, at Louvain, and at Paris. Years before, when he went to Paris, Quesnel had prophesied that he would some day be Archbishop of Utrecht.[3] As in the case of Steenoven, the chapter announced the election to the Pope, and asked for the confirmation of the archbishop-elect, and for a dispensation for consecration by a single bishop. Every effort was made by Rome to prevent the consecration. Already diplomatic pressure had been applied to the Dutch Republic by Venice, and by the Roman Catholic Electors of the Empire, to induce it to forbid the consecration of a successor to Steenoven; but the Dutch Government replied to the Doge of Venice that it intended to protect both parties among its Roman Catholic subjects, because it believed that in matters of religion persuasion and not constraint should alone be practised, and that it could not admit the right of the Pope to exercise unlimited authority over its subjects.[4]

On this the Ultramontane party asked that they might be allowed a vicar-apostolic, and there was a rumour that Rome might permit him to take the title of Bishop of Haarlem; but the Government thought this would only prolong the schism, and refused its consent.[5]

Persuasion having failed, an attempt was made to try force. The Bishop of Babylon (upon whom, of course, the possibility of the consecration depended) was staying with the parish priest, Pastoor Verheul, at Helder, at the entrance to the Zuyder Zee (where there is still an Old Catholic parish).[6] He was told

---

[1] Bellegarde, p. 320.                [2] Bellegarde, p. 328; Neale, p. 269.
[3] Bellegarde, p. 334.                [4] Bellegarde, p. 329.
[5] Bellegarde, p. 336; Neale, p. 266.
[6] The church and rectory here were destroyed during the German occupation of the Netherlands.

that a lady warmly attached to the other party had boasted that he would not trouble the country much longer. A few days later he was invited to dinner by the captain of an unknown ship. On his refusal, the ship set sail, and he had no doubt that there had been a plot to kidnap him.[1]

An attempt was next made to reconcile the Bishop of Babylon to Rome by means of his old friend, M. de Montigny, the agent at Rome of the Society of Foreign Missions at Paris; but he saw clearly that the sole aim of this attempt was to delay or prevent the consecration of Barchman Wuytiers. On August 23, however, a papal brief was published, which condemned the election of Barchman Wuytiers in still more violent terms than that of Steenoven, but which made the Pope ridiculous by mentioning as visible signs of Divine vengeance, not only the death of Archbishop Steenoven, but also that of " the layman Doncker ", and by asserting that the archbishop had been consecrated in his house.[2] Theodore Doncker, one of the assistants at the consecration of Steenoven, was a priest, not a layman, and was not dead, but alive and well.

It will be remembered that one of the points at issue was the duty of good Roman Catholics to accept without doubt facts officially stated by the Pope, such as the presence of the Five Propositions in the " Augustinus ". Doncker, standing in his pulpit at Amsterdam, with the brief in his hand, asked his people how the Pope, who had declared him to be dead, could expect his own decrees to be treated as infallible oracles.[3]

As before, the neighbouring bishops were invited to consecrate the new archbishop, but no answer was received from them. The Bishop of Babylon was then approached, and on September 30, 1725, the 18th Sunday after Trinity, in the Church of St. James and St. Augustine at The Hague (which is still in use),[4] he consecrated Cornelius John Barchman Wuytiers Archbishop of Utrecht. As before, the archbishop announced his consecration to the Pope, who replied by excommunicating him and all his clergy and all who should in any way assist or encourage him. He answered by appealing to the future General Council and by a letter to the Pope, in which he offered to resign for the sake of peace, but only on condition that he and his clergy should

---

[1] Bellegarde, p. 332.     [2] Compare the Nag's Head Fable.
[3] Bellegarde, p. 340; Neale, p. 267.
[4] Since the destruction of the English church this church has been used regularly for Anglican services, by the courtesy of the parish priest.

not be asked to accept the " Formulary " or the " Unigenitus ",
and that the rights of the chapters should be recognized.[1]

In the meantime the Chapter of Haarlem, which, though
maintaining its right to exist (denied by Rome), had deserted
the cause of Utrecht, had elected a vicar-general on the express
condition that he should not exercise the functions of his office
in any way.  But before it did this, the Chapter of Utrecht,
after inquiring of the canonists of Louvain whether it had a right,
as chapter of the metropolitical see, to appoint a vicar-general
for Haarlem if the Chapter of Haarlem refused or delayed to do
so, appointed Barchman Wuytiers, afterwards archbishop, as
vicar-general of the diocese of Haarlem.  As archbishop he
continued to govern the parishes in the diocese of Haarlem, which
recognized his authority, in the capacity of vicar-general as
well as of metropolitan.

About this time Hoynck van Papenbrecht, a canon of Malines,
published a *History of the Church of Utrecht*, which marked a change
in the Ultramontane theory of the ecclesiastical position in the
United Provinces.  Hitherto the Jesuits had taught that Vosmeer
and Rovenius were Archbishops of Utrecht, but that as the
United Provinces had been recognized by Spain as an independent
State in 1648, and as no ordinary Catholic jurisdiction could exist
in a state the government of which was heretical, there had been
no archbishops or diocesan organization in Dutch territory
since that year.  Hoynck van Papenbrecht saw that this was
absurd (for in that case there had been no diocesan organization
at all before Constantine), and maintained that the Dutch
dioceses had disappeared during the Reformation, so completely
that even the Pope could not restore them if he wished, and that
Vosmeer and Rovenius had in consequence never been anything
more than vicars-apostolic.  Another work on the same lines,
but not quite so extreme, was written by an anonymous writer,
who is believed to have been directed to do so by the internuncio.

These writers' arguments were completely refuted by Van
Erkel, the Dean of Utrecht, by Broedersen, one of the members
of the chapter, by the Bishop of Babylon in his *Second Apology*,
and by Van Espen, in his *Vindication of the Resolution of the Doctors
of Louvain*.[2]

Van Espen, however, at the end of his long life, had to suffer
for his firm defence of the cause of Utrecht.  Hermann Damen,

---

[1] Bellegarde, p. 341.          [2] Bellegarde, p. 327; Neale, p. 264.

doctor of Louvain, had written a treatise to show that the consecration of Steenoven was not only illicit and irregular, as the
Pope had declared it to be, but invalid—that is, null and
void, because Steenoven had been consecrated by only one
bishop. (In this and other cases the priests who took the
part of assisting bishops did not lay their hands on the
head of the candidate.[1] Such action would have been both
illogical and uncanonical. The contemporary accounts of the
consecration show that nothing of the sort took place.[2])

Damen's contention was that consecration by less than three
bishops is valid only by special dispensation from the Pope.
Van Espen, consulted by Van Erkel, wrote a learned treatise
in reply, known as the *Responsio Epistolaris*, in which he showed
by many examples, both ancient and modern, that consecration
by less than three bishops is perfectly valid even without a papal
dispensation. Among the instances which he quoted were the
consecrations performed in England by St. Augustine of Canterbury, and the consecration of a bishop of Paraguay in 1657,
without any dispensation, by less than three bishops, which had
been accepted as valid by the Congregation of Rites. But the
editor of this treatise added a preface, in which he maintained
that the consecration of Steenoven was not only valid, but lawful,
in direct opposition to the papal brief. Damen appealed to the
Council of Brabant, accusing Van Espen of having written the
preface; and the famous canonist, at the age of eighty-two, was
condemned by the university whose greatest ornament he was,
and compelled to flee from Louvain to Maestricht. When his
niece, who lived with him, begged him to make some concession
that would satisfy his opponents, he answered that if he hesitated
to defend the cause of the clergy of Utrecht, he would be afraid
to appear before the judgment seat of Christ.[3]

Van Espen reached Maestricht in February 1728, but soon
afterwards moved to Amersfoort, where he died, October 2,
1728, in communion with the Church of Utrecht. He was
buried in the Reformed church,[4] at the entrance to the choir, in
the family vault of the Foeyts; in 1928, two centuries later, the

---

[1] It has been suggested that they did, and that this is a precedent for proposed
consecrations in South India; but the suggestion is based on a mistake.
[2] Letter to the author from the present Archbishop of Utrecht, Mgr.
Rinkel.
[3] Bellegarde, *Vie de M. van Espen*; Neale, p. 265.
[4] That is, the old medieval parish church.

Old Catholic Congress at Utrecht paid a special visit to his tomb, at which I was present.

Archbishop Barchman Wuytiers received more letters of congratulation and communion after his consecration than any of his predecessors or successors. They numbered more than 100, and were signed by at least 2000 ecclesiastics in France and the Austrian Netherlands. Among them were all the bishops who had congratulated Steenoven, and there were said to be thirty others in France who were in sympathy; a list of these was sent in October 1725 to the archbishop by M. Dilhe. There were also letters of congratulation from many distinguished laymen. Thirty-one Carthusian and fourteen Cistercian monks, driven from France because they had refused to accept the Bull "Unigenitus", fled to Holland and placed themselves under the Archbishop of Utrecht.

The archbishop drew up rules for these monks, suitable to the conditions of the country, and also statutes for the seminary at Amersfoort. Since candidates for ordination from Utrecht were no longer allowed at Louvain (for the Rector of the University had seized the two seminaries) and since the seminary begun at Huissen by Archbishop van Neercassel had been closed, a new seminary was founded at Amersfoort in 1724, in which the Old Catholic priests of Holland have been trained ever since. The first statutes were those drawn up by Archbishop Wuytiers.[1] He also took part in an attempt to bring about reunion with the Russian Church. The Emperor Peter the Great, when staying at Paris in 1717, had been in communication with some of the doctors of the University, then strongly Gallican.[2] In 1727 Princess Irene Galitzin, the wife of Prince Sergius Dolgorouki, who was staying in Holland, was received into the Latin Faith by the Archbishop of Utrecht, who sent M. Jubé, the former parish priest of Asnières, near Paris, who had had to take refuge in Holland because he would not accept the "Unigenitus", to accompany her to Russia as her chaplain. Jubé, after visiting Paris, and receiving the blessing of Cardinal de Noailles and the support of the Oratorian Fathers, went to Moscow, where he was favourably received. The doctors of the Sorbonne (the Theological Faculty of Paris) had given him a letter authorizing him to enter into negotiations with the Russian bishops, some of whom

[1] Bellegarde, *Histoire Abregée*, p. 324.
[2] See Chapter V. The correspondence with Archbishop Wake was in 1718.

were believed to be favourable to reunion: there was even a proposal to make him a bishop, so that he might treat with them on equal terms, but it came to nothing. Bellegarde says that the Metropolitan of Kiev, the Archbishop of Riazan, and the Bishop of Tver were so well disposed to reunion that they were afterwards deposed and exiled. The death of Peter II in 1730 brought the whole affair to an end; for his successor Anne persecuted the Dolgorouki family,[1] and Jubé had to leave Russia.[2] The incident may be compared with the negotiations between the English Non-Jurors and the Orthodox Patriarchs, a few years earlier, and also those between Archbishops Wake and Dupin (see Chapter V).

Archbishop Barchman Wuytiers also tried to form a mission in Indo-China, independent of the Congregation *de propaganda Fide*, to be staffed by the French missionaries who had refused to accept the Bull " Unigenitus ". M. Terrasson of the Oratory was to be the leader, and they were to preach the Gospel in Laos (which Neale thought was an island off the Malabar coast, but it was evidently the country of that name on the eastern frontier of Siam). The scheme came to nothing, because the missionaries in Indo-China feared that the support promised them would not be forthcoming.[3]

As the Bishop of Babylon was getting old, the archbishop was anxious to secure the succession by consecrating a Bishop of Haarlem. After consulting Van Espen and others, he gave notice to the Chapter of Haarlem that unless they elected a bishop within three months he would exercise his right as metropolitan and nominate one. The three months passed, the archbishop assembled his chapter, and Theodore Doncker was unanimously elected. But owing to a controversy about usury, which was then raging, the consecration was postponed, and Doncker died in 1731. On May 13, 1733, Archbishop Barchman Wuytiers died suddenly at his house at Rhynwyck, near Utrecht.

On July 22 in the same year, Theodore van der Croon, parish priest of Gouda, who had been associated with the party of the chapter since the days of Archbishop Codde, was unanimously elected archbishop. The same formalities and excommunications

---

[1] Peter II's wife was a Dolgorouki, and the Empress Anne was jealous. The Dolgoroukis were a branch of the House of Rurik, which reigned before the Romanovs.

[2] Bellegarde, p. 347; Neale, p. 270, does not distinguish clearly between Peter I and Peter II.

[3] Bellegarde, p. 348.

took place as in the case of Steenoven and Barchman Wuytiers. An attempt was made by the French and Portuguese ambassadors to bribe the Bishop of Babylon to return to France. An interview was arranged at the castle of Zeist; the bishop was accompanied by M. Jubé, the priest who had been in Russia; but instead of finding there the Portuguese ambassador, as he expected, he found the French ambassador, who offered him, in the name of Cardinal Fleury (who was practically Prime Minister of France), benefices sufficient for him to live in episcopal state. The bishop asked for two days to consider the offer, as a polite way of refusing; but Acunha, the Portuguese ambassador, bitterly reproached his French colleague for not having kidnapped the bishop. He answered that such methods were not to his taste, and also might offend the Dutch Government.[1]

On October 28, 1734, the Bishop of Babylon consecrated Theodore van der Croon. The new archbishop was a man of particularly gentle disposition, and he asked the Archbishop of Malines to use his influence at Rome in his favour, but only provoked a violent controversy, in which, as in all the other controversies on the subject, the supporters of the chapter had the last word.[2] The archbishop died on June 9, 1739.

He was succeeded by a man of much more determined character, Peter John Meindaerts, who had been ordained in Ireland by Bishop Fagan, and who was now Archpriest of Leeuwarden and Dean of Friesland. The usual forms were observed, and Meindaerts was consecrated on St. Luke's Day, October 18, 1739. He announced his consecration to the Pope, and declared himself ready to resign, if by doing so he could bring peace to the Church. It is from Archbishop Meindaerts that all the later Old Catholic bishops derive their succession, for the Bishop of Babylon, after having consecrated four archbishops, died on May 14, 1742, at The Hague, and it became necessary to consecrate another bishop in order to provide for the succession.

Meanwhile, Prospero Lambertini, the great canonist, had in 1740 become Pope, under the name of Benedict XIV. This modest and learned Pope, the greatest occupant of the Roman see in the eighteenth century, might have been expected, perhaps, to heal the schism. But Benedict XIV, though not as much under the influence of the Jesuits as some of his predecessors, was a thorough Ultramontane. Professor von Schulte, the

[1] Bellegarde, p. 350.                    [2] Neale, p. 280.

great Old Catholic canonist (of whom more hereafter), says that Benedict XIV did for canon law what the Vatican Council did for dogmatic theology: he brought it completely under Papal control.[1] He thought that the Bull " Unigenitus " had been a mistake, perhaps did not even believe it, but he felt bound, in loyalty to his predecessors, to insist on its being accepted; and he not only excommunicated Archbishop Meindaerts, but abused him in language exceeding that of his predecessors, as " a child of iniquity, a most unnatural son of the tenderest of fathers, a deceitful and savage wolf, an accomplished deceiver, a madman whose case was almost desperate ".[2] The reason for this violence was that Meindaerts was supposed to have directly disobeyed the brief of Clement XII declaring the election invalid, although in reality that brief had not, and indeed could not have, reached Holland before the consecration.[3]

Archbishop Meindaerts lost no time in providing for the succession. The Chapter of Haarlem had continued to refuse to exercise their right of election, and the metropolitan therefore had the right to nominate the bishop (per jus devolutionis). With the consent of those of the clergy of Haarlem who acknowledged his jurisdiction, he nominated Hieronymus de Bock, who had also been ordained in Ireland, and who was in charge of one of the parishes at Amsterdam, to the see of Haarlem, vacant since 1587, and consecrated him on September 2, 1742. As usual, the Pope excommunicated everyone concerned. Bishop de Bock died within three years, and John van Stiphout was nominated as his successor, and was consecrated on July 11, 1745.[4]

At this period there were fifty-two parishes which acknowledged the archbishop's jurisdiction, thirty-three in the diocese of Utrecht, seventeen in Haarlem, one in Leeuwarden, and the island of Noordstrand. In the city of Utrecht there were six parishes and in Amsterdam eight.[5]

Three different attempts to bring the schism to an end were now made. The first failed, because Rome insisted that the archbishop and his clergy should accept the " Formulary " and the " Unigenitus " and revoke all their appeals to the future General Council, and that the archbishop should ask for absolu-

---

[1] Schulte, *Sources of the History of Canon Law*, quoted by G. W. O. Addleshaw, Church Quarterly Review, 1936.
[2] Neale, p. 283; Bellegarde, p. 358.     [3] Bellegarde, p. 359.
[4] Bellegarde, p. 367.     [5] Neale, p. 284.

tion.  Then a certain Father Norbert proposed that the Dutch clergy should not be required to accept the " Unigenitus ", on the ground that if they did so, they would be breaking the civil law.  But they found that they were being represented as really accepting the " Unigenitus ", and only refusing to do so publicly for fear of civil penalties.  As honest men, they could not permit themselves to be placed in such a false position: they explained their real attitude towards the " Unigenitus ", whereupon the negotiations came to an end.  A third attempt failed through the death of Benedict XIV.  The Marquis Nicolini, a Florentine, who made this attempt, declared his astonishment that Rome should accept the regicides of Portugal (see p. 135) but anathematize the best Catholics in the Church.[1]  Cardinal Tamburini promised that if he were elected Pope he would at once reconcile the Church of Utrecht; but he was not elected, and nothing was to be hoped for from Clement XIII,[2] a weak man, who could not resist the Jesuits.

As reunion appeared to be hopeless, at any rate for the present, Archbishop Meindaerts decided to strengthen his position by consecrating a third bishop.  There was one faithful congregation in the diocese of Leeuwarden, and it appeared desirable to appoint a bishop for that see, but some of the clergy preferred a coadjutor-bishop.  The canonists of Paris and Caen were consulted, and agreed unanimously that the archbishop had the right to consecrate a bishop for Leeuwarden, and indeed for all the other vacant sees.  This opinion was supported by Bishop Verthamon of Luçon.  But as the Government of Friesland objected to the consecration of a bishop for that province, the archbishop, with the unanimous consent of the chapter, nominated as Bishop of Deventer Bartholomew John Byeveld, a canon of Utrecht, who was in charge of one of the parishes at Rotterdam.  He was consecrated on the Feast of the Conversion of St. Paul, January 25, 1758.[3]  The revived bishopric of Deventer has never been more than a titular one, as there have never been any parishes in that diocese which have accepted the archbishop's jurisdiction.  The one parish in Leeuwarden was lost for want of episcopal superintendence.  The nomination of Byeveld was denounced by the Pope, as usual, and the archbishop replied with a letter which was translated into French, Latin, Italian, Spanish, and Portuguese, and went through three editions in France in less

[1] Bellegarde, p. 383.          [2] Neale, p. 292.
[3] Bellegarde, p. 386.

than a month; it also made a great impression at Vienna.[1]   No
brief was issued against the consecration though it had been
forbidden.

In 1763 Archbishop Meindaerts decided to hold a provincial
synod.   Though the Council of Trent had ordered that provincial synods should be held every three years, it had not been
possible to hold one at Utrecht since 1565.   The main purpose
of the synod was to condemn the erroneous teaching published
by Pierre Le Clerc, a French subdeacon living at Amsterdam,
by which means it was hoped that the Pope might be induced
to judge the Church of Utrecht favourably; and at the same time
to condemn the teaching of Hardouin, Berruyer, Pichon, and other
Jesuits.   A long account of this synod is given by Dr. Neale,
Chapter 14.   Bellegarde only concerns himself with the proceedings against Le Clerc.   It can only be briefly described here.
The members of the synod were the three bishops, the Dean and
Chapter of Utrecht, and representatives of the clergy of both
dioceses, twenty in all.   They met in the cathedral church of St.
Gertrude at Utrecht (which since the erection of the new cathedral
in 1914 has been turned into an Old Catholic museum).

The synod began by securing the rights of the rest of the
clergy of the province if at any future time they should submit to
the authority of their lawful bishops; and then formally recited
the Nicene Creed, anathematized all errors and heresies which the
Council of Trent had anathematized, and adopted Bossuet's
*Exposition de la Foi* (Exposition of the Faith) as the expression
of its own faith.

Le Clerc had declared that the Five Propositions attributed to
Jansen contained the Catholic Faith on the question of grace.
This opinion was formally condemned by the Synod; for the contention of the Dutch " Jansenists " had always been, not that the
Five Propositions were true or orthodox, but that they were not
to be found in Jansen's *Augustinus*.   In condemning Le Clerc's
account of the schism between Rome and Constantinople, the
synod most injudiciously declared the Greek Churches to be
schismatic because they were separated from the " chair of Peter " :
a statement which, as Dr. Neale observes, applied to the Church
of Utrecht with equal force.[2]   But no doubt the synod was not
acquainted with the case for the other side.   It also condemned
Le Clerc's opinion that the Church is never infallible except when

[1] Bellegarde, p. 389; Neale, p. 293.          [2] Neale, p. 302.

it is assembled in Œcumenical Councils, and that bishops and priests are equal; and it renewed its adhesion to the creed of Pius IV, which Le Clerc had rejected. It condemned various doctrinal errors of the most serious kind taught by the Jesuits, Hardouin and Berruyer [1] (the former of whom had put forward the remarkable theory that all the classical literature was composed in medieval monasteriès!) and errors in moral theology taught by Pichon, another Jesuit. It also condemned several works on Probabilism, one of which had already been condemned at Rome. In opposition to the opinion of the Jesuits, that the Pope might dispense subjects from their civil allegiance, and that regicide was in certain cases permissible, the Synod rejected this dispensing power, and asserted the Divine right of kings.[2] (This was one of the main issues between the Roman and English Churches in the century after the Reformation: Pius V had declared Queen Elizabeth deposed, and released her subjects from allegiance to her, which had been the chief reason for the persecution of Romanists in England; attempts to murder her, as well as Henri IV of France and William the Silent in the Netherlands, successful in the last two cases, had been defended on the principles now condemned. The Jesuits had been accused of attempting to murder King Joseph of Portugal, September 3, 1758, and this had led to their expulsion from the kingdom.)[3]

The synod also passed twenty-four canons on discipline. The most interesting of these directed that those who neglected the opportunity of being confirmed risked their salvation (those who adhered to Rome could not be confirmed in the Dutch Republic, from 1703 to 1827, for there were no bishops there except the excommunicated archbishops and their suffragans); that there should be no music during the Mass between the Elevation of the Host and the Lord's Prayer (as already directed by Archbishop Rovenius); and that marriages between Catholics and non-Catholics, even when performed without the forms required by the Council of Trent, were valid, but, on the part of the Catholic partner, sinful. This was in accordance with the instructions of Pope Benedict XIV (based on the distinctions drawn by Archbishop van Neercassel), since the decrees of the Council of Trent had not been published in the United Provinces.

---

[1] Chiefly on the doctrine of the Holy Trinity.
[2] Neale, p. 318.
[3] F. Nielsen, *History of the Papacy in the Nineteenth Century*, vol. i, p. 41.

Le Clerc, while his case was before the Synod, declared that he accepted as his judge an Œcumenical Council only; such a Council must include all the Eastern Churches as well as the Latin Church (he mentioned the "Nestorians" especially). But there is no precedent for the gathering of an Œcumenical Council to judge the teaching of a subdeacon.

A copy of the acts of the synod was sent to Pope Clement XIII, and at the same time Gabriel Dupac de Bellegarde was entrusted with the duty of preparing them for the press. This French priest had edited the works of Arnauld and Van Espen, and had written a life of Van Espen; he afterwards wrote the *Histoire Abregée de l'Eglise Metropolitaine d'Utrecht*, which is the principal source of this narrative. He was born at Château de Bellegarde, in the diocese of Narbonne, and educated at Toulouse and Paris. When D'Étemare, one of the leaders of the Gallican party in France, had to take refuge at Rhynwyck, near Utrecht, Bellegarde went with him, and devoted his life to the defence of the Church of Utrecht. In 1761, in spite of his well-known connexion with Utrecht, he was made a canon of Lyons Cathedral (the primatial cathedral of France), with the title of count. He resigned this preferment after a few years, in order to devote himself more completely to the cause of the Church of Utrecht. He died at Utrecht on December 13, 1789.[1]

The acts of the synod were very well received throughout Roman Catholic Europe, and many bishops sent letters of congratulation and communion to Archbishop Meindaerts. The Archbishop of Trier, who was one of the Electors of the Empire, proposed to circularize all the German bishops on behalf of Utrecht. (This archbishop had as his suffragan Bishop Hontheim, generally known as Febronius, concerning whom see the next chapter.) Dr. Barthel, a learned canonist of Würzburg, wrote strongly in favour of the Synod of Utrecht. Letters of sympathy were received from several Italian bishops, who had the support of the Kings of Naples and Sardinia, and from many French ecclesiastics.

Pope Clement XIII was much pleased with the acts of the synod, but the Jesuits (whose dissolution was now at hand) insisted that it should be condemned. A commission of six cardinals was appointed to decide the matter; four of them

---

[1] Neale, pp. 320, 338.

prepared a formal condemnation, which was duly issued. It began with the words " Non sine acerbo dolore ", and politely described the members of the synod as " men given over to destruction, children of iniquity, impious, headstrong, rebels against the judgement of the Church, and schismatics chased from her bosom ".[1] Bottari, the librarian of the Vatican, who declared that the majority of the commission had not the slightest knowledge of theology, observed that even if they burned the acts of the synod on the steps of St. Peter's, they would only add fresh testimony to the affection and reverence of the synod towards the Roman see.

On receiving this document, the synod reassembled, and sent a letter to the Pope, which was more effective in winning support for the Church of Utrecht than any of its other publications. But the University of Cologne declared that it was better to communicate with Lutherans or Calvinists than with the Church of Utrecht; the Elector-Archbishop of Cologne called the members of the Synod " vipers ", and the Prince-Bishop of Liége called them " ravening wolves " : even the Assembly of the Clergy of France, from which support might have been expected, if the appointment of the French bishops had not been so long in the hands of the supporters of the " Unigenitus ", condemned the synod, without giving themselves more than a few hours to study its acts. Bellegarde, however, asserts that he is authorized to say that this condemnation did not really represent the general opinion of the French bishops, or even of those who signed it.[2]

Archbishop Meindaerts died on October 31, 1767. Walter Michael van Nieuwenhuisen, the parish priest of Dordrecht, was unanimously elected as his successor, and after notice had been given to the Pope, and the neighbouring bishops had been invited to take part in his consecration, he was consecrated on Sexagesima Sunday, February 7, 1768, by the Bishops of Haarlem and Deventer. The usual bull of excommunication followed. Nevertheless, the new archbishop received letters of communion from bishops in France, Germany, Italy, and Spain, and from a large number of priests,[3] who recognized fully, not only that the Church of Utrecht was orthodox in doctrine, but also that her claims to canonical jurisdiction were sound.

In 1769 a very curious incident occurred in Spain. The

[1] Bellegarde, p. 417, translated by Neale, p. 326.
[2] Bellegarde, p. 430.     [3] Bellegarde, pp. 432–434.

beatification of Juan de Palafox, Bishop of Osma in Spain, a determined foe of the Jesuits, who had died in 1659, was being pressed forward by the King, but bitterly opposed by the Jesuits. Joseph Climent, Bishop of Barcelona, issued a pastoral letter, in which he praised the Dutch bishops, and regretted that so few of their episcopal brethren had come to their assistance. He was accused by the Inquisitor-General of want of deference to the see of Rome, but was acquitted by the Ecclesiastical Council, before which, by the King's orders, the case was brought, and which added to its decision the remark that the Bishop of Barcelona might without blame have asked the King to use his influence with the Vatican for reconciliation with Utrecht. The Jesuits, who were anxious to prevent this, and were already annoyed with the King because he was supporting the beatification of Palafox, forged a letter from Archbishop Meindaerts, in which he was made to say that if Palafox, who had been (according to them) devoted to the Five Propositions, were canonized, Rome would thereby withdraw the condemnation of those propositions, and would acknowledge that the Jansenists had been right all the time. The letter was sent to Rome, and " the exposure of a new Jansenist plot " was announced publicly. The three Dutch bishops at once drew up a formal reply. They pointed out that Archbishop Meindaerts had died in 1767, whereas the letter was dated December 15, 1770; that the Provincial Synod of Utrecht, at which Archbishop Meindaerts had presided, had formally condemned the Five Propositions as heretical; and that the Church of Utrecht could not have produced a document so injurious to the see of Rome, as well as to Palafox himself, as that letter was. The archbishop sent this reply to Pope Clement XIV with a letter expressing in the strongest terms his veneration for the see of Rome, and begging the Pope to observe how dishonestly the enemies of the Church of Utrecht had behaved. The Pope sent a gracious reply, promising to do all he could for reconciliation, if the Church of Utrecht would send deputies to Rome. Negotiations were begun; the King of Spain and the Empress Maria Theresa wrote to the Pope in favour of Utrecht; the canons of Salzburg, assembled to elect a new prince-archbishop, agreed that whoever should be elected would do all he could for Utrecht, and Count Colloredo, the successful candidate, kept his promise. Rome, however, began by insisting on the withdrawal of all appeals to a future Council. The Pope was busy with the bull suppressing the Society of Jesus, which was published on July 21, 1773, and soon afterwards he fell ill; he became worse through fear of the vengeance of the Jesuits, and he died on September 22, 1774.[1] With him the opportunity of reconciliation perished; for his successor, Pius VI, had no sympathy with the Church of Utrecht, and it was during his pontificate that the outbreak of the French Revolution diverted all men's thoughts in a very different direction.

Bishop van Stiphout of Haarlem died on December 16, 1777. The archbishop, since the Chapter of Haarlem still refused to elect his successor, nominated to the vacant see Adrian Johannes Broekman, the President of Amersfoort Seminary, and consecrated him in the Seminary Church at Amersfoort, the 1st Sunday after Trinity, June 21, 1778. The Bishop of Deventer had died the day before, and was succeeded by Nicolas Nellemans, the parish priest of Delft, who was consecrated on the feast of St. Simon and St. Jude, October 28, 1778. In this case the bull of excommunication was published with greater solemnity than usual, on January 18, 1779, the feast of the Chains of St. Peter. At the moment of publication, the great bell of St. Peter's split, and the huge lamp that hung before the Pope's throne fell to the ground, but without hurting anyone, though the basilica was crowded.[2]

The history of the Church of Utrecht at this period, and indeed much later, shows that her members were still, though excommunicated by the Pope, faithful Roman Catholics, desiring nothing so much as reconciliation with Rome, and that many Roman Catholic bishops in several countries maintained communion with Utrecht, in spite of all that the Pope might say. The Dutch bishops still hoped that a change of policy at Rome, such as might have occurred if Clement XIV had lived longer, would bring the schism to an end. The point in dispute was really the right of the Pope to blind obedience. The Dutch bishops and their flocks, like all Gallicans, held that he was a constitutional monarch, who could not enforce new dogmas upon his subjects without the consent of a General Council, nor deprive local churches of their ancient canonical rights; and they would not sign any document which they did not believe to be true, even for the sake of reconciliation with him whom they still believed to be the Vicar of Christ. But the Popes, with all their advisers

[1] Neale, pp. 331-337; Nielsen, op. cit., vol. i, p. 86.
[2] Neale, p. 338; Bellegarde, p. 484.

at Rome, and the great majority of Roman Catholics, especially in the southern countries, where Romanism was strongest and where the Jesuits had long been in control of the schools, held that the Papacy was an absolute monarchy, whose right to blind obedience came straight from God.

The Gallican position was not permanently tenable. To believe that the Pope is sovereign by Divine right and yet refuse to obey him, except on conditions which he declines to recognize, is as inconsistent as to levy war against the King in the King's name. This is the difficulty which confronts all those who hope that a reformed, constitutional, or decentralized Papacy may some day bring about reunion. Constitutional monarchy is alien to the whole tradition and historical development of the see of Rome. Whatever concessions the Papacy has made, it has never made one limiting its own authority, or admitting itself to have been wrong.

Reconciliation with Rome means, and as long as Rome remains Rome, always must mean, unconditional submission.

# CHAPTER IX

FEBRONIUS

HITHERTO the nation which was to take the leading part in the Old Catholic movement had had hardly any part in its origins. Germany was not, like the kingdom of France or the Dutch republic, a single state. In theory, the German principalities were members of " the Holy Roman Empire of the German Nation "; but since the thirteenth century the Emperor, nominally supreme, had derived his real power and importance from his hereditary dominions. Since the fifteenth century the emperors had all been of the House of Hapsburg, [1] though the imperial title was not hereditary, but elective (the original seven electors, princes with the right to elect the Emperor, had by the eighteenth century been increased to nine; strictly speaking, the emperors were only " emperors elect ", for the Emperor received his title by being crowned by the Pope, and the last Emperor to be crowned so was Charles V). In Germany, unlike France and England, the sovereign had no crown lands of his own. The monarchy was elective, and in theory anyone might be elected emperor, but in practice only someone with large hereditary dominions had any chance. The Reformation, and other historical causes, had made the great vassals independent of their sovereign, and their independence was sealed by the Treaty of Westphalia (1648). Since that time Germany had been a collection of large and small states; each ruler had most of the rights of an independent sovereign, including the right to decide the religion of his subjects. The Emperor was the master of Austria, Bohemia, Hungary, and the southern part of the Netherlands (now Belgium), which was his share of the inheritance of Charles V (the Belgian provinces, originally Spanish, were transferred to Austria by the Treaty of Utrecht, 1713), increased by victorious wars against the Turks; and he had certain rights of a ceremonial kind over the rest of Germany.

Many of the German states were governed by ecclesiastics, archbishops, bishops, or abbots. These states had originally been great fiefs held by ecclesiastics (like Durham in England),

[1] Francis of Lorraine, who married Maria Theresa, was the only exception.

but they had become independent, like the other states. The most important of these ecclesiastical rulers were the Elector-Archbishops of Mainz, Cologne, and Trier. These sees were reserved for members of royal and noble families, who lived much the same life as other German princes, keeping a coadjutor bishop to perform their spiritual functions.

In 1740 the male line of the House of Hapsburg became extinct at the death of the Emperor Charles VI. By the instrument called the Pragmatic Sanction he had bequeathed his hereditary territories to his daughter, Maria Theresa, and he had done his best to ensure that her husband, Francis of Lorraine, should be elected emperor.

When the electors met to choose a new emperor, Doria, the Papal Nuncio, tried to induce them to annul one of the obligations imposed by the constitution on the elected candidate, according to which he had to promise to oppose certain papal encroachments, and to recognize the rights of the Protestant members of the empire, which had been guaranteed by the Treaty of Westphalia. But the electors replied by expressing a wish that the Pope would satisfy the long-standing complaints known as the *gravamina nationis Germanicae*, the grievances of the German nation.[1] The ten *gravamina* had first appeared in a letter from Martin Mayr, chancellor of the archbishopric of Mainz, to Cardinal Æneas Sylvius Piccolomini, afterwards Pope Pius II, in 1457, and had been renewed by Jakob Wimpheling, by order of the Emperor (strictly speaking, King of the Romans and Emperor elect) Maximilian I in 1510. Mayr complained that the Pope disregarded the decrees of Constance and Basle, that elections to bishoprics were arbitrarily annulled, that benefices were reserved for cardinals and papal secretaries, that grants of expectancies were given, that annates were rigorously exacted, and that bishoprics were given, not to the most worthy, but to the man who offered the largest bribe. Other complaints referred to indulgences, taxation for defence against the Turks, and usurpation by the Pope of the judicial rights of the bishops : the German nation groaned under its slavery.[2]

The electors appointed Johann von Hontheim, a professor in Trier University, to inquire into these grievances, and specially to investigate how far the constitution of the Church in Germany

[1] F. Nielsen, *History of the Papacy in the Nineteenth Century*, vol. i, p. 109.
[2] M. Creighton, *History of the Papacy*, vol. iii, p. 189.

was in accordance with the civil law. The result of Hontheim's inquiries appeared twenty-two years later, in 1763, in the book *De statu ecclesiae et legitima potestate Romani pontificis*, which was the source of the movement called Febronianism.

Johann Nicolaus von Hontheim, better known by his pen-name Febronius (which he took from the name of his brother's daughter Justine, a nun at Juvigny near Clermont, who was called Sister Febronia), was born at Trier in 1701, and educated at a Jesuit school and at the University of Louvain, where he came under the influence of the great canonist, Zegers van Espen, then nearly eighty years old. Hontheim learned Gallican principles at Louvain, but he never became a Jansenist. He also attended the Protestant University of Leyden. On his return home he became a professor at the University of Trier, head of the seminary for priests at Coblenz, and canon of St. Florian's collegiate church there. The Elector-Archbishop, Franz Georg von Schönborn, began to employ Hontheim, first in political matters, and later as his coadjutor bishop. Hontheim was consecrated Bishop of Myriophyti *in partibus infidelium* in 1748. The next Elector, Johann Philipp von Walderdorff, was more interested in hunting than in Church affairs, which he handed over almost completely to Hontheim.[1]

Hontheim wrote his most famous book under the pseudonym of Justinus Febronius, in order to avoid the inevitable consequences of publishing a book opposed to the policy of the Vatican. But he did not escape. The book appeared in 1763, and was condemned at Rome and put on the Index the following year. Nevertheless, a German translation of most of it was published the same year; two years later Italian, Spanish, and Portuguese translations appeared. The Pope had called upon the German princes and bishops to suppress it; and the Elector of Trier, among others, did so. Hontheim offered to resign his offices on the ground of age, but the Elector would not accept his resignation. He then wrote to one or two local newspapers, denying that he was Febronius, but nobody believed him; and the next Elector, Prince Clement Wenzel, who succeeded in 1768, made him a privy councillor and put all dealings with the Vatican into his hands, in spite of the Pope's protests. But at last an ex-Jesuit named Beck undermined Hontheim's influence with the Elector, and he was driven by moral pressure to recant.

[1] Nielsen, vol. i, p. 110.

So delighted was Pope Pius VI that he solemnly announced this recantation to the cardinals on Christmas Eve, 1778, and afterwards published it to the whole Roman Catholic world. But Hontheim's recantation was not sincere: his subsequent writings show that he had not changed his opinions, and had only recanted in order to avoid trouble. He lived until 1790.

The teaching of Hontheim was based on that of the great Gallicans, but with a difference. Hontheim was a German, not a Frenchman; a statesman rather than a theologian; his purpose, as he stated on the title-page of his book, was to reunite Christians who differ in religion (*ad reuniendos dissidentes in religione Christianos compositus*), a purpose rather different from that of the Gallican divines who had applauded the Revocation of the Edict of Nantes, as indeed it must always have taken a different form in the ecclesiastical circumstances of Germany. He addressed himself to the Pope, the princes, the bishops, and the doctors of divinity and canon law; he defended the rights of the bishops and of the State against the Papacy; he demanded that all claims based on the pseudo-Isidorian decretals should be dropped, and that the constitution of the Church in the first four centuries should be restored. He went so far as to deny that the passages of Scripture on which the papal claims were based had anything to do with the Papacy. Though he naïvely dedicated the book to Pope Clement XIII, he had no hope that the Papacy would be willing to limit its own authority: he therefore appealed to the princes to defend the rights of national churches. The bishops were the successors of the Apostles, therefore they possessed Divine right; St. Peter was only the first among equals, and the Pope had received his primacy in commission from the Church. The doctrines of his infallibility and universal jurisdiction were false, and the doctors of theology and of canon law must cease to teach them. The Church must be governed by the bishops; national councils of bishops should be summoned in the different countries, and if possible a General Council, which alone represented the whole Church. The Catholic princes were invited to set limits to the power of the Papacy.

There is another significant difference between Hontheim and his predecessors. Bossuet and the French Gallicans had fought for the privileges of the Church of France, the Dutch bishops and the Chapter of Utrecht for the canonical rights of their own church. They did not demand any change in other countries. But

Hontheim's Gallicanism was universal. He claimed that the whole system on which Latin Christendom had been governed for a thousand years was based on unsound foundations, and must be changed. Thus he was intellectually in a far stronger position. If Ultramontanism is true anywhere, it is true everywhere; if it is false at Paris or Utrecht (or in London), it is equally false in Rome. The Gallicanism of Bossuet was a claim for special privileges which had survived in one country. The Gallicanism of Febronius was a demand for an ecclesiastical revolution in all countries. But in 1763 revolution was in the air. The Jesuits, who had dominated Roman Catholic education for so long, were being dethroned. The Encyclopædists in France and the so-called Enlightenment (*Aufklärung*) in Germany were injecting scepticism into the educated classes of Europe, and the autocracy of the Counter-Reformation, both in religion and politics, was threatened. In 1769 representatives of the three Elector-Archbishops met at Coblenz, and after deliberating for three months, drew up thirty "Articles of Coblenz", which, if they were not written by Hontheim, were certainly influenced by him, and which were sent to the Emperor Joseph II, the son of Maria Theresa. Nothing was done immediately, but the suppression of the Jesuits in 1773 led to the rapid spread of Febronianism in Germany. The Benedictines and other orders, which took the place of the Jesuits, taught the doctrine of Constance, that a general council was superior to the Pope.[1] Joseph II's plan of Church reform, so well-meant, so irritating and, in the end, so unsuccessful, was influenced by Febronianism; but it was not certain whether Voltaire did not lurk behind Febronius.[2]

Meanwhile the Emperor Joseph's brother, Leopold, had succeeded to the Grand Duchy of Tuscany, and set himself to reform the Church there. His agent for this purpose was Scipione de Ricci, Bishop of Pistoia and Prato, who is described by Nielsen as " an enlightened, virtuous, and zealous prelate, but at the same time violent, impatient, and reckless ".[3] Ricci, who was born in 1741, and belonged to one of the oldest Tuscan families, of which Lorenzo Ricci, the last General of the Jesuits, was also a member, was educated first by the Jesuits, later by the Benedictines, and became Vicar-General to the Archbishop of Florence. He began to study St. Paul's Epistles and Gallican

---

[1] See above, p. 18.  [2] J. N. Figgis, in *Our Place in Christendom*, p. 125.
[3] Nielsen, vol. i, 125.

canon law, and became an enthusiastic convert to Jansenism and Febronianism. The Grand Duke Leopold, his sovereign, appointed him in 1780 to the bishopric of Pistoia and Prato. When he went to Rome to be consecrated, he gave offence by his disapproval of the favourite Jesuit devotion, adoration of the Sacred Heart of Jesus, which he called *cardiolatria*. This devotion was originated by Marguérite Marie Alacoque (beatified 1864, canonized 1922), a French nun, who claimed to have seen a vision in which our Lord's heart, burning like a furnace with love, received her heart placed within it; and is by some supposed to be due to the influence of the mystical writings of a Puritan divine named Goodwin, chaplain to Oliver Cromwell.[1]   The Jansenists at all periods protested against the cult of the Sacred Heart, on the ground that it is Nestorian heresy to offer Divine worship (*latria*) to our Lord's human nature, still more to a particular part of it, such as His heart, since we may only offer it to Himself who is both Divine and human, as well as because it is a serious mistake to confuse the word " heart " used as a metaphor for the seat of the emotions with the physical heart in the body. However that may be, the cult of the Sacred Heart has always been a favourite devotion of the Jesuits, and it had spread to the Italian Dominicans, who had succeeded the suppressed Society of Jesus as the leading order in Ricci's diocese.

Ricci proceeded to make himself unpopular by imposing necessary reforms (which were sanctioned by Rome) on some convents of Dominican nuns; by refusing certain dispensations from fasting which he thought unnecessary; by substituting catechizing, from a catechism with Jansenist tendencies, for the usual Lenten preaching; by removing certain unedifying legends from the Breviary, on his own authority; by insisting on provision of proper libraries for the books in the convents. He was told that he did not believe in the Pope (" as if ", he says in his Memoirs, " this new article of the faith were the watchword of Catholicism "), and his zeal for enlightenment was suspected by a population which had been accustomed for generations to the principle of uncritical obedience taught by the Jesuits.

In 1786 the Grand Duke Leopold, following the example of his brother the Emperor, who had introduced reforms into the Church not only in Austria but in his Italian province of Lombardy, sent

---

[1] G. Salmon, *Infallibility of the Church*, p. 224. G. L. Prestige, *Fathers and Heretics* (1940), pp. 411–414, traces the devotion back to St. Bernard's influence.

to the bishops of Tuscany a scheme of church reforms to be considered by their synods. Ricci accordingly held a synod of his clergy, 250 in number, at Pistoia, omitting in his formal summons the usual style of bishops, " by the grace of the Holy See ".[1]

The proceedings at this synod were later condemned by Pius VI in the Bull " Auctorem Fidei ", August 28, 1794; the condemnation of various propositions covers twenty-four pages in Denzinger's *Enchiridion Symbolorum et Definitionum.* The synod accepted the whole of the scheme proposed by the Grand Duke Leopold, and also adopted the four Gallican Articles, of which it made a solemn profession, and declared them to be " of faith " (which the French divines who drew them up had carefully refrained from doing). This, together with two other accusations, that the synod had declared that God was not *in tribus personis distinctus* (distinct in three Persons) but *in tribus personis distinctis* (in three distinct Persons), and that it was more correct to say " the Father, the Word, and the Holy Ghost " than to use the word " Son ", were the principal charges made by the Pope against the Synod of Pistoia. Besides these, the synod was condemned on the following grounds, amongst others :—

(1) that it declared that power was given by God to the Church, that it might be communicated to the pastors, who were its ministers for the salvation of souls;

(2) that the Pope was but a ministerial head, receiving his authority not direct from Christ in the person of St. Peter, but from the Church;

(3) that the Church had no right to extend her authority beyond matters of faith and morals, still less to exact obedience to her decrees by external force;

(4) that bishops had received from Christ all rights necessary for governing their dioceses;

(5) that bishops and priests should act together as judges in matters of faith; and that decisions of even the greater sees should not be accepted, unless approved by the diocesan synod;

(6) that it approved of the distinction between " matters of law " and " matters of fact " by which Clement IX was said to have restored peace to the Church (here the Jansenist controversy was revived);

[1] Nielsen, vol. i, p. 128.

(7) various statements of a Jansenist character about sin and grace;

(8) that Communion is an essential part of the sacrifice of the Mass, and that a Mass at which nobody but the priest communicates is only lawful if someone present makes an act of spiritual communion;

(9) that in its definition on the Eucharist it made no mention of Transubstantiation;

(10) that it condemned the opinion that the priest can apply the fruit (fructus) of a particular Mass to a special purpose, and that those who pay for that Mass enjoy special advantage from it (a condemnation which would have ruined the financial system of the Roman Communion);

(11) that it declared that there ought to be only one altar in each church;

(12) that indulgences were only the remission of part of the canonical penalty of sin, that belief in the Treasury of Merits was due to the excessive subtlety of the Schoolmen, and that in any case such merits could not be applied for the dead;

(13) various objections to the current practice of the Roman Communion with regard to ordination;

(14) that the synod requested the civil power to abolish diriment impediments to marriage arising from spiritual affinity (e.g., from the parties being god-parents to the same child), and from kinship and affinity beyond the fourth degree according to the reckoning of civil law, and to provide that within these limits there should be no dispensations (the rules proposed are exactly the same as those of the Church of England until recently);

(15) that it asserted that to adore the human nature of Christ is to give Divine worship to a creature, and, therefore, to adore the Sacred Heart is erroneous, or at least dangerous;

(16) that it condemned the use of a prayer "so many times";

(17) that it asserted that it is contrary to apostolic practice that the people should not join with their voices in public worship (which implied the use of the vernacular);

(18) that nothing but inability to do so excuses anyone from the duty of reading the Bible;

(19) that the works of Quesnel ought to be read by parish priests to their people (this was, of course, to defy the "Unigenitus");

(20) that there should be no pictures of the Holy Trinity, no special devotions to particular pictures, and no pictures of the Blessed Virgin under particular titles;

(21) that the assembling of a national council was one of the canonical ways of terminating religious controversies.[1]

These decisions, taken from the bull which condemned them, are important as showing what the programme of reforming ecclesiastics was at the end of the eighteenth century, and as furnishing a link between the Jansenist and Gallican movements of the seventeenth century and the Old Catholic movement of the nineteenth. In the Declaration of Utrecht, the Old Catholic doctrinal basis, the Bull " Auctorem Fidei ", which condemned the Synod of Pistoia, is rejected along with the Bull " Unigenitus ".

The Grand Duke Leopold took the greatest interest in the synod, and had a daily report of its proceedings sent to him. The next year, 1787, he summoned a " National Synod " of all the bishops of Tuscany, to meet in the Pitti Palace at Florence. This was contrary to Ricci's advice; for the archbishop had no sympathy with Ricci's ideas, and Florence was the residence of the Papal Nuncio; also it was full of fanatical monks, who would stir up the people against the Grand Duke. As Ricci had foreseen, the " National Synod " was a complete failure; only two other bishops supported him, and the opposition was so strong that he had thoughts of resigning his see. A report was spread that he intended to destroy an altar in Prato Cathedral which contained what was supposed to be the girdle of the Blessed Virgin. The mob became so threatening both at Prato and Pistoia that Ricci had to flee from his palace; and in the country, where he had taken refuge, everyone left the church as soon as he began to say Mass, so that he had to use a private chapel.[2] Three years later Joseph II died, and Leopold succeeded him at Vienna, where his time was so much occupied with European politics (the French Revolution had just broken out, and Queen Marie Antoinette was his sister) that he could not pay any attention to church reform. Ricci thus lost his main support, and had to resign his see, which he did in 1791. Because of his sympathy with the " constitutional bishops " in France, he was suspected of Jacobinism; in 1794 Pius VI published the Bull " Auctorem Fidei "

[1] H. Denzinger, *Enchiridion Symbolum et Definitionum*, 20th ed., 415-422.
[2] Nielsen, vol. i, p. 129.

condemning the Synod of Pistoia. During the troubled years which followed, Ricci was for some time imprisoned. In 1805 he signed a mild form of recantation, not because he had changed his opinions, but because he felt that he was a cause of offence to many people in Tuscany. He was received by Pope Pius VII, whose confessor actually asserted that the cause of the French Revolution and the Wars of Napoleon was the Divine anger caused by the Synod of Pistoia.[1] Ricci died in 1810.

Meanwhile the great ecclesiastical princes of Germany had accepted Febronian ideas. In 1786 the Pope proposed to establish a new Nuncio at Munich, with whom, and not with the archbishop, the Bavarian Government should transact ecclesiastical business. The three Elector-Archbishops of Mainz, Cologne, and Trier, with the Prince-Archbishop of Salzburg, protested against this invasion of the rights of the archbishops, and their representatives assembled at Ems, a watering-place seven miles from Coblenz, and agreed on what was called the Points of Ems (Emser Punktat). This was practically a repetition of the Articles of Coblenz seventeen years earlier. The archbishops declared that they recognized the primacy of the Pope but rejected the authority which he had usurped in consequence of the Pseudo-Isidorian Decretals. They called upon the Emperor to summon a national German Synod to re-establish the rights of the bishops. Hontheim, now eighty-five years of age, was not present at the meeting, but was delighted with its results, though he doubted whether a synod would effect much, since it had been shown by the Council of Trent that members of synods were inclined to intrigue for their own advantage rather than to promote the good of the Church.[2]

Joseph II received the appeal of the archbishops favourably, and urged them to shake off the Roman yoke. But the bishops were not willing to break with Rome in order to give more power to the archbishops, and the great majority of the clergy and laity had no sympathy with the Points of Ems. The four archbishops were worldly men, quite unfit to reform the Church: the Archbishop of Mainz was only interested in society and hunting, and the Archbishop of Cologne, a younger brother of Joseph II and Leopold, was neither devout nor intelligent. They began to issue, on their own authority, dispensations for marriage within the prohibited degrees, for which they were publicly rebuked by Pacca, the young Papal Nuncio at Cologne, who declared that

[1] Nielsen, vol. i, p. 130.          [2] Nielsen, vol. i, p. 132.

children born of such marriages were born in incest.  In 1788 the question of the nunciature at Munich was brought before the Diet of the Empire, and the Bavarian Government successfully claimed the right to deal with the Vatican in whatever way it chose; and the next year an official answer to the Points of Ems was published by order of the Roman Curia.  But the archbishops themselves were not profoundly interested, and their own authority was about to perish.  The whole system, on which Europe, and Germany in particular, had been governed ever since the Wars of Religion had been ended by the Treaty of Westphalia in 1648, was about to be broken up; and bishops and archbishops, Gallican and Ultramontane, Empire and Papacy, were all alike sucked into the roaring whirlpool of the French Revolution.

Febronianism, therefore, had no immediate result.  There was no popular feeling behind Hontheim and his disciples: they relied on the " enlightened despotism " of the princes of the House of Hapsburg-Lorraine, which was almost on its deathbed, and was in any case an unsound basis for Church reform.  Hontheim could no doubt appeal, as the English reformers of all schools, from Stephen Gardiner to William Tyndale, and innumerable Anglican and Gallican divines after them have appealed, to the Ghibelline tradition of the " godly prince ", to Constantine, Justinian, Charlemagne, and many other emperors, both Greek and German.  There was something to be said for this appeal as long as the medieval synthesis continued, as long as Church and State were one and the emperor or king had the interests of the Church at heart.  But it was not really in accordance with the nature of the Church, for the medieval synthesis was not true; Church and State cannot be one society without the gravest damage to both.  Since the French Revolution the modern European State has arisen, in which all citizens are equal before the law, and it is not the duty of the government to defend or propagate any particular religion.  Therefore the theory of the " godly prince " is an anachronism in the modern world.

Nevertheless, the work of Hontheim did not perish.  It was to bear fruit in another age, in more fortunate circumstances.  The tradition which Hontheim received from Van Espen he handed on to Wessenberg and Döllinger, having enriched it by showing that the Gallican claims were not the privileges of a particular church, but the rights of all churches, and that the Papal claims to Divine right had no basis in Scripture.

# CHAPTER X

## AFTER THE FRENCH REVOLUTION

THE French Revolution was the enemy of despotism in Church and State: wherever it spread, it swept the despotic governments favoured by the Counter-Reformation (and by the Lutheran form of the Reformation). The history of Europe for nearly a century is chiefly the history of the struggle between the principles of the French Revolution and those of the old order, of which the Papacy was one of the principal supports.

The struggles of Gallicanism and Jansenism against Ultramontanism had been one of the chief causes of the Revolution. It may be thought, therefore, that the Revolution might have been favourable to Gallicanism and Jansenism. It was not. The Revolution was even more fundamentally opposed to privilege than to despotism. Napoleon, though certainly a despot, marched through Europe as the instrument of the Revolution, everywhere sweeping away ancient privileges, and setting up in their place a legal system founded on the " Rights of Man ".

But Gallicanism was a system of privileges. It is conceivable that at an earlier period the Gallican privileges might, if they had been undisputed, have become gradually extended to all parts of the Roman Communion, as English freedom is the extension to the whole nation of privileges once enjoyed by only one class. But the ideas and methods of the French Revolution were entirely opposed to any such development.

The leaders of the French Revolution were for the most part either deists or atheists. The philosophy of Rousseau, who taught that man was originally and naturally good, was incompatible with the Christian doctrine that man is fallen, and still more with the Augustinian emphasis laid upon that doctrine by the Jansenists, and the philosophy of Rousseau was the philosophy of the French Revolution.

On the other hand, the opponents of the Revolution claimed that Gallicanism had led to disaster, and that what was needed, if the Church was to recover the lost ground, was a Papacy stronger

and more unbending than ever.  As the Reformation was followed
by the Counter-Reformation, which rejected the ideas of Erasmus
and Pope Hadrian VI as well as those of Luther, so the French
Revolution was followed by a revived Ultramontanism, which
was farther than ever from accepting the teaching of Bossuet,
Van Espen, and " Febronius ".

It is unnecessary to relate in detail the stormy history of the
Church in France during the Revolution.  One of the first acts
of the National Assembly was to confiscate all the property of the
Church and to pass the " Civil Constitution of the Clergy ",
which deprived both the King and the Pope of their rights over
appointments, rearranged the bishoprics according to the new
division of the country into departments (many sees being
suppressed), and ordered that bishops and priests should be elected
by all who had the political franchise, whether Roman Catholics
or not.  The Constitution was, of course, condemned by the
Pope, and the majority of the bishops and clergy refused to accept
it, with the result that they were severely persecuted, and many
suffered martyrdom.  The " constitutional bishops " and their
followers, headed by Grégoire, Bishop of Blois, hoped to
Christianize the Revolution, but in vain.  The Republic set up
the cult of " the Goddess of Reason " in place of Christianity,
and abolished the Christian kalendar and even the seven-day
week; this was followed, under the Directory, by the artificial
religion of " the Supreme Being ".  In 1797 a Gallican synod
was held in Paris by the " constitutional " party, which was
attended by twenty-six bishops and one bishop-elect.  It received
messages of sympathy from Spain, and also from the Church of
Utrecht.[1]  It did not succeed in restoring peace in the Church.
Napoleon saw that it was necessary for him to come to terms with
the Papacy.  The " constitutional " bishops and priests were
sincere republicans, whom he could not use for his own purposes.
He perceived that France must have a religion; that that religion
could only be Catholicism; and that the people could not conceive
of Catholicism without the Pope.  Accordingly, he arranged
a Concordat with the Pope, which was signed July 15, 1801.

By this Concordat, the whole French Church was swept away;
all the existing sees, twenty-three archbishoprics and 133 bishoprics,
were suppressed; all previous rights were abolished.  All the
bishops were asked by the Pope to resign; and they all did

[1] W. H. Jervis, *Gallican Church during the Revolution*, pp. 309–316.

so, both " constitutional " and " non-juring ", except some royalist bishops who had taken refuge in England.  France was divided into new bishoprics, corresponding to the new departments; there were to be ten archbishoprics and fifty bishoprics; the new bishops were chosen by Napoleon, and confirmed by the Pope.  (Napoleon added to the Concordat certain "organic articles ", which re-established the Gallican control of the church by the civil government, and required all professors in seminaries to teach the four Gallican articles, but the "organic articles" were never accepted by the Papacy.)[1]

There was no longer any possibility of appeal to the ancient Gallican privileges.  The new French Church had been erected by the Pope on the Ultramontane theory of his jurisdiction.  By a fresh arrangement made in 1817 the Pope re-erected, on the same theory, thirty of the suppressed sees.  The destruction of the ancient Church of France did not take place unopposed. A formal protest against the Concordat was issued by thirty-six bishops in 1803.  Some of them continued to govern a church composed of those French Roman Catholics who refused to recognize the Concordat.  This became known as the Petite Église (the Little Church).  The adherents of the Petite Église held that they were the true Church of France, and that the Church of the Concordat was schismatical.  But their bishops consecrated no successors.  The last of them, Lauzières de Themines, Bishop of Blois, died in 1829.[2]  Since that time the Petite Église has continued to exist without bishops, and after a time without priests.  Its members possess no Sacrament but Baptism, administered by a layman appointed for that purpose, who also has to read publicly the offices from the old Paris Breviary, now suppressed in the Roman Communion.  The members of the Petite Église. are peasants in remote country districts.  About 1912 M. Volet, the priest in charge of the Old Catholic congregation in Paris, and the Rev. G. E. Barber made an attempt to unite them with the Old Catholics, which came to nothing through the death of these two priests and the outbreak of the European War shortly afterwards.

The agreement between Napoleon and the Pope nearly brought the independent Church of Utrecht to an end.

[1] Jervis, pp. 333, 368.        [2] Jervis, pp. 393-395.  An article in the *Edinburgh Magazine*, March 1, 1833, shows that the Petite Église was by then somewhat revolutionary both in doctrine and practice.

AFTER THE FRENCH REVOLUTION

Archbishop Van Nieuwenhuisen died on Good Friday, April 14, 1797,[1] soon after the " Batavian Republic ", according to the principles of the French Revolution, had been substituted by the French invaders for the old Dutch Republic of the United Provinces. He was succeeded by Johannes Jacobus van Rhijn, a parish priest at Utrecht, who was consecrated on July 5, 1797, by Bishops Broekman of Haarlem and Nellemans of Deventer. The usual excommunication followed. The Church of Utrecht sympathized with the " Constitutional " Church of France and its Gallican council held the same year. Bishop Broekman died on November 28, 1800, and was succeeded by Johannes Nieuwenhuis, who was consecrated on October 28, 1801. Bishop Nellemans died on May 5, 1805, and was succeeded by Gisbertus de Jong, who was consecrated on November 7, 1805.[2]

The following year the nominal " Batavian Republic " was made into a kingdom for Louis Bonaparte, Napoleon's brother. (Strange that a republic which had existed for more than two centuries should have been transformed by the French Revolution into a kingdom, which has remained a kingdom to this day.) Napoleon, who was now the real ruler of the Netherlands, was determined to put an end to the independence of the Church of Utrecht. Archbishop van Rhijn died suddenly, June 24, 1808. Dr. Neale suggests that he was poisoned through a letter which he received.[3] The Chapter was forbidden by the Government to elect his successor. They sent an urgent petition to King Louis, but it was curtly refused. On January 14, 1810, Bishop Nieuwenhuis died; and the succession depended once again on a single life. The same year King Louis resigned, and the kingdom was annexed to the French Empire. Napoleon visited Utrecht in 1811. Willibrord van Os, one of the Grand-Vicars of the vacant archbishopric, was presented to him. He resisted the Emperor's plan to confiscate the revenues of the Church (Dr. Neale says, " He boldly and resolutely withstood the man to whose iron will Pius VII had yielded ") ;[4] but he could not persuade him to allow the election and consecration of a new archbishop. " I will myself treat with the Pope, and arrange the organization of the Church of Holland," said Napoleon;

[1] W. H. de Voil, *Origin and Development of Old Catholic Churches*; Neale, p. 339.
[2] J. M. Neale, *History of the Church of Holland*, p. 343.
[3] Neale, p. 344.
[4] Neale, p. 347.

and he intended to bring about the submission of Utrecht to Rome, when he came back from Russia.

Meanwhile the episcopal succession almost came to an end. Bishop de Jong, on his way home one dark night, fell into a canal, and was with difficulty kept above water till help arrived. As soon as the French were driven from the Netherlands the Chapter of Utrecht elected Willibrord van Os to succeed Van Rhijn. He was consecrated by Bishop de Jong, April 24, 1814.[1] The government's consent had not been asked, and the archbishop received a sharp rebuke. Accordingly, he asked for permission to consecrate a new Bishop of Haarlem, but his request was refused, and permission was only given in 1819. Johannes Bon was then consecrated Bishop of Haarlem, April 25, 1819, and the vacant sees were at last filled. Bon was the only bishop of the independent Utrecht succession who was never excommunicated; indeed, in 1827 he was actually nominated by the King of Holland to the see of Bruges. No difficulites were raised at Rome; one cardinal said, "Dominus Bonus non potest esse pastor malus." (Good cannot be a bad pastor).[2] But for other reasons he never became Bishop of Bruges.

However, the position of the Church of Utrecht was now very different from what it had been in the eighteenth century. Only a section of the clergy and people had adhered to the bishops and the chapter; there had always been a large number of Dutch Roman Catholics who remained in communion with Rome, though without bishops. The numbers of what we must now call the Old Catholic party had long been declining. Threefifths of the clergy had sided with Archbishop Codde. In 1736 there were fifty-two parishes under Archbishop Meindaerts; by 1814 there were only twenty-seven parishes and about 5,000 peóple, while there were a million in communion with Rome.[3] The state of Europe was altogether different from what it had been : a new world had come into existence, to which the controversies over the Bull " Unigenitus " were of no interest. The Powers of Europe were modern secular States, with no interest in theological questions, and the relations of Utrecht with Rome had ceased to have any political importance.

[1] Neale, p. 347.        [2] Neale, p. 348.        [3] Neale, p. 349.

# CHAPTER XI

## WESSENBERG [1]

THE ancient and somewhat chaotic divisions of Germany, both political and ecclesiastical, were swept away by the French Revolution in the person of Napoleon. The states governed by bishops and abbots, which were numerous, and some of which, as we have seen, were strongholds of Febronianism, disappeared altogether; the religious orders were dispersed and their churches confiscated; the principle that the religion of subjects must be decided by their ruler (" cujus regio, ejus religio "), which had been the basis of the last settlement, the Treaty of Westphalia, was replaced by religious toleration and the equality of all citizens before the law.

The Congress of Vienna, at which the representatives of the Powers assembled after the fall of Napoleon, had to legislate for a new world. It was impossible to restore the state of things before the Revolution. The Holy Roman Empire, which had long been moribund, and the ecclesiastical states, which were survivals from an entirely different stage of civilization, had finally disappeared. But the new arrangements which took their place were the product of the principles, prejudices, and interests of the Powers which had at last beaten Napoleon.

It was an unique opportunity for the establishment of a self-governing German Catholic Church, according to the ideas of Febronius. The innumerable vested interests had been swept away, and the road was clear for a single German Catholic Church with its own primate, subordinate but not subservient to the Pope, which might have been a model for a future United Germany. This was the scheme laid before the Congress of Vienna by Ignaz Heinrich von Wessenberg, who became, more than any other man, the forerunner of the Old Catholic movement in Central Europe.

Wessenberg was born November 4, 1774, of a noble Saxon

[1] Based on a life of Wessenberg by Dr. Wilhelm Schirmer, Old Catholic parish priest at Constance: for Sailer and Werkmeister, see W. H. de Voil, *Origin and Development of the Old Catholic Churches.*

family which had originally come from Aargau; his father was one of the ministers of the Elector of Saxony. He was educated at the University of Dillingen, where he came under the influence of the warm piety of Bishop Sailer (Johann Michael von Sailer, Bishop of Regensburg (Ratisbon); born 1751, died 1832), a strong opponent of Jesuit influence; and later at Würzburg and Vienna. In 1800 he was appointed by Dalberg, Prince Bishop of Constance, to be vicar-general of the diocese. In 1812 he was ordained priest at Fulda by Dalberg, and in 1814 named as his coadjutor; in the latter year he took part in the Congress of Vienna.

Wessenberg was a man of determined character combined with earnest devotion and enlightened outlook. He found the huge scattered diocese, half in Germany and half in Switzerland, which he had to administer (for his bishop, Charles, Prince of Dalberg, was also Archbishop of Regensburg), in a deplorable state: the clergy were ignorant and sleepy, and the people were exposed to the influence of the " religion of humanity " spread by the French Revolution. He set himself to restore the spiritual life of the diocese by providing a more educated clergy. He paid special attention to the diocesan seminary, and established pastoral conferences for the promotion of spiritual and intellectual life; he set up elementary schools, in which the newest educational methods were to be used, and founded libraries. He encouraged the study of the Bible by the laity. In 1812 he published a book of prayers and hymns in German. He was so bold as to issue, by his own authority, a *German Rituale*, from which many exorcisms and other obsolete formulas were omitted. He was extremely popular with both clergy and people, and he had the full confidence both of his bishop and of his sovereign, the Grand Duke of Baden.

Unfortunately for Wessenberg, his scheme for a self-governing German Catholic Church was not accepted by the Congress of Vienna. The strongest supporters of Febronianism had been the ecclesiastical princes of Germany; but they no longer existed. Metternich, of course, had no sympathy with nationalism, or political idealism of any kind; Consalvi, the representative of the Pope, fought with all his influence against the scheme; England and Prussia took no interest in the strengthening of German Catholicism. Bavaria, anxious to show its independence, made a separate Concordat with Rome. The truth was, Gallicanism was out of fashion: the reaction against the French Revolution had combined with the Romantic Movement to encourage the rise of a new Ultramontanism. Just as there was no room for the ideas of Erasmus in the struggle between the Reformation and the Counter-Reformation, so there was no room for the ideas of Febronius in the struggle between the Holy Alliance and the heirs of the French Revolution.

So the bishoprics of Germany were rearranged by Rome, as those of France had been. Mainz, the ancient seat of the primacy of Germany, had welcomed the French invaders with open arms, and had been in French hands from 1797 to 1814. It was now reduced to a simple bishopric; and the hope that it might become a sort of German Canterbury vanished. In 1817, Archbishop von Dalberg, who had been the last Elector-Archbishop of Mainz, and had been given the see of Regensburg instead of it when Mainz was definitely annexed by France in 1803, died. The Chapter of Constance elected Wessenberg as his successor in the see of Constance, and sent his name to the Pope, supported also by the Government of Baden. Pius VII was very much annoyed, and severely rebuked the chapter for recommending a man whom the Roman see had been unwilling to accept even as vicar-general. The Grand Duke forbade the Pope's brief to be published in his dominions, and at his request Wessenberg, though he was never consecrated, continued to administer the diocese.

Wessenberg, however, decided to go to Rome himself and plead his own cause. Although he had the full support of the Grand Duke his sovereign, he received nothing but rebuffs. The Pope would not give him an audience; Cardinal Consalvi, the Secretary of State, thought that Wessenberg would submit, but he was wrong; and on September 2, 1817, he issued a letter containing forml accusations against Wessenberg which has been described as " one of the strangest documents ever issued by the Roman Chancery ". Wessenberg was charged with issuing, as vicar-general of the diocese, ordinances annulling "sponsalia"; with supporting an ex-monk named Heckelsmüller, who had censured the veneration of saints and drawn a distinction between Catholicism and Romanism; with recommending " scandalous " books and expressing in his own writings opinions tending to schism; with preventing the clergy from appealing to Rome, permitting encroachments on the exemptions and privileges of religious orders, and introducing the vernacular and other abuses into the liturgy. These accusations are described by his biographer as a glaring mixture of truth and fiction. Being unable to obtain a hearing, Wessenberg left Rome and returned to Constance, where the assemblies of the clergy in the various divisions of the diocese gave him their full support. The real point at issue was his determination to govern his diocese according to the principles of Febronius, and not to be a mere local officer of the Vatican.

But in 1821 the Pope cut the ground from under his feet by abolishing the ancient see of Constance, which dated from the fourth century, and making Freiburg-in-Breisgau a bishopric in its place. The establishment of the new see was delayed till 1827, and in that year Pope Leo XII made Freiburg an archbishopric. The archbishopric of Mainz (the see of St. Boniface and the Primates of Germany his successors) was now a simple bishopric in the new province of Freiburg. Wessenberg's official career was at an end, and he retired into private life. He lived until August 9, 1860, beloved by a large circle of friends and disciples.

Although Wessenberg appeared to be a failure, because his ideas were out of fashion in the age in which he lived, his work bore fruit in the future. He had put the system of Febronius into practice, with success, just as the Ritualists in England put Tractarianism into practice, and his influence was the cause of the prevalence of Old Catholicism in Southern Germany and Northern Switzerland.[1]

[1] Another forerunner of the Old Catholic movement was Benedikt Maria von Werkmeister, 1745–1823, Court chaplain at Stuttgart. He produced a Mass in German, all but the canon; it was used in the royal chapel, to which the public were admitted. Georg Hermes (1775–1831), Professor of Dogmatic Theology in the University of Bonn, belonged to the same school of thought. He was condemned after his death for teaching that a man could only believe what he recognized to be true by the evidence of his reason.

# CHAPTER XII

# THE CHURCH OF UTRECHT AND THE KINGDOM OF THE NETHERLANDS

ACCORDING to the settlement made by the Congress of Vienna, the territory of the Dutch Republic was united with the Belgian provinces formerly belonging to Austria in the new Kingdom of the Netherlands, under the House of Orange. In this kingdom Protestants and Roman Catholics had equal rights: it was not, like the old Dutch Republic, an officially Protestant State.

In 1823 Archbishop Nazalli was sent as nuncio to The Hague, to arrange, if possible, a concordat for the new kingdom. The three Dutch bishops were eager to make use of this opportunity to become reconciled with Rome; the King was favourable; and they addressed a letter to the nuncio, which they signed without their ecclesiastical titles, hoping that this concession would propitiate him. His reply was so insolent that they were obliged to take a stronger line. Two members of the chapter had an interview with Belli, Nazalli's secretary, and were told that the Church of Utrecht could only be received back into communion if all the bishops and clergy would sign the following statement:

"I, the undersigned, declare my submission to the Apostolic Constitution of Pope Innocent X, dated May 31, 1653, and the 'Vineam Domini Sabaoth' of Pope Clement XI, dated July 16, 1703. I reject and condemn, with all my heart, the Five Propositions extracted from the book of Cornelius Jansenius, in the sense of the author, as condemned by the Apostolic See and the aforesaid constitutions. Further, I submit, without any distinction, reservation, or explanation, to the Constitution of Pope Clement XI, dated September 8, 1713, and beginning with the word 'Unigenitus'. I accept it purely and simply, and swear thereto, so help me God and the holy Gospels." [1]

The bishops answered by proposing their own terms, which were as follows: "We accept, with the greatest willingness, and without any exception whatever, all the articles of the holy Catholic faith; we will neither hold nor teach, now or afterwards, any other

[1] J. M. Neale, *History of the Church of Holland*, p. 351.

opinions than those which have been decreed, determined, and published by our mother, the holy Church, conformably to holy scripture, tradition, the acts of Œcumenical councils, and those of the Council of Trent; we reject and condemn everything opposed to them, especially all heresies, without any single exception, which the Church has rejected and condemned; we also detest every schism which may separate us from the communion of the Catholic, Apostolic, and Roman Church, and of its visible head upon earth; in particular we reject and condemn the Five Propositions condemned by the Holy See, which are stated to be found in the book of Jansenius called ' Augustinus '; we promise, as well for the future as for the present, fidelity, obedience, and submission, in all things, to His Holiness the present Pope Leo XII, and his successors, according to the canons of the Church; and also to maintain respectfully, to teach, and to maintain, in accordance with the same canons, the decrees and constitutions of the Apostolic See." [1]

But Nazalli would not accept this proposal. Unconditional submission to his own terms was required. In consequence the negotiations were broken off.

Gisbert de Jong, Bishop of Deventer, who had been for four years (1810–14) the only bishop in the Church of Utrecht, and whose narrow escape from drowning had preserved the succession, died on July 9, 1824. Archbishop van Os nominated William Vet, parish priest at The Hague, as his successor. In his letter to the Pope to announce the nomination, the archbishop said that the only point really at issue between his church and her opponents was, whether the Church of Holland should be turned into a simple mission, and be deprived, by one stroke of the pen, of its bishops and cathedral chapters. No answer to this letter was received. The archbishop died at Amersfoort, February 28, 1825, and again the succession hung on one life. The Bishop of Haarlem, at the request of the Chapter of Utrecht, consecrated William Vet to be Bishop of Deventer on June 12, 1825 (the 2nd Sunday after Trinity), in the parish church at The Hague.[2] This consecration, to which the King's assent had been given, was performed with some splendour, and received much attention. Two days later the chapter elected Johannes van Santen, parish priest of Schiedam, to be archbishop, and he was consecrated in the cathedral of St. Gertrude at Utrecht, November 13 (the Sunday

[1] Neale, p. 352.    [2] Neale, p. 357.

within the octave of St. Willibrord), the governor of the province being present. The Pope was, as usual, informed, but for the first time the new archbishop, in addressing the Pope, called himself " brother ", not " son ". The usual excommunication followed.

The government of the Netherlands admitted the three bishops to an audience with the King, paid them salaries, and also paid a secretary-general for the Church. (After the French Revolution, it became usual in Continental countries for the clergy of recognized denominations to be paid salaries by the state. In France and other countries the salaries paid to the Roman Catholic clergy were compensation for the Church lands which had been confiscated; and the system was extended to other denominations. In English-speaking countries, where the clergy are never paid by the state, even when the Church is "established", the Continental practice is not generally known. It has this great disadvantage, that it gives the state excessive control over the Church, especially as regards appointments.)

But the Dutch Government would not recognize the titles of the bishops as " of " Utrecht, Haarlem, and Deventer, but only " at " those cities. In the following February the three bishops issued an encyclical letter to all bishops of the (Roman) Catholic Church, stating their case, begging the bishops to intercede for them with the Court of Rome, and ending with an appeal to the future Œcumenical Council. The Government consented to send this letter through its ambassadors to the bishops in various countries.

In 1827 Mgr. Capaccini was sent as nuncio to bring about a concordat with the Dutch Government, which was agreed to, but not ratified until the accession of King William II in 1841. Unlike his predecessor Nazalli, Capaccini invited the Archbishop of Utrecht to a conference, which is of great interest, as it was the last attempt to reconcile the Churches of Rome and Utrecht; the question had not yet been made more complicated by the creation of a rival hierarchy in the Netherlands, or by the definition of new dogmas.

The first conference was entirely occupied by compliments paid by Capaccini to the " Jansenists " in general and to Archbishop van Santen in particular; he praised their steadfastness in a Protestant country, their firm adhesion to Rome, the stand they had made against lax casuistry, the carefulness and prudence of the archbishop. At the second conference, after more compliments, Capaccini said that all the differences might be reduced to one small point, a thing about which so prudent and regular person as the archbishop could not possibly make any difficulty. "I see what you mean," said Van Santen: "it is the 'Formulary'." "It is but a form," replied the Nuncio; "all that is asked is, that you will write your name on a slip of paper, and then all will be well." The archbishop indignantly refused to sign a document, and confirm it with an oath, without being certain of the truth of it. "But," said the nuncio, "you are bound in your conscience before God to acknowledge the authority of the Holy Father; and as he assures you that the Formulary is true, you need have no further scruple. Any doubt in your mind is only a private opinion; but the authority of the Church teaches you that the statement is true, and requires you to acknowledge it." The archbishop answered, "I have read the *Augustinus* of Jansen more than once: I know that the Five Propositions, as condemned, are not contained in that book; how can I, then, as an honest man and a Christian, sign a declaration which denies the fact? I must obey God and my conscience, even if the Pope and the whole Church are misinformed. They cannot alter the fact, and they can have no authority from God to require me to sign a declaration which contradicts it." The nuncio next tried to convince the archbishop by a remarkable illustration. "Suppose," he said, "that the father of a family forbids his children to enter or look into a room, in which the table is covered with a green cloth. One of the children disobediently looks in, and sees that the table-cloth is green. The father makes an inventory of the furniture, in which he states, whether by accident or design does not matter, that the table-cloth is red. He then orders the children to sign the inventory as correct. Surely the child who had seen the table-cloth would have no right to refuse to sign the inventory, on the ground that the table-cloth was green. The father had a right to forbid his children to look into the room, and a right to order them to sign the inventory; the disobedience of the child cannot remove his obligation to do what he is told. He is bound to obey his father, even to the point of surrendering his own opinion. Now, the *Augustinus* of Jansen was condemned by the Bull 'in Eminenti' of Pope Urban VIII. Any knowledge of its contents can only be obtained by disobedience to that bull. You ought therefore, as a submissive child, not to insist on acting

on the knowledge obtained through disobedience, but to own
with humility, that when you read the condemned book you must
have been mistaken, that God did not give you clear light when
you were thus acting presumptuously.  All you have to do is to
sign the Formulary, and you will receive the blessing which will
result from giving up your own will, and thus restoring peace to
the Church."

The archbishop asked why the Pope should break the peace
of the Church by attaching so much importance to this signature
if it were a mere form.  Capaccini answered that he could not
believe that the archbishop would obstinately defend his own
opinion against that of so many wise and learned men.  The
archbishop then made the same suggestion as had been made by
Isaac Barrow 175 years before.  " I do not wish to set my judgment above that of others;  I only ask, let the Five Propositions
be shown me in Jansen's book, stated in the sense in which they
were condemned—that is, not in the sense in which anything
similar is found in St. Augustine, for the Pope never professed to
condemn St. Augustine."  Capaccini replied that he was not
there to argue, but to demand simple submission, and that it was
easy to misunderstand St. Augustine; but the archbishop said
that he could not solemnly declare that Jansen had misrepresented
St. Augustine, without knowing what the doctrine of St. Augustine
was, and whether it had been misrepresented or not.  Capaccini
again begged him to take the Pope's word for it.  But Van
Santen answered, " Am I, then, to understand that His Holiness
asks that I should call God to witness that I do believe what I
do not believe, what the Pope knows that I do not believe, what
Almighty God knows that I do not believe?  Is Catholic unity
to be maintained by perjury? "

" The Holy Father only requires," said Capaccini, " what lies
within the province of his authority.  When the Church instructs
you what to believe, you are bound to silence all trifling scruples."

" I cannot conceal my indignation," said the archbishop,
" at your efforts to make me declare that I believe what I do not
believe.  My conscience is subject to God, and I will act by His
aid; I must continue to refuse to sign the Formulary which I do
not believe in my heart." [1]

The refusal of Archbishop van Santen to purchase unity at
the price of falsehood is worthy to stand beside Luther's famous

[1] Neale, pp. 359-364.

(though doubtfully historical) words, "I can no other." It is true that Van Santen was in no danger of death, as Luther was, though if the Dutch Government, which had every reason for promoting reunion, had withdrawn his salary, he might have been reduced to poverty. But Van Santen was no revolutionary leader, like Luther; he had not behind him the ardent youth of a whole nation, burning for far-reaching reforms. He was an elderly bishop, cautious and conservative by temperament, the head of a small community of not more than 5,000 people, without a friend in the world outside their ranks. If he had accepted the Formulary, and his two suffragans with him, their names would have been acclaimed throughout the Roman Catholic world (for them, the only world that mattered) as the men who by their submission had healed the "Jansenist schism"; for the Church of Utrecht could not have continued without bishops. Moreover, he was a Roman Catholic, and the Papacy was to him what it is to all Roman Catholics—the Divinely-appointed centre of unity, as his predecessors had often declared. And yet he would not, for any advantage in this world or the next, declare that to be true which he was quite sure was false. He knew that conscience has a more binding authority than either Pope or Church.

The separation of Belgium from Holland in 1830 made no difference to the Church of Utrecht, which had no members in the Belgian provinces. On June 25, 1841, Bishop Bon of Haarlem died. The Government, hoping that the two other bishops would soon be dead and the schism be at an end, delayed its permission for the election of his successor. However, the archbishop consecrated Henricus Johannes Buul to the vacant see, without the consent of the King or the government, on May 10, 1843. As he had been consecrated without permission, he was for two years ignored by the government, and only recognized in 1845.[1]

The concordat between the Dutch Government and Rome, though concluded through the mission of Capaccini in 1827, was not ratified till after the death of King William I in 1841. The Roman Communion in Holland now numbered nearly 1,172,000, and had five missionary bishops. On March 4, 1853, after some negotiation with the Dutch Government, Pope Pius IX set up a new hierarchy in the Netherlands. Utrecht was to be the see of the new archbishop, but the other sees did not corre-

[1] Neale, p. 365.

spond, either in name or boundaries, to the old sees erected in 1559. Thus the Roman Catholic dioceses of Utrecht and Haarlem are quite differently arranged from the Old Catholic ones; and the other Roman Catholic sees are not Deventer, Groningen, Leeuwarden, and Middelburg, but Breda, Bois-le-Duc (Hertogenbosch), and Roermonde; the last two had in the sixteenth century belonged to the province of Malines, and all three are in Brabant and Limburg, which, not having been originally part of the Dutch Republic, but annexed at a later time, are and always have been mainly Roman Catholic. It is because the Kingdom of the Netherlands includes these Roman Catholic districts that it has such a large Roman Catholic minority; but though Neale wrote in 1857, " It needs no prophetic power to foretell that the commencement of next century will see Holland a Roman Catholic country," [1] his prophecy remains unfulfilled.

The erection of the new hierarchy caused great popular disturbances. Neale says that the (Anglican) Bishop of Glasgow, while visiting Utrecht, was taken by the mob for a Roman Catholic bishop, and had to take refuge in a house.

The Archbishop of Utrecht and the Bishop of Haarlem, as the canonical occupants of those sees, issued a formal protest against the new hierarchy (Bishop Vet of Deventer had died on March 7, 1853). They pointed out that the statement of the Pope's Bull, that Sasbold Vosmeer had been assisted in his work of restoration by large numbers of members of religious orders, was untrue, and that it was contrary to the rights of the Churches of Utrecht and Haarlem to set up rival bishops for sees which were already occupied.

In the following year Hermann Heykamp was consecrated Bishop of Deventer, in succession to William Vet. Bishop van Buul of Haarlem died in 1862, and a difficulty arose about the appointment of his successor. Hitherto, since the Chapter of Haarlem, which had submitted to Rome, refused to elect a bishop, the Bishops of Haarlem had been appointed by the archbishop. But in 1853 Pius IX had suppressed the Chapter of Haarlem. As there was now no chapter, the clergy of the diocese claimed the right to elect their bishop; but the archbishop would not agree. At last, in 1865, Lambert de Jong, whom the clergy of Haarlem had elected, was consecrated by the archbishop. He proceeded to draw up, with the unanimous consent of his

[1] Neale, p. 366.

clergy, a formal instruction for the administration of the diocese during a vacancy, and for the election of the bishop. The Bishop of Deventer approved, but not the archbishop. Bishop de Jong died the next year, and the clergy elected Gaspard Johannes Rinkel as his successor. But Archbishop Loos refused to consecrate him, and the see remained vacant until 1873.[1]

[1] G. Volet, *Histoire de l'Eglise d'Utrecht*, chap. 18.

# CHAPTER XIII

# THE DOGMA OF THE IMMACULATE CONCEPTION OF THE BLESSED VIRGIN MARY

DURING the greater part of the nineteenth century the struggle between authority and liberty was going on all over Europe. The principles of the French Revolution were matched, in Roman Catholic countries, against the principles of the Counter-Reformation; the Papacy, which had maintained for centuries absolute authority in its most extreme form, not to be resisted or even criticized, was naturally the rallying-point for those who feared and hated " liberalism ", whether in religion or in politics. Certainly there was much in the liberal programme which was incompatible, not only with Roman Catholicism, but also with historic Christianity generally. It was remembered that the French Jacobins had set up the cult of the Goddess of Reason in the place of the religion of Christ. The principle of complete equality of citizens before the law, combined (as it was in the Code Napoléon) with the principle of the omnicompetence of the State, now a completely secular institution, raised great difficulties for those whose forefathers had been accustomed for fourteen centuries to regard the promotion of true religion as one of the duties of the civil authorities. On the other hand, the revolutionary party introduced many reforms, such as the abolition of slavery and of religious persecution, which were required by the spirit of the Christian religion, but were neglected by its official guardians.

In France the struggle between the Counter-Reformation and the Revolution was complicated by the relations between Church and State. There were always two kinds of Gallicanism: the defence of the rights of the bishops against the Pope, and the defence of the rights of the Crown and the lawyers against the Church. Napoleon had destroyed the independence of the bishops, both of Pope and State; they were still appointed by the government, but national and diocesan synods and consistory courts had disappeared with the *ancien régime*, and the clergy were far more in the power of the bishops than formerly. Episcopal

Gallicanism had perished, but " royal " Gallicanism remained.
Spiritually-minded men, such as Lacordaire and Montalembert,
looked to the Pope as the only hope of the independence of the
Church from the State, and urged him to make terms with the
Revolution; they were followed into the Ultramontane party by
the great majority of French Catholics. Thus the way was
prepared for the " new Ultramontanism " of Pius IX and the
suppression of all survivals of local freedom, such as the diocesan
rites. The leader of this party in France was the layman, Louis
Veuillot, editor of the *Univers*. The local breviaries of France
had been purged of medieval superstitions by the Gallican divines
of the seventeenth and eighteenth centuries; but this reform had
never been agreeable to Rome. The alteration of diocesan
boundaries after the Revolution led to great confusion; and
gradually the Roman Breviary was substituted for the local
breviaries. The first diocese to make the change was Langres,
in 1839; the last was Orleans, in 1875. At the same time
florid Italian devotions to the Blessed Sacrament, the Sacred
Heart, and the Blessed Virgin, took the place of the old grave
piety of the French Church.

Meanwhile the Liberal Catholics, such as Lacordaire and
Montalembert, who had rebelled against the official Gallicanism
of the bishops, found that their hopes of reconciliation between
the Pope and the Revolution were in vain. Lacordaire in
France and Rosmini in Italy received even less encouragement
than Erasmus had,[1] three centuries earlier. In 1853 Montalembert wrote to Archbishop Sibour, " When we Ultramontanes
defended the rights of the Holy See, of justice and liberty, against
the Gallicanism of the lawyers and the universities, the Ultramontane school was a school of liberty. The attempt is now
made to turn it into a school of slavery, with only too much
success." [2]

It is not surprising that the Papacy placed itself on the side of
authority, or that, as the Reformation was followed by the
Counter-Reformation, the French Revolution was followed by
the Ultramontane revival. The struggle against the new ideas,
by which the whole of Europe was being so profoundly changed,
came to a head in the pontificate of Pope Pius IX, whose attempt
to strengthen and centralize his authority was carried out in three

[1] F. Nielsen, *History of the Papacy in the Nineteenth Century*, vol. ii, pp. 69, 173.
[2] C. S. Phillips, *Church in France*, 1848-1907, pp. 1-21.

stages: the definition of the Dogma of the Immaculate Conception of our Lady, in 1854; the promulgation of the Syllabus of Errors, in 1864; and the summoning of the Vatican Council, in 1869.

Giovanni Mastai-Ferretti was born in 1792, of a noble family at Sinigaglia. In his childhood he was taught to pray for Pius VI, persecuted by the French Revolution; he was growing up when the conquests of Napoleon were making the future of the Church and of the Papacy uncertain. As a boy he suffered from epilepsy, and was for that reason refused admission to the Papal Guards. He then decided to seek ordination, and in spite of his scanty theological education and his disease, he was ordained in 1819. At first he was only allowed to say Mass when another priest was present, but after he had been for a long time completely free from epileptic fits, this prohibition was removed. He became Archbishop of Spoleto, his native diocese, in 1827, and later Bishop of Imola. He was made cardinal in 1840, and elected Pope, with the name of Pius IX, in 1846.[1]

As priest and bishop he had always been specially devoted to the orphans and the poor; and he had friends among the liberals, for which reason he was distrusted at the Vatican. On becoming Pope, he at once proceeded to introduce a number of reforms into the government of the Papal States, and for a time was very popular as a liberal Pope. He was the first Pope to appear on foot in the streets of Rome since Clement XIV. Then came the year of the revolution, 1848. Mazzini and Garibaldi set up a republic at Rome, and the Pope had to take refuge at Gaeta, in the kingdom of Naples. The Roman Republic was soon overthrown by the French, and Pius IX was restored. But he had learned his lesson. .He would have no more to do with liberalism or Italian national aspirations: he became the firmest champion of reaction, both in theology and politics.

During his exile Pius IX had promised the Blessed Virgin Mary that if she would by her prayers restore him to his throne, he would make her Immaculate Conception a dogma which all Roman Catholics must accept as necessary to their salvation.[2] Even before his return he ordered the bishops to report to him how much desire there was in their dioceses for the definition of the dogma. On December 8, 1854 (the Feast of the Conception of the Blessed Virgin), Pius IX, by his own authority and without the support

[1] Nielsen, vol. ii, pp. 110-114.　　[2] Nielsen, vol. ii, p. 188.

of any council, decreed that " the doctrine which teaches that the most blessed Virgin Mary, in the first moment of her conception, by a special gift of grace from Almighty God, in consideration of the merits of Jesus Christ the Saviour of mankind, was preserved pure from all taint of original sin, is revealed by God, wherefore it shall also be the object of sure and certain faith on the part of all believers ".[1] This was followed by the usual anathema against those who denied the dogma.

The doctrine of the Immaculate Conception had had a long history before this. It must not, of course, be confused, as it is by some ignorant persons, with the doctrine of the Virgin Birth. All orthodox Christians believe, as the Gospels teach, that our Lord Jesus Christ was born of a Virgin, and that he was entirely free, at every moment of His life, both from " original sin " and from actual sin. The Immaculate Conception is not that of our Lord, but of His Mother. From the earliest times the Church has regarded with the greatest veneration the gracious and holy figure of the Virgin Mary, who was called by the Fathers " the second Eve ", because she was the means of the Incarnation of the Son of God, through which we are saved, as Eve, according to Genesis, was the means by which man fell. All orthodox Christians accept the decree of the Council of Ephesus, which, in order to safeguard the Godhead of her Son, declared that she is rightly called θεοτόκος, Mother of God. Devotion to her has played an immense part in the development of Christian civilization, though it cannot be denied that it has been influenced by the cult of the Mother-Goddess, the worship of whom under various titles was the most popular religion in all Mediterranean countries in pre-Christian times.[2]

It would have been well if the theologians had been content to venerate the Blessed Virgin as the first and holiest of saints. To us, accustomed to require à posteriori evidence for what we believe, the question whether the Blessed Virgin was sinless appears both profane and futile. For we know nothing about her life, apart from the New Testament, which gives us no evidence one way or the other. Unfortunately the medieval mind did not work in this way. Whereas we argue from particulars to general notions—that is, inductively—the old divines formed their general notions first, and argued from them deductively. " If

---

[1] Nielsen, vol. ii, p. 194; Denzinger, *Enchiridion*, 20th ed., p. 458.
[2] E. O. James, *The Christian Faith in the Modern World*, pp. 199 ff.

the Lord's Mother is so close to Him, and therefore so holy, it is impossible to suppose that she can have been separated from Him by sin, even for a moment. If Jeremiah and St. John the Baptist were sanctified from the womb, much more must this grace have been bestowed on the Mother of God." Thus it came to be generally believed, at any rate in the West, that she was by the special favour of God entirely free from actual sin; though St. Paul had taught that " all have sinned, and come short of the glory of God ",[1] and though many of the Fathers had followed him. St. John Chrysostom, indeed, went so far as to teach that the Blessed Virgin's interference at the wedding in Cana was a fault, though a small one.[2]

But speculation went farther than this. St. Augustine taught that in fallen man conception cannot take place without sin, which causes every child that is conceived to be stained with sin, and hateful in God's sight, from the first moment of its existence. This doctrine of " original guilt " is to be distinguished from the milder teaching of the Greek Fathers, that " original sin " is a loss of supernatural grace and a hereditary tendency to sin, but not a stain or taint. But the teaching of St. Augustine was dominant in the West for many centuries, and it is not surprising that the combination of his severe doctrine of " original guilt " with extreme veneration for the Blessed Virgin, and the à priori or deductive method (" it must have been so, therefore it was so ") universal in that age, should have led to the rise of the doctrine of the Immaculate Conception.[3]

The ordinary medieval teaching was, that the Blessed Virgin was free from all actual sin, by a special grace conferred upon her at birth. The contrary view, that she was freed from original sin also by grace bestowed at her conception, appears to have first arisen in the twelfth century. (It is sometimes said that it appears in the Koran, but this seems to be a mistake.) Various passages from earlier writers, both Greek and Latin, quoted in its defence, are shown by Dr. Pusey [4] to be irrelevant. The words of Petavius are only too true: " In most of them " (writings in favour of the Immaculate Conception), " while I am wont to

[1] Rom. 3. 23.
[2] Gieseler, *Compendium of Ecclesiastical History*, vol. ii, p. 35. St. John Chrysostom, *Hom.* 45 *in Matth.*, *Hom.* 21 *in Johann.* Origen in *Lucam, Hom.* 17 : St. Basil, *Ep.* 260 (*ad Optimum*). Tertullian, *De Carne Christi*, 7.
[3] N. P. Williams, *Idea of the Fall and Original Sin*, p. 417, note.
[4] E. B. Pusey, *First Eirenicon*, part ii, pp. 297 ff.

approve of the piety, and the effort and zeal to adorn the most holy Mother of God, I miss diligence and critical sagacity in the treatment of this question. . . . For if among the ancients, especially the Greeks, there occurs anything which sounds, as to the Blessed Virgin, like ἄχραντος, ἄφθαρτος, ἀμίαντος—i.e., ' undefiled, uncorrupted, unpolluted,' and more of this sort—they fly upon it eagerly, as a godsend, and adapt it to their purpose. But it does not follow. . . . They are mistaken who, from those and similar words, which signify the highest purity and integrity in the Blessed Virgin, think that their task is done, and employ those, in whom they find these expressions, in witness of the intact and immaculate conception, which they wish to prove." [1]

The Feast of the Conception of the Blessed Virgin Mary came originally from the Greeks, who commemorated on December 9 the legend that St. Anne was barren and conceived the Blessed Virgin by a special Divine gift. It reached the Latin churches through the Greeks of Sicily; it was kept at Lyons, then at St. Alban's Abbey, between 1119 and 1146, and elsewhere in England.[2] St. Bernard condemned it as a novelty, in a letter written to the canons of Lyons in 1140, saying that it should not be kept, because the Conception of the Blessed Virgin was not holy, like her Nativity.[3] Nevertheless, the opinion and the devotion based on it became widely spread. St. Thomas Aquinas was opposed to it, while Duns Scotus supported it; in consequence, it became the subject of a controversy, which lasted for centuries, between the Dominicans, following St. Thomas, and the Franciscans, following Scotus. The question was raised at the Council of Basle, and Cardinal Giovanni de Turrecremata, one of the most learned theologians of the age, who afterwards received the title of " Defender and Protector of the Faith " from Pope Pius II, wrote an elaborate treatise against the Immaculate Conception; but it was not presented to the Council, because Pope Eugenius, one of whose envoys Turrecremata was, withdrew him from Basle on account of the dispute between the Pope and the Council about the Greeks.[4] So the Council, without hearing the case against the doctrine, passed a decree in favour of it, which was received in France, though not at Rome. Thus the Immaculate Conception, at that period, became connected with the Gallican party. Turrecremata collected 100

---

[1] Petavius, *De Incarnatione*, xiv, 3, 9, ap. Pusey, p. 295.
[2] Pusey, pp. 250–361.      [3] Pusey, p. 171.      [4] Pusey, p. 517.

authorities against the doctrine. An epitome of his book is given by Pusey in an appendix.[1] He points out that, according to Scripture, all were subject to sin, " original " as well as " actual ", except our Lord Himself; and answers the attempts, mostly exceedingly captious, to escape from this conclusion. He then deals with the subject on the ground of tradition and reason, answering objections, according to the scholastic method. There was an immense literature on the subject; Dr. Pusey gives quotations from a vast number of writers, whose arguments now appear unreal, because we cannot accept either their premises or their methods.

However, the success of the supporters of the doctrine was not due to argument, but to popular devotion. Anything that was believed to give more honour to the Blessed Virgin was popular; arguments in opposition made no appeal to any but theologians. The Franciscans were supported by the Jesuits, who spread the doctrine, as part of their devotional system, throughout the Roman Communion. It was this devotional system which was the real cause of the definition of the Immaculate Conception as a dogma. Dr. Pusey says that the difference between him and the party in the Roman Communion whose teaching he regards as the main obstacle to reunion between the Roman and English Churches does not relate to the greatness of the sanctification which we may well believe that God bestowed upon her, whom He willed to bring into so near a relation to Himself; nor to the singular eminence to which He willed thereby to raise her, alone in His whole creation; nor to the fact that she, with all the saints in glory, intercedes for us; nor to its being permissible, in the way explained by Bishop Milner, to ask for her prayers as we ask for the prayers of other our fellow-creatures, only, of course, that she is far more exalted and acceptable to God; but to this, whether God has constituted her in such sort *the* Mediatrix with Him our Mediator, that as we have no approach to God except through Jesus, so our approach to Jesus must be through her; or again, as all grace comes to us through Jesus alone and for His merits, so all grace is transmitted from Him through her; or whether again, He has delegated her as the dispensatrix of His graces (the pictures of the Immaculate Conception represent her no longer, as in the representations of the Catacombs, as holding up her hands to

[1] Pusey, p. 456.

God, but raining down graces upon us); or whether she is
" the gate of Heaven " in such sort, that " no one can enter
heaven unless he pass through Mary as through a door " (St.
Bonaventura, quoted by Liguori, Glories of Mary, V. i, p.
237); or again, whether she be " the hope of sinners ", so that the
first step for returning sinners is to betake themselves to her, as
their approach to Jesus; or whether " she restrains her Son,
that He may not inflict chastisement, and saves sinners " (St.
Bonaventura).[1]

Against this popular devotion the learning of the Dominican
scholars could not prevail, even though, pandering to popular
superstition, they claimed that their denial of the doctrine had
been revealed in a vision to St. Catherine of Siena. The vision
of St. Catherine, against the doctrine, was confronted with that
of St. Birgitta of Sweden, for the doctrine. In 1387, the University
of Paris condemned a Dominican who denied this doctrine, and
ordered that all members of the University should pledge themselves to accept it; an appeal to Rome against this decision
failed. The Gallican Council of Basle passed a decree in favour
of the doctrine. In 1483, Pope Sixtus IV, hoping to still the
controversy, issued a bull forbidding the condemnation of either
side. The Council of Trent, following instructions from Rome,
confirmed the bull of Sixtus IV, and left the question un-
determined. At Berne, in 1509, four Dominicans were burned at
the stake for feigning miracles with the object of discrediting the
doctrine. At Valencia in Spain, on December 8, 1530, the denial
of the doctrine from the pulpit led to a riot. In Portugal, in
1646, the three estates of the realm bound themselves to defend
this doctrine, if need be with their lives. Long before the nineteenth century it had become dangerous, in Latin countries, to
oppose the doctrine.[2]

The supporters of the doctrine went farther than this. In
1588 Ramón de la Higuera, a Jesuit, claimed to have discovered
at Granada a manuscript and some leaden tablets which proved
that St. James the Apostle had visited Spain and had borne
witness to the Immaculate Conception. The Dominicans had
no difficulty in proving that these pretended discoveries were a
forgery; and in 1639 Pope Urban VIII forbade any appeal to
the " Laminae Granatenses " (tablets of Granada). However,

---

[1] Pusey, pp. 41–42.
[2] Connop Thirlwall (Bishop of St. David's), 6th Charge to his Clergy.

it became in Spain a point of national honour to defend the tablets as authentic. In 1651, a Jesuit who appealed to them, contrary to the Pope's prohibition, had to withdraw; and after a fresh investigation, in 1682 Pope Innocent XI declared the tablets as human figments likely to corrupt the Catholic Faith, and put them on the Index.[1]

Some have claimed that the authorization of the festival of the Conception on December 8 meant that the Church sanctioned the doctrine of the Immaculate Conception. I have even heard it argued that because the festival was retained in the Anglican kalendar (the Revised Prayer Book of 1928 added a " proper " of the day), the Church of England encourages belief in the doctrine. But the history of the festival forbids any such claims.[2] It originated among the Greeks, who have always rejected the doctrine of the Immaculate Conception (because, for one thing, they have never held the Augustinian doctrine of " original guilt ", without which it is meaningless). The Feast of the Conception commemorated one of the events which led to the Incarnation; this was the reason given by the Provincial Synod of Canterbury in 1328, for the first known direction for its observance in England.[3] The Carthusians kept it as the " Sanctification " of the Blessed Virgin until 1509.[4] As late as 1708, Pope Clement XI, in ordering the festival to be kept, was careful to call it the feast of the Conception of the Blessed Virgin Mary immaculate, and so not to commit himself to the Immaculate Conception. Other evidence could be given, such as that of Bellarmine, who, though believing in the Immaculate Conception, asserted that it was not the chief foundation of the festival;[5] but this is sufficient to show that the observance of the festival does not necessarily involve the acceptance of the doctrine (which, so far as the Anglican Communion is concerned, is rejected by implication in Article XV (" Of Christ alone without sin "), which is strictly in accordance with Holy Scripture and with all the Fathers).

It is not, then, surprising that Pope Gregory XVI received many petitions that he would make the Immaculate Conception a necessary dogma,[6] or that Pope Pius IX decided to carry out what a large part of the Roman Catholic world had so long eagerly desired. Already the use of the phrase " immaculately

[1] Nielsen, vol. ii, p 189.      [2] Pusey, p. 351.      [3] Pusey, p. 365.
[4] Pusey, p. 369.      [5] Pusey, p. 380.      [6] Nielsen, vol. ii, p. 77.

conceived" had been allowed in a preface in the Liturgy. In 1847 Giovanni Perrone, Professor of Dogmatic Theology in the Collegium Romanum, published a book to prove that a dogma may be defined, without any basis in Scripture or written tradition, if it has existed as a secret tradition in the consciousness of the faithful.[1] The only passage in Scripture which Perrone could find to support the Immaculate Conception was Gen. iii. 15, in the Vulgate, according to the reading, " *ipsa conteret, she* shall bruise thy head ";[2] though even if this reading were the true one, it is difficult to see what this passage has to do with the Immaculate Conception.

The theological faculties of Munich and Tübingen were asked to give their opinion on Perrone's theory, and they were opposed to it.[3] Pius IX began by asking the bishops to report how far the devotion to the Immaculate Conception had extended in their dioceses. The Italian, Spanish, Portuguese and Irish bishops, and many others, answered with enthusiasm, though even there there were doubts; almost all the professors at Maynooth, for instance, were in opposition. Many of them seem to have regarded the proposed definition as a gift to the Blessed Virgin, to induce her to crush all heresies and give peace to the Church! On the other hand, grave doubts as to the wisdom of the definition were expressed in France, Germany, Austria and the Uniat Churches. Out of forty-nine bishops in the United States, only one sent any answer.

On receiving the replies, the Pope appointed a theological commission to examine Perrone's theory. The commission reported that Tradition by itself, without Scripture, is sufficient for the definition of a dogma, and that " the existence of a Catholic tradition was proved when the general agreement of the Church at any period could be verified, or when a certain number of decisive pieces of evidence which presume it could be produced ".

Accordingly, on December 8, 1854, Pius IX issued the Bull " Ineffabilis Deus ", proclaiming the Immaculate Conception of the Blessed Virgin Mary as a dogma necessary to salvation, and anathematizing all who should fail to believe it sincerely.[4] The new dogma was received with tremendous enthusiasm wherever the teaching of the Jesuits prevailed; for instance, by the

---

[1] Nielsen, vol. ii, p. 191.    Max Kopp, *Die Altkatholische Bewegung*, p. 81, note.
[2] Pusey, pp. 382 ff.      [3] Nielsen, vol. ii, p. 191.      [4] Denzinger, p. 458.

Courts of Vienna, Naples, and Madrid. But there were some protests by individuals. Laborde and Guettée in France, Carillo in Spain, and an Austrian priest at Passau, protested, with unhappy results for themselves. On January 3, 1857, Archbishop Sibour of Paris was murdered by an excommunicated priest, shouting as he did it, " Away with goddesses! " [1] As it happened, Sibour had been one of the bishops who had urged that the definition of the dogma was inopportune.

But the only formal protest was made by the three bishops of the Old Catholic Church of Holland. On September 14, 1856, Archbishop van Santen and his two suffragans, Bishops van Buul of Haarlem and Heykamp of Deventer, addressed a letter to the Pope. They protested against the new dogma on three grounds: it was contrary both to Scripture and tradition; the bishops of the Universal Church had never been consulted about it; it was a new doctrine, and therefore, according to Tertullian and St. Vincent of Lerins, a false one. They reminded the Pope that his predecessor, Alexander VII, when asked by Philip IV of Spain for a decision on this question, had consulted Cardinal Bona, who had told him that even if the Holy Ghost had specially revealed a truth to the Pope, he would have had no right to enforce it on the faithful, though it would be binding on himself as an individual. And they appealed, once again, to the future Œcumenical Council.[2]

It was not long before the new dogma was supported by the most famous " revelation " of modern times. On March 15, 1858, Bernadette Soubirous, a French girl of fourteen, saw a white figure with a rosary, who said to her in French, " I am the Immaculate Conception ", and showed her where to find a hitherto unknown spring of water. This was the origin of Lourdes, which has become the most frequented place of pilgrimage in the Roman Catholic world.[3]

The proclamation of the dogma of the Immaculate Conception is of enormous importance, for two reasons: one of faith, and one of order. It illustrates the method by which the opening made by the Council of Trent, when it set Tradition on a level with Scripture, can be used to introduce any novelty that appeals to popular devotion. Here was a doctrine which was clearly

---

[1] Nielsen, vol. ii, 196.
[2] J. M. Neale, *History of the Church of Holland*, pp. 374-378.
[3] Nielsen, vol. ii, p. 197.

contrary both to Scripture and to the teaching of the Fathers, all of whom held that Christ alone was without sin; unheard of before the twelfth century, condemned by the greatest divines of the Middle Ages, St. Bernard and St. Thomas Aquinas, and based on the Augustinian theory of " original guilt " (to be distinguished from " original sin "), which had never been formally defined by the Church as necessary, and which is specially difficult for most modern Christians to accept, but without which the Immaculate Conception is meaningless. Yet it was taken up by powerful religious orders for party reasons, and made popular by means of devotions based upon it, and at last came to be so widely accepted that it could be made into a necessary dogma without serious opposition; the Spanish bishops actually told Pius IX that it had been believed in Spain since the beginning of Christianity there! It was not defined in order to meet any heresy; it had no connexion with the Catholic dogmatic scheme, which is quite complete without it. There is nothing to prevent any popular superstition from being defined as a dogma in the same way.

As a matter of order, the Bull " Ineffabilis " was an entirely new departure, and was universally recognized as being so. Never before had any Pope added a fresh dogma to the Faith without a Council. The Bull " Unigenitus " was the nearest precedent, but that was only the condemnation of a set of pro-positions, not the definition of a new dogma. Indeed, Dr. Neale calls the " Ineffabilis " " a second and worse ' Unigenitus ' ".[1] The Bull was inconsistent with the Gallican opinion that the judgment of the Pope is not irreversible until confirmed by the consent of the Church; for the Immaculate Conception was proclaimed as an irreversible dogma, though the consent of the Church had never been asked. Therefore the infallibility of the Pope, by himself and not by the consent of the Church, decreed sixteen years later by the Vatican Council, was already implied by the Bull " Ineffabilis ". The contrast between the long and fierce opposition to the " Unigenitus ", and the almost universal acceptance of the " Ineffabilis ", marks the decline of Gallicanism. Still, it must be remembered that the laity will not fight for the constitutional rights of the bishops unless those rights protect some principle that they value. The opposition to the Bull " Uni-genitus " had behind it the national feeling of France, and hatred

[1] p. 374.

of the political intrigues and moral subtlety of the Jesuits. The Bull " Ineffabilis ", on the contrary, had behind it the vast system of popular devotion to the Blessed Virgin, against which the doubts and difficulties of the theologians counted for nothing.

If I may express a personal opinion, I think that the real cause of the erroneous beliefs, that the Blessed Virgin is the dispenser of grace and that the Pope is the representative of Christ on earth, was popular neglect of God the Holy Ghost, the real dispenser of grace to men, and the only true Vicar of Christ.

CHAPTER XIV

# THE SYLLABUS OF ERRORS

THE second stage in Pius IX's programme of reaction was the Encyclical " Quanta Cura " against the errors of modern times, to which was attached a list or syllabus of these errors. It was issued exactly ten years after the Bull " Ineffabilis ", on December 8, 1864.[1]

The immediate cause of the encyclical was the great political change which had taken place in Italy during those ten years. When Pius IX had been crowned as Pope, Italy was divided among a number of despotic sovereigns, of whom the Pope was one. Lombardy and Venetia belonged to Austria, which was the great supporter of all despotic monarchies throughout Europe. Some of these states had a long history. The Papal States dated from the eighth century, and had been much enlarged by the Renaissance Popes; the kingdom of Naples had been founded by the Normans in the eleventh century. Victor Emmanuel, King of Sardinia (which included Piedmont), had given his subjects a constitution, and made himself the hope of the moderate Liberals, who aimed at the union of Italy under the House of Savoy. He had also annoyed the Pope by the introduction of the " Siccardi Laws ", which abolished the medieval exemption of the clergy from the civil courts (the privilege which had been the cause of the dispute between Henry II of England and St. Thomas of Canterbury nearly seven centuries earlier) and the right of sanctuary for criminals.[2] Between 1859 and 1862 the whole of Italy and Sicily, except Venetia and a small district round Rome, had been annexed by King Victor Emmanuel partly through the skill of Cavour, his great Minister, and partly through the campaign of Garibaldi. The Pope had lost fifteen of his twenty provinces, and retained only what was called " the Patrimony of St. Peter ", surrounded on all sides by the constitutional kingdom of Italy, with its capital at Florence. The remnant of the Papal States was the only part of Italy (except Venetia) which still was despotically governed. So

[1] F. Nielsen, *History of the Papacy in the Nineteenth Century*, vol. ii, p. 261.
[2] Nielsen, vol. ii, p. 200.

far from being a model to other countries, as might have been expected from the claim of its ruler to be the Vicar of Christ, it was notoriously the most inefficiently and corruptly governed state in Europe.[1] The annexation of the rest of the Papal States had been carried out after an overwhelming vote of the inhabitants in favour of it; and it was only the protection of the Emperor Napoleon III, who needed the support of the large clerical party in France, that prevented the Italians from annexing Rome too, and making it their capital.

The Pope therefore found himself no longer one of many despotic rulers, but an isolated despot surrounded on all sides by a country governed constitutionally, a country which had annexed three-quarters of his former dominions. The difference was not confined to the form of government. The kingdom of Italy was a modern state in which all religions were equal and the privileges of the clergy had been abolished. At Rome the government was in the hands of the clergy, and no other services than those of the Church were allowed within the city.

In these circumstances Pius IX issued the encyclical " Quanta Cura ", together with the " Syllabus of Errors ". Eighty errors of various kinds were condemned. They were divided into ten groups: the first those of pantheism, naturalism, and absolute rationalism; the second those of moderate rationalism (for instance, "All the dogmas of the Christian religion indiscriminately are the object of natural science or philosophy "); the third those of indifferentism and latitudinarism (such as " Human beings can find the way of eternal salvation and obtain salvation in the observance of any religion," " we may at any rate hope for the eternal salvation of all those who are not living in the true Church of Christ," " Protestantism is nothing but a different form of the same true Christian religion, in which one may please God as well as in the Catholic Church "). The fourth group included the secret societies, Bible societies, and clerico-liberal societies. The fifth consisted of errors as to the Church and her rights; the sixth of errors as to civil society, in itself and in its relation to the Church; the seventh of errors as to natural and Christian morals (such as, that authority is nothing but numbers and material strength, that the laws of morals need no Divine sanction, that to break the most solemn oath is laudable when done for the love

[1] The Rev. Montagu Noel, first vicar of St. Barnabas, Oxford, who had stayed in Rome before 1870, assured me of this.

of one's country). The eighth group was concerned with marriage; the ninth with the Pope's temporal power; and the tenth with religious toleration and the opinion that "the Roman Pontiff can and ought to be reconciled to liberalism and modern civilization".[1]

The first three classes of propositions condemned are only such as any Christian church, certainly at that period, would have condemned; that one may please God equally by Protestantism and by Catholicism would have been denied by most Protestants as strongly as by the Pope. The condemnation of secret societies can easily be justified; and when it is remembered that George Borrow was one of the best-known agents of the Bible Society, and also that the Bull " Unigenitus " had condemned the Bible Society's fundamental principle that to read the Bible is the right and duty of all men, we cannot expect the Pope's approval for the Bible Society. The chief problems raised by the Syllabus of Errors were concerned with the relations of Church and State; it was a final protest against and challenge to the apparently invincible progress of the liberal conception of the secular state, represented by Cavour's slogan " A free Church in a free State ".

We can now perhaps judge this controversy more impartially than could the politicians and historians of the nineteenth century. The liberal programme had grave defects, and in some countries the progress of liberalism, which the optimists of the last century thought would last for ever, has been actually reversed. But to understand Pius IX's position it is necessary to review briefly the past history of this problem.

In the Middle Ages Church and State were regarded as one society with two sets of officials, at the head of which sat Pope and Emperor on equal thrones. This old conception of the Church-State went back to Theodosius (379–95), and implied the persecution, in a greater or lesser degree, of all who dissented from the religion of the community. Though it continued in England and in Lutheran countries on a national instead of an imperial scale (with the King supreme over both hierarchies, ecclesiastical and civil), it was dropped by Rome in the seventeenth century, under the influence of the Jesuits. The theory of the Counter-Reformation, and also of the Calvinists (as is shown clearly in the history of Scotland), was that the Church and the State were different societies, but that in all that concerned religion and morals it was the duty of the magistrates of the State to accept

[1] H. Denzinger, *Enchiridion Symbolorum*, 20th ed., pp. 477–490.

the authority of the clergy, and in particular to defend and promote the true religion by the suppression of heresy. The principle is illustrated alike by the Solemn League and Covenant, the Revocation of the Edict of Nantes, and the persecution of the Jansenists.

In opposition to this, the French Revolution, which sought to destroy privilege in all its forms, had (in theory) made all citizens, whatever their religion, equal before the law. The governments which had accepted " liberal " principles no longer regarded it as part of their duty to promote any one religion, or even religion in general. The spiritual life of man was the business of the Church and the other denominations; the State was concerned only with his life in this world. This was the principle accepted in theory by almost all European states until the last few years; among others, by the new Kingdom of Italy. Already, while he was still only King of Sardinia, Victor Emmanuel had angered the Pope by the introduction of the " Siccardi Laws ", which had abolished the right of the clergy to be tried in their own courts [1] even for criminal offences, together with the right of asylum in certain churches, and some of the public holidays which were Church festivals. Cavour had begun his career in Parliament by defending these laws, and he was never forgiven by the Vatican.

For Pius IX was entirely opposed to the secularization of the State and to the liberal conception of progress. Among the propositions condemned by the Syllabus were these: " The Church has no power to employ force, nor any temporal power direct or indirect " (24). " The immunity of the Church and of ecclesiastical persons had its origin from civil law "(30). " The ecclesiastical court for the temporal causes of clerics, whether civil or criminal, ought to be altogether done away with, even against the will of the Apostolic See " (31). "The abolition of the civil sovereignty, which the Apostolic See possesses, would conduce in a very high degree to the freedom and prosperity of the Church " (76). " In this age of ours it is not any longer expedient that the Catholic religion should be regarded as the only religion of the State, to the exclusion of any other religions " (77). " The Roman Pontiff can, and ought to, reconcile himself to progress, liberalism, and modern civilization."

There were, it is true, many other propositions condemned by the Syllabus, concerning which we cannot but sympathize with

[1] The restoration of this right was one of the most objectionable features of the Concordat proposed in Yugoslavia, 1937.

the Pope. Among them are: "Authority is nothing else but numbers and material strength" (60). "The violation of all the most solemn oaths, and any criminal action contrary to the eternal law, is lawful and highly praiseworthy when committed for love of country" (64). Others were claims made by the State to interfere with the government of the Church, with religious teaching in the schools, and with the ecclesiastical control of marriage.

It is easier for us than it was for our grandparents to see that the growing power of the secular State is a very serious menace to the Christian religion. At that time the State did not perform such extensive functions as it does today; but even then there was continual friction between Church and State over the control of marriage, education, and, in Roman Catholic countries, the religious orders (which are sometimes great industrial concerns). Moreover, the neutrality of the State towards religion, carried out more or less successfully in English-speaking countries (though even there not always real), has never been complete on the Continent. Particularly in Latin countries, where there is only one religion of any importance and everyone is either for it or against it, the problem presents much greater difficulties than where religion is represented by many denominations. In the German-speaking countries the principle of " a free Church in a free State " is so far from being recognized that the State controls religious denominations to an extent which would not be tolerated in England, still less in Scotland, the Dominions, or the United States. Certain denominations are " recognized ", and their clergy are paid by the State, which thereby secures power over the life and work of the denomination. Everyone is registered as a member of one of the " recognized confessions ", or else as " without religion ". No denomination may baptize, marry, or bury anyone not registered as a member of it; those who wish to change their religion must obtain leave to do so from the civil authority. A denomination which is not " recognized " has hardly any rights at all; for instance, the children of its members have to receive religious teaching in the schools as members of one of the " recognized confessions ". In Germany, no minister of any denomination may be appointed unless he has a university degree; and the heads of all denominations have to receive the sanction of the government on their appointment.[1]

[1] All this refers to Central Europe before the rise of Hitler.

Such rights as these were exercised by Continental states even in the nineteenth century; the Roman Communion was secured by " concordats " made between the Pope and the government concerned. In English-speaking countries, where religious denominations (apart from the Church of England) are free from state control, such concordats have not been found necessary.

In Germany and Italy the omnicompetent State of the nineteenth century, neutral (in theory) towards religion, became the totalitarian State of the twentieth century, with a tendency to set itself up as an object of worship, a rival to the God revealed in Christ. We have seen the defects, and in some countries the overthrow, of liberalism; and we may even be inclined to regard the Syllabus of Errors, not as a reactionary protest against the invincible march of progress, but as a courageous challenge to the growing secular State, whose demands have since become so monstrous and menacing. For there can be no doubt in any Christian mind that the State has no right to that absolute and unconditional obedience, even within its own sphere, which belongs to God alone.

But though the Papacy is indeed one of the most powerful opponents of civil interference with spiritual things, and has been so for more than a thousand years, the character of its opposition must not be misunderstood. The Syllabus of Errors certainly did not promote religious freedom. It demanded liberty for the Church from the control of the State, and liberty for Roman Catholics in Protestant or Orthodox countries; but it explicitly refused the same liberty to minorities in Roman Catholic countries. Two instances, of perhaps an extreme kind, show what might happen under the governments of which Pius IX approved. In 1852 Francesco Madiai and his wife were condemned by the Government of the Grand Duke of Tuscany to four years' penal servitude for having read the Bible in an Italian translation and spread this translation at Florence; and were only released because Lord Palmerston threatened to send English warships against Tuscany.[1] In 1858, at Bologna, then in the Papal States, a Christian nurse in the family of a Jew named Mortara secretly christened her master's little boy without his parents' consent, whereupon the child was taken away from his parents and brought up at Rome in a house for converted Jews, nor was

[1] Bolton King, *History of Italian Unity*, vol. i, p. 374.

the indignation that arose in all parts of Europe successful in restoring him to his family.[1]

What Rome desired, and, as there is evidence to show, still desires, is that the State should be totalitarian in a Christian sense. Christ, as the argument runs, is Lord of all men, corporately as well as individually: the State ought therefore to be Christian (that is, of course, Roman Catholic, since that is the only true form of the Christian religion), and ought to suppress, as far as possible, all other forms of religion. The Papacy has never believed in the principles of religious freedom, but has only supported religious freedom in the interests of its own subjects. It is the support of this principle, the lordship of Christ (identified with the lordship of His Vicar, the Pope) over all human life, that is the object of the new festival of Christ the King.[2]

While therefore we can agree that many of the propositions condemned by the Syllabus of Errors were rightly condemned, and that the Pope was fully justified in protesting against the secularization of society and the interference of the State with the rights of the Church over her members, we cannot regard the Papacy as a trustworthy champion of religious freedom against the secular State. In spite of specious arguments to the contrary, Christianity has everything to gain by freedom; and the Church ought to seek freedom from State interference, not only for her own members, but for all Christians and also for non-Christians. The claim which she makes for freedom to govern her own members she ought to be willing, and indeed eager, to grant to others: at least, it seems so to the English mind. That is, however, not the Roman view. Heresy is regarded as an absolute evil no more to be tolerated than disorder or brigandage: even less, indeed, for it injures not worldly goods, but souls.

This digression is necessary, because the Old Catholic revolt, which broke out only seven years after the publication of the Syllabus of Errors, was to some extent the result of the tension between the Papacy and the modern State; and that attitude is not easy for English people to understand. In English-speaking countries, where there are always many denominations, we are accustomed to two ecclesiastical conditions: the "established

---

[1] Nielsen, vol. ii, p. 205.
[2] " La Ligue Universelle du Christ-Roi " has as one of its objects " un esprit de totale soumission aux directives du Souverain Pontife, soumission née da la conviction que toute parole du Pape est parole de Dieu." (Dom Lucien Chambat, *La Royauté du Christ selon la Doctrine Catholique*, 1931, p. 71.)

Church ", in theory, though no longer in practice, identical with the State in the medieval sense, but in such a way that the civil power dominates (and even domineers) over the ecclesiastical; and the " free " Church, secured against State interference by its constitution, and completely self-governing. Neither of these ecclesiastical conditions existed, on a large scale, in that part of Europe with which we are concerned in this book. The conception of " a free Church in a free State " has its difficulties and its limitations: perhaps it is not compatible with either Roman law, so jealous of the right of association, or the Latin temperament, so impatient of illogical compromises. In countries where neither the Church nor the State really believes in it, we cannot expect it to work well. We, who live in a country where the State has for centuries been much stronger than the Church, find it difficult to understand the position in countries where the Church claims, and sometimes possesses, enough power to interfere seriously with the State, not always or necessarily in the interests of justice.

The Syllabus caused much alarm in several Roman Catholic countries. In Belgium it became necessary for the Church to proclaim that there was nothing in the Syllabus inconsistent with the oath to defend the Belgian constitution. In France, Bishop Dupanloup of Orleans published a defence of the Syllabus, in which he argued that the Pope had asserted absolute truths, which could not always be maintained strictly, the necessities of the time being relative.[1] He thus became recognized as the leader of the moderate party among the bishops, which was opposed by the extreme Ultramontanes under Bishop Pie of Poitiers.

[1] Nielsen, vol. ii, p. 267.

# CHAPTER XV

# THE VATICAN COUNCIL

THE third and final part of Pius IX's programme was the Vatican Council. Since the Council of Trent had been closed in 1563, no General Council had been held. This was a longer period without a council than had ever elapsed before. According to the Roman reckoning, the Council of Trent was the 19th Œcumenical Council.[1] (Only the first seven councils are recognized by the Orthodox Eastern churches, and the Anglican churches have never accepted more than the first six.)

Why had there been no council since Trent? Not because no problems had arisen for a council to solve, but because the system of government which had been practised since the Counter-Reformation had made councils unnecessary. The government of the Church had been centralized, as never before; the Jesuits were usually dominant at Rome, and their doctrine, that the Pope was infallible, was taught wherever their influence extended, and had become the assumption on which the administration of the Church was based. The opponents of the Bull " Unigenitus " had appealed again and again " to the future council ", and their appeals had been forbidden. The very word "council", we are told, was regarded at Rome as sacrilegious.

But by the middle of the nineteenth century " Jansenism " and Gallicanism were no longer dangers to be feared. Pius IX thought that an Œcumenical Council would carry out his policy and would fix for ever the principles which he believed to be the necessary remedies against the dangers which surrounded the Church. Two days before the proclamation of the Syllabus of Errors he began privately to consult the cardinals in the Congregation of Rites about the expediency of a council.[2] The following year, 1865, he appointed a commission to consider the proposal; in 1867 he mentioned it in a public allocution to the bishops assembled in St. Peter's for the 1,800th anniversary of the martyrdom of St. Peter.[3]

[1] Denzinger, *Enchiridion*, 20th ed., p. 491.
[2] Dom Cuthbert Butler, *Vatican Council*, vol. i, p. 81.
[3] Butler, vol. i, p. 85.

On February 6, 1869, the *Civilta Cattolica*, the organ of the Jesuits at Rome, published a letter suggesting agenda for the Council. The writer hoped that the doctrine of the Syllabus of Errors would be confirmed, the Infallibility of the Pope declared by acclamation to be a necessary dogma, and the bodily assumption of the Blessed Virgin into heaven decreed to be a dogma necessary to salvation. The Pope repudiated responsibility for this letter, but it was generally thought to be extremely significant.[1] Prince von Hohenlohe, the Foreign Minister of Bavaria, was much alarmed by the suggestion that the Syllabus might be confirmed, and tried to induce other Governments to join him in protest, but he got no support.[2] Bishop von Ketteler of Mainz feared that if the infallibility, universal ordinary jurisdiction, and temporal power of the Pope were made dogmas, there would be a schism. Twenty-two leading German laymen met at Berlin and drew up an address to the bishops opposing the suggestions of the *Civilta*; but it was never presented.[3]

On the other hand, an important manifesto was published by a Bohemian priest, entitled *The Reform of the Church in Head and Members*.[4] He urged that the Council should stop the centralization of the Church, reduce the authority of Rome to a primacy, as in ancient times, restore to the bishops the rights of which the Papacy had deprived them, abolish the temporal power of the Pope, revise the marriage laws, suppress many of the religious orders and abolish permanent vows, permit exceptions to the rule of clerical celibacy, allow the liturgy to be said in the language of the people, give the laity a larger share in the government of the Church, encourage the education of priests at universities, and renounce the medieval claims of the Papacy to universal temporal sovereignty.

The Infallibility of the Pope, in the sense taught by Bellarmine, had become the almost universal opinion of the Roman Communion outside Germany, Switzerland, and Austria-Hungary. The old Gallican party in France, which denied it, had been declining ever since the Revolution. The proclamation of the dogma of the Immaculate Conception in 1854, which implied the Infallibility of the Pope, had been universally accepted. Bishop

---

[1] Nielsen, *History of the Papacy in the Nineteenth Century*, vol. ii, p. 300.
[2] Nielsen, vol. ii, p. 301.
[3] Nielsen, vol. ii, p. 305; Lord Acton, *History of Liberty*, p. 503.
[4] Acton, p. 494.

de Ségur wrote to Bishop Pie: " Pius IX has said to Mary, Thou art immaculate! Mary has answered, Thou art infallible!" [1]

But there was a new Ultramontane party, especially in France, which went far beyond this. Bellarmine had laid down that when the Pope teaches the whole Church in things pertaining to faith, or in moral precepts prescribed for the whole Church, and relating to things necessary to salvation, or in themselves good or evil, he cannot err. Nevertheless, he ought not to neglect the ordinary means of arriving at a true knowledge of the matter in question; and the ordinary means is a council.[2] It is his duty to ascertain the mind of the Church beforehand; but his decision does not require the subsequent consent of the Church, as the Gallicans held.

But the new Ultramontanes held that all doctrinal pronouncements by Popes are infallible. W. G. Ward, who as an Anglican priest had nearly wrecked the Oxford Movement by founding within it a Romanizing group opposed to its original principles, was now a lay professor of theology in the Roman mission in England. He held that all bulls and encyclicals, so far as they were doctrinal, and the decrees of the Roman Congregations, if published by the Pope's authority, were infallible. According to him, the Bull " Quanta Cura " must be accepted as the word of God.[3] He declared that he hoped for an infallible decision " every morning with the toast "! And he insisted that his view of infallibility was the only orthodox one, necessary to eternal salvation.

Veuillot, the editor of the *Univers*, who was, of course, not a theologian, but a journalist, wrote, " We all know certainly only one thing, that no man knows anything except the man with whom God is for ever, the man who carries the thought of God (namely, the Pope). We must unswervingly follow his inspired directions." [4] Veuillot had the full approval of Pius IX, who, as a " private theologian," was a " pronounced neo-Ultramontane ".[5]

The most blasphemous flattery of the Pope was practised in this circle. The hymn for the ninth hour in the Breviary, " Rerum Deus tenax vigor " (O God, creation's secret force), was paraphrased, with the name of Pius substituted for that of God. One devotee wrote, " To Pius IX who represents my God on the

---

[1] Nielsen, vol. ii, p. 293.    [2] Butler, vol. ii, p. 37.
[3] Butler, vol. ii, pp. 73-74.    [4] Butler, vol. ii, p. 75.
[5] Butler, vol. ii, p. 202.

earth: he is my God and I will glorify him, my father's God, and I will exalt him." Another applied to the Pope, Heb. vii. 26, " A pontiff holy, harmless, undefiled, separated from sinners, and made higher than the heavens ". Even the *Civilta Cattolica*, the Jesuit organ, said, " When the Pope thinks, it is God Who is thinking in him ".[1] On January 9, 1870, Bishop Mermillod preached, at St. Andrea della Valle in Rome, a sermon on the three Bethlehems, in which the weak things had confounded the mighty: the manger, the tabernacle, the Vatican.[2] It is hard to say how far these extravagances found support among the bishops. Certainly they were widely held in France, Italy, and even Germany; Archbishop Manning of Westminster, the head of the mission in England, was more than disposed to agree with W. G. Ward, though he did not put forward these views at the Council.[3] And he has been described as the " chief whip " of the Ultramontane party, which was found to include four-fifths of all the bishops, and of which the leader was Mgr. Dechamps, Archbishop of Malines, an Ultramontane of the old Bellarmine type.

The opposition consisted chiefly of " Inopportunists ": bishops who believed indeed that the Pope was infallible, but thought that to define his infallibility as a dogma was inexpedient. The best-known and most active of this group was Bishop Dupanloup of Orleans, who declared explicitly before the Council met that he had always believed and taught that the Pope was infallible, and that he would accept without question whatever the Council should decree. But in a pastoral letter to his clergy (November 11, 1869) he said that he opposed the definition of Papal Infallibility for the following reasons:—

(1) It was unnecessary.

(2) It was shelved at Trent, in order to avoid division among the bishops.

(3) Its definition would prevent the reconciliation of the Eastern Churches and the Protestants with Rome.

(4) It would antagonize civil governments.

(5) There were theological difficulties in defining it.

(6) There were historical difficulties, questions of fact.

(7) The bishops would thereby be lowered in the eyes of the people.[4]

[1] Butler, vol. ii, pp. 76–77.  [2] Nielsen, vol. ii, p. 328.
[3] Butler, vol. ii, p. 77.  [4] Butler, vol. ii, p. 124.

This position was shared by Archbishop Darboy of Paris and other French bishops, and many in England, America, and the churches of the Eastern rites.

But these men were completely devoid of the modern scientific spirit. The history written by Montalembert and Lacordaire, the French Liberal Catholic leaders, was quite uncritical. When Lord Acton met Bishop Dupanloup in Germany in 1869 he was appalled at his ignorance; and said to Döllinger, " What is to be expected if this is one of the best specimens? " As " Quirinus " said, the term Liberal Catholic obscured rather than expressed the real difference. The French opponents of Papal Infallibility opposed it on grounds of expediency; they knew nothing of the modern critical methods of studying history, which render it incredible.[1]

But beyond them there were some who held that the Infallibility of the Pope was untrue. This school of thought was not well represented among the bishops: Hefele of Rottenburg, Vérot of Savannah, and perhaps ten or twelve others, belonged to it. But it contained the three most learned historians in the Roman Communion: Bishop Hefele, the historian of the Councils; Döllinger, Professor of Church History at Munich; and Lord Acton, afterwards Professor of History at Cambridge. The leader of this group was Döllinger.

Johann Josef Ignaz von Döllinger was born at Bamberg in February 1799. He was educated at Würzburg, and ordained in 1822. He became professor at Munich in 1826; he represented the university in the Bavarian Parliament for two years, and in 1848 was elected as a Liberal to the German National Parliament, where he spoke strongly in favour of religious liberty. For many years he was regarded as a leader of the Ultramontanes; as late as 1861 he published a book called *The Church and the Churches*, with the object of showing the necessity of the Papacy to the reunion of Christendom. In this book he made statements about the Christians separated from Rome which are strange reading to-day. The English Church must sooner or later fall to pieces: it was only a question of time.[2] The first characteristic of Scottish Presbyterianism was the absence of theology. Protestantism had no organization that could negotiate with Rome, even if it wanted to. Such were the results of separation from the Papacy.[3]

---

[1] C. S. Phillips, *Church in France*, 1848–1907, p. 60.
[2] Acton, pp. 333–335.    [3] Acton, p. 341.

However, Döllinger's historical researches had for some years been leading him far away from Ultramontanism. His progress was assisted by his profound belief in religious freedom; whereas Bishop Dupanloup, the leader of the opposition in France, had, in his defence of the Syllabus, declared that the Pope could not be expected to accept religious freedom as a principle.[1]

In 1863 Döllinger had supported Professor Frohschammer in defence of the liberty of science: but Frohschammer's teaching had been condemned by the Pope, and Döllinger had submitted without hesitation.[2] Nevertheless, he was regarded at Rome as the real leader of the German opposition: " all the threads of the movement converge at Munich ", said the *Civilta Cattolica* (September 4, 1869).

The letter in the *Civilta* proposing agenda for the Council had greatly alarmed Döllinger, and he and his friend Professor Huber wrote a series of articles in the Augsburg *Allgemeine Zeitung*, which were afterwards recast and published under the title *The Pope and the Council*, on July 31, 1869. The authors took the pseudonym of " Janus ".

This book, which was called by Bishop Ullathorne of Birmingham " the gravest and severest attack on the Holy See and the Jesuits, and especially on the policy of Rome, for a thousand years ", and by Dom Cuthbert Butler " an imposing onslaught on the Popes, perhaps the most damaging ever compiled ",[3] consisted of three chapters, preceded by an introduction which pointed out that there were other signs of what was coming besides the article in the *Civilta*. Provincial synods held in Germany, Holland, Hungary, and the United States had accepted the Papal Infallibility; and since provincial synods were not allowed to decide doctrinal controversies, this belief was evidently regarded as no longer controversial.

The first chapter was a warning of the consequences of making the Syllabus dogmatic. To do so would be to impose on the Roman Catholic world the following principles:—

(1) The Church has the right to employ temporal and civil punishment (proposition 24).

(2) The Popes have never exceeded the bounds of their power, nor usurped the rights of princes (proposition

[1] Nielsen, vol. ii, p. 267.
[2] *Theodorus* (J. B. Mullinger), *New Reformation*, p. 58.
[3] Butler, vol. i, p. 111.

23); therefore the Pope still claims the right to depose sovereigns.

(3) The immunities of the clergy did not have a civil origin (which is well known to be historically untrue).

(4) Religious freedom must not be granted to non-Catholics.

(5) They are in damnable error who regard the reconciliation of the Pope with modern civilization as possible or desirable—that is, the modern State, with its religious and political freedom and equality for all citizens, and the right of the people to govern and tax themselves, is condemned.

The second chapter dealt with the Assumption, or bodily translation to heaven, of the Blessed Virgin Mary; and the authors had no difficulty in showing that it was a legend of the fourth century, and that even the Martyrology of Usuard (used at Rome in the ninth century) declared " that nothing was known of the Blessed Virgin's death, or of the subsequent condition of her body ".

The third chapter, which occupies more than nine-tenths of the book, was devoted to exposing the falsity of the doctrine that the Infallibility of the Pope had always been the teaching of the Church. " Janus " admits that the primacy of the Pope, as the successor of St. Peter, is by Divine right. It is hard to see why, for he says (p. 81): " For a long time nothing was known in Rome of definite rights bequeathed by St. Peter to his successors. Nothing but a care for the weal of the Church, and the duty of watching over the observance of the canons, was ascribed to them." He entirely rejects the Papal Supremacy: " There were many national Churches which were never under Rome, and never even had any intercourse by letter with Rome, without this being considered a defect, or causing any difficulty about Church communion ". He gives as instances the Armenian Church, " the great Syro-Persian Church in Mesopotamia, and the Irish and ancient British Churches, which remained for centuries autonomous, and under no sort of influence of Rome " (p. 84). The appellate jurisdiction of the Roman see, granted by the Emperor Valentianian I, is regarded by " Janus " as a usurpation. " The Bishops of Rome could exclude neither individuals nor churches from the communion of the Church Universal " (p. 81). " In early times the Church is organized in dioceses, provinces, patriarchates (national churches were added afterwards in the West), with the Bishop of Rome at the head as first patriarch, the centre and representative of unity, and, as such, the bond between . . . the churches of the Greek and the Latin tongue, the chief watcher and guardian of the, as yet very few, common laws of the Church (for a long time only the Nicene); but he does not encroach on the rights of patriarchs, metropolitans, and bishops." After describing at length the inconsistency of one Pope's teaching with another, the forgeries by means of which the papal power was increased, and the evil effects of the belief in infallibility on the character of the Popes themselves, etc., "Janus" expresses great discontent with the Council of Trent, implying, though he does not actually say so, that it was not a free Council; and declares that a Council's decisions are not binding unless it has complete freedom, and that its infallibility depends on the subsequent consent of the Church; the whole Church, not the Council, is the ultimate judge. Thus "Janus" went far beyond Bossuet, Van Espen, or Febronius; he had already come very near the Orthodox and Anglican position, though still divided profoundly from it by his belief in the Divine origin of the Papal Primacy. And he had come to it, not through traditional opposition to the Papal claims, but by independent and critical research.

*The Pope and the Council* is not a judicial statement: it is the work of the counsel for the prosecution. It may be one-sided and exaggerated;[1] it was declared even by Bishop Ketteler, one of the " inopportunist " bishops, to be as untruthful as Pascal's *Provincial Letters*.[2] But its main argument has never really been answered. Professor Hergenröther at once issued an *Anti-Janus* (for illustrations of his methods, see G. C. Coulton, *Papal Infallibility*, pp. 22, 259), and on November 26 *The Pope and the Council* was placed on the Index. Bishop Dupanloup was afraid that the Council would offend Napoleon III, that the Emperor would withdraw his garrisons from Rome, and that the Italians would thereupon annex the city and destroy the Pope's temporal power. He therefore decided to combine with the German bishops: he sent a statement of his own to them, he visited Germany, he had an interview with Döllinger.[3] This scandalized the Ultramontane party, which shows that a great difference was

---

[1] G. C. Coulton, *Papal Infallibility*, p. 259.
[2] Nielsen, vol. ii, p. 308.
[3] Nielsen, vol. ii, p. 309.

recognized between the " inopportunists ", of whom Dupanloup was a leader in France, and the school of " Janus ".

On September 6 the German bishops, assembled at Fulda, issued a pastoral letter the object of which was to calm the public excitement.  They declared that the Council would neither introduce new dogmas nor interfere with the State; that it would not lay down principles other than those which all Catholics believed already, or formulate doctrines not contained in Scripture and tradition, but would only set the old truth in a clearer light. But this agreed statement had not been easily reached.  Most of the German bishops were " inopportunists "; but Hefele of Rottenburg,[1] formerly Professor of Church History at Tübingen, declared boldly that he did not believe the doctrine of Papal Infallibility, since he had studied Church History for thirty years without finding any evidence that the ancient Church believed it; upon which Canon Molitor, who represented the Bishop of Speier, said that Rome would soon pull the heretical skin off the Bishop of Rottenburg.   There were also some who were in favour of defining the doctrine, such as Senestrey of Regensburg (Ratisbon).

Fourteen of the twenty-two German bishops also wrote a private letter to the Pope, begging him not to have the dogma defined, because of the dangers which would follow; and the bishops of Austria and Hungary sent similar requests.   But the letter of the German bishops was carefully concealed from the public: and " a diplomatist was able to report, on the authority of Cardinal Antonelli" (the Papal Secretary of State) "that it did not exist".[2]

In Hungary a new constitution for the Church, giving supreme power to the laity in all that was not dogma or liturgy, was approved by the King, with the unanimous consent of the bishops, on October 25, 1869; and it was thought that the Hungarian bishops would not support in the Council any proposals likely to destroy what had been done.[3]   In France, Bishop Maret, Dean of the Sorbonne, published a pamphlet on *The Council and Religious Peace*, in which he defended the old Gallican position of Bossuet, and hoped that the Council, assembled by the Pope, would utter the real voice of the Church.  He differed both from Dupanloup, who held the Papal Infallibility to be true, but its immediate definition inopportune, and from Döllinger, who held

---

[1] Rottenburg in Württemburg, not to be confused with Rothenburg in Bavaria.
[2] Acton, p. 518.              [3] Acton, pp. 509 ff.

that nothing could be expected from a Council held in such conditions.[1]

At this juncture Père Hyacinthe Loyson, one of the most celebrated preachers in France, withdrew from the Carmelite Order, of which he was a member. He was excommunicated shortly afterwards. His withdrawal was an advantage to the Ultramontane party, which they could use as a weapon against Dupanloup and his friends. Montalembert, the historian of Western monasticism, who was a member of Dupanloup's party and a friend of Loyson, tried in vain to persuade the latter to submit.[2]

The Vatican Council opened on December 8 (Pius IX's favourite date), 1869. The total number present at the Council, when the late-comers had arrived, was 744, nearly four-fifths of all the bishops in communion with Rome. Invitations had been sent to the bishops of the Eastern Communions, both Orthodox and Separated, but none of them accepted, because to have done so would have been to have acknowledged the papal claims. The Anglican bishops were, of course, not invited, since the validity of their orders was not recognized. The only bishops in the world whose orders were recognized at Rome but who were not invited to the Council were the Archbishop of Utrecht, Henricus Loos, and the Bishop of Deventer, Hermann Heykamp (the see of Haarlem had been vacant since 1867). The council to which their predecessors had so often appealed had at last met, and they were not even invited to it!

Of the 744 members of the Council, about 150 belonged to the minority. The leaders of the party were Cardinal Schwarzenberg, Archbishop of Prague, and Cardinal Rauscher, Archbishop of Vienna; Simor, the Primate of Hungary, Haynald, Archbishop of Kalocsa, and Strossmayer, Bishop of Diakovar in Bosnia; Melchers, Archbishop of Cologne, and Hefele, Bishop of Rottenburg; Cardinal Mathieu, Archbishop of Besançon, Darboy, Archbishop of Paris, Dupanloup, Bishop of Orleans, and Ginoulhiac, Bishop of Grenoble; MacHale, Archbishop of Tuam; Kenrick, Archbishop of St. Louis, and Vérot, Bishop of Savannah. Many of the bishops of the Eastern rites were also with the

[1] Acton, p. 511; Nielsen, vol. ii, p. 310; Butler, vol. i, p. 120.
[2] Nielsen, vol. ii, p. 311.
[3] Butler, vol. i, p. 95: he is badly informed on Dutch affairs, cf. vol. i, p. 262, vol. ii, p. 189.

opposition, among others the Patriarch of Babylon (whose flock were the " Chaldeans ", the minority of the Assyrian nation in communion with Rome). The Spanish and Italian bishops were almost solid for the majority. In general, it may be said that in countries where the bishops had hopes of reconciling Eastern churches or Protestants with Rome, many opposed the definition of Papal Infallibility, as likely to hinder reunion; but where there was no great rival form of Christianity the bishops were enthusiastically in favour of the definition.

The minority complained that by the Bull " Multiplices inter ", published at the beginning of the Council, the Pope alone could lay proposals before it, whereas at Trent all bishops had had the right to do so; [1] that the procedure was so arranged as to favour the majority; that the opposition could not even publish literature in defence of their case at Rome, since the Pope had autocratic power, and the Roman press was strictly censored.[2]

Another complaint was that the Italian bishops, whose dioceses were small, and whose ignorance was great, outnumbered all the other bishops in Europe, whereas the northern countries, from which most of the minority came, had but few bishops and vast dioceses. This was an old difficulty, which had been dealt with at the Council of Constance by the device of voting by nations.[3] The Pope was determined to get his decrees passed, and used his enormous personal influence for that purpose. For instance, he said solemnly to Cardinal Schwarzenberg, " I, Giovanni Mastai, believe in the infallibility." [4] He opened an audience which he gave to Bishop Ketteler of Mainz with the words " Lovest thou me? " [5] When, towards the end of the Council, Cardinal Guidi, Archbishop of Bologna, an eminent Dominican theologian, opposed the infallibility of the Pope apart from the bishops, saying that it was unknown before the nineteenth century, and calling St. Thomas Aquinas to witness, Pius IX sent for him and said to him, " You are my enemy. You are the coryphaeus of the opposition, and ungrateful. You have taught heretical doctrines." Guidi appealed to tradition, but the Pope replied " I am tradition " (La tradizione son'io). Guidi left with the words, " Holy Father, have the kindness to read my speech! " [6]

[1] Nielsen, vol. ii, p. 316.
[2] Nielsen, vol. ii, p. 333; Coulton, p. 133.
[3] Butler, vol. i, p. 264.
[4] Nielsen, vol. ii, p. 323.
[5] Nielsen, vol. ii, p. 325.
[6] Nielsen, vol. ii, p. 361.

The Chaldean Patriarch Audu, head of the Uniat minority of the Assyrian nation, made a strong protest against a proposal to require of Uniat bishops papal confirmation before consecration (as if they were Latin bishops), instead of papal ratification with an oath of fidelity after consecration. The Pope sent for him the same evening, and offered him the choice between immediate deposition and his signed promise to consecrate two bishops whom the Pope had nominated, but whom he had not consecrated because of the disturbance it would cause. He signed, but told his friends that he did not consider the promise binding.[1]

It must be remembered that every bishop had been appointed with the approval of Pius IX or his predecessors. We have seen, in the cases of Steenoven and Wessenberg, how impossible it was for anyone of whom the Pope did not approve to be consecrated bishop. Pius IX had rejected the nominee of the Chapter of Westminster, and appointed Manning instead of him. All bishops had, of course, taken an oath of obedience to the Pope; but on January 6, 1870, they were compelled to renew it, a ceremony which took the whole day.[2]

The Council began by electing the members of the commission on the Faith. They were all members of the majority, and its strength became known. Some hoped that the dogma of Papal Infallibility would be carried by acclamation; but the 150 bishops of the opposition were too many for this to be possible. Archbishop Darboy threatened that he and his friends would leave the Council if it were attempted.[3] On February 22, with the object of hastening the business of the Council, new regulations were introduced. In future what was passed by the majority would be held to be passed by the Council; the majority was given the right to closure the debate; and the presidents were given the right to cut short any speech.[4]

The first of these innovations was fundamental; the opposition held the traditional doctrine that the decrees of a council must be unanimous, or nearly so. If they accepted the new regulation, they could not prevent the Council from decreeing anything that the Pope chose. All sections of the minority were agreed on this point. On March 22, Bishop Strossmayer, after protesting against a statement in a scheme of doctrine laid before the Council, that Protestantism was the origin of rationalism (his defence

[1] Butler, vol. i, p. 225; Nielsen, vol. ii, p. 333.
[2] Butler, vol. i, p. 194.   [3] Acton, p. 533.   [4] Acton, p. 539.

of the Protestants against this unjust attack caused some disturb-ance), attacked the abrogation of the ancient rule of moral unanimity. A tumult of indignation arose: the bishops refused to listen, calling out, " He is Lucifer, anathema, anathema "; " He is another Luther, let him be cast out "; " These people don't want the Infallibility of the Pope; is this man infallible himself? "[1]

The next day Strossmayer sent in a protest, which had been approved by the German bishops and others, declaring that he could not acknowledge the validity of the Council if dogmas were to be passed by a majority. Accordingly, the preamble to the proposed dogmatic degree, with its attack on Protestantism, was altered; and all were prepared to accept the decree. But at the last moment attention was called to the last paragraph of the decree, which ran as follows:

" And since it is not sufficient to shun heretical pravity, unless those errors also be diligently avoided which more or less nearly approach it, we admonish all men of the further duty of observing those constitutions and decrees, by which such erroneous opinions, as are not here specifically enumerated, have been proscribed and condemned by this Holy See."

This paragraph was not to be separated from the rest of the decree, which was to be taken as a whole. If the bishops of the opposition accepted it, they accepted by implication the Infalli-bility of the Pope. If they voted against it, they would vote that the acts of the Pope had no claim to be obeyed. They were caught in a trap. Strossmayer stayed away, but the rest voted for the decree. All that they could hope to do, after this, was to set limits to the conditions of Papal Infallibility.[2]

On May 9 the dogmatic constitution on the Church, in four chapters, was introduced. The first defined the institution of the apostolic primacy of St. Peter, a primacy of true and proper jurisdiction, not merely of honour; the second the perpetuity of this primacy of jurisdiction in the Roman Pontiffs; the third the universal ordinary jurisdiction of the Pope over all churches, together and separately and all and each of the pastors and the faithful; the fourth that the Pope, when he speaks *ex cathedra*, is infallible, and his decisions are irreformable.[3] The debate on the constitution in general was closured, in accordance with the new regulations, on June 3. The opposition protested, and

---

[1] Butler, vol. i, p. 272.    [2] Acton, p. 543.    [3] Butler, vol. ii, p. 271 ff.

appealed to the procedure at the Council of Trent, against that which was enforced by Pius IX; but the Tridentine rules had never been published, and the Pope dismissed Augustine Theiner, the keeper of the archives, from his post, because he was supposed to have allowed bishops of the opposition to examine them.[1]

The first two chapters were passed without opposition; the debate on the third chapter ended on June 14; the debate on the fourth on July 4. It was during this last debate that Cardinal Guidi made the speech for which he was rebuked by the Pope, as was related above. The vote on the third and fourth chapters took place on July 13; 451 bishops voted for it; sixty-two voted for it with reservations (*placet juxta modum*), but some of these thought it not strong enough; eighty-eight voted against it, among whom were all the leaders of the opposition. They made one more attempt to persuade the Pope to modify the decree by adding the words " based on the testimony of the churches "; but in vain.[2] They therefore decided to leave Rome rather than vote " Non placet " at the public session. Hefele, Haynald, and Ginouilhac (now Archbishop of Lyons and Primate of France) opposed this plan, but they were over-persuaded. Accordingly they departed. " Monseigneur," said Haynald to Dupanloup, in the train, " we have made a great mistake "; but it was irreparable.[3]

Only July 18 the final vote took place; 533 voted for the decrees, and two against, Biccio, Bishop of Cajazzo in Naples, and Fitzgerald, Bishop of Little Rock in America. The voting took place during a tremendous thunderstorm. Both the bishops who voted against the decrees submitted immediately.

The Council dispersed for the summer; the bishops were ordered to meet again on November 11, St. Martin's Day. But before that day came great changes had taken place. War broke out between France and Prussia on July 19; soon afterwards the French garrison was withdrawn from Rome. On September 20 the Italians occupied the city; and the " States of the Church ", which had been under the civil government of the Popes for 1,100 years, came to an end. On October 20 the Pope suspended the Council indefinitely; and it is held by some to be still sitting, by a kind of legal fiction (though not a single member of it is still alive), because it was never formally closed.

[1] Nielsen, vol. ii, p. 360.     [2] Butler, vol. ii, p. 157; Nielsen, p. 364.
[3] Nielsen, vol. ii, p. 370.

The Vatican Council put an end to Gallicanism in all its forms. The controversy between the conciliar and the papal supremacy, which had lasted for five centuries, was now at an end.

From the historical standpoint every one of the four chapters of the constitution on the Church is false. That St. Peter had a primacy of jurisdiction over the other Apostles is contrary to the evidence of the New Testament.[1] That the Bishops of Rome are in a special sense the successors of St. Peter is a statement for which there is no real evidence at all.[2] That " it is necessary that every church should agree with the Roman Church " is a false interpretation of St. Irenaeus.[3] That the Pope has always been held to have immediate ordinary jurisdiction over each and all of the faithful, and to be infallible when he speaks *ex cathedra* on faith and morals, is contrary to the plainest facts of history. But to all this every Roman Catholic, since the Vatican Council, is irrevocably committed.

On the other hand, the Vatican Council, like the Council of Trent before it, only defined what had long been believed by most members of the Roman Communion. If the Church is to be governed by an infallible authority, as Gallicans no less than Ultramontanes believed, the Pope, who is always there, is a more effective infallible authority than a council, which may not meet for centuries. Ever since Trent, the Church had been governed on the assumption that there was no appeal from the decisions of the Pope. The belief of some that a council was above the Pope, a council, however, which only the Pope could summon, was a source of weakness. The Vatican Council did no more than fill up the gaps in the Tridentine system. Gallicanism was not a permanently tenable theory; for it gave the Pope either too much, or not enough. Since the whole working system of the Roman Communion was Ultramontane, it was perhaps better that the outside world should be under no illusions. Even Dr. Pusey, who had long been working for reunion with Rome on the basis of the dogmas of Trent and no more, gave up all hope after the Vatican Council.[4] At the same time the infallibility defined by the Council was the old doctrine of Bellarmine, not the wild ideas of Veuillot and W. G.

[1] E. Denny, *Papalism*, 75 ff, 903–913; Nielsen, vol. ii, p. 370.
[2] Denny, 464–493. (See above, p. 8.)  [3] Denny, 508 ff. (See above, p. 10.)
[4] He altered the title of his Eirenicon to " Healthful Reunion as conceived possible before the Vatican Council."

Ward. According to the Council, the Pope is infallible only when "in discharge of his office as pastor and teacher of all Christians, by virtue of his supreme apostolic authority he defines a doctrine regarding faith or morals to be held by the universal Church ".

It has never been officially stated which papal utterances are regarded as infallible. Father Dublanchy, in the *Dictionnaire de Théologie Catholique*, gives a list of twelve, which are commonly regarded as certainly infallible.[1] They include six positive statements, from the Tome of Leo to the proclamation of the Immaculate Conception; and six sentences of condemnation, those against Luther (among the propositions of Luther which were condemned was " Hereticos comburi est contra voluntatem Spiritus "—" The burning of heretics is contrary to the will of the Spirit "; the righteousness of burning heretics is therefore asserted by an infallible utterance), Jansen (the Five Propositions), Molinos, Fénélon, Quesnel (the Bull " Unigenitus "), and the Council of Pistoia (Febronianism). Some have added to these the condemnation of Anglican Orders by Leo XIII, and the decrees of Pius X against Modernism. The Syllabus of Errors is not now commonly held to be an infallible utterance. But the subjects of the Pope are obliged to accept " with sincere interior assent " many of his utterances which are not infallible.

The dogma of the universal ordinary jurisdiction of the Pope has not received the same attention as the dogma of his infallibility; but, as Dom Cuthbert Butler says,[2] it presents even greater difficulties to those outside the Roman Communion.

I have described the efforts of those who from time to time tried to reform the Roman Communion by decentralizing it, to reduce the papal supremacy to a mere office of inspection and direction (as in the proposals made to Archbishop Wake), and to bring about reunion with other churches on this basis. (It was said at the time of the " Malines Conversations ",[3] whether correctly or not I do not know, that Cardinal Mercier had some such object in view.) But any such attempt was ruled out for ever by the Vatican Council. Henceforward, no constitutional or modified Papacy is possible. Either the complete Ultramontane claims, as defined by the Vatican Council, must be accepted as part of the Divine revelation, or the Papacy must be rejected altogether.

[1] Butler, vol. ii, p. 227.    [2] Butler, vol. ii, p. 79.
[3] A discussion between some Anglican and Belgian theologians in 1921–1925, sanctioned by Archbishop Davidson and Cardinal Mercier.

### Appendix C.—The Constitution " Pastor Æternus ".

Pius, Bishop, Servant of the Servants of God, with the approval of the Sacred Council, for a perpetual remembrance.

The Eternal Pastor and Bishop of our souls, in order to continue for all time the life-giving work of His redemption, determined to build up the Holy Church, wherein, as in the house of the living God, all who believe might be united in the bond of one faith and one charity. Wherefore, before He entered into His glory, he prayed unto the Father, not for the apostles only, but for those who through their preaching should come to believe in Him, that all might be one even as He the Son and the Father are one.[1] As then He sent the apostles whom He had chosen to Himself from the world, as He Himself had been sent by the Father: so He willed that there should be pastors and teachers in His Church even to the end of the world. And in order that the episcopate also might be one and undivided, and that by means of a closely united priesthood the multitude of the faithful might be kept secure in the unity of faith and communion, He set Blessed Peter over the rest of the apostles, and fixed in him the perpetual principle of the twofold unity, and its visible foundation, in the strength of which the everlasting temple should be erected, and the Church in the firmness of his faith should lift her majestic front to heaven.[2] And seeing that the gates of hell with daily increase of hatred are gathering their strength on every side against the foundation laid by God's own hand, in order to overthrow the Church, if that might be: We, therefore, for the preservation, safe-keeping, and increase of the Catholic flock, with the approval of the sacred Council, judge it to be necessary to propose for the belief and acceptance of all the faithful, in accordance with the ancient and constant faith of the universal Church, the doctrine concerning the institution, perpetuity, and nature of the sacred Apostolic primacy, in which is found the strength and solidity of the entire Church, and at the same time to proscribe and condemn the contrary errors, so full of destruction to the Lord's flock.

[1] St. John 17. 41.
[2] St. Leo, Sermon IV, ch. 2 (St. Leo was the first Pope to make this extensive claim).

### CHAPTER I OF THE INSTITUTION OF THE APOSTOLIC PRIMACY IN BLESSED PETER

We, therefore, teach and declare that, according to the testimony of the Gospel, the primacy of jurisdiction over the universal Church of God was immediately and directly promised and given to Blessed Peter the Apostle by Christ the Lord. For it was to Simon alone, to whom He had already said, " Thou shalt be called Cephas ",[1] that the Lord, after he had uttered his confession, saying, " Thou art the Christ, the Son of the living God ", addressed these solemn words: " Blessed art thou, Simon Bar-Jona; because flesh and blood hath not revealed it unto thee, but My Father which is in heaven. And I say unto thee that thou art Peter, and upon this rock I will build My Church, and the gates of hell shall not prevail against it; and I will give unto thee the keys of the kingdom of heaven; and whatsoever thou shalt have bound on earth, shall be bound also in heaven; and whatsoever thou shalt have loosed on earth, shall be loosed also in heaven." [2] And it was upon Simon alone that Jesus after His resurrection bestowed the jurisdiction of chief pastor and ruler over all His fold, saying, " Feed My lambs: feed My sheep." [3] At open variance with this clear doctrine of Holy Scripture, as it has been always understood by the Catholic Church, are the perverse opinions of those who, while they distort the form of government established by Christ the Lord in His Church, deny that Peter in his single person, before all the other apostles, either singly or all together, was endowed by Christ with a true and proper primacy of jurisdiction; or of those who assert that the same primacy was not bestowed immediately and directly upon Blessed Peter himself, but upon the Church, and through the Church on Peter as her minister.

If anyone, therefore, shall say that Blessed Peter the Apostle was not appointed the Prince of all the apostles and the visible head of the whole Church militant; or that he directly and immediately received from our Lord Jesus Christ a primacy of honour only, and not of true and proper jurisdiction: let him be anathema.

[1] St. John 1. 42.
[2] St. Matt. 16. 16–19.
[3] St. John 21. 15–17.

CHAPTER II.  OF THE PERPETUITY OF THE PRIMACY OF
BLESSED PETER IN THE ROMAN PONTIFFS

That which the Prince of Shepherds and great Shepherd of the
sheep, the Lord Jesus Christ, established in the person of the
Blessed Apostle Peter for the perpetual welfare and lasting good
of the Church, must, by the same institution, necessarily remain
unceasingly in the Church, which, being founded upon a rock,
will stand firm to the end of the world.  For no one can doubt,
and it is known to all ages, that the holy and most blessed Peter,
the prince and head of the apostles, the pillar of faith and foundation of the Catholic Church, received the keys of the kingdom
from our Lord Jesus Christ, the Saviour and Redeemer of the
human race, and lives, presides, and judges, to this day and always,
in his successors the bishops of the holy see of Rome, which was
founded by him, and consecrated by his blood.[1]  Whence, who-
soever succeeds to Peter in this see, obtains, by the institution
of Christ Himself, the primacy of Peter over the whole Church.
The disposition of the truth therefore remains, and Blessed
Peter, abiding in the strength of the rock that he received, has not
given up the direction of the Church undertaken by him.[2]
Wherefore it has at all times been necessary that the Church, that
is, the faithful throughout the world, should agree with the Roman
Church, on account of its more powerful principality;[3] that
in that see, from which the rights of communion flow forth to all,
being associated as members with the head, they may grow
together into one compacted body.[4]

If then, anyone shall say that it is not by the institution of

[1] *Acts of the Council of Ephesus*, Session 3.  (This statement, as far as the words
"his successors", was made at the Council by Philip, the Roman legate.  It
is not certain that by "the successors of St. Peter" he meant the Bishops of
Rome *only*, and not all bishops: the last words of the sentence are no part of
what he said.  If he did mean what the Vatican Council thought he meant,
the Council of Ephesus did not endorse it, but acted afterwards in a manner
inconsistent with it.  See Denny, *Papalism*, 736 ff.).

[2] St. Leo, Sermon 3, ch. 3.

[3] St. Irenæus, *Against Heresies*, III, 3 (see above, page 28.  The words *convenire
ad* do not mean "agree with", but "resort to": and *principalitas* means "pre-
eminence among equals", not "sovereignty".  Also, "necesse" means not
"ought", but "must by the nature of things": it must happen that Christians
from all parts of the Empire are found in the capital.  See F. W. Puller, *Primitive
Saints and the See of Rome*, pp. 26 ff; Denny, *op. cit.*, 501–516.)

[4] *Acts of the Synod of Aquileia*, A.D. 381.  (Quoted here in a sense inconsistent
with the circumstances and context of the original passage, and with other
statements made elsewhere by its authors.  See Denny, *op. cit.*, 536–543.)

Christ the Lord, or by Divine right, that blessed Peter should have a perpetual line of successors in the primacy over the universal Church: or that the Roman Pontiff is not the successor of Blessed Peter in the primacy : let him be anathema.

### CHAPTER III. OF THE POWER AND NATURE OF THE PRIMACY OF THE ROMAN PONTIFF

Wherefore, relying on plain testimonies of the sacred writings, and adhering to the clear and express decrees both of our predecessors, the Roman Pontiffs, and of the general councils, we renew the definition of the œcumenical Council of Florence, in virtue of which all the faithful must believe that the holy apostolic see and the Roman Pontiff possesses the primacy over the whole world, and that the Roman Pontiff is the successor of Blessed Peter, Prince of the Apostles, and is the true Vicar of Christ, and Head of the whole Church, and the father and teacher of all Christians: and that full power was given to him in Blessed Peter to feed, rule, and govern the Universal Church, by our Lord Jesus Christ; as is also contained in the acts of the œcumenical councils, and in the sacred canons.

Hence we teach and declare that by the appointment of our Lord the Roman Church possesses a superiority of ordinary power over all other churches, and that this power of jurisdiction of the Roman Pontiff, which is truly episcopal, is immediate; to which all, of whatever rite and dignity, both pastors and faithful, both individually and collectively, are bound, by their duty of hierarchical subordination and true obedience, to submit, not only in matters which belong to faith and morals, but also in those that appertain to the discipline and government of the Church throughout the world, so that the Church of Christ may be one flock under one supreme pastor through the preservation of unity both of communion and of profession of the same faith with the Roman Pontiff. This is the teaching of Catholic truth, from which no one can deviate without loss of faith and salvation.

But so far is the power of the Supreme Pontiff from being opposed to the ordinary and immediate power of episcopal jurisdiction, by which bishops, who have been set by the Holy Ghost to succeed and hold the place of the Apostles,[1] feed and govern, each in his own flock, as true pastors, that their episcopal

[1] *Council of Trent,* 33rd session, ch. 4.

authority is really asserted, strengthened, and protected by the supreme and universal pastor; in accordance with the words of St. Gregory the Great: " My honour is the honour of the whole Church. My honour is the firm strength of my brother. I am truly honoured, when the honour due to each and all is not withheld." [1]

Further, from this supreme power of governing the Universal Church possessed by the Roman Pontiff, it follows that he has the right of free communication with the pastors of the whole Church, and with their flocks, that these may be taught and ruled by him in the way of salvation. Wherefore we condemn and reject the opinions of those who hold that the communication between this supreme Head and the pastors and their flocks can lawfully be impeded; or who make this communication subject to the will of the secular power, so as to maintain that whatever is done by the Apostolic See, or by its authority, for the government of the Church, cannot have force or value unless it be confirmed by the assent of the secular power. And since by the Divine right of the apostolic primacy, the Roman Pontiff is placed over the Universal Church, we further teach and declare that he is the supreme judge of the faithful,[2] and that in all causes, the decision of which belongs to the Church, recourse may be had to his tribunal,[3] and that none may reopen the judgment of the Apostolic See, than the authority of which there is none greater, nor can any lawfully review its judgment.[4] Wherefore they err from the right path of truth, who assert that it is lawful to appeal from the judgments of the Roman Pontiffs to an Œcumenical Council, as to an authority higher than that of the Roman Pontiff.

---

[1] St. Gregory the Great, *Letters*, VIII, 30. (The words occur in a letter to Eulogius, Patriarch of Alexandria, announcing the success of St. Augustine's mission to the English, and are preceded by the words, " Nor do I consider that an honour, by which I acknowledge that my brethren lose their own ". The Vatican Council deliberately refused to add these words: but without them the quotation is misleading, for St. Gregory is protesting against being addressed as " Universal Pope ". See Denny, *op. cit.*, 1104 ff.)

[2] Pius VI, Brief " Super soliditate ", November 28, 1786.

[3] *Acts of the Council of Lyons*, A.D. 1274. (This statement was based on forged interpolations in the writings of the Greek Fathers, universally accepted as genuine by the Latins at that period, but always recognized as forgeries by the Greeks. See Denny, *op. cit.*, 819 ff.)

[4] Pope Nicholas I, Letter 8, to the Emperor Michael III, A.D. 858. (This statement was based on a fictitious account of the non-existent Council of Sinuessa, which was accepted as genuine in ninth-century Rome, but has long been universally recognized to be unhistorical. See Denny, *op. cit.*, 970–972.)

If then anyone shall say that the Roman Pontiff has the office merely of inspection or direction, but not full and supreme power of jurisdiction over the Universal Church, not only in those things which belong to faith and morals, but also in those things which belong to the discipline and government of the Church spread throughout the world; or that he possesses merely the principal part, and not the whole fulness of this supreme power; or that this power which he enjoys is not ordinary and immediate, both over all and each of the churches and over all and each of the pastors and the faithful : let him be anathema.

CHAPTER IV.   OF THE INFALLIBLE TEACHING POWER OF THE
ROMAN PONTIFF

Moreover, that the supreme power of teaching is also included in the apostolic primacy, which the Roman Pontiff, as the successor of Peter, Prince of the Apostles, possesses over the whole Church, this holy see has always held, the perpetual practice of the Church confirms, and œcumenical councils also have declared, especially those in which the East with the West met in the union of faith and charity.   For the Fathers of the Fourth Council of Constantinople, following in the footsteps of their predecessors, gave forth this solemn profession: " The first condition of salvation is to keep the rule of the true faith.   And because the sentence of our Lord Jesus Christ cannot be passed over, Who said, ' Thou art Peter, and upon this rock I will build My Church ',[1] these things which have been said are approved by events, because in the apostolic see the catholic religion has always been kept undefiled, and its holy doctrine proclaimed.   Desiring, therefore, not to be in the least degree separated from the faith and doctrine of that see, we hope that we may deserve to be in the one communion, which the apostolic see preaches, in which is the entire and true solidity of the Christian religion." [2]   And, with the approval of the 2nd Council of Lyons,

[1] St. Matt. 17. 18.
[2] From the Formula of St. Hormisdas the Pope, as proposed by Hadrian II and the Fathers of the eighth General Council (fourth of Constantinople) and signed by them, A.D. 869.   (This Council, though now regarded by Rome as the eighth Œcumenical Council, has been rejected by the whole Eastern Orthodox Communion since 879.   This rejection was admitted by the Council of Florence, which in its own acts called itself the eighth Œcumenical Council, and was also so called by Pope Clement VI, though Rome now regards it as the seventeenth.   See Denny, op. cit., 919.   The researches of Professor Dvornik have shown that this Council was not œcumenical, and was only

the Greeks professed that the holy Roman Church enjoys supreme and full primacy over the whole Catholic Church, which it truly and humbly recognizes that it has received with the plenitude of power from our Lord Himself in the person of Blessed Peter, Prince or Head of the apostles, whose successor the Roman Pontiff is; and as the apostolic see is bound before all others to defend the truth of faith, so also if any questions regarding faith shall arise, they must be defined by its judgment.[1]   Finally, the Council of Florence defined: That the Roman Pontiff is the true Vicar of Christ, and the Head of the whole Church, and the father and teacher of all Christians; and that to him in Blessed Peter was delivered by our Lord Jesus Christ the full power of feeding, ruling, and governing the Universal Church.[2]

To satisfy this pastoral duty our predecessors always made unwearied efforts that the salutary doctrine of Christ should be propagated among all the nations of the earth, and with equal care watched, that it might be preserved genuine and pure where it had been received.   Therefore, the bishops of the whole world, now singly, now assembled in synods, following the long-established custom of churches,[3] and the form of the ancient rule,[4] sent word to this apostolic see of those dangers especially which sprang up in matters of faith, that the losses of faith might there

---

reckoned as being so by a later error.   The formula of Hormisdas was written in 516, for the purpose of reconciling Constantinople.   Some of its statements are contrary to well-known historic facts.   It was accepted by Constantinople in the sense that Rome and Constantinople constitute one see, which is not the sense intended by the Vatican Council.   The rest of the Greek churches refused to accept it, and were ultimately reconciled to Rome through a different formula.   Further, it seems probable that the text of the formula, as accepted by the Greek bishops at the Council of 869, did not contain the words about the prerogatives of the Roman see, which were only in the Latin text. In any case, the Greek churches repudiated this Council ten years later, as we have seen, and also at the Council of Florence, 1439.   See Denny, op. cit., 800–813 and 918).

[1] Acts of the Fourteenth General Council (second of Lyons), A.D. 1274.   (The Greeks present at this Council were merely the ambassadors of the Emperor Michael VIII, who was anxious for union with Rome for political reasons. The Council was from the first repudiated by the Greek bishops and people.)

[2] Acts of the Seventeenth General Council of Florence, A.D. 1438.   (This Council was not only rejected by all the Eastern Churches, the Greek bishops who signed it being repudiated as soon as they returned home, but also by the Gallicans, on the ground that the Pope had no right to remove the Council from Basle. See Denny, op. cit., 259, 1191.)

[3] Letter of Cyril of Alexandria to Celestine I of Rome, A.D. 422.

[4] Rescript of Innocent I of Rome to the Council of Milevis (in Africa). (See Denny, op. cit., 633–638, who shows that Innocent's claims were not founded on fact.)

be most effectually repaired where the faith cannot fail.[1] And the Roman Pontiffs, according to the needs of times and circumstances, sometimes assembling œcumenical councils, or asking for the mind of the Church scattered throughout the world, sometimes by particular synods, sometimes using other helps which Divine providence supplied, defined those things to be held, which with the help of God they had recognized as agreeing with the Sacred Scriptures and apostolic traditions. For the Holy Spirit was not promised to the successors of Peter that by His revelation they might make known new doctrine, but that by His assistance they might inviolably keep and faithfully expound the revelation or deposit of faith delivered through the Apostles. And indeed all the venerable Fathers have embraced and the holy orthodox doctors have venerated and followed their apostolic doctrine; knowing most fully that this see of St. Peter remains ever free from all blemish of error, according to the Divine promise of the Lord our Saviour made to the prince of His disciples: " I have prayed for thee that thy faith fail not, and when thou art converted, strengthen thy brethren." [2]

This gift, then, of truth and never-failing faith was Divinely conferred upon Peter and his successors in this chair, that they might perform their high office for the salvation of all: that the whole flock of Christ being kept away by them from the poisonous food of error, might be nourished with the pasture of heavenly doctrine; that by the removal of the opportunity of schism, the whole Church might be kept one, and, resting on its foundation, might stand firm against the gates of hell.

But since in this very age, in which the salutary efficacy of the apostolic office is most of all required, not a few are found who take away from its authority, we judge it altogether necessary solemnly to assert the prerogative which the only begotten Son of God deigned to join with the supreme pastoral office.

Therefore, faithfully adhering to the tradition received from the

[1] St. Bernard, Epistle 191, to Pope Innocent II. (St. Bernard, of course, accepted the Pseudo-Isidorian Decretals as genuine, see above, pp. 12, 110.)
[2] St. Luke 22. 32. See also the *Acts of the Sixth General Council.* (This is an unfortunate reference. Pope Agatho, writing to the Sixth General Council, was the first to interpret the passage in this way. The Council did not agree with him, for it condemned his predecessor, Pope Honorius, as a heretic. Archbishop Kenrick, of St. Louis, U.S.A., in the speech which he prepared for the Vatican Council, but was not allowed to deliver, pointed out that the words "when thou art converted" make this interpretation of the passage impossible; Denny, *op. cit.*, 159.)

beginning of the Christian faith, for the glory of God our Saviour, the exaltation of the catholic religion, and the salvation of Christian nations, we, with the approval of the sacred Council, teach and define that it is a dogma Divinely revealed that the Roman Pontiff, when he speaks " ex cathedra ", that is, when discharging his office of pastor and teacher of all Christians, by virtue of his supreme apostolic authority, he defines a doctrine regarding faith or morals to be held by the Universal Church, by the Divine assistance promised to him in Blessed Peter, possesses that infallibility with which the Divine Redeemer willed that His Church should be endowed for defining doctrine regarding faith or morals : and that therefore such definitions of the Roman Pontiff are irreformable of themselves, and not from the consent of the Church.

But if anyone presumes to contradict this our definition (which may God avert), let him be anathema.

(The translation is based on Dom Cuthbert Butler's *Vatican Council*, vol. ii, pp. 277–295.)

The references in the notes are part of the text of the Constitution " Pastor Aeternus ". The sentences in brackets are my comments on them.

# CHAPTER XVI

## THE SUBMISSION OF THE BISHOPS

THE Vatican Council had defined its new dogmas, and laid an anathema on all who should refuse to accept them. Every bishop was required to accept them formally himself, and to publish them in his diocese. What would the bishops of the opposition and their supporters do?

Most of them had been "inopportunists": they believed the dogmas to be true, but thought it a mistake to define them formally. For these there was nothing to prevent acceptance of the decision of the Council. But there were a few who held the dogmas to be not merely inopportune but false; and some of these found themselves faced by a most difficult conflict of duties.

The bishops of the opposition had agreed, before they left Rome, to do nothing without consulting one another.[1] But they could not keep their promise. The French and German bishops could not communicate with one another, for their countries were at war. Early in September, Cardinal Schwarzenberg, Archbishop of Prague, wrote to Cardinal Mathieu, Archbishop of Besançon, to ask what the French bishops would do.[2] Mathieu, who had already, on August 8, made his submission,[3] replied that the French bishops of the minority would make no further objection to the œcumenical character of the Council. Before the end of the year they had all come in, except Archbishop Darboy of Paris; and he sent his submission to the Pope as soon as the siege of Paris was over.

According to the older teaching of the Church, the definitions of an œcumenical council required to be confirmed by the whole Church, either through the bishops, or with the assent of the clergy and laity. The latter is the doctrine of the Orthodox Eastern Communion (at any rate according to the teaching of some of its divines);[4] it denies the Latin distinction between "*ecclesia*

[1] Hefele to Döllinger, ap. Schulte, *Das Altkatholizismus*, p. 221.
[2] Butler, *Vatican Council*, vol. ii, p. 173.          [3] Butler, vol. ii, p. 170.
[4] Stefan Zankov, *Orthodox Eastern Church*, tr. Lowrie, p. 94 (he follows Khomiakov).

*docens* " (teaching Church) and " *ecclesia discens* " (learning Church), and claims that even the laity has sometimes remained faithful to orthodoxy when the bishops have fallen away from it. The history of general councils shows that in earlier times their ratification by the bishops who had not been present was considered necessary. Thus St. Athanasius, when arguing against the Arians, did not claim that the decrees of the First Council of Nicæa were binding, before they had been received by all the local churches, but that they were in accordance with the traditional faith.[1] The Council of Nicæa was not known to or accepted by the Assyrian Church until eighty years after it took place.[2] Nor were later councils regarded as having authority in a local church until they had been ratified there. The Fifth General Council was not confirmed at Aquileia until A.D. 700. The acts of the Sixth General Council were sent by Pope Agatho to the Spanish bishops, and confirmed by them at the Fourteenth Council of Toledo, A.D. 684; otherwise they would have had no authority in Spain.[3] The Second Council of Nicæa was rejected by the Council of Frankfort, A.D. 794, representing the Churches of Germany, France, and England (under a misapprehension, no doubt, of its actual teaching); it does not appear to have been formally accepted by these churches before the fifteenth century, if then. The Council of Florence was rejected by all the Eastern churches, though some of the leading Greek bishops had accepted its decrees for political reasons (see above, ch. III, p. 80).

Even as late as 1864 Lord Acton could write : " The Church exists expressly for the purpose of preserving a definite body of truths, the knowledge of which she can never lose. Whatever authority, therefore, expresses that knowledge of which she is the keeper must be obeyed. But there is no institution from which this knowledge can be obtained with immediate certainty. A Council is not *à priori* œcumenical; the Holy See is not separately infallible. The one has to await a sanction, the other has repeatedly erred." [4]

But Lord Acton, with all his learning, belonged to the extreme left wing of the Roman Communion. Both Ultramontanes and Gallicans had long held that the decrees of an œcumenical

---

[1] Denny, *Papalism*, 1281; Athanasius, Encyclical, in Migne, *Patres Græci*, vol. 25, p. 549.
[2] W. A. Wigram, *The Assyrians and their Neighbours*, p. 52.
[3] Bossuet, *Defensio Declarationis Cleri Gallicani*, vol. ii, p. 52, ap. Denny, 1042.
[4] Lord Acton, *History of Freedom* and other essays, p. 477.

council required only the ratification of the Pope, not that of the Church at large.  Archbishop Laud gave as his first reason for rejecting the legality of the Council of Trent, that it claimed the right " to conclude any controversy." [1]  According to Gallican principles, at any rate as held in the nineteenth century, an œcumenical council, ratified by the Pope, was infallible, and required no further confirmation.  Therefore the Vatican Council could only be rejected, by those who held this view, on the ground that it was not œcumenical, as being not free, or not representative, or that it was not yet finished.  But when the vast majority of the bishops, including those of the opposition, had submitted, it became difficult for individual bishops to maintain that the Council did not really represent the mind of the Church; and when the Pope had prorogued it, the plea that it was not finished ceased to be more than technically true.

The real objections to accepting the Council, felt by those who led the revolt against it, were more profound.  They were, that the new dogmas were not " the ancient and constant faith of the Universal Church ", since they were unknown for many centuries, and since their later acceptance was largely based on forged documents;  and that the claim to direct authority over every individual might involve the revival of the medieval claims of the Papacy to interfere with the rights of civil governments, and even to depose kings.

The Vatican Council did not permit the defence of the papal claims as a development.  This would have cut the ground from under the feet of the opposition, but it was too dangerous a weapon for Rome to employ.  For if the papal claims have increased, they may hereafter decrease;  if Papalism is a development, so are other forms of Christianity.  The Vatican Council laid down explicitly that the infallibility and universal ordinary jurisdiction of the Pope had been held by the whole Church ever since St. Peter.

To show the absurdity of such a claim, we need not go beyond the nineteenth century.  *Keenan's Catechism* was a controversial book, carrying the imprimatur of four bishops, and widely circulated throughout the British Isles, 1846–60.  It contained the following question and answer:—

" Must not Catholics believe the Pope in himself to be infallible? "

[1] William Laud, *Conference with Fisher*, sect. 27;  More and Cross, *Anglicanism*, p. 74.

" This is a Protestant invention: it is no article of the Catholic faith; no decision of his can oblige, under pain of heresy, unless it be received and enforced by the teaching body; that is, by the bishops of the Church ".[1]

In 1788 a document repudiating the right of the Pope to absolve subjects from allegiance to their sovereign, the theory that princes excommunicated by the Pope may be deposed or murdered, and the doctrine of the Infallibility of the Pope, was signed by 1,523 English Romanists, including all the four bishops (vicars-apostolic) (one of them afterwards withdrew his signature), and 240 priests, the great majority of the clergy of the Roman Communion in England at that time. This protest was the cause of the Relief Act of 1790.[2]   In 1793 a similar Bill was passed in Ireland giving relief from civil disabilities to those who would take an oath repudiating Papal Infallibility. Again, before the Roman Catholic Emancipation Act of 1827, the Irish Romanist bishops gave evidence before a Parliamentary committee that they and their flocks rejected the infallibility and unlimited spiritual authority of the Pope and his right to absolve subjects from their civil allegiance. It was in consequence of this that the Emancipation Act was passed.[3]   Among those who at that time repudiated the Papal Infallibility was John MacHale, who survived to sit in the Vatican Council as Archbishop of Tuam and speak and vote for the opposition.[4]

The truth is that the Infallibility and Universal Ordinary Jurisdiction of the Pope, far from being " the ancient and constant faith of the Church ", had in quite modern times not reached many parts of the Roman Communion. Though taken for granted at Rome and in Southern Europe, at least since the days of Bellarmine, they were formally rejected in France, under the Gallican Articles, until the Revolution; they had not penetrated into the British Isles before 1831, but then became widespread through the work of Cardinal Wiseman in England and Cardinal Cullen in Ireland; and in the German-speaking countries there was still at the time of the Vatican Council a large party which had never held them.

---

[1] G. Salmon, *Infallibility of the Church*, p. 25;   W. J. Sparrow-Simpson, *Papal Infallibility*, pp. 111 ff.
[2] Sparrow-Simpson, p. 100.
[3] Salmon, p. 264; Archbishop Kenrick, ap. G. C. Coulton, *Papal Infallibility*, p. 188.
[4] *Theodorus* (J. B. Mullinger), *The New Reformation*, p. 83.

The second objection to the acceptance of the new dogmas—the fear that the medieval claim of the Papacy to temporal sovereignty over all Christian countries was being revived—was, whether justified or not, widely spread, especially among the laity; and was supported by W. E. Gladstone in his book on *Vaticanism* (1874).

Why was it, that though the intellectual difficulty of accepting the new dogmas was so great, the bishops of the opposition did all at last submit? It is not enough to say that they yielded to pressure, or that they could not face the consequences of refusal. No doubt these reasons had their effect. But the bishops were also controlled by the dogma of the oracular infallibility of general councils. In the words of the German bishops' Pastoral of August 30, 1870: "These decisions (of general councils), according to the unanimous and undoubted tradition of the Church, have always been held to be preserved from error by a Divine and supernatural assistance. Hence the faithful in all times have submitted themselves to these decisions as to the infallible utterances of the Holy Ghost Himself." [1]    Dom Cuthbert Butler says: "I have been met with the question: 'What, do you say it was right for these bishops to go against their intellectual convictions?' Yes, surely; that is what it is to be a Catholic." [2] This is called "the sacrifice of the intellect", and is regarded by Roman Catholics as a highly praiseworthy and meritorious act. It was, however, as we have seen, indignantly refused by Archbishop van Santen of Utrecht (ch. XII, p. 190). It presents an ethical difference between Rome and the rest of Christendom, as great as any dogmatic difference.

But in what sense is the oracular infallibility of general councils a unanimous tradition of the Church? The tradition which the Council of Trent made equal to Scripture was apostolic tradition. But neither Scripture nor apostolic tradition could teach the infallibility of general councils, for there was no general council before A.D. 325. The oracular infallibility of general councils is a tradition created, not received, by Rome. The promise made by our Lord, that the gates of Hades should not prevail against His Church and that the Holy Ghost should lead His disciples into all truth, did not necessarily bestow inability to err. The distinction is made clear by Archbishop Laud: "Into all truth, is a limited 'all': into all truth absolutely necessary to

---

[1] Butler, vol. ii, p. 180.          [2] Butler, vol. ii, p. 168.

salvation. A Church may err, and dangerously too, and yet not fall from the foundation." [1] So also William Chillingworth says: "You must . . . be so acute as to distinguish between being infallible in fundamentals, and being an infallible guide in fundamentals. That there shall always be a Church infallible in fundamentals, we freely grant; for it comes to no more than this, that there shall always be a Church. That there shall always be such a Church which shall be an infallible guide in fundamentals, this we deny." [2]

The French bishops of the opposition, as we have seen, had all submitted by the end of 1870; and there was no popular opposition in France to the acceptance of the Vatican Council. Bishop Las Cases, of Constantine and Hippo in Algeria (the see of St. Augustine), left in his will a statement that he had never been an "inopportunist", but that on the morrow of the Council God had given him grace to say with entire truth, "I believe to-day in the infallibility as fully as I disbelieved in it yesterday"! [3]

In the United States, Archbishop Kenrick of St. Louis was the only bishop who found difficulty in accepting the new dogmas. Nevertheless in October he submitted unreservedly to the decision of the Council, as an act of pure obedience, without in any way withdrawing his objections to the new dogmas on historical grounds. In a letter to Lord Acton, written March 29, 1871, he explained his position at length. He tried to reconcile himself to the new dogmas by means of Newman's theory of development, arguing that the Papal Supremacy was now very different from what it appeared to have been in the early Church, so it might be the same with the Infallibility (a plea which, as has been shown, the terms of the Constitution "Pastor Aeternus" do not allow). However, he declared that, in spite of his submission, he would never teach the doctrine of Papal Infallibility, so as to argue from Scripture or tradition in its support, but would confine himself in future to his administrative functions. [4] Dr. Sparrow-Simpson's comment is: "The records of intellectual servitude present few more painful documents than this. Whether one regards the doctrine, the Archbishop, or the facts of history, such an attitude bristles with intellectual, if not moral, inconsistencies. . . . The

---

[1] Laud, *Conference with Fisher*, section 33, ap. More and Cross, p. 158.
[2] W. Chillingworth, *Religion of Protestants*, ap. More and Cross, p. 113.
[3] Butler, vol. ii, p. 171.
[4] J. F. von Schulte, *Das Altkatholizismus*, p. 269.

sole virtue by which everything else is supposed to be redeemed is the virtue of submission. Theories such as this can only exist as a dark background to enhance the moral and spiritual superiority of sincere unbelief and genuine schism." [1]

In Ireland there were two bishops, Archbishop MacHale of Tuam and Bishop Moriarty of Kerry, who were never required to submit formally or to promulgate the decrees. In 1875 they signed with the other Roman Catholic bishops a joint pastoral enforcing the Infallibility as being of faith. [2]

In Germany there were at that time twenty-three bishoprics, one of which—Gnesen-Posen—was regarded by its occupant as Polish rather than German. Of the remaining twenty-two bishops, seventeen met at Fulda on August 30, and issued a pastoral enforcing the new dogmas, of which more hereafter. The five who did not sign this pastoral were Deinlein of Bamberg, Förster of Breslau, Beckmann of Osnabrück, Hefele of Rottenburg, and Forwerk, Bishop of Leontopolis and Vicar-Apostolic in Saxony. Archbishop Deinlein, in a letter written on November 13, 1870, declared that he had only opposed the new dogmas as inopportune. [3] Förster, the Prince-Bishop of Breslau, found himself in a specially difficult position, pressed by the professors of the university, headed by Joseph Hubert Reinkens, to resist the new dogmas, and by the majority of his people to accept them. He asked the Pope to allow him to resign his see, but permission was refused. He accordingly proclaimed the new dogmas in a pastoral dated October 20, 1870.

Bishop Beckmann of Osnabrück published the decrees, January 19, 1871.

Bishop Hefele's position was more difficult: of all the bishops of the opposition he was the most learned, and the most firmly convinced that the new dogmas were contrary to the facts of history. Being the author of the standard history of Church Councils, he had every reason for knowing. He was in close sympathy with Döllinger, to whom he wrote as follows, on August 10, 1870: "I am in no uncertainty as to what I have to do, and in this I am in agreement with the cathedral chapter and the faculty (of theology). I shall, in the first place be in no hurry with my answer, and I shall do all I can to call into existence a meeting of our German friends. Moreover, I will *never* recognize

---

[1] Sparrow-Simpson, p. 302.  [2] Butler, vol. ii, p. 177.
[3] Schulte, pp. 208 ff.

the new dogma without the limitations which we desire, and I will deny the validity and the freedom of the Council. The Romans may then suspend and excommunicate me, and put an administrator in my diocese."

On September 14 he wrote again: " I refused the invitation to Fulda quite firmly, because the intention there was clean contrary to our agreement at Rome. Now Ketteler and Melchers (the Bishop of Mainz and the Archbishop of Cologne) are willing to deny the existence of such an agreement. They seem to have forgotten everything, even what they themselves did and said at Rome. . . . As long as nothing is directly demanded from Rome, I keep silent: thus I shall refuse to publish the decrees, and wait quietly for my suspension. Indeed, I did think already of resigning my bishopric, but have given up that idea, and am willing to drink the cup which is forced upon me. At least I do not know anything else to do. To recognize as Divinely revealed something *that is not true in itself*, let him who can, do it. I cannot."

Writing on November 11 to the Bonn Committee (see next chapter), he is still certain that the new dogmas have no basis in Scripture or tradition. He is astonished that nearly the whole German episcopate has changed its convictions, but he again declares that he will not publish the new dogmas in his diocese. He would rather give up his bishopric than act against his conscience. Delay without formal schism is his policy, in the hope that God may in some unexpected way intervene. On December 3, writing to a priest of the Cologne diocese, he says that he is neither willing nor able to take part in a formal schism: he does not think that such a schism is possible, for the individual opponents of the new dogmas are scattered all over the world, and the bulk of the clergy and laity are completely indifferent. On December 17 he tells Döllinger that he is being pressed on all sides, even from France and America, to submit; but he is still determined to refuse, even if he is suspended. On January 25 he writes to his friend at Bonn: " Unfortunately I must say with Schulte, ' I lived many years in a deep delusion ': I believed I was serving the Catholic Church when I was serving the caricature which Romanism and Jesuitism have made of it. It was at Rome that I first realized that all that is done and practised there has no longer more than the appearance and name of Christianity: only the husk, the kernel is gone." He goes on to say that his power to give dispensations for marriages within the prohibited degrees has. been taken away. (Roman Catholics are forbidden by canon law to marry relatives as remote as third cousins, unless by dispensation; the right to give such dispensations belongs to the bishop, but has to be renewed every five years, and can be taken away at any time. This is one of the methods by which, since the Counter-Reformation, the Pope is able to keep the bishops subservient.) In consequence, many people in Hefele's diocese were living together without marriage, or resorting to civil marriage (which is regarded by Roman Catholics as no marriage at all).

On March 11 he wrote a final letter of despair to Döllinger. His position is impossible. His clergy are in revolt; he would not have believed that the new dogma could have made so much progress in his diocese. Sixteen couples have been unable to marry for want of dispensations. He cannot bear the thought of being a suspended and excommunicated bishop. He must either resign his see or submit. A letter from his friend at Bonn brought the reply that he had already once submitted to a dogma which he knew to be false (the Immaculate Conception, in 1854). Accordingly, on April 10 he made " the sacrifice of the intellect", and published the decrees of the Vatican Council.[1]

But his humiliation was not complete. He was compelled to falsify history. In the second edition of his great *History of the Councils* he had to modify his assertion that Pope Honorius fell into heresy, in such a way as to make it appear that his alteration was due to fresh research and not to the Vatican Council.[2] And he had to show that Pope Julius I claimed that " the churches might come to no conclusion without the approval of the Bishop of Rome ", by deliberately mistranslating the text of the Pope's letter so as to apply to himself words which really refer to all the Latin bishops (*omnibus nobis*, πᾶσιν ἡμῖν), and show plainly that the Pope made no such claim.[3]

In Switzerland, Greith of St. Gall was the only bishop in opposition to the new dogmas; he stood by Hefele for some months, but had submitted by December 1870.[4]

In Austria, Cardinal Schwarzenberg, Archbishop of Prague

---

[1] Schulte, pp. 222–230; Coulton, pp. 199–202; Sparrow-Simpson, pp. 307–310.
[2] Schulte, p. 310.    [3] Coulton, pp. 202–203.    [4] Schulte, p. 226.

(then, of course, in the Austrian Empire), held out for some time. On August 2 Professor Schulte had an interview with him, and was convinced that he would publish the new dogmas. Schulte, who as Professor of Canon Law in the University of Prague belonged to the Cardinal's diocese, says that he could have resisted the Council, and would have been followed by his diocese, where hardly anyone believed in the Infallibility of the Pope; but that he was afraid that if he did, the result might be the strengthening of Czech nationalism (Schwarzenberg was an Austrian), and the revival of Hussitism. He published the decrees of the Council on January 11, 1871, but he did not really change his convictions, he did not obey the order to condemn Schulte's book *The Strength of the Popes*, and he remained on good terms with him until Schulte left Prague for Bonn in 1872.[1]

In Hungary, Archbishop Haynald of Kalocza held out until October 1871, when he submitted under pressure from Rome.[2] But Bishop Strossmayer of Diakovar remained firm. He and Hefele were the strongest members of the opposition; but whereas Hefele was a scholar, Strossmayer was a nationalist politician. In spite of his name, he was a Croat, and the cause of Croat independence was the main purpose of his life. The Pope dared not interfere with him, because of his influence among his own people. There is in Croatia an old tradition of independence, shown by the use of Old Slavonic as the liturgical language in the Glagolithic rite (the Roman liturgy in Slavonic), which has been used in certain churches for a thousand years. As late as October 2, 1871, Strossmayer wrote to Reinkens that " Rome uses its power for destruction " and that true Catholics ought to say to St. Peter, as St. Paul did, " Thou walkest not in the truth of the Gospel ". In a letter to Lord Acton, a little earlier, he expresses the hope that a really free council may yet take place. But his Vicar-General published the decrees, December 26, 1872, whether with or without his consent is uncertain. Ultimately, on February 28, 1881, Strossmayer accepted Papal Infallibility, with the object of winning the support of Pope Leo XIII for the cause of the Croats. He was the last of all the bishops to submit.[3]

It may be mentioned here, though it is outside the scope of this book, that the Vatican Council aroused resistance in the

---

[1] Schulte, p. 249.  [2] Schulte, p. 251.
[3] Schulte, pp. 251–264.

Uniat Churches. There was a schism among the Chaldeans,[1] but it did not prove to be permanent. In South India some thousands of people separated from the Uniat Church of Malabar and placed themselves under the Patriarch of the East, who sent them a bishop; and this Indian diocese still continues as a constituent part of the Assyrian Church.

[1] Butler, vol. i, p. 226.

# CHAPTER XVII

# THE GERMAN REVOLT

THERE were, however, men who were determined to refuse the new dogmas of the Vatican Council, no matter what the cost might be. Respect for learning, and for research with the sole object of discovering the truth, is one of the most honourable German traditions. The resistance to the Vatican Council began among the professors in the Roman Catholic universities of Germany. Again, as at the time of the Reformation, there was a complete difference of outlook between the Italians and the Germans. In the Italian universities, except at Rome, there were no theological faculties; and more religious books were published in England or Germany in one year than in Italy in half a century.[1] The backbone of the majority at the Vatican Council was composed of Italian, Spanish, and South American bishops, whose learning was quite insufficient to decide the questions raised by the new dogmas. But many of the theological professors of Germany, when they found themselves called upon to accept the new dogmas, could not bring themselves to deny what they had always taught and to accept what they knew to be untrue.

Archbishop Scherr of Munich returned home the day after the solemn publication of the new dogmas. He at once summoned the professors of the theological faculty of the university to meet him. He told them that Rome had spoken (the famous words " Roma locuta est, causa finita est " are based on a forged interpolation into St. Augustine), and that they could not do anything but submit. He then tried to give the dogma of Papal Infallibility as favourable an interpretation as he could. " Ought we not," he said to Döllinger, " to be ready to begin to labour afresh in the cause of the Holy Church? " " Yes," replied Döllinger, with great firmness, " for the old Church." " There is but one Church," said the Archbishop, " and that is neither new nor old." " But they have made a new one," answered Döllinger. The Archbishop went on talking, and at last said, " You know, of course, that there have always been changes in the Church and

---

[1] Quirinus (Friedrich), *Letters from Rome on the Council*, pp. 95, 192.

in her doctrines." The words caused a sensation, and the Archbishop added, " At least, you know that dogmas have often required to be defined." [1]

At first the leaders of the opposition thought that many of the bishops, at any rate in Germany, Austria, and Hungary, would continue to resist and would be glad of their support. At the end of July the Roman Catholic professors of Munich University issued a declaration, that for several reasons, which they gave, they felt bound in conscience to refuse to recognize the " Vatican Assembly " as a free œcumenical council, or its decisions as valid; and especially bound to reject the personal infallibility of the Pope, because it was a new doctrine not based on Holy Scripture, and contrary to the tradition of ecclesiastical antiquity and to Church history. [2]

On August 11 Cardinal Antonelli wrote to the papal nuncio at Brussels that the decrees of the Vatican were now binding on the whole (Roman) Catholic world, without requiring any further publication. [3] Nevertheless, the German opponents of the new dogmas continued their propaganda.

The chief organizer of the movement was Johann Friedrich von Schulte, Professor of Canon Law in the University of Prague. Schulte was born at Winterberg in Westphalia, in 1827, and had been professor at Prague since 1855. He began immediately after the Vatican Council to organize a meeting of professors of various universities to protest against the new dogmas. The meeting was held at Nuremberg on August 25–26, 1870. Fourteen were present at it, including Döllinger, Friedrich, and Reischl from Munich, Knoodt, Langen, and Reusch from Bonn, Dittrich and Michelis from Braunsberg, Löwe, Mayer, and Schulte from Prague (Löwe and Mayer went by the express wish of Cardinal Schwarzenberg). They drew up a formal manifesto in which they declared that the Vatican Council was not a true œcumenical council, because it was neither free nor morally unanimous; that the third and fourth chapters of the constitution " Pastor Æternus " lacked the necessary conditions of dogma, since they had not been believed always, or everywhere, or by all: on the contrary, the opposite doctrines had been hitherto freely taught in many dioceses; that the third chapter of the

[1] *Theodorus* (J. B. Mullinger), *The New Reformation*, p. 95 ff.
[2] Schulte, *Das Altkatholizismus*, p. 189.
[3] Schulte, p. 108.

constitution (the immediate ordinary jurisdiction of the Pope) completely destroyed the Divinely appointed nature of the episcopate; and that the dogma of the Papal Infallibility would revive the control of the Pope over civil affairs, and destroy the understanding between Church and State, clergy and laity, Catholics and those of other religions. Accordingly, they undertook to stand by the bishops of the opposition, and demanded a real and free general council, not in Italy, but on the German side of the Alps.[1]

This declaration was signed by thirty-three professors and teachers, both priests and laymen, representing seven universities: Bonn, Braunsberg, Breslau, Giessen, Munich, Prague, and Ratisbon. Twelve days earlier, on August 14, a meeting of laymen had taken place at Königswinter, near Bonn. At this meeting it was agreed to issue a declaration that, because the Vatican Council was neither free nor unanimous, they did not recognize its decrees on the infallibility and universal ordinary jurisdiction of the Pope, but rejected them as contrary to the traditional belief of the Church. This was signed by 1,359 persons of various professions, including thirty-two members of the staffs of universities, seventy-five school teachers, ten burgomasters, forty-three doctors, twelve officers, and twenty-eight magistrates. The time was most unsuitable for the beginning of such a movement: for everyone's mind was occupied by the war with France, which had just begun. Nevertheless, the challenge had been made.[2]

It was not long before the German bishops gave their answer. On August 30 they assembled at Fulda, beside the tomb of St. Boniface, and issued a pastoral letter, in which they made the following assertions:

(1) " When the children of the Church receive with faith the decrees of a general council, they do it with a conviction that God, Who is the eternal truth and is alone infallible in His own right, co-operates with it in a supernatural manner, and preserves it from error." This is based on the " unanimous and undoubted tradition of the Church ".

(2) The Vatican Council was such a council, and the Holy Ghost spoke by it.

(3) The Vatican Council did not propound any new

---

[1] Schulte, pp. 97–105.    [2] Schulte, pp. 105–107.

doctrine differing from the ancient teaching, any more than any other general council, but simply developed and threw light upon the old truth faithfully preserved and contained in the deposit of faith.

(4) These decrees, through having been solemnly published by the Pope, were now binding on all the faithful.

A translation of the complete text of the pastoral letter is given by Dom Cuthbert Butler.[1]

This declaration was signed by seventeen of the German bishops. There were five who did not sign: the Archbishop of Bamberg, the Bishops of Breslau, Osnabrück, and Rottenburg, and the Vicar-Apostolic of Saxony (Bishop of Leontopolis). Cardinal Melchers and the other bishops of the opposition who signed this pastoral letter had forgotten the promise they had made at Rome only six weeks earlier, to do nothing without consulting the rest.[2] The publication of the Fulda pastoral letter destroyed all hope that the German bishops would lead a national revolt against the new dogmas. The most that could now be expected was that individual bishops, such as Hefele or Strossmayer, would join it, but this did not happen. Those who had protested against the new dogmas were, if priests, compelled to choose between submission and suspension, to be followed, if they still remained obstinate, by excommunication. They would lose their means of subsistence in this world, and their principal means of preparing for the next. Even the laymen found themselves in an extremely difficult position. At that time, in most parts of Germany, Church and State were still closely connected. There was no civil marriage (which in any case was regarded by Roman Catholics, since the Council of Trent, as invalid); and since excommunicated persons were refused ecclesiastical marriage, it was impossible for them and their families to get married. Moreover, though excommunicated, they would still be regarded by the State as Roman Catholics, and would have to pay the tax for the support of the Church and the clergy—that is, for the propagation of the new dogmas in which they did not believe. Their children would have to receive Roman Catholic teaching, and they would have to pay for it, and for the administration of the sacraments, by which they were forbidden to benefit. If they

[1] Dom Cuthbert Butler, *Vatican Council*, vol. ii, pp. 180–183.
[2] Schulte, p. 110.

died, they could not have the bells rung (to which Germans attach great importance), nor could they have any funeral service read over their graves. In many places they could only be buried in the place set apart for suicides; for all the consecrated ground would be closed to the excommunicated.[1]

And they would have to undergo all this, not for believing any new doctrine, but for continuing to believe what they and all their forefathers had always believed, and what some of the very bishops who inflicted the excommunication had themselves maintained until the end of the Vatican Council a few months before : for refusing to declare in spite of this, that the new dogmas were " the ancient and constant faith of the Church ".

On the other hand, it was impossible for the Pope and the bishops to adopt any other policy. They had committed themselves finally to the necessity of the new dogmas to salvation : they could not permit any priest or official teacher to reject them. It is true that Lord Acton was never required to submit to the new dogmas. But Lord Acton was not a priest, nor an official teacher, nor did he make any public protest, or join any organized opposition. (One may perhaps add, that he was a member of the House of Lords, a friend of the British Prime Minister, and a scholar of international reputation, in a country where Roman Catholics of such eminence were not common.) He was allowed to continue till his death in that communion with Rome which he declared to be dearer to him than life; but he never changed his belief, or accepted the new dogmas. In 1876 he wrote to Gladstone, on the latter's writings against the Vatican Council : " I think you are too hard on Ultramontanes and too gentle with Ultramontanism. You say, for instance, that it promotes untruthfulness. I don't think that is fair. It not only promotes, it inculcates distinct mendacity and deceitfulness. In certain cases it is made a duty to lie. But those who teach this doctrine do not become habitual liars in other respects."[2]

One after another, the leaders of the opposition were suspended " from order and jurisdiction " : that is, deprived of their posts, and forbidden to say Mass or to perform any ecclesiastical function. Besides the professors, there were parish priests among them, such as Wilhelm Tangermann, the parish priest of Unkel, in the diocese of Cologne. Reinkens, at Breslau, was suspended in August

---

[1] Schulte, pp. 119–121.
[2] J. N. Figgis and Lawrence, *Lord Acton's Correspondence*, p. 93.

for publishing a book called *Pope and Papacy*:[1] Michelis about the same time. The professors of Bonn were suspended on November 4.[2] There were some who submitted. Professor Haneberg of Munich, formerly a Benedictine abbot, did so on the honourable ground that he could not bear to be responsible for the danger to the unlearned which the continuance of the struggle would bring about.[3] Professor Thiel of Braunsberg submitted, and was soon afterwards made Canon and Vicar-General.[4] But the principal centre of interest was Munich. All Europe, even in the midst of the Franco-German War and the siege of Paris, was watching Döllinger. On November 29, seven professors of Munich, among them Reischl, who had signed the Protest of Nuremberg, published a declaration that they accepted the œcumenical character of the Vatican Council.[5]

On January 4, the archbishop commanded Döllinger to submit. He asked for time to think it over, which was granted, and extended at his request. At last, on March 28, Döllinger wrote to the archbishop, giving the reasons why he could not accept the Vatican Council and its decrees. His words were: " As a Christian, as a theologian, as a historian, as a citizen, I cannot accept this doctrine ". He could not accept it as a Christian because it was contrary to the clear teaching of Christ and His apostles; as a theologian, because it was contrary to the genuine tradition of the Church; as a historian, because he knew that this theory had cost Europe rivers of blood, overthrown the constitution of the ancient Church, and brought many abuses into it; as a citizen because, by its claim to submit the whole political order to papal authority, and by the exemptions demanded for the clergy, it would cause endless and fatal divisions between Church and State, and between clergy and laity.[6]

The archbishop replied with a pastoral letter, warning Döllinger of the consequences of continued disobedience. The professors of the university, all but three, signed an address expressing their sympathy with Döllinger. A large meeting of laymen, held on April 10, resolved to petition the King of Bavaria to use his prerogative against the new dogmas, and to forbid them to be taught in the university or the schools.[7] Other addresses of sympathy were received, including one from the

[1] Schulte, p. 186.    [2] Schulte, pp. 134, 136.
[3] Schulte, p. 100.    [4] Schulte, p. 183.    [5] Schulte, p. 190.
[6] *Theodorus*, p. 100; Butler, vol. ii, p. 185; Schulte, p. 203.
[7] *Theodorus*, p. 110.

City Council of Vienna. Father Dalgairns, in the *Contemporary Review*, wrote that by the light of burning Paris men were still watching every move of the combat going on between the Archbishop of Munich and Dr. Döllinger.[1]

On Sunday, April 23, a notice proclaiming that Professors Döllinger and Friedrich were placed under the greater excommunication was read from all the pulpits in the diocese of Munich. By this not only were they deprived of the sacraments, but the faithful were forbidden to have any dealings with them:[2] according to canon law (and it was expressly stated that the excommunication was followed by all the canonical consequences) their lives were forfeit. Döllinger made no appeal to the ecclesiastical courts. Josef Renftle, the parish priest of Mehring, near Augsburg, who had been excommunicated for protesting from his pulpit against the new dogmas, continued, with the support of his congregation, to occupy his parish, and the Bavarian Government would not let the Bishop of Augsburg expel him by force. He remained in possession until August 1878.[3]

Now that there was no longer any hope that even one bishop would lead the opposition to the new dogmas, the future was exceedingly dark, but Döllinger and his friends determined to act together. On May 28, Döllinger invited the members of the party at Munich to meet at his house. They agreed to make public a declaration that they rejected the Papal Infallibility and did not recognize the validity of the suspensions and excommunications.[4]

Upon this the German bishops issued a reply, in the form of two pastoral letters, one addressed to the clergy, the other to the laity. In the first they insisted that the decrees of the Vatican Council must be accepted by all, but they minimized as much as possible the effect of the decrees. They said, for instance, that the Papal Infallibility was not personal, but official, and carefully defined; and that the new decrees would in no way interfere with the rights of the State. In the second they appealed to the prejudices of the laity against the new critical methods employed by modern scholars, and asserted that the dogma of Papal Infallibility was necessary, in order to maintain the authority of the Church against the independence of modern thought. These

---

[1] *Theodorus*, p. 111.  [2] Schulte, p. 205.
[3] Schulte, p. 207; *Theodorus*, p. 112.
[4] Schulte, p. 338.

pastoral letters appeared at Whitsuntide, 1871.[1] About the same time, Pope Pius IX, addressing a deputation of French Roman Catholics, told them that the leaders of the opposition to the Vatican Council were more formidable than those of the French Revolution, and more to be dreaded than the Communists, " those fiends let loose from hell ", who had just set fire to Paris and shot Archbishop Darboy.[2]

In June, Dr. Zenger, Professor of Roman Law at Munich, who was one of Döllinger's supporters, died. The last sacraments were refused to him unless he would withdraw his signature to the address to Döllinger: but he received absolution from Messmer, and the viaticum and extreme unction from Friedrich, with the assistance of Renftle, who sent in the Blessed Sacrament and the holy oils from his parish. The day after Zenger's death, a petition, signed by 18,000 Roman Catholics, was sent to the government, asking that they might be allowed to have one church in Munich, with its furniture and its revenues, in which they might practise their religion without accepting the Vatican decrees, and that parish priests might be compelled to give the necessary civil sanction to marriages celebrated by the excommunicated priests of the " Old Catholic " party (there being at that time no civil marriage in Bavaria). Zenger was buried by Friedrich, and several government officials, nearly all the professors of the university, and a great crowd of students and others, attended the funeral: there was even a students' torchlight procession to the grave.[3] In August, Döllinger, in spite of his excommunication, was elected Rector of the University, and the six new members of the University Senate were all members of his party.

The Old Catholics, as we must now call them (that is, those who maintained the Roman Catholic religion as it was before the Vatican Council), were finding support in other countries also. What was happening in Switzerland will be related in the next chapter. Van Vlooten, the parish priest of St. Augustine's, The Hague, had written a letter expressing his admiration of the " wise, powerful, and spirited opposition " to the Vatican Dogmas shown by the committee at Munich. Accordingly, Renftle wrote to the Archbishop of Utrecht (Henricus Loos), asking him to give confirmation in his parish, as his own bishop refused to do

---

[1] *Theodorus*, pp. 113-116.     [2] *Theodorus*, p. 116.
[3] *Theodorus*, pp. 118-120; Schulte, p. 340.

so. On August 19, 1871, the archbishop answered that he would, subject to the approval of his chapter, but that he hoped that the Creed of Pope Pius IV would be the doctrinal basis of the new movement.[1]

At the meeting held at Munich on May 28 it had been decided to organize a congress. This was held on September 22–24, at Munich, and was the first of a long series of Old Catholic congresses. The chairman was Professor von Schulte of Prague (see above, p. 227), who was a layman; the vice-chairmen Professor Windscheid of Heidelberg and Dr. Keller from Aarau in Switzerland, an eminent Swiss statesman. It was an international congress, for there were several members from Austria and Switzerland, four priests from the Church of Utrecht, Hyacinthe Loyson from France, and Roman Catholics from Spain, Ireland, and Brazil. In all, there were 300 Old Catholic sympathizers present.[2]

There were also visitors from other communions at the congress. The Bishop of Ely (Harold Browne) sent his sympathy by telegram; the Bishop of Lincoln (Christopher Wordsworth) and his diocesan synod sent a formal letter assuring the congress of their brotherly feeling and promising co-operation in whatever way might be in their power. The Rev. F. S. May attended the congress, with commendatory letters from both bishops; he was also directed to go to Utrecht and see the three Dutch bishops (the English bishops were unaware that the see of Haarlem was vacant).[3] Members of the American Episcopal Church and the Greek Orthodox Church, and some Protestants from Germany and Switzerland, were also present at the congress.[4]

Among the members of the congress committee were Döllinger, Friedrich, Langen of Bonn, Reinkens of Breslau, Huber, who had shared with Döllinger the authorship of The Pope and the Council (" Janus "), and Professor Maassen of Vienna.

The purpose of the congress was not to form a schism, but to provide for the spiritual needs of those who had been excommunicated for refusing to submit to the Vatican Council. As it turned out, this was impossible without forming a schism. But the Old Catholics did not leave the Roman Communion of their own free will. They were expelled, and it was necessary, if they were to continue to live as Catholic Christians, to form an

---

[1] *Theodorus*, p. 131.    [2] Schulte, pp. 342 ff.
[3] *Theodorus*, p. 124.    [4] *Theodorus*, p. 343.

organization.. This organization was ultimately, as we shall see, given a canonical status through the Church of Utrecht. The work of the congress, which was partly done in private, was of two kinds. A doctrinal basis was drawn up, and a programme for organization was agreed to. The doctrinal basis consisted of seven resolutions. The first repudiated both the new dogmas of the Vatican Council and the ecclesiastical censures based upon them, and maintained the Creed of Pope Pius IV, issued by the Council of Trent. The second acknowledged " the primacy of the Roman bishop as it was received by the Fathers on the ground of Scripture ", but rejected " every attempt to thrust out the bishops from the immediate and independent direction of the separate churches, and declared that dogmas of faith can only be defined in accordance with Scripture, and that the dogmatic decisions of a council must be shown to be in harmony with the originally delivered faith of the Church, in the direct consciousness of belief of the Catholic people and in theological science ". The right to a voice in the enunciation of rules of faith was claimed for the Catholic laity.

The third resolution demanded reforms in the Church, and a constitutional share for the laity in Church affairs. It declared that the accusation of " Jansenism " against the Church of Utrecht was baseless, and that the congress had no dogmatic differ-ence from that church. It expressed hope for reunion with the Orthodox Eastern churches, and for gradual understanding with the Anglican and Protestant churches.

The fourth resolution demanded a broader education for the clergy, and protection against the arbitrary power of the bishops.

The fifth resolution was a declaration of loyalty to the civil governments, especially in any conflict with the principles of the Syllabus of Errors.

The sixth was a demand for the expulsion of the Jesuits.

The seventh claimed the right of the Old Catholics to a share in the property of the Church.[1]

The proposals for organization were as follows:—

(1) " In all places where the necessity exists and the persons are close by, a regular cure of souls is to be set up. The local committees can decide whether these conditions are fulfilled.

(2) " We have a right to see our priests recognized by the

[1] *Theodorus*, pp. 126–134; Schulte, pp. 22–24.

State as entitled to perform ecclesiastical functions, wherever, and so long as, these are presumed by the rights of citizens (that is, wherever the law of the land assumes that citizens have the right to be married, buried, etc., by the Church).

(3) " Where possible, these rights should be claimed.

(4) " Individuals are justified by our circumstances in asking foreign bishops to perform episcopal functions: and we are justified, as soon as the proper time shall have arrived, in providing for the introduction of a regular episcopal jurisdiction." [1]

These proposals were resisted by Döllinger, but he afterwards came to accept them wholeheartedly.

It will be observed that the Congress of Munich was transitional. On the one hand, its members still adhered to the Council of Trent, and claimed to be within the Roman Communion. They stood precisely where the Church of Utrecht had stood for 150 years, and it was significant that they explicitly declared themselves in full agreement with Utrecht.

On the other hand, they had not got an existing organization like the Church of Utrecht, no bishop or diocesan chapter, and their demand for reform was sharper than Utrecht's had ever been. Their decision to set up opposing congregations, and a rival bishopric, was necessary if they were to continue to exist, but it was undoubtedly an act of schism, though, if their doctrinal position was true, their schism was justified: no one is bound to adhere to bishops whom he believes to be heretical. But since they were setting up a rival organization to that of Rome (however justifiably), it is doubtful whether they had a moral right to claim a share in the property of the church which was now Ultramontane. The Roman Communion had established new dogmas; those who could not accept them were obliged to separate, and to set up what was in their eyes the true Catholic Church, free from the Vatican heresy. They had a right to freedom in the practice of their religion, but they had not necessarily a right to a share in the property of the communion which they had left.

At any rate, the Congress of Munich in 1871 was a parting of the ways. From this time the Old Catholics were in fact no longer a party within the Roman Communion, but a separate communion.

[1] *Theodorus*, pp. 125–126; Schulte, p. 345.

During the next few months many Old Catholic congregations were formed, not only in Germany, but in Austria: before the end of 1871 there were twenty-three.[1] At Munich regular Old Catholic services were begun in October by Professor Friedrich. The Grand Duchy of Baden was from the first the part of Germany where the Old Catholic movement was most widespread; the reason for this was the influence of Wessenberg a generation earlier. The first Old Catholic service at Cologne was held by Pfarrer Tangermann at St. Pantaleon's Church, on February 1, 1872.[2] This was a garrison church, which the Government permitted the Old Catholics to use; it had long been used by Protestants without any objection being made, but when the Old Catholics began to use it, the army bishop, Mgr. Namzanowski, declared that it was desecrated, no doubt because it was used for schismatic Masses, while the Protestants had only used it for prayers and preaching. However, the Prussian Government deprived him of his office, and soon afterwards freed the Old Catholics from their obligation to pay the church tax.

A series of lectures was given at Munich by the Old Catholic leaders, and was so successful that Reinkens went to give similar lectures in other large cities, and thus became well known throughout Germany. He was more than twenty years younger than Döllinger, and was coming more and more into the foremost rank of the movement. At this time an important recruit appeared from France, the Abbé Michaud, who had been a curate at the Church of the Madeleine in Paris; like Loyson, he adopted a much more radical position than the German leaders, and it was probably his influence which caused the rapid development of ideas between the Congress of Munich in 1871 and the Congress of Cologne in 1872.[3] Meanwhile the committee at Munich, moved to vigorous action by the formal excommunication of Reinkens and three of his colleagues, invited the Archbishop of Utrecht to make a confirmation tour in Bavaria. No such invitation had been received at Utrecht since the breach with Rome 150 years before; and the archbishop, after some hesitation, accepted it. He went first to Cologne, then to Munich, where he arrived on July 5, and the following Sunday he held a confirmation at St. Nicholas' Church. He was entertained at dinner by the committee; an Anglican sympathizer was present. The following day he went to confirm at Kiefersfelden, and on

[1] *Theodorus*, p. 135.    [2] *Theodorus*, p. 140.    [3] *Theodorus*, pp. 140–146.

Wednesday at Mehring: in both parishes priest and people were entirely Old Catholic. From Munich he went to Kempten, where he confirmed seventy-one children; thence to Constance, to see the memorials of Wessenberg; from there to Kaiserslautern, Zweibrücken, and Landau (all these towns are in Bavaria), in all of which he held confirmations. On his return to Utrecht he was presented with a jewelled cross and ring in memory of this historic tour.

By thus administering a sacrament outside his own province, the Archbishop of Utrecht took a long step away from Rome; for it implied that since the Vatican Council he did not acknowledge the jurisdiction of the German bishops. One of his predecessors had consented to help the Gallicans in this way, but had not done so. There was, of course, a Dutch precedent: the famous confirmation held by Bishop Varlet at Amsterdam. The archbishop's tour made many thousands of people familiar with the idea, entirely new to them, that the services of a bishop could be enjoyed apart from Rome. It was another step towards the breaking of the papal dominance over the imagination.

The second Old Catholic Congress was held at Cologne, on September 22–24, 1872. It had been arranged by the central committee, meeting at Munich on March 17, and including ninety members, from several German States.

There were 350 Old Catholic members of the congress, the great majority of whom were Germans. The Archbishop of Utrecht was there with four of his priests; [2] there were seven Austrians, among them Schulte, who was again elected chairman; two from France (Loyson and Michaud), three from Belgium, one each from England and Italy. The Swiss Old Catholics were represented by Herzog and some laymen.

This time there were far more visitors from other communions than at Munich. Bishop Christopher Wordsworth of Lincoln was sent a special invitation, which he accepted. He was accompanied by the Bishops of Ely and Maryland, and twenty-two Anglican priests, among whom were Dr. A. P. Stanley, Dean of Westminster, the Rev. F. S. May, and the two sons of the Bishop of Lincoln, both recently ordained. One afterwards became Bishop of Salisbury, and the other, afterwards Canon Wordsworth,

---

[1] *Theodorus*, pp. 146–152; Schulte, p. 352.

[2] According to an Anglican eye-witness, the archbishop took little part in the Congress, because he could not speak French or German easily (*Monthly Packet*, 1872).

Master of St. Nicholas' Hospital, Salisbury, was probably the last survivor of the members of the Congress. (He died February, 1938.) There were also present the Archpriest Janyschev, Rector of the Theological Academy at St. Petersburg, and General Kiréev from Russia; and twenty-one German Protestant pastors, some of their laymen, one Dutch Protestant, Edmond de Préssensé, one Swiss, and one Hungarian Protestant. The total number of visitors was seventy-two.[1]

Two open meetings were held, which were attended by large crowds; and there were four closed meetings, at which only members and invited visitors were present.

The work done by the congress was of three kinds: organization, reunion, and Church reform. Fifteen resolutions on the organization of pastoral work were accepted by the congress. They laid down that in the circumstances in which the Old Catholics found themselves they might organize parishes, appoint priests without institution by a bishop, use Protestant churches or other buildings where no Catholic church was to be had, do without consecrated altars and other church furniture where necessary; priests were to avoid ecclesiastical controversy in their sermons, marriages might be solemnized without the usual dispensations, and where ecclesiastical marriage was refused, civil marriage was sufficient; and other regulations for immediate necessities were made.

As the German Old Catholics had no bishop, they agreed that foreign bishops, especially the bishops of the Church of Utrecht *and of the Armenian Church*, might be asked to give confirmation and ordination, until they could have German Old Catholic bishops consecrated.[2]

The question of reunion aroused much interest. Bishop Christopher Wordsworth was probably the most learned Anglican bishop of his day. Like his uncle, the famous poet, he was a High Churchman of the pre-Tractarian kind (being a Cambridge man, he had never come under the influence of Newman), and was thoroughly acquainted with the Fathers. He pointed out that it was impossible for the Church of England, which appealed to the undivided Church, to accept the Council of Trent or the Creed of Pope Pius IV, and that as long as the Old Catholics adhered to the dogmas of Pius IV they would never be able to oppose effectual resistance to those of Pius IX.

[1] *Theodorus*, p. 154; Schulte, p. 353.     [2] Schulte, p. 27.

The Abbé Michaud proposed that the congress should declare that it accepted the first seven œumenical councils, but did not regard the western councils, including Trent, as œcumenical. But Reinkens said that this proposal was premature. The question of the western councils would have to be investigated, and it was the business of the Reunion Committee to organize research, and to make the results of it known by popular books and articles.[1] Accordingly, a committee of ten was appointed to study the problem of reunion; its members were Döllinger, who was chairman, Friedrich, Schulte, Langen, Reusch, Michelis, and Michaud, Professor Lutterbeck of Giessen, and Herr Rottels, with power to co-opt others.[2]

On the subject of Church reform, various speakers condemned existing abuses, but the congress was content with passing resolutions asserting the claim of the Old Catholics to be the Catholic, as opposed to the Ultramontane, Church, and laying down principles as to the relations of Church and State.

After the congress, the formation of Old Catholic congregations (Gemeinden) made rapid progress. In some places the government gave the Old Catholics either full use or part use of a church. The governments of Prussia, Baden, and Hessen showed some sympathy towards the Old Catholics; but the Bavarian Government, in spite of the personal sympathy of King Ludwig II with Döllinger and his cause, was consistently hostile, and it was more than sixty years before the Old Catholics were fully recognized there.

On March 24, 1873, the papal nuncio issued instructions to the German bishops, that where the civil authorities had given the Old Catholics (who were called the " New Heretics ") a share in the use of any church, they were to forbid their people to make any use of it, and to provide for their spiritual needs in some other way.[3] (All who attended Old Catholic services or meetings had been already excommunicated.)

Early in 1873 the " Falk Laws " limiting the power of the Church in various ways were introduced by Prince Bismarck. We are not concerned with the effect of these laws on the Roman Communion in Germany, or with the " Kulturkampf ", the struggle between Church and State to which they led. But they recognized the Old Catholic Church and gave it a legal position.

---

[1] *Theodorus*, pp. 156–163.     [2] *Theodorus*, p. 161; Schulte, p. 29.
[3] Schulte, p. 359.

The appointment and consecration of a bishop were now necessary; the consent of the government was obtained by Professor von Schulte, and the commission appointed for the purpose by the Congress of Cologne chose Langen, Michelis, Reinkens, and Reusch, and submitted their names to the government for its approval. (It may appear strange to the English reader that such approval was needed; but Continental governments, which pay the clergy, enforce church taxes on members of religious communions, and provide teaching in accordance with the religion in which the parents are registered, exercise much more control over religious bodies than is tolerated in English-speaking countries.) The Archbishop of Utrecht promised to consecrate the elected candidate; and a constitution was drawn up, which he would have to swear to observe after his consecration.[1]

On June 4 the election was held at the Frankenskapelle near St. Pantaleon's Church at Cologne. There were seventy-seven electors, twenty-one priests and fifty-six lay representatives of the parishes and unions (Vereine). Professor Reinkens received sixty-nine votes, Professor Reusch five, Professors Langen and Michelis one each.[2]

Reinkens was very unwilling to accept the office. Schulte and others persuaded him to yield. He insisted that the vow of the clergy should be of love and reverence, not of obedience, and bound himself by a similar vow.[3] The news was declared to the waiting crowd by Tangermann from the pulpit of the church, the bells were rung, and the Te Deum was sung. Probably it was the first popular election of a bishop in Germany since the days of St. Boniface. The assembly burst into tears of joy, and Schulte calls the scene " a most inspiring moment, such as the Church has not seen since the apostolic times ".

On the very day of the election Archbishop Loos died. The Ultramontanes were jubilant, and said it was a judgment from heaven. For the last time, the Church of Utrecht was left with only one bishop, Hermann Heykamp, Bishop of Deventer. He was asked to perform the consecration; the bishop-elect, with Professors Knoodt, Reusch, and von Schulte, paid him a visit at Rotterdam, and arrangements were made for the consecration to take place there. In the church of St. Lawrence and St. Mary

[1] Schulte, p. 361.          [2] Schulte, p. 379.
[3] *Theodorus*, p. 184.

Magdalene at Rotterdam,[1] on August 11, 1873, the Bishop of Deventer consecrated Josef Hubert Reinkens to be Bishop of the Old Catholic Church in Germany, and Caspar Johannes Rinkel to be Bishop of Haarlem. The assistants, in the absence of other bishops, were Canons Verhay and Hardenwyk, vicars-general of the dioceses of Utrecht and Haarlem. The formal proofs of the elections were read instead of the papal mandate, and the two bishops did not notify their consecration to the Pope.[2]

*Note.*—Dom Cuthbert Butler (*Vatican Council*, vol. ii, p. 189) says that Bishop Reinkens was consecrated by " the Jansenist Bishop of Utrecht ". The see of Utrecht had been an arch-bishopric since 1560; and, as we have seen, it was at that moment vacant. This is not Butler's only mistake in dealing with Dutch affairs. He says (vol. ii, p. 262) that the Dutch bishops at the Vatican Council were only vicars-apostolic, but Pius IX had set up rival diocesan bishops in the Netherlands in 1853 (Neale, *History of the Church of Holland*, p. 367).

---

[1] Destroyed by the Germans in 1940.
[2] *Theodorus*, p. 185; Schulte, p. 383.

# CHAPTER XVIII

# THE SWISS REVOLT

THE Vatican Council was followed by a revolt in Switzerland also. But whereas the German revolt was led by theological professors, the Swiss revolt was led by laymen. The German objection to the decrees of the Council was primarily historical; the Swiss objection was primarily political.

Switzerland, unlike Germany and Austria, was a republic, or rather a federation of small republics, some Roman Catholic and others Protestant. As they differed in religion, ecclesiastical affairs were controlled by the cantons, not by the Federal Government. The French Revolution had destroyed the old constitution of the Swiss Federation, and put in its place the " Helvetic Republic ". In 1815 this had been succeeded by the new Swiss Federation, which included, for the first time, Geneva, which had been independent since the Reformation, and the hitherto subject districts of Vaud, Valais, and Ticino. Thus Switzerland, originally a German-speaking country, became a trilingual one. Gradually the cantons, one after another, became more " liberal ". In 1847 seven Roman Catholic cantons formed the Sonderbund, a federation within the Federation, in consequence of the suppression by the Canton Aargau of the eight convents in its territory and, on the other side, the admission of the Jesuits to Lucerne. The other cantons objected, and in a civil war lasting three weeks suppressed the Sonderbund. But the tension between the two parties remained. Under the Constitution of 1848 the Jesuits were not allowed to settle in any Swiss Canton.

Opposition to the Papacy had a long history in Switzerland. It was not forgotten that the two great Gallican councils had been held, one just beyond the frontier at Constance, the other in Swiss territory at Basle. Northern Switzerland had been in the diocese of Constance when Wessenberg was administering it, and his influence over all that region had been great. John Baptist Hirscher, who began to teach theology in the high school at Fribourg in 1837, was already in 1849 urging the introduction of the practical reforms afterwards carried out by the Old

Catholics.[1]  He suggested the reform of the Breviary, and even of the Canon of Scripture: the abolition of clerical celibacy, the use of the language of the country in the services, changes in the laws about indulgences and dispensations, and the reunion of Christendom.  Philipp Anton von Segesser, President of the Council of Lucerne, declared that the definition of Papal Infallibility by a council was impossible because absurd.[2]  Paulin Gschwind, the parish priest of Starrkirch with Dullikon, in Canton Solothurn, wrote a book, anonymously, in 1869, suggesting that the Vatican Council might well abolish clerical celibacy.[3]

On April 3, 1870, during the Vatican Council, Landammann Augustin Keller addressed a meeting at Langenthal, which passed strong resolutions protesting against the Syllabus of Errors and the new dogmas proposed by the Council.[4]  A short-lived paper called *The Catholic Voice from the Forest Cantons* was started by a young priest and a layman at Lucerne, to oppose the new dogmas: the name of the priest was Eduard Herzog.[5]  On August 18, 1870, the Diocesan Conference of Basle, a council representing the cantonal governments, agreed unanimously, with the exception of the representatives of Cantons Lucerne and Zug, to ask the Bishop of Basle not to publish the dogma of Papal Infallibility, the Federal Government to maintain the rights of its citizens against the papal claims, and the governments of the cantons to support their petition.  On October 27 the Diocesan Conference asked for a commission to inquire about the possibility of setting up a national archbishopric the next time the constitution should be revised, and a Roman Catholic theological faculty at Berne.[6]

Naturally, such suggestions were regarded with horror in Ultramontane circles.  The revision of the Swiss Constitution was expected, and it was suggested in a " clerical " paper that the result of revision might be similar to the murder of Archbishop Darboy by the Communists of Paris.[7]

The Swiss bishops, unlike those of Germany and Austria, had all voted with the majority at the council, except Bishop Greith of St. Gall, who submitted, as we have seen, before the end of 1870.  There was therefore never any possibility of a revolt led

---

[1] Paulin Gschwind, *Geschichte der Entstehung der christkatholischer Kirche in der Schweiz*, p. 8.
[2] Gschwind, p. 21.                        [3] Gschwind, p. 37.
[4] Gschwind, p. 80.                        [5] Gschwind, pp. 82–84.
[6] Gschwind, pp. 126–127.                  [7] Gschwind, p. 141.

by the bishops; and the clergy were almost all on the same side. The opposition in Switzerland came from the laity. The whole history of the Swiss Federation had been one long resistance to despotism: it is not surprising that many Swiss Roman Catholics resented the new despotism of the Vatican decrees, especially as they were believed to give dogmatic sanction to the Syllabus of Errors.

Eugen Lachat, Bishop of Basle, who resided at Solothurn, the headquarters of the diocese since the Reformation, published the Vatican decrees, although in several of the cantons within his diocese the government had forbidden the publication of them. Only two priests refused to read the document publishing the decrees: Johann Baptist Egli, the prison chaplain at Lucerne, and Paulin Gschwind, parish priest of Starrkirch with Dullikon, near Olten. Egli was excommunicated on March 10, 1871. His flock at the prison were devoted to him, but he had to leave them. Secular work was found for him in the Civil Service at Berne.[1] Later, he was put in charge of the Old Catholic congregation at Olsberg, in Canton Aargau.

Gschwind was in a stronger position; for parish priests, who were paid by the canton, could not be removed by the bishop without the consent of the cantonal government. He was sent by the Bishop of Basle a letter of excommunication, but he tore up the letter in the presence of the messengers, and declared the bishop excommunicated, as holding a heretical dogma.[2] He was supported by the majority of his parishioners, and also by the government of Canton Solothurn, whose leave for his removal the bishop had not sought.

Large meetings of Roman Catholics at Solothurn on April 29, 1871, and at Berne on May 1, passed resolutions rejecting the Vatican decrees, demanding the revision of the constitution for the protection of citizens against clerical demands, and supporting the suspended priests. A clerical committee was formed, and three representatives—Landammann Keller, Professor Munzinger, and Senator (Nationalrat) Anderwert—were sent to the first Old Catholic Congress at Munich,[3] which was also attended by Gschwind.

On May 12, 1872, the proposed revision of the constitution,

[1] Gschwind, pp. 152–156.
[2] *Theodorus, New Reformation*, p. 170.
[3] Gschwind, p. 164.

from which the Old Catholics had hoped much, was rejected. On September 23, Eduard Herzog, Professor of Theology at Lucerne, who had kept quiet since the failure of the *Catholic Voice*, wrote to Bishop Lachat resigning his post, and soon afterwards took charge of the Old Catholic congregation at Krefeld in Germany.[1] That autumn Professor Reinkens of Breslau was invited by the central committee, of which Professor Munzinger was the chairman, to come and give an address at Olten.[2] In spite of ill health, Dr. Reinkens accepted the invitation. On Sunday, December 1, a great meeting of protest against the Syllabus of Errors and the Infallibility of the Pope was held at Olten, and was attended by men from most of the German-speaking cantons. At this meeting Professor Munzinger put forward a programme of seven points, which was passed unanimously. The seven points were:—

(1) The establishment of local branches of the movement.

(2) The local branches would protest against the despotic system of the Papacy, especially against the Syllabus of Errors and the Infallibility of the Pope, and would stand by any priests who might be punished for rejecting these doctrines.

(3) The local branches would do all they could to see that priests who rejected the Infallibility of the Pope were appointed to vacant parishes.

(4) The central committee was entrusted with the duty of bringing influence to bear on the cantonal governments to appoint Old Catholic teachers in theology in schools and colleges, or else to give scholarships to colleges in Germany where the leaders of scientific Catholic theology were teaching.

(5) The necessary reforms in worship and discipline could only be introduced when the increase of the movement had led to the establishment of a new constitution for the Church.

(6) In the existing circumstances the central committee should have the right to invite foreign bishops to give confirmation and ordination, until a Swiss anti-infallibilist bishop should be appointed.

(7) The ultimate object of the movement was the reunion of all Christian Churches.

After this, Professor Reinkens addressed the meeting. He said that the existence of the Church and religion was Light, Life,

[1] Gschwind, pp. 191–193.          [2] Gschwind, p. 224.

Love, and Freedom. He refused to say anything about the abuse cast at them except to implore his audience never to imitate the language of the Ultramontane newspapers. The difference between them and the Ultramontanes was that the Ultramontanes, when they said the Church, meant the Pope, whereas they, when they said the Church, meant the Fellowship, the People of God. He pointed out that when Austria had passed a law granting religious freedom to all denominations, the Pope had declared that law null and void. And he concluded by attacking the favourite doctrine of the Jesuits, that it is man's duty to " sacrifice his reason " to obedience.[1] This address made a tremendous impression; and as eleven cantons and thirty-six towns and villages were represented at the meeting, the movement began to spread rapidly. On December 16 the Bishop of Basle sent an uncompromising answer to the demands of the Diocesan Conference, whereby, as Keller said, " the bridge was broken ".[2] He was supported by the other Swiss bishops, who issued a joint pastoral against the " new heresy ". On January 28, 1873, the Diocesan Conference met at Solothurn, and proceeded to depose the bishop and to invite the cathedral chapter of Solothurn to elect his successor.[3] (Under the constitution they apparently had the power to do this.) The cantons of Lucerne and Zug did not consent, but in the other five cantons—Solothurn, Aargau, Thurgau, Berne, and Basel-Land: the canton of Basle is divided into two parts, Basel-Stadt (town) and Basel-Land (country)—Eugen Lachat was no longer recognized as Bishop of Basle by the civil governments. The decision to refuse recognition was passed by a large majority in each case.[4] The bishop was, however, supported by his chapter, which refused to elect a successor, and by the great majority of his clergy.

In the meantime the Council of Canton Solothurn had passed a law requiring parish priests to submit, after six years, to re-election by their parishes; if the parish rejected its priest, the living became vacant, and the patron proceeded to present a new priest. Similar laws had already been passed in other cantons.

The Bishop of Basle protested that this regulation was contrary to canon law. The cantonal government, however, claimed that in a matter of this kind the civil law was supreme. The

---

[1] Gschwind, pp. 226–229.
[2] Gschwind, p. 244.
[3] Gschwind, p. 249.
[4] Gschwind, p. 252.

result was that parishes which wished to get rid of an Ultramontane priest had an opportunity of carrying out their wishes. One case was the town parish of Olten. Here Pfarrer Bläsi, the parish priest, was an extreme and aggressive Ultramontane. Making use of the new law, the parish meeting decided by 291 votes to 30 to depose him. The " Stift " of Schönenwerd, the patron, refused by a majority to make any appointment, and the right of presentation passed to the " Regierungsrat ", which, in accordance with a petition from the parish, called Eduard Herzog back from Krefeld to take charge of Olten. Herzog was born at Schöngau, in Canton Lucerne, so that he was returning to his native land. His parishioners at Krefeld wrote to Olten that they were very sorry to lose him, but that they could not refuse to recognize that Switzerland had the first claim on a Swiss. He was inducted at the large parish church of Olten at Easter 1873, and a banquet followed in the hall of the railway station, at which all the Swiss leaders of the movement were present. On this occasion Benedict von Arx, a member of the Government of the canton, pointed out that the success of the movement was due to the parishioners of Starrkirch with Dullikon; for that country parish had been the fulcrum of the movement, and if its people had not supported their priest in his resistance to the Vatican Council, nothing more would have happened.[1]

The fourth parish, after Starrkirch-Dullikon, Olsberg, and Olten, to join the movement was Trimbach, where Pfarrer Kilchmann was elected on March 16, 1873, by 167 votes to 57, in the place of Pfarrer Hausherr. But Kilchmann died on April 7, 1874, having occupied the parish not quite a year.[2]

The separation of these parishes from the Roman Communion was accompanied by practical difficulties. On March 12, 1873, the Pope issued orders that in no case might churches which had been profaned by Old Catholic services be used by Roman Catholics. Appeal must be made to the civil courts, and if they would not allow Roman Catholics the exclusive use of the church, a " Notkirche " (emergency church) must be built.

There was no such rule forbidding the use of the same church by Roman Catholics and Protestants, which was a common practice in Canton Thurgau. But Gschwind points out that the Roman Catholics could not treat the Old Catholics as they did the Protestants. For one thing, since the services were similar,

[1] Gschwind, pp. 275–279.     [2] Gschwind, p. 284.

the uneducated might easily mistake an Old Catholic for a Roman Catholic service (at this time the only difference was doctrinal, though later on the Old Catholics abolished the use of Latin and made other changes).[1] Also, since the Protestants had no priests, and did not celebrate Mass, they were not setting up altar against altar, and their services, which consisted only of preaching and prayers conducted by laymen (for Rome naturally does not regard a Protestant minister as anything more than a layman), were not nearly so offensive to the Roman Catholics as the rival Mass of the Old Catholics.

Accordingly, the Roman Catholics built " emergency churches " at Olten and Starrkirch-Dullikon. The question arose whether the bells as well as the church were defiled by Old Catholic use, and whether Roman Catholics who died might have the passing bell and the funeral bell rung for them in such a church. But though they were not allowed to use the church for services, the " extra pious " had no objection to misusing it, so that it had to be closed when not in use.

At the beginning of 1873 the " committee of the Society of Independent Catholics " started a paper called *Katholische Blätter* (Catholic Leaves), which was edited by Professor Dietschi of Olten and Pfarrer Gschwind.[2] In 1878 it became *Der Katholik*, and still continues under this name.

On April 20, 1873, a great meeting was held at Arlesheim near Basle, to protest against Ultramontanism. An organized attempt was made to break it up, but the Basle Government, warned at the last moment, prevented this by sending troops, and arresting four rioters. Resolutions were passed against " intrusion and misuse of the spiritual power ".[3] A few days earlier the government of Solothurn, which no longer recognized Mgr. Lachat as Bishop of Basle, compelled him to leave his palace at Solothurn and to take refuge in Canton Lucerne. The Canton of Berne, which also refused to recognize him, ordered the Roman Catholic priests in its territory to break off their relations with him. The cause of the dispute in Berne was not the Vatican Council, but a cantonal law of 1874 ordering the election of all ministers of religion by their congregations. Pius IX forbade Roman Catholics to take part in such elections. Berne is a Protestant canton; but in 1815 its territory had been increased

[1] Gschwind, pp. 289–293.  [2] Gschwind, p. 297.
[3] Gschwind, pp. 299–306.

by the addition of a district in the Jura which was French-speaking and Roman Catholic. The clergy of this district, with four exceptions, refused to break off relations with Bishop Lachat, and signed a protest against the action of the cantonal government. On this the government deprived the priests who had signed the protest of their parishes. They were permitted to say Mass in private, but not to perform any public functions, because, being paid by the State, they had transgressed the law of the State. They were supported by the Pope, and by Roman Catholics in other countries; the priests who were instituted in their place, some of whom were men of inferior character, were roughly treated by the laity, who refused, and indeed were forbidden by the Pope, to attend their services. Appeals to the supreme federal courts of Switzerland only resulted in the confirmation of the action of the Bernese government. But in Aargau, Thurgau, Solothurn, and Basel-Land, some of the clergy broke off relations with Bishop Lachat at the bidding of their governments:[1] it was in the French-speaking district of Berne and its neighbourhood that the most serious resistance was organized. On January 17, 1874, the Canton Berne passed a new law confirming its action, which was sanctioned, in spite of papal protests, by the Federal Council on September 17; and the appeal of Bishop Lachat against his deposition was likewise rejected.

A similar dispute broke out in Geneva. Until the French Revolution, Roman Catholic services had been entirely prohibited in the city of Calvin; and the ancient bishopric of Geneva had been transferred to Annecy in Savoy (it will be remembered that St. Francis de Sales was Bishop of Geneva, but only once visited his nominal see city, and then at the risk of his life). When Geneva was annexed by the revolutionary French government, which abolished Calvin's independent city-state, Roman Catholic services were again held (the first was in 1799, in a private house), and in the reorganized Church of France Geneva was attached to the diocese of Chambéry. In 1815 Geneva became for the first time a canton in the Swiss Federation; it received an addition of twenty Roman Catholic parishes, and on September 20, 1819, under pressure from the cantonal government, the Pope transferred the city to the diocese of Lausanne. In 1864 Mermillod, who had been a parish priest at Geneva, was consecrated by Pope

[1] Gschwind, p. 348.

Pius IX as suffragan bishop to the Bishop of Lausanne, with the title of Bishop of Hebron. (It was Mermillod who afterwards preached the sermon on the three Bethlehems—the manger, the tabernacle, and the Vatican.)[1] The cantonal government, however, refused to allow Bishop Mermillod to live within its territory: it did not want a bishop in Geneva at all, and least of all Mermillod. On March 23, 1873, the Canton of Geneva passed a law that all Roman Catholic priests must be elected by the Roman Catholic citizens of their parishes, who must also have a share in the government of the church. This was the answer of the canton to the Pope, who had a few weeks before created Geneva an " apostolic vicariate " and put Mermillod in charge of it. Attempts were made by the bishop and his friends to induce the French Government to interfere, and to appeal to the Powers which had taken part in the Congress of Vienna, because that congress had guaranteed freedom of religion in Switzerland; but in vain. The Genevan government held that in making such a law it was not interfering with religious freedom, but only with church government; the Roman Catholics answered that the right of the Pope to control appointments was an essential part of their religion. Eleven priests were deprived of their posts, and their successors had to take the following oath:—

" I swear before God to conform strictly to the provisions of the constitution and the law as to the organization of Catholic worship in the Republic, and to observe all the commands of the constitutions and laws of the canton and the Federation. I swear also to do nothing contrary to the security and tranquillity of the State: to preach to my parishioners obedience to the law, respect towards the magistrates, and union with all their fellow-citizens."

Mermillod was expelled from the canton.

Hyacinthe Loyson, the celebrated French preacher, who had resigned his post at Paris in 1869 on doctrinal grounds, and who had given a series of lectures in Geneva on Church reform, at the invitation of the Old Catholic party, was in October 1873 elected to one of the three vacant parishes in the city. He and his two colleagues were accordingly placed under the greater excommunication. Loyson, however, did not possess the gifts of either a statesman or a pastor. He wanted to abolish at once such customs as compulsory celibacy for the clergy and compulsory confession; for this the time was not yet come. His preaching

[1] See above, ch. 15, p. 193.

drew crowds to his church, but he could not build them up into a congregation. His ministry at Geneva was not altogether a success, and his later career showed that he had not the stability necessary for a leader in a new religious movement.[1] Loyson had, moreover, committed what must be regarded, at the very least, as a grave error of judgment. Though a Roman Catholic priest and a religious, he had married, as early as 1872. The marriage took place in London. Whatever opinions may be held on clerical marriage in general, it is evident that a man who has been ordained on condition that he remains celibate has no right to marry, without being released from his obligations by some competent authority, and still claim to exercise his functions as a priest. Much more is this true if he has taken a vow of celibacy, as Loyson, who was a Carmelite, had. His defence was that many Roman Catholic priests in France, including one very well-known one, were secretly married, and that he wished to show that a priest who marries should do so openly. But this is not a convincing defence of his breach of his vows. Nor can it be claimed that he had a right to marry as an Old Catholic priest; for the Old Catholic Church was not yet constituted, and in any case did not permit priests to marry till some years later. Unfortunately Loyson was not the only priest to marry without authority: Gschwind tells us that he did the same, hoping to hasten the formal abolition of compulsory clerical celibacy.[2] (For the rest of Loyson's career, see p. 283.)

On the other hand, Loyson's departure from Geneva was entirely to his honour. Because of the struggle between the canton and the Papacy, all the Catholic churches, except Notre Dame, were handed over to the " Liberal Catholics ", as they called themselves—that is, the supporters of the new laws of the canton. They demanded the possession of Notre Dame as well, and Loyson held that this was unjust: for the " Liberal Catholics " were really only a minority of the Catholics of Geneva. He declared that they were neither liberal nor Catholic;[3] he saw that their motives were not religious, but political, and he left Geneva and returned to France.

Meanwhile the movement was gathering strength in German-speaking Switzerland. A second meeting of delegates from all the Old Catholic congregations in Switzerland was held at Olten

---

[1] Gschwind. pp. 368–384;  *Theodorus*, pp. 180–182.
[2] Gschwind, p. 468.          [3] *Theodorus*, p. 220.

on August 31, 1873 (the first one had been held on December 1, 1872: see above). At this meeting resolutions were unanimously passed declaring that the Old Catholics were independent of the Roman hierarchy, and that they had a right to elect their own bishop and to introduce various reforms, such as the use of the mother-tongue in the church services, the abolition of ecclesiastical impediments to marriage, and the secularization of churchyards.[1] Eighteen delegates were elected to represent the Swiss at the International Old Catholic Congress at Constance (see next chapter).

The following year, 1874, the Swiss Federation adopted a new constitution, which came into force on May 29. Among its provisions were the establishment of compulsory education, freedom of access to the State schools for children of all denominations, a State university, complete freedom of religion, the expulsion of the Jesuits and their affiliated organizations from Swiss territory, and other articles in accordance with the programme of contemporary Liberalism. The new constitution made it possible, as Gschwind says, for the Swiss Old Catholic Church to build its own house without being continually threatened with an unequal struggle against the Roman hierarchy.[2]

It was necessary to provide for the future education of the clergy, apart from the Roman Catholic seminaries, in which the instruction was in accordance with the obscurantist ideas favoured by Pius IX. Accordingly, a Catholic theological faculty was set up by the Canton of Berne in the new university at the capital. At the end of November the new faculty started, with five professors and eight students. At its head was Professor Friedrich of Munich, who was closely associated with Döllinger; the other professors were Franz Hirschwälder, a Silesian pupil of Döllinger's, Dr. Georgens of Metz, Eduard Herzog, and Dr. Gareis of Würzburg, a layman. At the same time, the large church of St. Peter and St. Paul at Berne, which had not long been built, passed into Old Catholic hands. The professors in the theological faculty were given by the government the right to use the church, whereupon the parish priest, Stephen Perroulaz, deserted it, and held his services elsewhere. The parochial church council was against him, and ultimately he was deprived of his office as the parish priest recognized and paid by the canton, and

[1] Gschwind, p. 409; see *Theodorus*, p. 188, for a somewhat different account.
[2] Gschwind, p. 419.

Professor Herzog, who had till then been in charge of Olten, was elected in his place.[1] The next step in the progress of the movement was the formation of a constitution, including the election of a bishop. On June 14, 1874, a meeting of representatives of the congregations was held at Berne for this purpose. How far the revolt had gone is shown by the startling fact that the lay representatives of Berne, Zürich, and St. Gall saw no need for a bishop: he would, they said, be either a little Pope or an unnecessary figurehead. But Herzog, Loyson, and Gschwind pointed out that they must have a bishop, both as the necessary minister of confirmation and ordination, and as the centre of unity without which the different congregations could not be held together. Landammann Keller, too, roundly warned them "not to make a constitution for the moon"! In consequence, they decided by a large majority to maintain episcopacy, and to appoint a committee to draw up the constitution. An Anglican priest, the Rev. L. M. Hogg, who was present, exclaimed to Gschwind, " Vous avez sauvé l'église " (You have saved the church).[2]

The next meeting was held on September 21 at Berne: and a long discussion took place about the rights of the future bishop. It was decided that the bishop should have such powers as the national synod should bestow upon him. The next question was whether the bishop, like the parish priests, should be liable to re-election every six years; Deramey, a priest from the Jura, thought that the same rule should apply to bishops as to priests. But this proposal was rejected: it was decided, however, that the synod should have the power to depose the bishop for neglecting his duties, but only by a two-thirds majority. The question of his stipend was to be settled after consultation with the cantonal governments.

On October 14 Dr. Watterich, formerly of Strasbourg, was appointed the first Old Catholic parish priest at Basle, where the church formerly belonging to the Dominicans was assigned to the Old Catholics. Dr. Watterich, without opposition from anyone, abolished the hearing of confessions, said Mass in German, and reduced the vestments to alb and stole; and at the Synod in the following year the representatives of Basle demanded that these reforms should be universally adopted, together with the abolition of clerical celibacy.[3]

---

[1] Gschwind, pp. 434–442.     [2] Gschwind, p. 444; *Theodorus*, p. 218.
[3] Gschwind, p. 450.

The first National Synod of the Old Catholic Church of Switzerland met at Olten, June 14, 1875, and was composed of forty-six clerical and 115 lay members. It declared the constitution drawn up the previous year to be now in force, and proceeded to arrange for the election of a bishop. This required the sanction of the State, which was given by the Federal Council on April 28, 1876, on condition that the bishop should be a Swiss citizen, should be resident in Switzerland, and should perform no spiritual functions outside Swiss territory. Within a year eight cantons had given their approval: they were Aargau, Solothurn, Geneva, Neuchatel, Zürich, Berne, Basel-Land, and Basel-Stadt. Accordingly, the National Synod, which now represented fifty-five ecclesiastical parishes and seventeen other communities, spread over ten cantons, and numbering in all 73,380 persons, met on June 7–8, 1876, to elect a bishop. It had fifty-four clerical and 108 lay members. The executive council laid before the Synod a proposal to identify itself with the efforts of the German Old Catholic Church for union with the Protestant, Greek, and Anglican Churches. Professor Michaud moved that the basis of any such union should be the seven first general councils. He was opposed by Gschwind, on the extraordinary ground that if the Vatican Council had erred so grievously, councils such as the Council of Nicæa, in an earlier age and with smaller numbers, might equally have been mistaken. (This was, of course, to destroy the foundation of the Old Catholic position, which is that the Vatican Council was not a true general council, and to make a present to the Ultramontanes of the witness of the Primitive Church.) Professor Michaud's proposal, however, was referred to a committee, and accepted by the Synod on its second day.

It was found that out of the fifty-four priests only thirteen were Swiss citizens, and therefore eligible. Professor Herzog received 117 votes, Karl Schröter of Rheinfelden thirty-four, and no one else more than two. Herzog at first refused the offer, but was persuaded by Keller and Schröter to accept it, for the good of the Church. The remaining business of the Synod was the consideration of the proposals from Basle already mentioned, of which the abolition of clerical celibacy was the most important; the provision of a German Missal and Ritual, which was entrusted to a committee consisting of the bishop-elect, Michaud, Watterich, Gschwind, and Weibel; and various financial arrangements.

The consecration of Bishop Herzog took place in the old parish church at Rheinfelden (where the whole Catholic population had become Old Catholic), on September 18, 1876. The consecrator was Bishop Reinkens. There were no bishops assisting him, for the Dutch bishops did not come.

The Old Catholic Church of Switzerland has from the beginning been officially called " Christkatholisch " (Christian Catholic), not " Altkatholisch " (Old Catholic), a term which is not used in Switzerland. But in this book, in order to avoid confusion, I always use the words " Old Catholic ". The story told in this chapter shows, perhaps, why the Swiss did not adopt the term " Old Catholic ". The movement was chiefly a lay one, and contained a revolutionary element strong enough to make the name " Old Catholic " unsuitable. Certainly the appeal to antiquity, though not absent, was far less powerful than the liberal and republican spirit in revolt against the whole Roman system, and not always careful to distinguish between what was ancient and Catholic, and what was modern and Roman. We cannot be surprised that the conservative Church of Utrecht was alarmed by the proceedings of the Swiss opponents of the Vatican Council; nor that a movement led by laymen of the middle class, liberal in politics and inclined to associate politics with ecclesiastical reform, should have ultimately failed to appeal to the conservative peasants who have always been the backbone of the Roman Communion in Switzerland, and who loved the ancient observances, the processions and the pilgrimages, which the liberals of the towns despised and sought to abolish, as inconsistent with the enlightenment of the nineteenth century.

# CHAPTER XIX

# THE REUNION CONFERENCES AT BONN

IN order to carry the story of the Old Catholic movement in Switzerland down to the consecration of Bishop Herzog, I have passed by several important events in Germany. I now return to the point which I reached at the end of Chapter 17, the consecration of Bishop Reinkens at Rotterdam on August 11, 1873.

A month later, on September 12, the third Old Catholic Congress (the two previous ones had been held at Munich and Cologne, see Ch. 17) met at Constance, in the same hall in which the famous Gallican Council had deposed Pope John XXIII, and had also condemned John Huss to the stake. Bishop Christopher Wordsworth of Lincoln, who was himself unable to be present, sent a message of greeting, with some Latin verses contrasting the congress with the Council:

"Inclyta qua tollit veteres Constantia turres,
    Jam video doctum se glomerare chorum:
Agnosco præsens in te, Constantia, Numen,
    Concilium Nemesis convocat ipsa tuum.
Tu famosa nimis synodo, Constantia, sævo
    Nunc es concilio nobilitanda pio.
Martyrum ubi quondam maduit tua sanguine tellus,
    Nunc seges albescit messis apostolicæ.
Ecce! novo cineres Hussi fulgore coruscant,
    Fitque evangelii fax pyra martyrii;
Pragensis video venerandam surgere formam,
    Inque tuo cœtu vivida verba loqui." [1]

Among those who were present were Bishop Reinkens, and most of the German Old Catholic leaders, though not Döllinger. Switzerland was represented by eighteen delegates, including Gschwind and Loyson; the latter was not permitted to speak, because he had broken his vow of celibacy, which, as Gschwind bitterly remarks, " shows the difference between Germany and Switzerland ".[2] (But it is also true that Loyson could not speak German.) The Church of Utrecht was represented by Pastoor [3]

---

[1] *Theodorus, New Reformation*, p. 189.
[2] Gschwind, op. cit., p. 411.
[3] "Pastoor" is the title of a Catholic priest in Dutch.

Rol of Utrecht, Pastoor van Vlooten of Amersfoort, and van Santen, a subdeacon. There were eleven Old Catholics from Austria, and five from other countries.[1]

Among the visitors were the Archpriest Vassiliev and Colonel Kiréev, from Russia; the Bishop of Albany (Dr. Doane) and the Assistant Bishop of South Carolina (Dr. Lyman); Dr. Howson, the Dean of Chester; the Rev. J. B. Mayor, Professor of Classics at King's College, London, and the Rev. C. F. Lowder, the famous Vicar of St. Peter's, London Docks.

The President of the Congress was Professor von Schulte, who was assisted by Professor Cornelius and Landammann Keller. It has always been the custom at Old Catholic Congresses to have a layman as president.

The business before the congress was first to record progress since the last congress; then to draw up a constitution for the German Old Catholic Church; lastly, to appoint committees to promote reunion. Professor von Schulte told the congress that there were now at least 50,000 registered Old Catholics and eighty-two congregations in Prussia, Bavaria, and Baden. The constitution, in seventy articles, was unanimously adopted and left for final confirmation by the synod. Professor Michelis proposed that two committees for reunion should be appointed: one to sit at Munich and correspond with the Eastern churches, the other to sit at Bonn and correspond with the Anglican and Protestant churches. They were to work together, and their ultimate object should be a general council. This proposal was adopted, together with a scheme for the maintenance of theological students and retired priests.

On the Sunday, Bishop Lyman celebrated, using the American liturgy, at 7.30 in the Evangelical church; and an Old Catholic Mass, in Latin, was sung at the Augustinian church at 9.0, at which Bishop Reinkens preached. The most complete agreement was felt by all who were present, and Old Catholics and Anglican visitors alike testify to the encouragement given by the congress.[2]

On September 20 the German government formally recognized Bishop Reinkens, and on October 7 he took the oath of allegiance, which included a promise to resign rather than oppose the government. This promise was severely criticized, especially in England, but the bishop maintained that to use

---

[1] Schulte, *Das Altkatholizismus*, p. 676.
[2] *Theodorus*, pp. 192–196.

against his sovereign the influence bestowed upon him by State recognition would be treason, and declared that he repudiated the doctrine of a State Church, and would never tolerate any interference by the government in the doctrine, liturgy, or internal discipline of the Church.[1]

The first synod of the German Old Catholic Church, appointed under the constitution drawn up at Constance, met at Bonn on May 27-29, 1874. It differed, of course, from a congress, in being the official organ of the diocese; it consisted of the clergy and representatives of the laity (for the Old Catholics have from the beginning admitted laymen to their synods), whereas the congresses are voluntary gatherings, open to all members of the Church.

This synod declared itself in favour of certain practical reforms, of which the chief were that confession should be voluntary, the mother tongue should be used for all church services (but this could only be carried out gradually), all fees for Masses should be abolished, and the rich and poor should be given equal treatment in church. As we have seen, these proposals were at once imitated in Switzerland, with less caution.

The fourth Old Catholic Congress was held at Freiburg-in-Breisgau, and began on September 6, 1874. Most of its members came from Baden: there were only four from Switzerland (Herzog, Watterich, Schröter, and Keller), and none from Holland. The Russians who had been at Constance came again, accompanied by Sukhotin from Moscow; from the English Church there were Dean Howson, Professor Mayor, the Warden of Keble (Edward Talbot, afterwards Bishop of Winchester), and nine others. The congress seems to have concerned itself mainly with the disputes between Old Catholics and Roman Catholics about the ownership of Church property. It asserted that Church property belonged to the parish, and not to the Church as a whole; therefore, if the majority of a congregation accepted Old Catholic principles, the church and all that was in it should pass to the Old Catholics.[2] (I doubt very much whether this claim was justified: it seems logically to involve a Congregationalist view of the nature of the Church.)

But the importance of this congress was completely overshadowed by the first of the two international conferences at Bonn, which was held the following week. These conferences

[1] *Theodorus*, p. 203.　　　　[2] *Theodorus*, pp. 222-230.

differed from the Old Catholic congresses in being, not meetings of Old Catholics at which visitors were welcomed, but inter-denominational assemblies summoned for the express purpose of promoting reunion. They were important because they were the first of their kind. No such conferences had ever been held in modern times; in them, for the first time, Latin, Anglican, and Orthodox theologians met to discuss the differences which separated them. We can see that the difficulties were greater than they realized, and that the " *imponderabilia* " were scarcely recognized at all. At that date this was inevitable; it is remarkable that they made so much progress as they did.

The Old Catholic leaders had no wish to confine their work to the section of Latin Christendom which rejected the Vatican Council. They perceived that their separation from the Papacy made possible the healing of the wounds in the unity of Christendom which had been open for centuries; and they intended the conferences at Bonn to lead to reunion both with the " Oriental " and with the Anglican Churches. These conferences, however, did not represent churches (like the Bonn Conference of 1931, which will be described later): they were private meetings of theologians invited by the Old Catholic leaders. The invitations to the conference of 1874 were sent to particular theologians in many countries, who had shown sympathy with the Old Catholic movement. The invitation ran as follows:—

" On September 14 and the following days a conference of members of different communions, actuated by the desire and hope of a future great reunion of Christians, will be held at Bonn.

" It is proposed to take, as the basis and standard of limitation of the endeavours of the conference, the confessions, teaching, and institutions recognized by the Church in the first centuries, and regarded as essential by both the Eastern and the Western communions before the Great Schism.

" The aim specially proposed by the conference is not an union of different sections of the Church whereby each should become absorbed in the general body and lose its distinctive characteristics, but the re-establishment of intercommunion between the churches on the basis of ' unitas in necessariis ', without interference with those particular tenets of individual churches which do not affect the essentials of the ancient Church confession."

The Committee for the Promotion of Church Reunion.[1]

<hr>

[1] *Theodorus*, pp. 230–231.

It will be observed that no mention was made of Trent. Two years before, at the Congress of Cologne, the question of the recognition of the later Latin councils had been raised by Michaud, and shelved. The Church of Utrecht still held fast by Trent, and it was probably for this reason that no Dutch theologians appeared at Bonn; indeed, there appears from this time a certain coolness between the Church of Utrecht and the newer Old Catholic movement, which lasted until the Declaration of Utrecht fifteen years later. It was clearly necessary to lay Trent aside, if reunion with either the Orthodox or the Anglican Communion was desired;[1] but in doing so, Döllinger and his colleagues had moved farther in two years than the Church of Utrecht in 150.

The Old Catholic members of the Bonn Conference were Bishop Reinkens, Döllinger, Langen, Reusch, Knoodt, and Lutterbeck, professors, and four other Germans; Quily, a priest from Geneva; and Dr. Michaud, from Paris. The Orthodox members were Professor Z. Rhossis from Athens, and four Russians—the Archpriest Janyschev, Rector of the Clerical Academy at St. Petersburg; Arsenius Tatschalov, the Russian chaplain at Wiesbaden; Alexander Kiréev, and Theodor von Sukhotin, of the Society of Friends of Spiritual Enlightenment.

The Anglican members were: from England, the Bishop of Winchester (Dr. Harold Browne), the Dean of Chester (Dr. Howson), Dr. H. P. Liddon, the Warden of Keble (the Rev. E. S. Talbot), the Master of University College, Durham (Dr. A. Plummer), Professor Mayor, Canon Conway of Westminster Abbey, seven other priests, among whom were the Rev. L. M. Hogg and the Rev. H. N. Oxenham, and three laymen; from America, the Bishop of Pittsburg (Dr. Kerfoot), and his chaplain, Dr. Hartmann, the Rev. R. J. Nevin, American chaplain at Rome, and several other priests.

There were also nine German Protestants, including Professors Kamphausen, Krafft, and J. P. Lange; the Revs. J. Victor Bloch and Pastor Schöler from Denmark; an English Congregational minister, the Rev. J. Macmillan, and Professor Auguste Kerckhoff of Melun, France.[2]

At the opening meeting, on September 14, Professor Reusch asked those present to be discreet in making public what might

[1] *Theodorus*, p. 156 (Bishop Wordsworth's Letter to the Congress of Cologne).
[2] *Theodorus*, pp. 231-233.

be said.   A short account of the proceedings would be published, but no detailed report.   The members of the conference represented no one but themselves, and he therefore proposed that the chair should be taken, not by a dignitary of the Church, but by one who was known simply for his learning, Dr. Döllinger. The proposal was agreed to by acclamation.   The learning and skill of Döllinger, as chairman, and his European reputation, were one of the main causes of the success of the conference.

Döllinger then explained that their business was to discuss the points of difference between the Old Catholics and the Anglicans, and between the Old Catholics and the Orientals.   He proposed to limit the discussion with the Anglicans to certain points, but he was prepared to accept any other course, such as the discussion of the Thirty-Nine Articles.   When Mr. Hogg remarked that if they confined themselves to the first five or six centuries they need not discuss either the Thirty-Nine Articles or the Tridentine Decrees, Döllinger made the following important statement:—

" As regards the Council of Trent, I believe I am at liberty to state, not only in my own name, but also in that of my colleagues, that we in no way consider ourselves bound by all the decrees of that Council, which cannot be regarded as œcumenical." [1]

It is clear that by making this statement Döllinger and his friends had shut the door behind them, and were no longer in any sense Roman Catholics.

The first subject to be discussed was the " Filioque " clause in the Nicene Creed.   Döllinger pointed out that this question was twofold:   there was a question about the truth of the clause " And the Son ", and a question whether its insertion into the Creed was lawful.   He proposed to confine the discussion to the latter point, leaving the former point for future consideration.   The proposal for discussion was, that the way in which the Filioque had been inserted was illegal, and that, for the sake of unity, the original form of the Creed ought to be restored.   The Englishmen would not accept this:   the Americans were less intransigeant.   After the proposal had been amended by the Bishop of Winchester, and rejected, in its amended form, by the Orientals, it was unanimously accepted in the following form:—

" We agree that the way in which the Filioque was inserted into the Nicene Creed was illegal, and that, with a view to future peace and unity, it is much to be desired that the whole Church should

---

[1] *Theodorus*, p. 235.

set itself seriously to consider whether the Creed could possibly be restored to its primitive form, without sacrifice of any true doctrine which is expressed in the present Western form." [1]

After this, fourteen articles dealing with points supposed to be in dispute between the Old Catholic and Anglican Communions were unanimously agreed to.  They were as follows:—

(1) We agree that the apocryphal or deutero-canonical books of the Old Testament are not of the same canonicity as the books in the Hebrew canon.

(2) We agree that no translation of the Holy Scriptures can claim an authority superior to that of the original text.

(3) We agree that the reading of Holy Scripture in the vulgar tongue cannot lawfully be forbidden.

(4) We agree that, in general, it is more fitting, and in accordance with the spirit of the Church, that the Liturgy should be in the tongue understood by the people.

(5) We agree that faith working by love, not faith without love, is the means and condition of man's justification before God.

(6) Salvation cannot be merited by " Merit of condignity ", because there is no proportion between the infinite worth of the salvation promised by God and the finite worth of man's works.

(7) We agree that the doctrine of " works of supereroga-tion ", and of a " treasury of the merits of the saints "—*i.e.*, that the overflowing merits of the saints can be transferred to others, either by the rulers of the Church or by the authors of the good works themselves—is untenable.

(8) (*a*) We acknowledge that the number of the sacra-ments was first fixed at seven, in the twelfth century, and was then received into the general teaching of the Church, not as a tradition coming down from the Apostles or from the earliest times, but as the result of theological speculation.

(*b*) Catholic theologians (*e.g.*, Bellarmine) acknowledge, and we acknowledge with them, that Baptism and the Eucharist are " principalia, præcipua, eximia salutis nostræ sacramenta ".

(9) (*a*) The Holy Scriptures being recognized as the primary rule of faith, we agree that the genuine tradition

<hr>

[1] *Theodorus*, p. 254.

(*i.e.*, the unbroken transmission, partly oral, partly in writing, of the doctrine delivered by Christ and the Apostles) is an authoritative source of teaching for all successive generations of Christians. This tradition is partly to be found in the consensus of the great ecclesiastical bodies standing in historical continuity with the primitive Church, partly to be gathered by scientific method from the written documents of all centuries.

(*b*) We acknowledge that the Church of England, and the churches derived through her, have maintained unbroken the episcopal succession.

(10) We reject the new Roman doctrine of the Immaculate Conception of the Blessed Virgin Mary, as being contrary to the tradition of the first thirteen centuries, according to which Christ alone was conceived without sin.

(11) We agree that the practice of confession of sins before the congregation or a priest, with the exercise of the power of the keys, has come down to us from the Primitive Church, and, purged from abuses and freed from constraint, should be preserved in the Church.

(12) " Indulgences " can only refer to penalties actually imposed by the Church herself.

(13) We agree that the commemoration of the faithful departed—*i.e.*, a calling down of an outpouring of Christ's grace for them—has come down to us from the Primitive Church, and should be preserved in the Church.

(14) The Eucharistic celebration in the Church is not a continuous repetition or renewal of the propitiatory sacrifice offered once for ever by Christ upon the cross; but its sacrificial character consists in this, that it is the permanent memorial of it, and a representation and presentation (*Vergegenwärtigung*) on earth of the one oblation of Christ for the salvation of redeemed mankind, which according to Hebrews 9. 11.12. is continuously presented in heaven by Christ, Who now appears in the presence of God for us (Heb. 9. 24). While this is the character of the Eucharist in reference to the sacrifice of Christ, it is also a sacred feast, wherein the faithful, receiving the Body and Blood of our Lord, have communion one with another (1 Cor. 10. 17).[1]

[1] *Theodorus*, pp. 255–266.

(This article should be compared with the corresponding article in the Declaration of Utrecht, see next chapter.) The first four articles were passed with hardly any criticism; the fifth and sixth with slight amendments; the seventh and eighth unaltered. (The text given above is the text of the articles as they were finally passed.) The Bishop of Winchester had to leave at this point in the conference. The preamble to the ninth article, " The Holy Scriptures being recognized as the primary rule of faith ", was inserted to satisfy the Bishop of Pittsburg and the Dean of Chester, though Dr. Liddon claimed that it was not needed, in view of the twentieth Article of the English Church.

Archpriest Janyschev asked what " the great ecclesiastical bodies " referred to were. Döllinger answered, " First your own Church, and then the Western Church, except those sections of it which have severed their historical continuity ". Bloch asked whether the Churches of the Reformation were included, and Döllinger replied that he could not say that the Lutheran Church of Denmark had broken continuity in the same way as the Reformed Church of Geneva. But this did not satisfy Bloch, who refused to exclude any Church whose members were baptized; he would exclude the Baptists.

As to the continuity of the Church of England, the Russians said that the Metropolitan Philaret of Moscow had expressed doubts about it; but Döllinger and Bishop Reinkens spoke strongly in defence of it, and Liddon said that Philaret had told him, the year before his death, that he had never gone into the matter himself, but had taken his views from Roman Catholic writers.

The tenth article, on the Immaculate Conception, was opposed by Liddon, with the support of Oxenham (H. N. Oxenham subsequently joined the Roman Communion). Though he did not believe the doctrine himself, Liddon desired that those who wished to believe it, not as a dogma, but as a " pious opinion ", should be free to do so. He afterwards defended his attitude in a letter to *The Times*, September 30, 1874. Döllinger, however, protested with greater warmth than he showed on any other subject during the conference. He declared that he and his colleagues had two reasons for opposing the doctrine strongly. It had been introduced into the Church by a series of intrigues and falsehoods; and its promulgation as a dogma had prepared the way for the definition of the Papal Infallibility. It was for them "*fons et origo malorum* ", the source of all their troubles. He was warmly supported by the Bishop of Pittsburg and the Dean of Chester, and Liddon's amendment was rejected by twenty-five votes to nine. Liddon was primarily a dogmatic theologian, whereas Döllinger was a historian who could not admit that it was " pious " to believe what rested on no evidence at all. Liddon thought that if they were to condemn the speculation, they must logically condemn many other speculations. He was, however, convinced by Bishop Reinkens that there were other reasons why this condemnation was necessary.[1] (It is perhaps relevant to observe that Liddon had more in common with the French than with the German temperament, and that he did not accept or understand the critical methods of modern historians, as his attitude towards *Lux Mundi* afterwards showed.)

The eleventh and twelfth articles were passed without discussion. The thirteenth—on prayers for the dead—was criticized by the Dean of Chester, who refused to vote on it, but was carried by a large majority. At this point the following article was proposed : " We acknowledge that the Invocation of Saints is not commanded as a duty necessary to salvation for every Christian "; but the " Orientals " objected so strongly (referring to the Seventh Œcumenical Council) that it had to be dropped. The article on the Eucharist was left to the last, as likely to arouse the greatest differences of opinion; it was drafted by a committee consisting of Döllinger, Bishop Kerfoot (of Pittsburg), Dean Howson, Dr. Liddon, and Dr. Nevin. It was accepted both by the Orthodox and by the Danish Lutheran members of the Conference. The Rev. John Hunt asked whether it was meant that the Body and Blood of Christ were received in another sense in the Eucharist from that in which they were received in all other acts of worship; but he was sharply rebuked by Döllinger, who said that the opposite interpretation would be contrary to the teaching alike of the Eastern, Western, and Anglican churches, and that this was hardly the time to advance towards Calvinism.[2]

The last meeting of the conference was devoted to certain points raised by the " Orientals ". The dogmatic question of the Procession of the Holy Ghost was referred to a committee. The Eastern doctrine of the condition of the faithful departed was then discussed. According to this belief, the spirits of the faithful

[1] J. O. Johnston, *Henry Parry Liddon*, p. 196.          [2] *Theodorus*, p. 267.

departed are in a condition of light and peace, with a foretaste of eternal bliss, and in the case of the saints, including the sight of Jesus Christ Himself (Phil. 1. 23): but the full recompense of the entire man must be delayed till the resurrection of the body and the Last Judgment (2 Cor. 4. 10; Tim. 4. 8). Döllinger said that he did not know that this was the teaching of the Orthodox Church, and that they could not take any steps with regard to it immediately.[1] (Nevertheless, it appears to be the teaching of St. Irenæus, St. Justin, and other Fathers, and to be similar to the opinion held by Pope John XXII, and condemned by the University of Paris in the fourteenth century. It was maintained by Dean Luckock, A. J. Mason, and many other Anglican theologians, on the authority of Holy Scripture and the earlier Fathers.)[2]

The first Bonn Conference closed with the Te Deum, the Lord's Prayer, and an extempore prayer by Bishop Reinkens. It aroused much interest all over Europe, and especially in England. Indeed, when one considers how novel the venture was, amazing progress had been made.

The following year a second conference was held at Bonn, beginning on August 11, 1875. The invitations to this conference, unlike the invitations to its predecessor, were general: " everyone of sufficient theological knowledge, who was interested in the objects of the conference, was to consider himself invited ". Consequently, a much larger number was present; but the results were not so satisfactory, at any rate in Dr. Liddon's opinion. As before, Döllinger was in the chair.

The leading German Old Catholics who had been present the year before came again, and with them Dr. Herzog, the future Bishop in Switzerland. There were also several German Protestant pastors there. A very strong Orthodox contingent came to the Conference, headed by Lycurgus, Archbishop of Syra and Tenos in the Ægean Sea, and two Roumanian bishops. The Russians who had been at the first conference came again, with Professor Ossinin of St. Petersburg and others. With them were theologians from the Patriarchate of Constantinople, the Church of the Kingdom of Greece, the Serbian Church, and the Orthodox Church in Hungary. There was also present a certain Dr.

---

[1] *Theodorus*, p. 271.
[2] Charles Gore, *The Holy Spirit and the Church*, p. 311; H. M. Luckock, *After Death*, pp. 219–227; A. J. Mason, *Purgatory*, pp. 77–100; A. Lewis Innes, article in *Theology*, No. 41, November, 1923.

Overbeck, an English convert to Orthodoxy, who seems to have displayed the mentality of the convert in a manner which did not promote the success of the Conference.[1]

The Anglican contingent included the Bishop of Gibraltar (Dr. Sandford), Dean Howson, Dr. Liddon, Dr. Plummer, and Prebendary F. Meyrick, who was for many years secretary of the Anglo-Continental Society; the Rev. Malcolm MacColl, the well-known publicist; the Rev. L. M. Hogg; the Rev. F. W. Puller, afterwards Father Puller, S.S.J.E.; Professor Lias, the Rev. Albert Barff, of Cuddesdon, the Rev. J. A. Rivington (who afterwards joined the Roman Communion, and to refute whom Father Puller wrote his great book *The Primitive Saints and the See of Rome*), and many others. From the Church of Ireland came the Rev. Lord Plunket (afterwards Archbishop of Dublin), and the Right Hon. Master Brooke: these both belonged to the party which was then attempting to have all reference to Baptismal Regeneration and Priestly Absolution removed from the Irish Prayer Book. The American contingent did not include any bishop, but Dr. Henry L. Potter, Secretary of the House of Bishops (afterwards Bishop of New York), and Dr. W. S. Perry, Secretary of the House of Deputies of the General Convention, were there, together with Dr. Nevin, the American chaplain at Rome, and several other priests and laymen. There were no Danes this time, but the Rev. J. B. Paton, an English Congregationalist minister, and two Scottish Presbyterian ministers were present.[2]

The conference was concerned almost entirely with the dogmatic side of the Filioque question. The committee appointed by the conference to draw up an agreed statement consisted of the following members: Old Catholics, Döllinger, Bishop Reinkens, Langen; Anglicans, Liddon, Meyrick, Nevin; Orthodox, Archbishop Lycurgus, Anastasiadis, Bryennios, Janyschev, Ossinin; secretaries, Reusch, von Philippov, Rev. G. E. Broad (the English Chaplain at Düsseldorf, whose services as interpreter at both conferences were invaluable).

The agreed declaration was based on the language of St. John of Damascus. The choice of this Father, though unwelcome to Dr. Liddon, was made in order to satisfy the Orthodox. It ran as follows :—

---

[1] J. O. Johnston, p. 190.
[2] *Report of the Reunion Conference at Bonn*, August 10–16, 1875, pp. lv–lix.

(1) The Holy Ghost issues out of the Father (ἐκ τοῦ Πατρός) as the beginning (ἀρχή), the cause (αἰτία), the source (πηγή) of the Godhead (*De Recta Sententia*, n.1, *Contra Manich.* n. 4).

(2) The Holy Ghost does not issue out of the Son, because in the Godhead there is but one beginning (ἀρχή), one cause (αἰτία), through which all that is in the Godhead is produced (*De fide orthodoxa*, i. 8: ἐκ τοῦ Υἱοῦ δὲ τὸ Πνεῦμα οὐ λέγομεν, Πνεῦμα δὲ Υἱοῦ ὀνομάζομεν).

(3) The Holy Ghost issues out of the Father through the Son (*De fide orthodoxa*, i. 12; *Contra Manicheos*, n. 5; *De hymno Trisagion*, n. 28). To this was added at the special request of the Orthodox theologians, to enable them to accept the article: Homily in Sabb, s.n. 4: τοῦθ' ἡμῖν ἐστι τὸ λατρευόμενον.... Πνεῦμα ἁγίου τοῦ Θεοῦ καὶ Πατρός, ὡς ἐξ αὐτοῦ ἐκπορευόμενον, ὅπερ καὶ τοῦ Υἱοῦ λέγεται, ὡς δι' αὐτοῦ φανερούμενον καὶ τῇ κτίσει μεταδιδόμενον, ἀλλ' οὐκ ἐξ αὐτοῦ ἔχον τὴν ὕπαρξιν.

(4) The Holy Ghost is the image of the Son, Who is the image of the Father (*De fide orthodoxa*, i. 13); issuing out of the Father and resting in the Son as the power radiating from Him (*De fide orthodoxa*, i. 7).

(5) The Holy Ghost is the personal production out of the Father, belonging to the Son, but not out of the Son, because He is the Spirit of the mouth of the Deity, and utters the word (*De hymno Trisagion*, n. 28).

(6) The Holy Ghost forms the mediation between the Father and the Son, and is united to the Father through the Son (*De fide orthodoxa*, i, 13).[1]

This agreement on the doctrine of the Procession of the Holy Ghost has formed the starting-point of discussions on the subject ever since. It was not universally accepted in the English Church. Pusey, now an old man of seventy-five, was quite intransigeant in his opposition to any tampering with the Western tradition as to the Filioque. Pusey had had scarcely any contact with living Orthodoxy, and could hardly be expected to understand Orthodox thought and feeling on this point.[2]

No other subjects were discussed at the Conference. Döllinger, indeed, delivered a long historical address, defending the validity of Anglican ordinations, on the ground that the English

[1] *Report of the Reunion Conference at Bonn*, August 10-16, 1875, pp. 103-104.
[2] H. P. Liddon, *Life of Pusey*, vol. iv, pp. 292-302; Johnston, p. 189.

Church, in addition to possessing the historic succession, clearly taught that a grace of the Holy Spirit was conveyed by ordination, and rejecting the entire system of papal indulgences.

Döllinger intended to continue these conferences, but his intention was not fulfilled. First the machinations of Dr. Overbeck,[1] and then the rapidly increasing hostility between England and Russia over the future of the Turkish dominions, which in 1878 nearly led to war between the two empires, made it impossible to invite English and Russian theologians to meet in conference. After 1878 interest in the subject seems to have died down, and the Old Catholics were fully occupied with their own affairs. The vision that was seen at Bonn was a " vision of many days ", but the seed that was sown there ripened fifty years later, when the fifteen hundredth anniversary of the Council of Nicæa opened a new chapter in the relations between the Anglican and Orthodox Churches, and when, in the same year, the whole Old Catholic Communion officially recognized the validity of Anglican ordinations.

[1] Johnston, p. 207.

# CHAPTER XX

# THE CONSTITUTION OF THE OLD CATHOLIC CHURCHES

THE result of the protest against the Vatican Council was that in three countries—Germany, Switzerland, and Austria—new separate organizations had been formed, composed of the individuals whom the Pope had excommunicated. Their hopes, first that a large section of the Roman Communion would join them, and then that they would be able to bring about immediate reunion with the Orthodox or the Anglican churches, were not fulfilled. The organization which had at first been expected to be temporary became permanent.

The Old Catholics were determined to remain Catholic: they never even considered joining any Protestant organization. The creed, the seven sacraments, and the three-fold ministry were retained; the greatest care was taken to provide for a valid episcopal succession, and its validity has never been denied even by Rome. But it would be a great mistake to suppose that the Old Catholics only differ from Rome in their rejection of the Vatican Council and its dogmas.[1] Their divergence in faith and order goes much farther. While the Church of Utrecht has always been conservative and has made reforms in faith and order with great caution, it cannot be denied that in the German, Swiss, and Austrian Old Catholic movements, especially the two latter, there has been a certain revolutionary element. From the beginning the movement took the form of national churches, both on principle and through necessity.[2] It was contrary to Old Catholic principles, even if it had been permitted by the governments, for a bishop in one State to exercise ecclesiastical jurisdiction in another. The Swiss government expressly required Bishop Herzog to exercise no such jurisdiction, and gave its sanction to his consecration only on this condition. The three Old Catholic churches, though in full communion and close contact with one another, were entirely independent; and there

[1] Werner Stocker, *Die Kirchenrechtlichen Grundanschauungen des Altkatholizismus*, p. 79.  [2] Stocker, p. 32.

has never been any supreme authority over them all. When they act together, they do so by free consent.[1] The organ of this consent is the International Congress, which was first held at Munich in September 1871, and since 1889 the Bishops' Conference.[2]

Each of the three churches proceeded to draw up a constitution for itself, though the Austrian Old Catholic Church was not fully organized till later. These constitutions followed in general the same lines, but differed considerably in detail: the Swiss, because they were republicans, and because, as we have seen, the Swiss movement was lay rather than clerical, and the Austrians, possibly because the movement began among artisans, rather than in university circles, as in Germany, or among civil servants, as in Switzerland, made their constitutions more democratic than the Germans did. The chief principle adopted in these constitutions was the division of powers,[3] in accordance with English and American precedents. According to Roman Canon Law, the legislative, executive, and judicial powers are all exercised by the ordinary (normally the bishop), and in the last resort by the Pope. The Old Catholics were opposed on principle to any such autocracy. Their bishops are constitutional monarchs; the legislative power belongs to the synod, the executive power to the representative body (Synodalrat in Switzerland and Austria, Synodalvertretung in Germany), and the judicial power to the synodal court, with an appeal to the synod (the right of appeal to the synod is an exception to the general principle of division of powers). The bishop is *ex officio* a member of these three bodies, and in Germany, but not in Switzerland or Austria, he is the chairman. But, except in the smallest judicial cases, he has no power of sole decision.

Another principle is the equality of the clergy and the laity. The representatives of the laity sit in synod with the clergy, and also in the council and the court. But matters of faith, and matters purely spiritual, cannot be decided by the laity. The Synod cannot in any way alter or add to the dogmas of the Church.[4]

The bishop is elected by the synod.[5] He must have an absolute majority of the votes, in order to be elected. It is

---

[1] Stocker, p. 34.   [2] Stocker, p. 35.
[3] Stocker, p. 39.   [4] Stocker, p. 38.
[5] *Kirchliche Ordnungen und Satzungen fuer die deutschen Altkatholiken*, p. 1; *Verfassung der christkath. Kirche der Schweiz*, 9. c, p. 3.

THE CONSTITUTION OF OLD CATHOLIC CHURCHES

provided that no one may be elected without the previous approval of the government; but the government has no voice in the election itself. The bishop must be consecrated by one or more Catholic bishops: whenever circumstances permit it, at least three bishops take part in the consecration.[1] The actual words of consecration are said in Latin, and each bishop separately lays his hands on the head of the candidate (at any rate, this took place when Bishop Schindelaar, the first Austrian Old Catholic bishop, was consecrated at Berne, for I was present myself and saw it). In Germany the bishop may, with the consent of the Representative Body, appoint a coadjutor bishop; and he may appoint any priest in the council as his vicar-general, or, with the Representative Body's consent, any priest in the diocese.

In Switzerland the bishop-elect must have served at least two years in the cure of souls or as a teacher of theology, must possess Swiss citizenship, and must not be *persona minus grata* to the civil government.[2]

Apart from any restrictions imposed by positive law, an Old Catholic bishop possesses all the rights and privileges of other Catholic bishops. (He wears cope and mitre, of course, and carries a pastoral staff.) In practice, the power of the bishop is considerably greater than in theory. It was fortunate for the Old Catholic churches that their first bishops lived long enough to guide them through the period of reconstruction. Bishop Reinkens died in 1896, and Bishop Herzog not till 1924, after an episcopate of forty-eight years. In Austria, on the other hand, the Imperial Government would never allow the consecration of an Old Catholic bishop, and the Church had to be governed by a priest with the title of Bistumsverweser. The first bishops were Alois Paschek, consecrated for Czechoslovakia in 1924, and Adalbert Schindelaar, consecrated for Austria in 1925.

The supreme government of the Church is vested in the synod, which consists of the bishop, all members of the synodal council, all priests on the roll of the diocese, and lay representatives of the parishes. In Germany each parish sends one representative for every 300 members: in Switzerland each parish sends one, and extra representatives for larger parishes. The synod meets every

---

[1] The only recent exception was the consecration of Bishop van Vlijmen, see p. 317.
[2] *Verfassung*, p. 33.

year, usually in Whitsun Week.[1]   In Germany the bishop (in his absence, and during the vacancy of the see, the coadjutor bishop, or the vicar-general), is the chairman of the synod.   In Switzerland, but not in Germany, the synod has power to depose the bishop for neglect of his duties.   In Switzerland and Austria the chairman of the synod is a layman.

The members of the representative body, the board of examiners, and the ecclesiastical court are elected by the synod.

The representative body, both in Germany and Switzerland, consists of the bishop, three priests and five laymen.   In Germany the bishop is chairman *ex officio*; in Switzerland a layman is chairman.   In Germany two of the clerical and three of the lay members must be resident within easy reach of the bishop's house (at Bonn), where the meetings are held.   The representative body is responsible to the synod, and has to present a report of its work at every meeting of the synod.

Both in Germany and Switzerland the parish priest is elected by the parish, and instituted by the bishop, in accordance with the civil laws; if the bishop refuses to institute him, he has the right to appeal to the Synod.   In Germany he is appointed for life, and can only be removed by the synod, either on account of age, sickness, or infirmity, or in consequence of a formal judgment of the synod in its judicial capacity.   The clergy of all ranks are permitted to marry at their discretion; except that in Germany permission to marry has to be obtained from the bishop (with an appeal to the synod, in case of refusal), and this permission is not given to anyone within six years of his ordination as priest, and in the case of a priest not ordained in the German Old Catholic Church, also not within three years of his admission to the diocese.[2]   These restrictions are not in force in the other Old Catholic dioceses.

We have already seen how in Switzerland compulsory clerical celibacy was abolished as early as 1875.   In Germany the change was made in 1877, and was strongly opposed by Döllinger, Reusch, and many others, even though it was limited by the restrictions just described.   In Holland, clerical celibacy remained compulsory until 1922, and was then abolished without any serious opposition.   At the present day all the Old Catholic bishops, except the Bishops of Haarlem and Deventer, are married men.

---

[1] *Kirchliche Ordnungen*, pp. 18 ff.
[2] *Kirchliche Ordnungen*, p. 28; Schulte, *Das Altkatholizismus*, pp. 625–650.

The clergy are not under obligation to recite the Breviary, on the ground of freedom of conscience [1] (an Anglican priest, himself under obligation to recite Matins and Evensong daily, may perhaps be allowed the opinion that this change was a grave mistake); no special civil position is claimed for them, as for the Roman Catholic clergy. All payment for Masses was at once abolished, nor are there any indulgences.

The laity, as we have seen, have equal rights with the clergy in all matters of government, apart from purely spiritual matters—that is, matters of faith—and the discipline of the clergy. Confession is not compulsory:[2] the abolition of compulsory celibacy for the clergy and compulsory confession for the laity creates the danger that people may join the Old Catholic churches because their discipline is laxer, and also produces an immense, though indefinable, difference in the atmosphere: it is Anglican rather than Roman. The laity are left completely free in such matters as the observance of fast-days,[3] discussions with members of other communions about religion, and other things which are strictly regulated in the Roman Communion. It is hardly necessary to say that there is no censorship or Index Expurgatorius. The laity are completely free to read any book they wish; the reading of the Bible is, of course, encouraged. In practice, the discipline of the church is only exercised over the clergy.

In Germany there is a court of the synod, composed of three judges, who must have reached the standard for that office imposed by the civil law, and four jurymen. The judges are appointed by the bishop; the jurymen are elected by the synod on the motion of the bishop. All cases which cannot be settled by the bishop in person are tried by the court of the synod; there is in every case a right of appeal to the synod itself.[4] In Switzerland judicial authority is exercised by the representative body (Synodalrat).

The Old Catholic churches reject the medieval synthesis. They do not regard Church and State as a single community; and they repudiate all temporal power and privilege for the church and clergy.[5] They are forced by their history to reject the opinion that the visible Church cannot be divided by schism: from the time of the Bonn Conferences they recognized the

---

[1] Stocker, p. 52.    [2] Stocker, p. 55.
[3] *Kirchliche Ordnungen*, p. 35; Stocker, p. 35; Schulte, p. 621.
[4] *Kirchliche Ordnungen*, p. 50.    [5] Stocker, p. 27.

Catholicity of the Orthodox and of the Anglican Communions.[1]
They hold that the Church herself, not any organ of the Church,
such as a council of bishops, is the highest authority in Church
matters: in this they appear to be in agreement with the Orthodox churches.   Their democratic practice is defended not only
by modern, but by ancient precedents, though in some respects,
such as the permission given to the clergy to marry even after
ordination, they have gone beyond anything allowed in the early
Church.   However, this particular relaxation of ancient rules
appears to have been inevitable, though perhaps premature.
In the general atmosphere of individual liberty the Old Catholic
churches would probably not have been able permanently to
enforce celibacy on their clergy even if they had wanted to do
so.   (It will be remembered that the abolition of compulsory
celibacy was demanded by the French and German bishops even
at the Council of Trent.)   There is, indeed, much to be said for
the view that the celibacy of the clergy is impossible without a Pope
to enforce it; while, from the time of Gregory VII, the Papacy
has found clerical celibacy to be necessary to its system.

The Old Catholics do not pretend to stand exactly where they
stood before the Vatican Council.   They claim that their protest
was based upon learning (*Wissenschaft*) and must, apart from the
revealed Faith, which cannot change, progress with the progress
of learning.   Old Catholicism is therefore not so much a position
as a movement, in spite of its name.[2]

The relation of the Old Catholic churches to the State is
extremely complicated, especially in Switzerland, where the
cantonal governments make their own rules, subject to the
federal law of religious freedom for all.   The German Empire
was also federal, and the Old Catholic church was fully recognized
in Prussia and Baden, while in Bavaria it was merely a private
society.   In Austria, as I have already mentioned, the Imperial
Government did all it could to discourage the Old Catholic
movement, and forbade the consecration of a bishop:  the
church was for fifty years governed by an administrator (*Bistumsverweser*), who gave confirmation, but had to get bishops from
other countries to ordain priests.

In Germany the seat of the bishopric has always been Bonn;

---

[1] Schulte, pp. 652–656;  *Die Altkatholische Kirche*, ed. Siegmund-Schultze,
pp. 97 ff.
[2] Stocker, p. 4.

in Switzerland, Berne; in Austria, before the Revolution, Warnsdorf on the German frontier of Bohemia, which is now the seat of the bishopric for Czechoslovakia. The Old Catholic bishops in these countries have never used territorial titles; but this does not mean that they have any hope of reunion with Rome, whose Ultramontanism has shown no signs of modifying the spirit which promoted the Vatican Decrees.[1]

[1] Stocker, p. 78.

# CHAPTER XXI

## THE DECLARATION OF UTRECHT

WHILE the Old Catholics of Germany, Switzerland, and Austria were building their new church organizations and introducing drastic reforms, the Church of Utrecht, with its two dioceses, Utrecht and Haarlem, was maintaining its old traditions as before the Vatican Council. The Dutch Old Catholics had been separated from Rome for 150 years. The Vatican Council, to which their bishops had not been invited, had in practice made little difference to them. It is true that the gate into the Roman Communion was now bolted behind them. They had appealed to the future General Council against the Formulary of Alexander VII, and the Bull " Unigenitus ": the Council had met, and had not only not received their appeal, but had proclaimed two new dogmas which excluded them from the right to make such an appeal in the future. They had protested, as they had so often done before; and there the matter had ended.

When Archbishop Loos went on his confirmation tour in Germany, and when Bishop Hermann Heykamp consecrated Bishop Reinkens for the German Old Catholics, the isolation of Utrecht appeared to be ended. But the conservative Dutch were alarmed by the changes made by their German and Swiss friends; especially by the rejection of the authority of the Council of Trent (1874) and by the permission to marry given to the clergy (1877).

For 150 years the Dutch Old Catholics had asserted their full acceptance of the decrees of Trent, even though they had been excommunicated by Rome. Yet within two years of the consecration of Bishop Reinkens at Rotterdam their German and Swiss friends were ignoring Trent and discussing reunion with Orthodox and even Anglican divines. No representatives of the Church of Utrecht were at either of the Bonn Conferences. For a time it seemed likely that the Dutch would fall back into isolation, and that the German-speaking Old Catholics would attach themselves to Canterbury rather than to Utrecht. As we shall see in a later chapter, it was arranged that an Anglican bishop should have the oversight of the Old Catholic congregation in Paris. In 1879 Anglican bishops were admitted to Communion at the Old Catholic cathedral at Berne; in the same year the Swiss Old Catholic Synod passed a resolution admitting Anglicans to Communion, and in 1883 the German Old Catholic Synod passed a canon to the same effect. From all this the Dutch stood aloof. They remained exactly where they had always been. Fortunately, this coolness passed away. Canterbury could never have done for the German-speaking Old Catholics what Utrecht did for them; and, as subsequent experience has shown, the Anglican churches were not yet ready for reunion. Utrecht had given the Old Catholics their episcopal succession and their jurisdiction: it remained for Utrecht to give them a firm dogmatic basis.

Bishop Hermann Heykamp of Deventer, who had consecrated Bishop Reinkens and Bishop Rinkel of Haarlem on August 11, 1873, died the following year. The archbishopric, vacant since the death of Archbishop Loos on June 4, was filled by the election of Johannes Heykamp (not to be confused with Hermann Heykamp: Butler makes this mistake), parish priest of Schiedam, who was consecrated on April 8, 1875, by the Bishop of Haarlem, assisted by Bishop Reinkens. He at once nominated and consecrated Cornelius Diependaal to the bishopric of Deventer. So for the first time since the death of Bishop de Jong in 1867 all the three bishoprics were filled. Archbishop Heykamp was a learned and saintly divine of the old school, still living in thought within the Roman Catholic world, the gates of which had been closed upon him. In 1870 he had written, under the pseudonym "Adulfus", an attack on the "Infallibility of the Pope"; and also a protest against a petition for the restoration of the temporal power of the Pope, which had been sent by the Romanist bishops of the Netherlands to the King.

In 1880 Pope Leo XIII issued an encyclical declaring that for (Roman) Catholics civil marriage was no marriage at all. Archbishop Heykamp published a reply, in which he proved from Scripture, from the decrees of Councils, and from the teaching of some Popes, such as Benedict XIV, the great canonist, that marriage is of natural right, and may exist without the Christian sacrament of marriage, which is only its benediction.[1]

Archbishop Heykamp performed his greatest service to the Old Catholic cause by summoning the conference which led to the Declaration of Utrecht. This conference met on September 24, 1889. It consisted of the five Old Catholic bishops, the

[1] G. Volet, *Esquisse Historique de l'Église d'Utrecht*, ch. 19.

Archbishop of Utrecht, the Bishops of Haarlem (Rinkel) and Deventer (Diependaal), and Bishops Reinkens and Herzog, together with theologians representing the Dutch, German, and Swiss Old Catholic churches. The Austrian Bistumsverweser accepted its decisions later. The archbishop took the chair. The conference reached complete agreement, and decided to take three steps to unite the churches.

(1) The five bishops agreed to establish a Bishops' Conference for mutual consultation. No church was to have priority or jurisdiction over any other; all the bishops agreed that they would not consecrate any bishop without the consent of all the Old Catholic bishops, and without the acceptance of the Convention of Utrecht by the candidate.

(2) An International Old Catholic Congress was to be held every two years.

(3) The five bishops issued a declaration of doctrinal principles by which all Old Catholic bishops and priests were to be bound. This document, known as the Declaration of Utrecht (Utrechtserklärung), is still the doctrinal basis of Old Catholicism.

Its original text was in German, not in Latin. A translation of it will be found in an appendix to this chapter. The most significant point in the Declaration of Utrecht is its fifth article, which is as follows:—

" We refuse to accept the decrees of the Council of Trent in matters of discipline, and as for the dogmatic decisions of that council we accept them only so far as they are in harmony with the teaching of the Primitive Church."

That is to say, the Council of Trent has no infallible authority: its dogmas are only binding so far as they represent the teaching of the Primitive Church. The importance of this step does not seem to have been realized at the time; but by taking it, the Church of Utrecht ceased to be in any sense Roman Catholic, and placed herself, with the other Old Catholic churches, alongside the Orthodox and Anglican Communions: she opened the way to the future reunion of all non-papal Catholic churches, which her adherence to Trent had hitherto made impossible.[1]

By this declaration the tendency to disunity and drift was checked. The Old Catholic churches now possessed a firm

[1] Bishop Küry, in *Die Altkatholische Kirche*, p. 106.

basis of principle and of unity: to be an Old Catholic is to accept the Declaration of Utrecht. It was the turning-point in the history of the Old Catholic movement; it may yet prove to have been a turning-point in the history of the reunion of Christendom.

### APPENDIX: THE DECLARATION OF UTRECHT

(1) We adhere faithfully to the Rule of Faith laid down by St. Vincent of Lérins in these terms: " Id teneamus, quod ubique, quod semper, quod ab omnibus creditum est; hoc est etenim vere proprieque catholicum ". For this reason we persevere in professing the faith of the primitive Church, as formulated in the œcumenical symbols and specified precisely by the unanimously accepted decisions of the Œcumenical Councils held in the undivided Church of the first thousand years.

(2) We therefore reject the decrees of the so-called Council of the Vatican, which were promulgated July 18, 1870, concerning the infallibility and the universal episcopate of the Bishop of Rome—decrees which are in contradiction with the faith of the ancient Church and which destroy its ancient canonical constitution by attributing to the Pope all the plenitude of ecclesiastical powers over all dioceses and over all the faithful. By denial of his primatial jurisdiction we do not wish to deny the historic primacy which several œcumenical councils and the Fathers of the ancient Church have attributed to the Bishop of Rome by recognizing him as the *Primus inter pares*.

(3) We also reject the dogma of the Immaculate Conception promulgated by Pope Pius IX in 1854 in defiance of the Holy Scriptures and in contradiction with the tradition of the first centuries.

(4) As for encyclicals published by the Bishops of Rome in recent times, for example, the Bulls " Unigenitus " (see above, pp. 65, 80) and " Auctorem fidei " (see above, p. 147), and the Syllabus of 1864, we reject them on all such points as are in contradiction with the doctrine of the primitive Church, and we do not recognize them as binding on the consciences of the faithful. We also renew the ancient protests of the Catholic Church of Holland against the errors of the Roman Curia, and against its attacks upon the rights of national churches.

(5) We refuse to accept the decrees of the Council of Trent in matters of discipline, and as for the dogmatic decisions of that

Council we accept them only so far as they are in harmony with the teaching of the primitive Church.

(6) Considering that the Holy Eucharist has always been the true central point of Catholic worship, we consider it our duty to declare that we maintain with perfect fidelity the ancient Catholic doctrine concerning the Sacrament of the Altar, by believing that we receive the Body and the Blood of our Saviour Jesus Christ under the species of bread and wine. The Eucharistic celebration in the Church is neither a continual repetition nor a renewal of the expiatory sacrifice which Jesus offered once for all upon the Cross; but it is a sacrifice because it is the perpetual commemoration of the sacrifice offered upon the Cross, and it is the act by which we represent upon earth and appropriate to ourselves the one offering which Jesus Christ makes in Heaven, according to the Epistle to the Hebrews, 9.11-12, for the salvation of redeemed humanity, by appearing for us in the presence of God (Heb. 9. 24). The character of the Holy Eucharist being thus understood, it is, at the same time, a sacrificial feast, by means of which the faithful, in receiving the Body and Blood of our Saviour, enter into communion with one another (1 Cor. 1. 17).

(7) We hope that Catholic theologians, in maintaining the faith of the undivided Church, will succeed in establishing an agreement upon questions which have been controverted ever since the divisions which have arisen between the churches. We exhort the priests under our jurisdiction to teach, both by preaching and by the instruction of the young, especially the essential Christian truths professed by all the Christian confessions, to avoid, in discussing controverted doctrines, any violation of truth or charity, and in word and deed to set an example to the members of our churches in accordance with the spirit of Jesus Christ our Saviour.

(8) By maintaining and professing faithfully the doctrine of Jesus Christ, by refusing to admit those errors which by the fault of men have crept into the Catholic Church, by laying aside the abuses in ecclesiastical matters, together with the worldly tendencies of the hierarchy, we believe that we shall be able to combat efficaciously the great evils of our day, which are unbelief and indifference in matters of religion.

*Note.*—This translation is accepted by the Old Catholic bishops as correct, and was printed in the Report of the Lambeth Conference of 1930, p. 142.

# CHAPTER XXII

# THE OLD CATHOLIC MOVEMENT IN LATIN COUNTRIES

THE protest against the degrees of the Vatican Council was, as we have seen, almost entirely confined to German-speaking people. There were individuals in other countries who sympathized, but no Old Catholic bishopric was set up. It was not till much later, and for other reasons, that Old Catholic churches were organized among the Slavs.

But there were attempts to found Old Catholic movements in Latin countries. (By Latin countries I mean countries whose language is derived from Latin, such as France, Italy, and Spain.) These attempts must be briefly described. None of them led to any important or permanent result.

In France, Père Hyacinthe Loyson was from the first associated with the Old Catholic movement. He had been a Carmelite monk, and a famous popular preacher; he left the order in 1869, before the Vatican Council, and in 1872, before any Old Catholic church had been organized, he married (see above, pp. 255, 274, 276); this placed him in a false position, and the stricter Old Catholics would have nothing to do with him. For a time he was in charge of the Old Catholic parish at Geneva, which has always been the extreme left wing of the movement; but he came to the conclusion that the motives of his flock were political rather than religious, and in 1874 he returned to France. In 1879 he began to work independently in Paris, and gathered a congregation round him by his sermons. Loyson was, however, no organizer, and the crowds which attended his preaching did not join his congregation, which remained small. It was necessary that he should be under some episcopal jurisdiction; the Dutch bishops refused to have anything to do with him, except on conditions which he was unable to accept; a French congregation could not be expected to place itself under Bishop Reinkens, and Bishop Herzog was forbidden by his Government to exercise jurisdiction outside Switzerland.

At the request of the Archbishop of Canterbury, the Primus of the Scottish Church undertook to be responsible for Loyson, and in 1879 Bishop Herzog, commissioned by him, gave confirmation to candidates from Loyson's congregation, in the presence of one Swiss and three Anglican priests. From 1883 Bishop Jenner (who had been consecrated Bishop of Dunedin, New Zealand, but had never been accepted there) performed episcopal duties for this congregation, and after 1888 Bishop Cleveland Coxe of Western New York. In 1893 Loyson resigned, feeling that he needed to be more completely free: he had reached an extreme Liberal position akin to that of his friend Dean Stanley, of Westminster Abbey. Already some Parisian sympathizers with Old Catholicism had applied to Archbishop Heykamp for help, and he had promised to do what he could. Archbishop Gul was now approached, and he sent J. J. van Thiel, the President of Amersfoort Seminary (afterwards Bishop of Haarlem), to reorganize the community at Paris. Van Thiel united the congregation of Loyson with others who adhered to the Port Royal tradition. M. Georges Volet, a French priest ordained by Bishop Herzog, was placed in charge of the parish. Archbishop Gul took it under his jurisdiction, authorized the use of French in the services and Communion in both kinds, and on January 13, 1895, consecrated the new church of St. Denys at 96 Boulevard Auguste Blanqui (13th arrondissement). Volet died in 1914, and then the small congregation was administered by Canon X. Gouard, of St. Laurence and St. Mary Magdalene's, Rotterdam, who went to Paris one Sunday in each month for that purpose.[1] He perished in the bombardment of Rotterdam in 1940. Since 1950, there is in France an Old Catholic mission to lapsed Roman Catholics, under the jurisdiction of the Old Catholic Bishops: it is led by Abbé André Henri Bekkens in Paris, whose services are now held at the British Embassy Church.

In Italy there was at the time of the Wars of Italian Independence a large number of priests who were anti-papal, but on political rather than theological grounds. A small movement against the papal claims was begun in 1874 at Naples by a priest called Panelli, but it did not lead to anything. In 1881 Count Enrico di Campello, a canon of St. Peter's at Rome, resigned his post because he could not accept the Vatican decrees, and in 1882 he placed himself at the head of an Italian Old Catholic move-

[1] Max Kopp, *Die Altkatholische Bewegung*, p. 141; G. Volet, *Esquisse Historique de l'Eglise d'Utrecht*, ch. 22.

ment, with six parishes and seven out-stations. In 1888 he visited the Bishop of Salisbury in England, and met there Bishop Herzog, Amandus Czech the Administrator of the Austrian Old Catholics, Pastoor van Santen from the Church of Utrecht, and Juan Cabrera (afterwards bishop) from Spain, together with many Anglican bishops from different parts of the world: all these received Holy Communion together on August 3, in Bishop John Wordsworth's private chapel. In 1891 the first synod of the Italian Old Catholic church was held. Count Campello was elected bishop, but his consecration never took place. Bishop Herzog, with authority to act also as Bishop Reinkens' representative, took part in the synod; a constitution was drawn up, and a liturgy and other rites in Italian, following closely the Swiss Old Catholic rites, were issued. Campello's headquarters was at Arrone in Umbria. In 1902 Campello resigned through old age, and the next year he returned to the Roman Communion, and died soon afterwards, on July 2, 1903. He was succeeded by Professor Cicitti-Suriani, who had been ordained in 1884 by Bishop Herzog.[1] Much interest was taken in this movement in certain quarters in England, chiefly by Evangelicals anxious to support anything anti-papal. Archbishop Benson had to warn Campello and his adherents that their movement could not hope for success if it could be represented as an English mission: it must be national and self-supporting.[2] Bishop John Wordsworth of Salisbury was charged with the duty of inquiring into the state of the Italian Old Catholic church and reporting to the next Lambeth Conference. He found that the greatest caution was needed, because Campello, though himself above suspicion, was "too much of an orator to be a great leader", and that some of his followers were not to be trusted.[3] The movement, which never reached any great size, appears to have become completely extinct. The Swiss Old Catholic Church has some out-stations in Italy.

There were no other Old Catholic movements in Latin countries. Pfarrer Max Kopp mentions others, but he was mistaken in regarding them as Old Catholic. The Spanish Reformed Church owed its origin, not to the Vatican Council, but to the Spanish Revolution of 1867, when freedom of religion was proclaimed in Spain. The Spanish Reformed Church is episcopal

[1] Kopp, p. 139.
[2] A. C. Benson, *Life of Archbishop Benson*, vol. ii, p. 199.
[3] E. W. Watson, *Life of Bishop John Wordsworth*, p. 318.

in constitution, but its founders were under the influence of the conservative Evangelical section of the Anglican Communion. Juan Cabrera was for many years bishop-elect of this Church. In 1889 he asked the Dutch Old Catholic bishops to consecrate him; but they refused to do so, because the doctrinal basis of his Church was the Anglican Thirty-Nine Articles, which they only knew from Roman Catholic books, and regarded as a wholly heretical formulary. (This led to difficulties with the English Church later.) It has always been the policy of the English Church to abstain from interfering in countries where the Roman Communion is in possession, except so far as to provide for Anglicans living there. But in 1894 Lord Plunket, Archbishop of Dublin, assisted by two other Irish bishops, consecrated Juan Cabrera to be Bishop of the Spanish Reformed Church. The Anglican Communion, however, never recognized Cabrera as an Anglican bishop, and he died in 1916. He had no successor until the consecration of Bishop Santos M. Molina in 1956. Confirmation and ordination had been administered by the Archbishop of Armagh in the intervening period. The Lusitanian Church in Portugal has had a similar history, except that it had no bishop until the consecration of Bishop A. F. Fiandor in 1958, which was followed by that of Bishop Luis C. Pereira in 1962. Both have always been quite small (the total number of communicants in the two countries is said to be about 1100); neither has ever been Old Catholic. Bishop Cabrera sometimes attended Old Catholic congresses. The Archbishop of Utrecht and the Bishop of Deventer attended the consecration of Bishop Pereira. Understandably, however, relations between the Old Catholics and the Spanish and Portuguese Reformed Churches have not been close. The latter have little in common with the Churches of the Union of Utrecht.[1]

The Mexican movement under Bishop Riley, referred to by Kopp, was Evangelical, not Old Catholic, and its adherents have now been placed under the jurisdiction of the American Episcopal Church.[2] The movement in the Philippine Islands, of which Kopp speaks, was led by one Gregory Aglipay, who called himself archbishop, but was never consecrated. However, Mgr. Isabelo

---

[1] C. B. Moss, *Living Church*, February, 1934; *Life of Archbishop Plunket, Light and Truth*, etc.
[2] Kopp, p. 152.
[3] Kopp, p. 153; information supplied by American Episcopal Church Board of Foreign Missions.

de los Reyes and two other bishops were consecrated by the American Episcopal Church, with which the Philippine Independent Catholic Church works in close contact, and has now 30 bishops and two million members.

It may be asked why the Old Catholic Movement was confined to German-speaking countries. Without speculating on deeper causes, I think it is a sufficient explanation, that it was only in the German-speaking countries that there was a living anti-Ultramontane tradition, combined with an earnest belief in the value of historical research. In many German dioceses the Infallibility of the Pope had never been taught, and formed no part of the popular belief. The influence of Febronius, and of the reforms of Joseph II, had been widespread: it is significant that the Fricktal in Canton Aargau, where Old Catholicism took firm root, had been until the Congress of Vienna part of the Austrian lands. Also many of the districts where the Old Catholic movement spread were those which had been under the administration of Wessenberg. Again, the great influence of Döllinger over his pupils, and the overwhelming force of his attack on the papal claims, had their effect on a people with the traditional German respect for learning.

One might have expected that France, the classical home of Gallicanism, would have produced an Old Catholic movement. But Gallicanism, at the time of the Vatican Council, was on its death-bed. It still had its followers among the clergy, but the laity was Ultramontane. Besides, Gallicanism is very different from Old Catholicism. Gallicanism is essentially the doctrine that the collective episcopate is above the Pope. But the bishops had all accepted the Vatican Council. The logical French could not hold a theory of episcopal rights which the bishops themselves had abandoned. The Gallicans had always maintained the supremacy of the Pope, as the successor of St. Peter, subject to an œcumenical council. But the Old Catholics denied this, on historical grounds. They were not Gallicans; there was a wide gulf between Dupanloup, or even Bossuet, and Döllinger, who by 1874 had come to repudiate the authority of Trent. Besides, it was not to be expected that Frenchmen would join a movement mainly German, so soon after the Franco-German War.

In Italy and Spain Ultramontanism had long been taken for granted; the decrees of the Vatican Council were nothing new. The same may be said of Belgium. In Great Britain and Ireland, once a stronghold of Gallicanism, Manning and his followers, and similar people in Ireland, had spread Ultramontanism everywhere. It was only in the German-speaking countries that the background necessary to a revolt existed; and even there the revolt was confined to a small minority. There was no motive behind it which could appeal to great masses of men: perhaps it was not a period in which any religious movement could have won a great following on the Continent of Europe. The hopes of its friends and the fears of its enemies were not fulfilled. Old Catholicism never produced a great popular leader, a Luther or a Wesley; and it remains a small minority everywhere. But it is not without importance for the present, or without significance for the future.

# CHAPTER XXIII

# FURTHER SPREAD OF THE MOVEMENT

In 1890, the year after the Declaration of Utrecht, Ignaz von Döllinger, the great leader of the movement, died at the age of ninety-one. He is rightly regarded, both by the Old Catholics themselves and by the outside world, as the founder and inspirer of the Old Catholic movement, though he was over seventy at the time of the Vatican Council. As we have seen, he took a prominent part in organizing the German Old Catholic Church; he presided at the Bonn Conferences, the success of which was mainly due to his skill, his learning, and his great reputation; and he led the revolutionary change by which the Old Catholics rejected the authority of the Council of Trent. And yet, though he regarded his excommunication as unjust and indeed invalid, and though he refused appeals, repeated until the end of his life, to submit to Rome, he did not celebrate Mass or undertake any duties as a priest after his excommunication: it is hard to see why. Ultramontane writers have tried to show that he never joined the Old Catholic Church; but his letter to Pfarrer Widmann, written October 18, 1874, is enough by itself to show that he did. " As far as I am concerned," he wrote, " I reckon myself as belonging by conviction to the Old Catholic Communion, and I believe that it has a higher vocation given to it to fulfil, and that three-fold " (permanent protest against the Vatican dogmas, the example of a Catholic church free from error, the reuniting of Christendom).[1] He remained till his death on the roll of the Old Catholic clergy, he received the last sacraments from his friend Professor Friedrich, he was given Old Catholic burial.[2] It is true that he, like his friends, Franz Heinrich Reusch (1828–1900) and Josef Langen (1837–1901), was much opposed to the abolition of compulsory clerical celibacy, and from 1878 to 1883 his name does not appear in the list of Old Catholic priests; but in 1883 it was replaced there. The words from which Dom Cuthbert Butler and others argue that in 1888 he regarded himself

[1] Rudolf Keussen, *Internationale Kirchliche Zeitschrift*, October, 1936, p. 186.
[2] K. Neuhaus, in *Die Altkatholische Kirche*, p. 117.

as a Roman Catholic and not an Old Catholic will not, in view of these facts, bear the meaning put on them: he certainly never regarded the Old Catholic Church as a schismatic sect.[1] Döllinger was an old man, and a professor, not a parish priest; he was in a difficult position at Munich, for the Bavarian Government did not recognize the Old Catholic Church. But it is certain that he lived and died in that church. (In my book *The Old Catholic Churches and Reunion*, I was wrong on this point, and I hereby withdraw the statement which I made then.)

In accordance with the agreement made at Utrecht, an International Old Catholic Congress was held every two years. There had been such congresses before, ever since 1871, but those held at this period did not receive so much attention from outside as those held earlier; on the other hand, the Dutch Old Catholics now took their full share in the proceedings. Archbishop Heykamp and many of his priests attended the congress held at Cologne in September 1890; it was there that he received the deputation from Paris mentioned in the last chapter. He died on January 8, 1892, after a short but painful illness. He was succeeded by Gerardus Gul, parish priest of Hilversum, who was consecrated at Hilversum on May 11, 1892, by the Bishop of Haarlem, assisted by the Bishop of Deventer and Bishop Reinkens. The period when the irregularity of consecration by less than three bishops was necessary was now ended.

On November 22, 1893, Cornelius Diependaal, Bishop of Deventer, died, and was succeeded by Nicolas Bartholomew Peter Spit, parish priest of S.S. Peter and Paul, Rotterdam. He was consecrated at Rotterdam, May 30, 1894, by Archbishop Gul, assisted by Bishop Rinkel and Bishop Herzog. The congress of 1894 was held at Rotterdam—the first held in the Netherlands.

On August 4, 1895, Theodore Hubert Weber was consecrated at Berne to be coadjutor to Bishop Reinkens. Bishop Herzog consecrated him, and was assisted by Bishop Reinkens and the new Bishop of Deventer. Bishop Reinkens died January 4, 1896, and Bishop Weber then became the second bishop of the German Old Catholic Church.[2]

Josef Hubert Reinkens, as the first bishop, was, next to Döllinger, the man to whom the movement owed most. He was born at Burtscheid near Aachen in 1821, and was ordained in

---

[1] Dom Cuthbert Butler, *Vatican Council*, vol. ii, p. 190, is mistaken.
[2] G. Volet, *Esquisse Historique de l'Église d'Utrecht*, ch. 22.

1848. It was through his skill and under his guidance that the German Old Catholic Church was consolidated and that such reforms as the liturgical use of German and the introduction of clerical marriage were carried through with success; and it was fortunate that he lived long enough to see his church firmly established. His successor, who was fifteen years younger, had always been his intimate friend. Each was the author of a long list of books on religious and philosophical subjects.[1]

In September, 1897, the bishops issued a joint letter to all their people, announcing a remarkable extension of the movement: a new Old Catholic diocese was to be founded in the United States of America.

The spiritual care of the large number of Roman Catholic emigrants to America, of various nations, who refuse to submit to the Roman Catholic hierarchy in their new country, has long been a serious problem. The first attempt to solve this problem by Old Catholic means had been unfortunate. At the request of Bishop Hobart Brown, the Anglican Bishop of Fond du Lac, Bishop Herzog ordained a young Frenchman, Joseph René Vilatte, on June 7, 1885, to work among French-speaking emigrants in Wisconsin under the direction of the Bishop of Fond du Lac. The headquarters of the mission was at a place called Little Sturgeon.[2] Vilatte, however, was not content with this arrangement. In 1891 he went to India, and induced a Jacobite bishop, who had been formerly a Roman Catholic, to consecrate him as a bishop for America. The consecration took place at the Church of our Lady of Good Death, Colombo, Ceylon, May 28, 1892: the consecrators were Alvarez Julius I, a Portuguese convert to the Jacobite Church, who claimed to be Archbishop of Ceylon (though he does not appear to have had any considerable flock there), Mar Paul Athanasius, Bishop of Kottayam, and Mar George Gregorius, Bishop of Niranam. The rite used was the Latin, not the Jacobite. Alvarez was, if I may use the expression, an inverted Uniate, a Jacobite bishop using the Latin rite; and the consecration appears to have received the sanction of the Jacobite Patriarch, His Beatitude Ignatius Peter III, given December 29, 1891.[3]

Vilatte now claimed to be a Jacobite bishop (though the " Jaco-

[1] Neuhaus, *op. cit.*, p. 126.
[2] Max Kopp, *Altkatholische Bewegung*, p. 150.
[3] Copies of documents in the author's possession.

bite " Church did not recognize him or any of his acts), and his connexion with the Old Catholics had ceased; but he returned to America and took charge of a number of congregations, chiefly Polish. His later career does not concern us. It is enough to say that he behaved like an ecclesiastical adventurer, consecrating bishops and ordaining priests in different countries. The most celebrated person ordained by him was Father Ignatius Lyne of Llanthony Abbey, who was an Anglican deacon, but had never succeeded in being ordained priest by any Anglican bishop. Vilatte ultimately returned to Paris, and submitted to the Roman Communion, in which he died. Some of those who claim to have derived their succession from him call themselves Old Catholics, but falsely: Vilatte was consecrated by Jacobite bishops, as we have seen.

In 1897 a number of Polish congregations in Chicago and the neighbourhood, dissatisfied with the control exercised by the Roman Catholic bishops (who were mostly Irish) over their church property, formed an independent organization, entered into correspondence with the Old Catholic bishops in Europe, and elected Antonius Stanislas Kozlowski to be their bishop, with his headquarters at Chicago. On November 21, 1897, he was consecrated at Berne by Bishop Herzog, assisted by Archbishop Gul and Bishop Weber. Bishop Kozlowski died January 14, 1907. It appears that one section of the Poles in America separated from him in 1898, and attached themselves to Vilatte. Another group of Polish congregations had been formed in the Eastern States as early as 1900, and in 1904 elected as their bishop Francis Hodur, parish priest of St. Stanislas', Scranton, Pennsylvania. On the death of Bishop Kozlowski, the two groups united under Father Hodur, and on September 29, 1907, after attending the Old Catholic Congress of that year, he was consecrated at Utrecht by the three Dutch bishops. Bishop Hodur died in 1953. The Polish National Catholic Church in the United States, which is in full communion with the Old Catholic churches of Europe, includes four dioceses: a central diocese with its See at Scranton, Pa., under Bishop Grochowski, an eastern diocese with its See at Springfield, Massachusetts, under Bishop Lesniak, a western diocese with its See at Chicago, under Bishop Rowinski, and a northern diocese, with its See at Buffalo, and with some congregations in Canada, under Bishop Zielinski. On August 26, 1936, two new bishops, John Misiaszck and Joseph

Padewski, were consecrated. There are also four Lithuanian congregations, which for some years had a bishop of their own, Bishop Gritenas (now dead), and claim the title of the " Lithuanian National Catholic Church ". These dioceses in America differ considerably, both in doctrine and government, from the Old Catholic churches of Europe. In contrast to the democratic constitutions and annual synods of the European Old Catholics, the synod meets only every ten years (the distances to be covered are no doubt much greater), and the presiding bishop has supreme authority, subject only to the synod. In 1906 the synod pronounced that baptism and confirmation were one sacrament, and that the preaching of the word of God was the seventh sacrament. Some of their teaching does not appear to be consistent with the rule of St. Vincent of Lerins, which the Declaration of Utrecht emphasizes; still less with the Augustinian traditions of the see of Utrecht. The Polish National Church has shown a strong nationalist tendency by introducing into the kalendar festivals in commemoration of the Martyrs of the Polish Nation (the second Sunday in May) and of the national heroes Adam Mickewicz, Julius Slowacki, and Towanski. The liturgical use of the Polish language was at once introduced; on the other hand, the clergy were not allowed to marry till 1921, and in fact not many are married. This church has done much for the working class, to which most of its members belong, and probably owes its great increase to this; it is now much the largest Old Catholic church, and probably numbers at least 100,000. It had an extension in Poland, under Bishop Padewski. He died in a Communist prison in 1951. Bishop Grochowski, Hodur's successor in the U.S.A., in June 1959 consecrated at Utrecht Maximilian Rode as Bishop for Poland: he was assisted by four other Old Catholic bishops. There is now (1961) an assistant bishop, Joachim Pekala, for Poland. There are 100,000 Old Catholics, in 85 parishes and many out-stations, organized in 11 rural deaneries.

In the United States and Canada the National Polish Church has 370,000 members (1959), four dioceses, and 155 parishes; there are five active bishops and three retired bishops. In 1954 the Archbishop of Utrecht visited the United States, and was warmly welcomed by the Polish Old Catholics. Since then their doctrinal and liturgical unity with the Old Catholics of Europe has been much strengthened.

On January 12, 1906, Bishop Weber died, and was succeeded by Josef Demmel, who was consecrated as third bishop of the German Old Catholic Church on July 26, 1906, by the Archbishop of Utrecht, the Bishop of Deventer, and Bishop Herzog, at Bonn. On May 2 of the same year Bishop Rinkel of Haarlem, who had been consecrated with Reinkens in 1874, died at Haarlem, and on August 22 Dr. J. van Thiel, Principal of Amersfoort Seminary, was consecrated to be his successor by the Archbishop of Utrecht, assisted by Bishops Spit and Demmel.

The eighth Congress, held at Vienna in 1909, was remarkable for the appearance of the Mariavites (see next chapter). On March 16, 1911, Dr. Georg Moog, Professor of New Testament Exegesis at Bonn, was consecrated by the Archbishop of Utrecht, assisted by the Bishop of Haarlem and Bishop Herzog; Bishop Demmel had found himself forced by age and infirmity to ask for a coadjutor. The consecration took place at Krefeld, and was remarkable for the presence of Bishop Bury, the Anglican Bishop in North and Central Europe, attended by two Anglican priests as chaplains. He had been specially invited by the Bishop-elect, and he was given a place of honour in the chancel, and signed the certificate of consecration with the other bishops; but he took no part in the consecration itself. Bishop Demmel died on November 12, 1913, and Bishop Moog then took his place.

Bishop van Thiel died on May 29, 1911, and was succeeded by Nicolas Prins, parish priest of Haarlem, who was consecrated on October 1, 1911, by the Archbishop of Utrecht, assisted by the Bishop of Deventer and Bishop Moog.[1] Bishop Prins was the first Dutch Old Catholic bishop to visit England. The ninth congress, held at Cologne, was remarkable for the presence of no fewer than nine Old Catholic bishops, including Bishop Hodur and three Mariaviten bishops from Poland. The Archbishop of Canterbury was represented officially by the Bishop of Willesden, and the American Episcopal Church by the Bishop of Massachusetts. Early in 1914 the old cathedral of St. Gertrude at Utrecht was replaced by a new one, because it was too small, and was turned into a museum of Jansenist and Old Catholic antiquities.

Meanwhile an important increase in membership had taken

[1] Volet, ch. 23.

place in Austria. The difficulties of the Old Catholics in Austria had always been greater than in Germany or Switzerland because the imperial government did all it could to discourage them. There were two districts in which the movement began: the southern, with its centre at Vienna, and the northern, with its centre at Warnsdorf, a small industrial town in Bohemia, close to the German frontier. At Vienna the pioneer was Alois Anton, at Warnsdorf Anton Nittel; the former actually demanded, in the name of 3,000 families in Vienna, a share in the use of the cathedral of St. Stephen. This was of course refused, but the Old Catholics were granted by the city council the right to a share in the use of the medieval Chapel of St. Saviour in the Old Rathaus. The Roman Catholics thereupon ceased to use it, and it has been ever since the headquarters in Vienna of the Old Catholic Church. The first enthusiasm of the movement was damped by the discovery that it would be necessary to break permanently with Rome, and many of its adherents returned to the Roman Communion. Nevertheless, a conference was held in 1872, at which it was decided that the Austrian Old Catholics needed a bishop of their own. But the government would not permit the consecration of a bishop, or, until 1907, admit the validity of marriages performed by Old Catholic priests. The Old Catholics claimed that they were still Catholics, and that they had not left the Church, but that the hierarchy had left them. The government maintained that if they were Catholics they would accept the Vatican decrees, and if they were not Catholics they must formally declare that they had left the Catholic Church, which they refused to do. However, in 1877 the government recognized the three congregations at Vienna, Warnsdorf, and Ried as constituting the " Old Catholic Church "; but it would not allow the church tax paid by Old Catholics to be used for the support of the Old Catholic clergy, as in the case of all other denominations; consequently the Old Catholics, mostly working-class people, were constantly in financial straits. They were also much hampered by the difficulty of getting priests. In 1880 the first Austrian Old Catholic synod was held, and the usual Old Catholic changes were introduced, such as the abolition of the liturgical use of Latin, compulsory clerical celibacy, compulsory confession, fees paid for Masses, etc. At the Synod of 1881 the Breviary was altered, and Nittel was elected as administrator of the bishopric (Bistumsverweser), but his election was refused recognition by the government. In 1883 Communion in both kinds was restored. In 1885 the government forbade Bishop Reinkens to administer confirmation in Austria; three years later the synod elected Amandus Czech as administrator, and gave him the right to administer confirmation. (Whether such confirmation was valid, I do not discuss. The Pope grants to certain priests the right to administer confirmation, and in the Eastern churches the priest is the usual minister of confirmation, using chrism blessed by a bishop; but whether the Austrian Old Catholic synod, without any bishop, was entitled to introduce such a practice, I cannot say. However, they had to choose between confirmation administered thus and none at all.) The election of Czech was recognized by the Government, and the Church now had its head, though it still had to wait thirty-seven years for a bishop. In 1896 the headquarters of the diocese was removed from Vienna to Warnsdorf, the centre of the more important part of the Austrian Old Catholic Church.

In 1890 began what is called the " Los von Rom " (Away from Rome) movement. Rome was accused of giving undue favour to the Slavs in the Austrian Empire, because the German-speaking Austrians were regarded as too liberal. Czech priests were put in charge of German congregations, which was much resented. The movement was more political than religious, and the Evangelical Church gained a much larger number of adherents from it than the Old Catholic church, which refused to take part in political controversy. Nevertheless this movement led to the foundation of more than eight Old Catholic congregations. At the same time, a Czech-speaking Old Catholic congregation was founded at Prague by Dr. Iska. One unfortunate feature distinguished the Austrian Old Catholic Church from its sister churches. Whereas the Dutch, German, and Swiss Old Catholic churches maintain the Catholic doctrine of the indissolubility of marriage, the Austrian Old Catholic Church decided in 1902 to permit the marriage of persons divorced by the civil law. For this reason its increase of membership was not altogether due to religious conviction. A curious reason why some Austrians left the Roman for the Old Catholic Communion was that Rome prohibits cremation of the dead, which the Old Catholic church permits; [1] indeed, there is a special form of service for burial of the ashes after cremation, as in the English Prayer Book of 1928. [2]

[1] Neufeld, *op. cit.*, pp. 84–91.
[2] W. H. de Voil, *Origin and Development of the Old Catholic Churches.*

CHAPTER XXIV

# FALSE STARTS

THE Old Catholic organization has one very serious weakness. The small national churches, each with its own bishop, are completely self-governing, within the terms of the Agreement of Utrecht: it is not easy for foreign bishops, perhaps even speaking a different language, to be sure that the bishop elected is suitable for his office, or to reject him when he has been elected by his own countrymen; and if he should turn out to be unsatisfactory, there is no means of compelling him to resign. This weakness does not exist in the Orthodox and Anglican systems. An Orthodox church in a country where the Orthodox are a minority is usually " autonomous "—that is, self-governing for internal purposes, but under the superintendence of the Œcumenical Patriarch. The right to be " autocephalous "—completely self-governing—is only granted after careful inquiry, and guarantees that it will not be abused; an Orthodox church, founded in modern times, is not usually autocephalous unless the Orthodox form the majority of the nation (as in Roumania).

In the Anglican Communion there is a similar arrangement. Small churches are under the jurisdiction of the Archbishop of Canterbury, who appoints their bishops. A church does not become self-governing until it is sufficiently developed to form a province; and an Anglican province must contain at least four bishoprics, so that its bishops may be consecrated without the necessity of outside help. It is almost impossible for an unsatisfactory bishop to behave in a manner which will bring about a schism. The case of Bishop Colenso is not likely to be repeated.

But there have been at least three such cases among the Old Catholics. The best known of these cases is that of Bishop Mathew. I propose to tell the strange story of this bishop at greater length than it perhaps deserves, because it is of some importance that the misunderstandings which have arisen in some quarters should, if possible, be brought to an end. It is not easy, even now, to understand some parts of the story, but I

have done my best to find out what happened and to relate it
without prejudice.

As early as 1896 an attempt was made to begin an Old Catholic
movement in England, but it came to nothing, because the priest
proposed as bishop made his submission to Rome.  In 1902 an
application was made to the Dutch Old Catholic bishops to
consecrate an English Old Catholic bishop.[1]  The candidate was
the Rev. Richard O'Halloran, a Roman Catholic secular priest
at Ealing, who had quarrelled with his superiors.  O'Halloran
asked Bishop Herzog to come and give confirmation at his church.
Bishop Herzog consulted Bishop Wordsworth, who asked the advice of Bishop (later Archbishop) Davidson.  He made inquiries,
and advised great caution:[2]  so nothing was done.  In 1908
O'Halloran tried again, and this time the instrument of his
purpose was Dr. Mathew.

Arnold Harris Mathew was the son of an officer in the Army,
and was born in 1852.  His father claimed to be the third Earl
of Landaff in the peerage of Ireland, but neither he nor his son
could ever afford to prove their claim before the Committee of
Privileges of the House of Lords.  The boy was baptized by a
Roman Catholic priest in France; but at the age of two, to satisfy his mother's scruples, he was again given baptism (presumably
conditional) by an Anglican priest.[3]  This double baptism
appears to have foreshadowed his strange career of hesitation
between the two communions.  He was educated at Cheltenham
College, and when twenty went to an Anglican theological
college in the Isle of Cumbræ.  After a short time he left Cumbræ,
was received into the Roman Communion, and was ordained
priest at Glasgow, June 24, 1877, by Archbishop Eyre (then
titular Archbishop of Anazarba, afterwards Archbishop of Glasgow).  Soon afterwards he was given the degree of Doctor of
Divinity by the Pope.[4]  After being in charge of two or three
missions, he was appointed in 1889 to a mission at Bath.  There,
according to his own account, he suffered a severe mental shock,
due partly to his discovery of the real reason for the resignation of
his predecessor, partly to some critical books which he read and
to the conversation of an ex-Dominican priest named Suffield,

---

[1] Dutch Old Catholic Pastoral, quoted in *Guardian*, May 6, 1908.
[2] G. K. A. Bell, *Life of Archbishop Davidson*, vol. ii, pp. 404–406.
[3] A. H. Mathew, in *Times*, April 12, 1913; also in *An Episcopal Odyssey*.
[4] Mathew, *An Episcopal Odyssey*.

who had become an Unitarian. He began to doubt the Infallibility of the Pope and other doctrines which he had accepted on the papal authority. He afterwards said that his faith was completely shattered by a conversation with a leading Unitarian whom he met by accident in a train. He ceased to believe in the Virgin Birth and other fundamental Christian doctrines. Accordingly he resigned his mission and his orders, and retired into private life.[1] He was placed under the lesser excommunication in 1889.

At this point he changed his name by deed-poll, at his father's request, to Count Povoleri: the title was inherited from his grandmother. Two years later he had passed his mental crisis, and he was advised by Mr. Gladstone and his cousin, Lady Sandhurst, to return to the Church of England, and to seek for a curacy at Holy Trinity, Sloane Street. He had informal permission from Bishop Temple to officiate there, and he solemnized one or two marriages (signing the register as Count Povoleri), but, according to his own account, he was never formally received into the Church of England, because Archbishop Benson insisted, as a condition of his being received, that he must sign a renunciation of the errors of the Church of Rome; and this he could not do. In 1892 he was married in an Anglican church: his wife was, and continued to be, a member of the Church of England. In 1894 his father died, and as he now claimed to be Earl of Landaff, he resumed his own name, and gave up his Italian title.[2] He remained in retirement until 1907, though he appears sometimes to have communicated as a layman, in Roman Catholic churches, which of course he had no right to do. He tried to get his marriage recognized at Rome, so that he could live as a married layman; but the authorities were obdurate. By training and outlook he was a Roman Catholic, and a priest; but by marrying he had closed the door behind him. He could only have gone back by giving up his wife and declaring his marriage to be no marriage.

In 1907, on the advice of Father George Tyrrell, the Modernist leader, he again sought to be admitted into the Anglican ministry. But the Bishop of Rochester, in whose diocese he was living, gave him no encouragement.[3] Archbishop Davidson told him that

[1] Mathew, *Times*, April 12, 1913.
[2] Mathew, *An Episcopal Odyssey*.
[3] A. F. Winnington-Ingram (Bishop of London), *Times*, April 14, 1913.

he must be on probation for a time, but he would not accept this: he wanted a good living at once in order to be able to support his family.[1] In December of the same year he produced a scheme for removing the doubt about the validity of Anglican orders, by the appointment of an Old Catholic coadjutor bishop, and wrote to Archbishop Davidson about it.[2] A few days later he told Archbishop Davidson that he intended to open a mission in England under the Archbishop of Utrecht, for discontented Roman Catholics, " in a spirit of perfect and cordial amity with the Church of England ". The Archbishop naturally could not approve of such a proposal.[3] Early in 1908 Dr. Mathew was told by Father O'Halloran that he (Dr. Mathew) had been elected bishop by a meeting of seventeen priests and sixteen laymen at Chelsfield, called for the purpose of founding an Old Catholic movement in England. O'Halloran took Mathew to Holland, introduced him to the Old Catholic bishops, and produced a letter dated March 13, signed by three priests and three laymen, requesting the Archbishop of Utrecht to consecrate Dr. Mathew.[4] This letter, with other documents, was also shown to Bishop Herzog. O'Halloran prevented Bishop van Thiel from going to England to find out whether the need for a bishop was genuine. Archbishop Gul and his suffragans believed O'Halloran, without making any inquiry of the Anglican bishops (though they asked why O'Halloran and Mathew did not join the English Church); and the consecration of Dr. Mathew was arranged for April 8, 1908. He sent notice of this to the Archbishop of Canterbury. But the day before, April 7, the Dutch bishops discovered that Dr. Mathew was married, which he had not told them. No married priest had at that time been consecrated as an Old Catholic bishop. The Dutch bishops had no objection in principle to consecrating a married priest, but they wanted to be sure that he had not left the Roman Communion in order to marry. So the consecration was postponed. However, they were satisfied on this point, and Dr. Mathew was consecrated at St. Gertrude's Cathedral, Utrecht, on April 28, 1908, by Archbishop Gul, assisted by the Bishops of Haarlem and Deventer and Bishop Demmel from Germany.[5]

[1] Bell, *op. cit.*, vol. ii, p. 1016.
[2] Bell, p. 1017.          [3] Bell, p. 1018.
[4] W. H. de Voil, *Origin and Development of the Old Catholic Churches.*
[5] *Guardian*, May 6, 1908.

On his return to England, he found that the support which he had been led to expect did not exist. He afterwards declared that he had been grievously misled; he offered to retire, but the Dutch bishops refused his offer.[1] O'Halloran asked Dr. Mathew to make him a bishop, but he refused; O'Halloran would not accept the Declaration of Utrecht. In the *Guardian* of June 3 a letter from Bishop van Thiel of Haarlem was published, declaring that the Dutch bishops had complete confidence in Bishop Mathew, and asking for the support of " the British people and Church " for him. Bishop Mathew found himself a bishop without a flock. But he was joined by a Congregationalist minister, the Rev. Noel Lambert, who had a chapel at River Street, Islington, and whom he ordained priest on June 25, 1909.

At this time Bishop Mathew's purpose was to provide a resting-place for discontented and lapsed Roman Catholics who were not prepared to join the Church of England. He was ready to work with the Church of England, and lectured at the Queen's Hall in favour of the validity of Anglican orders; he joined the newly founded Society of St. Willibrord. But the Lambeth Conference of 1908 disapproved of what he was doing, and on February 22, 1909, the Archbishop of Canterbury wrote privately to the Editor of the *Guardian*, pointing out that there was no need for an Old Catholic movement in England, since the Church of England was in the same position as the Old Catholics.[2]

Meanwhile the Dutch Old Catholic church had revised the liturgy, which was translated into Dutch and simplified.[3] As we shall see, Bishop Mathew made this revision an excuse for his later separation. On October 13, 1909, Bishop Mathew took part in the consecration of the first Polish Mariaviten bishop, John Kowalski, at Utrecht (see below). In December 1909 he was led (according to his own account), by a passage in the Life of Bishop Chinnery-Haldane of Argyll and the Isles, to doubt the validity of Anglican orders, on the ground that several Anglican archbishops had received only Presbyterian baptism, and that the administration of baptism among Presbyterians, and even in the Church of England, was sometimes very careless. (An unbaptized person cannot be ordained or consecrated: if he is, his orders are invalid.) In March 1910 Bishop Mathew gave a public lecture at Carshalton, in which he expressed his doubts, and said

[1] Mathew, *An Episcopal Odyssey.*
[2] Bell, *op. cit.,* p. 1019.    [3] *Guardian,* January 27, 1909.

that many Anglican priests had applied to him for conditional ordination, but he had refused it.[1] On June 7, 1910, he issued an official rejection of Anglican orders; to which Bishop van Thiel of Haarlem replied that in doing this Bishop Mathew did not represent any of the continental Old Catholic churches: he was in full communion with them, but completely independent.[2]

Meanwhile, on June 13, 1910, Bishop Mathew had taken a step which is very difficult to defend. He secretly consecrated two Roman Catholic priests, the Rev. H. J. Beale of Nottingham and the Rev. A. W. Howarth of Corby, Lincs, to the episcopate. These two priests are said to have had the title of Monsignor, and to have been deprived of it. They did not cease to be Roman Catholic priests, they did not accept the Agreement of Utrecht (which Bishop Mathew seems to have consistently ignored); but they told him informally that they did not believe in the infallibility of the Pope. At this time Bishop Mathew had only one church under his jurisdiction, and perhaps two or three oratories. The reason he gave later for this consecration was the need of maintaining the succession; a need which the Old Catholic bishops in Germany and Switzerland, with their thousands of adherents, did not feel. It seems that ever since he had attended the Old Catholic Congress at Vienna in 1909, Bishop Mathew had thought the continental Old Catholics to be getting steadily more Protestant, and decided to make it unnecessary for his followers, if he should die, to get his successor consecrated by continental Old Catholic bishops.

During the autumn the story of this consecration leaked out. On September 20, 1910, the *Nottingham Guardian* published a letter from Father Howarth to his diocesan, Bishop Brindle, giving his reasons for accepting consecration. On December 1 the *Oud Katholiek*, the organ of the Dutch Old Catholics, published an article pointing out that Bishop Mathew had broken the Agreement of Utrecht, under which he had been consecrated, in four different ways; for he had consecrated Beale and Howarth, (a) without informing his fellow bishops, (b) in secret, (c) without assistants, (d) while the candidates were members of another communion.[3] Bishop Mathew's reply was to issue, on December 29, 1910, a "Declaration of Autonomy and Independence", which was published in the *Guardian*, January 6, 1911. He

[1] *Guardian*, March 11, 1910.     [2] *Guardian*, August, 5, 1910.
[3] *Guardian*, December 9, 1910.

proclaimed that he differed from the Church of Utrecht and the other continental Old Catholics on seven points (in the version published in his *Episcopal Odyssey* they were increased to nine). Because of these differences he would not allow the continental Old Catholics to interfere with him in any way.

The points of difference were these:—

(1) The refusal of the continental Old Catholics to accept the doctrine of the Synod of Jerusalem (a purely Greek Council, 1672).

(2) The omission of invocation of saints from the German and Swiss liturgies.

(3) Changes in the liturgies, in particular the abolition of the rite of Benediction (he appears to have been misinformed here).

(4) Changes in the new Dutch Missal, especially the omission of the Pope's name (as Patriarch) from the Canon of the Mass.

(5) The disuse of the daily Mass.

(6) The absence of statues and pictures from the churches (here again he must have been gravely misinformed).

(7) The admission of Anglicans to communion, and the permission given to Anglican priests to celebrate the Eucharist in Old Catholic churches.

The two further points mentioned in *An Episcopal Odyssey* are:—

(8) The abolition in some cases, optional character in others, of the Sacrament of Penance.

(9) The neglect of fast-days, and of the fast before Communion.

It will be observed that all these are points of discipline, rather than of doctrine, and therefore not such as to justify schism. Some of the charges were certainly false. The most important, perhaps, was the complaint that the Old Catholics no longer recognized the Pope as their patriarch. It seems unreasonable to reject the claim of the Bishop of Rome to be Pope, and to accept his claim to be patriarch; for the Roman claim to patriarchal jurisdiction in Northern Europe rests only on the Forged Decretals: Bishop Mathew was a learned scholar, who must have known this. The Council of Jerusalem (more properly, Bethlehem) was a regional Orthodox council, never accepted by anyone in the West, and not regarded even by the Orthodox churches as œcumenical.

On January 11, 1911, the *Oud Katholiek* replied that Bishop Mathew had known all this before he took part in the consecration of Bishop Kowalski; and that in the December number of his paper he had praised the Church of Utrecht. The reason for his sudden change was that the Archbishop of Utrecht had asked him to explain the consecration of Beale and Howarth. He was no longer an Old Catholic, and the Dutch Old Catholics did not regret it at all. From his mention of the Synod of Jerusalem, his intention seemed to be to unite himself with the Orthodox churches.[1]  (One obstacle would have been that he was married.)

On February 17, Bishop Mathew's defence was summarized in the *Guardian*. He maintained that he had not separated himself, but only declared his independence; that Reinkens had been consecrated by Archbishop Heykamp alone (here he confuses Hermann Heykamp, Bishop of Deventer, with John Heykamp, Archbishop of Utrecht, a confusion which he ought not to have made, especially as it affected his own succession);[2] that Reinkens had consecrated Herzog without the consent of the Dutch bishops; that his followers had always accepted the Synod of Jerusalem; that he had thought the Dutch Old Catholics still "Roman"; and that he had protested against the defects of the Old Catholics, and been rebuffed.[3]    On April 28 he again declared that he had not separated from the Old Catholics, but merely declared his autonomy. This, however, was not the view taken by the Old Catholics themselves. They regarded his Declaration of Autonomy as an act of separation.[4]  The next Old Catholic Conference of Bishops, in 1913, declared formally that it did not recognize Bishop Mathew or any of his acts. He had ceased to be an Old Catholic on December 29, 1910, after an episcopate of less than three years.

It is not difficult to show the weakness of his defence. It was unnecessary for him to assert his independence: Bishop van Thiel had expressly admitted it months before, and no one had ever doubted it. What he had really done was to refuse to be bound any longer by the Agreement of Utrecht. The consecration of Bishop Reinkens by one bishop was a necessity; this cannot be said of the consecration of Bishop Herzog, but that was

---

[1] *Guardian*, February 10, 1911.
[2] Hermann Heykamp had no choice: he was the only Old Catholic bishop surviving. Mathew was in communion with nine bishops.
[3] *Guardian*, February 17, 1911.        [4] *Guardian*, May 5, 1911.

in the transitional period before the Agreement of Utrecht. There was no reason why any western Catholic should feel bound by the Synod of Jerusalem. The other points, however deplorable Mathew might think them, were not points of dogma, and in any case he had known them, or might have known them, before; some of them, such as the small changes in the Dutch Missal, were frivolous (the only important change, the omission of the Filioque from the Nicene Creed, he had adopted himself, as well as the principle of the vernacular liturgy).

He had already on May 3, 1910, made his little church a " cathedral ", and appointed a Dean and five Canons (complete with robes). No other Old Catholic church possessed a Dean and Chapter (except, of course, the historic Chapter of Utrecht); but Bishop Mathew, with his one congregation and minute flock, must needs have one. After his Declaration of Autonomy, his dean, Noel Lambert, joined the Church of England, taking the " cathedral " with him; another priest preferred to remain Old Catholic (though he was not recognized by any Old Catholic bishop): he ultimately returned to Lutheranism. There were eight priests left; in January 1911, Bishop Mathew consecrated four of them, as titular Bishops of Durham, Hereford, Norwich, and Winchester, at their own request. [1] The same day the four newly consecrated bishops elected Mathew " Archbishop of London ". Notice of this consecration was sent to the Pope, with the result that Dr. Mathew was placed under the greater excommunication, February 28, 1911. This excommunication was published in *The Times*; in 1913 Archbishop Mathew sued *The Times* for libel, but he lost his case. A wealthy lady offered to build him a cathedral, and published documents giving him various elaborate titles, which he signed.[2] On February 28, 1911 he proposed to the Roman Catholic Bishop Hedley of Newport to found an " Uniat Church " in England, with himself at the head of it; he hoped that a large number of Anglican priests would join it. (This was, I believe, his real object: he thought that the publication of the Report of the Royal Commission on Ecclesiastical Disorders would lead to a large secession of priests from the Church of England.)[3] After his excommunication he withdrew his offer of submission to Rome. He next tried the Orthodox churches. The Holy Synod of

[1] Mathew, *Times*, April 14, 1913.
[2] Mathew, *Times*, April 14, 1913.      [3] de Voil, *op. cit.*

Russia would have nothing to do with him; but he claimed that Archbishop Gerasimos Mossarra of Beyrout had received him into the Orthodox Patriarchate of Antioch (the archbishop had no power to do this without the consent of the Patriarch of Antioch and his Synod, which was certainly never given). Archbishop Mathew consecrated many bishops, none of them particularly suitable for the office: one at least turned out to be a man of bad character. Most of them left him after a short time; some joined the Roman Communion, others the Anglican, while others founded independent sects, none of which are of any importance.

Early in 1915 Dr. Mathew offered to re-consecrate the Bishop of London![1] In May the Archbishop of Canterbury found it necessary to publish a statement about Dr. Mathew's history. On December 18, 1915, Dr. Mathew resigned, in order to make his personal submission to Rome; in the following January the Rev. Bernard Williams, who had been his chaplain, and was now " Grand Vicar in the vacancy of the see ", wrote to the *Guardian* that since Archbishop Mathew's submission to Rome the " Old Roman Catholic " movement had come to an end. But Dr. Mathew could not accept Rome's terms; on March 5, 1916, he resumed his former position, and on April 14 in his private chapel at Kingsdown, Deal, he consecrated Bernard Williams as his coadjutor with right of succession. On April 15 the Archbishop of Canterbury gave him a personal interview; it appears that he wanted work in the Church of England, but the Archbishop would only admit him as a layman. (Did he inform the Archbishop that he had consecrated a coadjutor the previous day?) A fresh attempt in this direction was made by his friends in 1917, but the Archbishop would not hear of it. In 1919 Dr. Mathew, now reduced to poverty, begged to be allowed to sit in the choir at South Mymms and read the lessons. While this request was being considered, he died, December 19, 1919.[2]

The protest of the Lambeth Conference of 1908 was answered by an apology from the Dutch Old Catholic bishops, and a promise that they would in future consult their Anglican colleagues before accepting candidates for consecration from England.

---

[1] *Guardian*, August 19, 1915 (letter from Archbishop of Canterbury's chaplain); *An Episcopal Odyssey* (defence of the proposal, by Bishop Mathew); Bell, *op. cit.*, p. 1020.

[2] Bell, *op. cit.*, pp. 1022–1023.

This was followed in 1920 by an assurance that the Old Catholics did not recognize Bishop Mathew in any way.[1] If the contact between the Anglican and Old Catholic communions had been as close in 1908 as it was thirty years earlier, this deplorable consecration would never have taken place.

The case of the Mariaviten bishops was very different from that of Bishop Mathew, and I do not think that the Old Catholic bishops can fairly be blamed for consecrating them. The Mariaviten Union (Mariæ Vita, Life of Mary) was founded in Poland in 1893 by a Franciscan abbess, for greater strictness of life and special devotion to our Lord in the Sacrament exposed. It was at first sanctioned by some Polish bishops; and a community of men was founded in connexion with it. It was, however, condemned at Rome on April 5, 1906; the leaders of it were excommunicated on December 5, 1906. It had made great progress among the peasants. After its condemnation Roman Catholic priests were explaining that the hosts consecrated by Mariaviten priests became the body, not of Christ, but of the Devil. (The atmosphere in which this was possible was evidently quite different from that of the Old Catholic revolt against the Vatican Council.) The cause of the Mariaviten Union was taken up by the Russian layman, General Kiréev, who had long been the leading supporter of the Old Catholics in the Russian Orthodox Church. He attended the Old Catholic Congress at Vienna in September 1909, with three Mariaviten priests. On October 5, 1909, John Marie Kowalski was consecrated bishop for the Mariaviten, at Utrecht, by the three Dutch bishops, Bishop Demmel, and Bishop Mathew.[2] The Rev. G. E. Barber, Secretary of the Society of St. Willibrord, was present by the special request of the consecrating bishops and the bishop-elect. At this time the Mariaviten were said to have thirty-two priests and 200,000 adherents. Soon afterwards two more bishops were consecrated at Plock in Poland. Anglican visitors spoke most highly of the zeal and piety of the Mariaviten. The Blessed Sacrament was perpetually exposed in all their churches, and they had large orders both of monks and nuns; these features were quite unknown in the other Old Catholic churches. Even Bishop Mathew (April 28, 1911) said that he was in complete agreement with the Polish Old Catholics. General Kiréev pre-

---

[1] *Report of Lambeth Conference*, 1920, p. 154.
[2] *Guardian*, October 13, 1909, p. 1616.

sented the three bishops to the Emperor of Russia, and they were given recognition: indeed, there was some fear that the Russian Government would use the Mariaviten Church as a means of dividing the Poles. During the German occupation of Poland they were severely treated, their churches were closed, and they were forbidden to hold services. Poland suffered as severely as any European country during the war; and it seems to have been some mental disorder due to the war that led Archbishop Kowalski to adopt his strange and immoral doctrine of mystical marriage. In consequence of this, the Old Catholic bishops in 1924 broke off all relations with the Mariaviten Church, which became greatly diminished and completely discredited.

(The Mariaviten Church has never had any connexion with the Polish National Church under Bishop Hodur, referred to in Chapter 23, which has one bishopric in Poland.)

Bishop Mathew ceased to be an Old Catholic bishop on December 29, 1910. The Old Catholic churches have not recognized him or any of his acts since that date; nor have they accepted anyone ordained or consecrated by him, either before or since he ceased to be an Old Catholic bishop. But there are several sects which claim to derive their episcopal succession from him, which are often confused with the Old Catholics, and which in some cases make use of the name " Old Catholic ". It cannot be too strongly emphasized that none of these sects is Old Catholic, or is recognized in any way by the genuine Old Catholic churches in communion with the Archbishop of Utrecht. For further information see H. R. T. Brandreth, *Episcopi Vagantes and the Anglican Church*.

It appears that all these sects reject the infallibility and ordinary jurisdiction of the Pope, omit the Filioque clause, employ married priests, and use the Roman Liturgy in a more or less modified form. None of them possesses any large number of members.

They all lay great stress on the validity of their orders, and it seems desirable to state the facts about this claim. The word " valid " is used in different senses, but in my opinion it has properly only one meaning: it means recognized by the competent authority. It is a legal term, and conveys an idea which no society can do without.

An ordination is valid when it is recognized by the Church

<hr />

[1] De Voil, *op. cit.*

(whatever is meant by the Church).[1]    It is not necessarily valid because the ordained man is effective or successful (any more than a marriage is valid because the couple live happily together). " Spiritually valid " can only mean " recognized by the spiritual or ecclesiastical authority ": not " recognized by God ", because we have no certain means of ascertaining what ministry or sacrament God recognizes, unless we believe that what the Church, as God's representative, recognizes is necessarily recognized by Him.

The ministry of every communion is valid for that communion. Disputes about validity only arise when the mutual recognition of different communions is proposed, or when a minister of one communion wishes to serve in another. Every communion has the right to decide for itself what conditions it requires for its ministry; so that, for instance, an Anglican priest has no right to complain that he cannot become a priest of the Roman Communion without a fresh ordination.

The Orthodox Eastern Communion retains the old discipline of the Church up to the fourth century, according to which no one ordained outside the Church can be received into the ministry without a fresh ordination; but this is qualified by the doctrine of " economy ", according to which the Church can in certain circumstances receive as valid, if she thinks it desirable, ordinations or other sacraments which are in themselves not valid. The Orthodox churches, therefore, are free to accept the clergy of these sects without ordination, or to require a fresh ordination, as they shall think fit. They have not, as far as I know, accepted any.

The Roman Communion, on the other hand, follows the rule introduced by St. Augustine with the object of reconciling the Donatists. Every ordination with the proper subject, matter, form, minister, and intention is valid; and the Roman Church is therefore forced to recognize the validity of the ordinations of all these sects if they can prove their succession. But in practice those who have received consecration or ordination from Bishop Mathew and his successors, and afterwards submit to Rome, are required to promise never to make use of the powers thus irregularly obtained. As far as I know, this has been the invariable practice of Rome.

The Old Catholic churches have simply refused to recognize

[1] See *Doctrine in the Church of England*, p. 131.

or accept any person ordained or consecrated by Bishop Mathew at any time. The question of validity is not raised.

The Anglican Communion certainly followed the same rule as the Roman until 1920. But the Lambeth Conference of that year decided that no person ordained or consecrated by Bishop Mathew or his successors or other irregular bishops should be admitted to the Anglican ministry without conditional ordination. This rule has been strictly observed. Beale was in Roman orders, and he was accepted as a priest, not as a bishop. Some have been ordained conditionally before they were allowed to serve as Anglican priests.

It has been argued that the Lambeth Conference, in making the recommendation (for resolutions of the Lambeth Conference have of themselves no binding force), departed from the traditional Western theory and reverted to the Eastern theory, which was universal before St. Augustine.[1] But it can also be argued (as it was by Puller)[2] that the Lambeth Conference only decided, that because of the difficulty of proving the facts (since Bishop Mathew and his successors often held their consecrations and ordinations in private chapels and rooms), and because of the untrustworthy character of some of the persons concerned, it was safer to make a general rule that no irregular consecrations or ordinations of this kind should be accepted as certain.

The question, however, remains, whether the practice of recognizing schismatic ordinations, introduced by St. Augustine in order to reconcile the Donatist Church, will bear application to the " wandering bishops " with irregular succession derived from Bishops Mathew and Vilatte. (There are other " wandering bishops " whose consecration is even more doubtful; but they have no connexion with the Old Catholics.) Dr. O. C. Quick criticizes the Augustinian theory, because " it makes the essence of a valid sacrament consist in a divine action performed in response to the utterance of a particular form by a person who has a *ministerial power inherent in himself*, rather than by a person who has a *ministerial authority in virtue of an office held* " (*The Christian Sacraments*, p. 154). A bishop is an officer of the Church, and has the right to consecrate bishops and ordain priests for the Church only because he holds that position. But according to the

---

[1] See *Doctrine in the Church of England*, p. 134, where this view seems to be maintained (1938).

[2] In conversation with the author.

traditional Western theory, an excommunicated bishop, even if completely isolated, can go about the world consecrating bishops and ordaining priests at his own discretion, and the Church is bound to recognize that they are bishops and priests, who cannot be consecrated or ordained again. It is this theory which has made possible the vagaries of the Mathew and Vilatte successions. And it is at any rate a possible view that the Church ought to have some means of preventing an unsatisfactory and irresponsible bishop, after he has been excommunicated and has ceased to have the authority of any church, even a heretical one, behind him, from filling the world with irregular bishops and priests, whose performances deceive the ignorant and unwary, and bring the sacraments and ministry of the Church into disrepute and ridicule.

# CHAPTER XXV

# THE OLD CATHOLIC CHURCHES AFTER THE FIRST WORLD WAR

DURING the first World War, 1914–19, the revolutions which followed it, and the collapse of the German and Austrian currency, the Old Catholic churches passed through storms which might easily have destroyed them. The Germans and Austrians were on one side, the Poles in Europe and America on the other, the Dutch and Swiss were neutral. No congresses could be held. The financial difficulties must have been enormous. Yet these small churches survived, and appeared in the new world after the War (with the exception of the Mariaviten Church), no weaker, if no stronger, than before.

In 1916 Bishop Prins of Haarlem died, and Mgr. Henricus Johannes Theodorus van Vlijmen was consecrated to succeed him by Archbishop Gul, assisted by Bishop Herzog only. Bishop Spit was too infirm to assist, and Bishop Moog was suddenly prevented from going to Holland, because of the War. This was the last Old Catholic consecration in which fewer than three bishops took part.

Archbishop Gul died in 1920, and was succeeded by Franciscus Kenninck, who had been President of Amersfoort Seminary. He was consecrated by the Bishop of Haarlem, assisted by Bishops Herzog and Moog.

The division of the dominions of the House of Hapsburg made it possible to establish new bishoprics. The Austrian Old Catholics had always been divided into two groups: one on the northern frontier of Bohemia and Moravia, with its centre at Warnsdorf; the other in and around Vienna. The northern group of congregations was now in the Czechoslovak Republic, though it was almost entirely composed of members of the German-speaking minority. Amanduš Czech remained the diocesan administrator (*Bistumsverweser*) until his death in 1922. His successor, Mgr. Alois Paschek,[1] was consecrated as the first Old Catholic bishop

---

[1] Now spelt Pašek, but I retain the German spelling, as easier for English readers.

in Czechoslovakia by the Archbishop of Utrecht, on September 14, 1924, together with Bishop Küry. For the veteran Bishop Herzog, the last survivor of the first generation of Old Catholics, died in 1924, at the age of eighty-two. It is impossible to over-estimate the importance to the Swiss Old Catholic Church of the firm hand of Bishop Herzog, whose episcopate lasted forty-eight years, and who guided the church through the critical period of its constitutional and liturgical settlement, until the time of crisis was past. He was succeeded by Mgr. Adolf Küry, who had been, and remained, Professor in the Old Catholic Theological Faculty at Berne. Bishop Küry has taken a prominent part in all the modern international Christian movements, such as those con-nected with the Stockholm and Lausanne Conferences.

Meanwhile the leadership of the Viennese group in the Austrian Old Catholic Church passed to Adalbert Schindelaar, who was consecrated first Bishop of the Old Catholic Church in Austria, during the International Old Catholic Congress at Berne, on September 1, 1925, by Bishop Küry, assisted by the Archbishop of Utrecht, the Bishop of Haarlem, and Bishops Moog, Paschek, and Bonczak. This was the largest number of Old Catholic bishops that had ever taken part in a consecration. I was present at it myself, and it was a most impressive sight, especially so soon after the War in which these bishops had been on different sides. Unfortunately, Bishop Schindelaar died thirteen months later; he was succeeded by Bishop Robert Tüchler, a Viennese, who had been a Barnabite monk in the Roman Communion and who was consecrated by Bishop Paschek on August 9, 1928. Under him the Austrian Old Catholic Church increased in numbers rapidly.

The five Churches of Holland, Germany, Switzerland, Austria, and Czechoslovakia are the nucleus of the Old Catholic commu-nion. But, as we have seen, bodies of Slavs, who have become discontented with the papal rule on national rather than religious grounds, have from time to time joined the Old Catholics. These Slavs are either Czechs, Yugoslavs, or Poles.

After the collapse of the Austrian Empire there was a great revolt against the Roman See among the Czechs; but as the Czechoslovak Old Catholic Church was almost entirely German-speaking, it did not gain much from this movement.[1]

There was also a revolt among the Roman Catholics of Yugo-

[1] Article by Bishop of Wakefield (J. B. Seaton) in *Church Quarterly Review*.

slavia after the war. The dispute with Italy about the possession of Dalmatia and Fiume had made many Croats unwilling to be subject to an Italian Pope. There were traditions of independence in that part of Europe: the Glagolithic rite, which is the Roman Liturgy in Old Slavonic, has been in use in some churches ever since the conversion of the Slavs; Gregory of Nin, a tenth-century bishop who led the defence of the Slavonic against the Latin rite, has been made a national hero, and his colossal statue by Mestrovitch occupies the small cathedral square at Spalato (now Split). It was not forgotten that Bishop Strossmayer, the leader of the Croat national party in his day, had also been the firmest member of the minority at the Vatican Council. A large group of priests asked the Pope for permission to say Mass in Croat. He answered that those churches in which the Old Slavonic Mass had been said for centuries might continue to enjoy that privilege; but that there was no reason why the Croats should be allowed to use their modern language for the Mass, any more than the French or Germans. Some priests were dissatisfied with this answer. In 1923 an Old Catholic church was formed, and spread rapidly throughout Yugoslavia, among the Croats and Slovenes (not, of course, among the Serbs, who are Orthodox). Marko Kalogjera, a " Domherr " (canon) of Split Cathedral, was elected bishop, and was consecrated at Utrecht by the archbishop, February 25, 1924. His residence was at Zagreb (Agram), the capital of Croatia. Unfortunately, in 1928 a dispute about the constitution of the church broke out. At the Old Catholic Congress of Utrecht in that year I talked to leaders on both sides, and the point in dispute appeared to be the question whether the democratic constitution of the Swiss Old Catholic Church or the more monarchical constitution of the German Old Catholic Church should be copied in Yugoslavia. In 1933 the bishop was accused of granting divorces to persons who had no right to them, for money. The Old Catholic Bishops' Conference, before which the accusation was brought, felt itself obliged to sever its relations with Bishop Kalogjera. But the Yugoslav government had recognized him as the Old Catholic Bishop, and paid him a salary (it is suggested that the Serbs were not unwilling to use the Old Catholic Church to divide the Croatian people). The Old Catholic bishops apparently omitted to give notice of their proceedings to the Yugoslav government, and Bishop Kalogjera persuaded the government that he was the victim of a Pan-German conspiracy, since all the members of the Old Catholic Bishops' Conference, except the Dutch, were German-speaking.

The Yugoslav Old Catholic Church was divided into two sections: one-third of it supported the bishop, was who recognized by the government; the other two-thirds remained in full communion with Utrecht, and elected as their bishop first Ivan Cerovski, and then a priest named Dònkovič, who was never consecrated.[1] It is clear that the consecration of Bishop Kalogjera is another instance of the weakness in the Old Catholic system, mentioned in the last chapter. The Old Catholic Church in Croatia, in communion with Utrecht, has now 4,000 members in 8 parishes. Its bishop, Vladimir Kos, died in 1959. Vilim Huzjak was elected by the synod to succeed him, and was consecrated in 1961. The bishops in Serbia and Slovenia are not in communion with Utrecht.

In 1925, after an interval of twelve years caused by the war and its results, the tenth International Old Catholic Congress was held at Berne. Two important events took place during this congress: the consecration of Bishop Schindelaar, which was mentioned above, and the formal recognition by the Old Catholic Bishops' Conference of the validity of Anglican ordinations, the effect of which will be explained in a later chapter.[2]

The Patriarch of Constantinople was represented by the Metropolitan of Thyatira, the Archbishop of Canterbury by the Dean of Salisbury (Dr. Burn), and the American Episcopal Church by the Bishop of Harrisburg (Dr. Darlington) and the Rev. Dr. W. Chauncey Emhardt. There were also present representatives of the High Church movement in the German Evangelical Church and the Swiss Reformed Church. The Anglican visitors were admitted to Communion on the first day of the Congress, in accordance with the rule of the Swiss Old Catholic Church since 1883: it was inspiring, so soon after the War, to see representatives of both sides, and of neutral nations, kneeling together at the altar.                                    •

The twelfth Old Catholic Congress, at Vienna in 1931, was notable for an alteration in the usual arrangements. The second day of the congress began with the celebration of the Russian Liturgy, in German, by a Russian Orthodox bishop; the third

[1] H. Neufeld in *Die Altkatholische Kirchen*, p. 91.
[2] *Internationale Kirchliche Zeitschrift*, October, 1925.

day with a Solemn Eucharist, celebrated according to the English Rite of 1928 by the Dean of Chichester, who represented the Archbishop of Canterbury at the Congress. The reason for this arrangement was the wish of the Austrian Old Catholics to promote closer relations with the Orthodox and Anglican communions: there were an English church and five Orthodox churches of different nationalities in Vienna.

In 1929 Bishop Spit of Deventer, who had long been infirm, died, and was succeeded by Johannes Hermannus Berends, the parish priest at The Hague, who was consecrated in his own church by the Archbishop of Utrecht. He remained in charge of his parish until 1934, as the bishopric is only titular.

The thirteenth Old Catholic Congress was held at Constance in 1934. The Archbishop of Canterbury was represented by the Bishop of Lincoln, who celebrated the Holy Eucharist, according to the English rite, early on the first day of the congress, when the Old Catholic bishops and a large number of others received the Holy Communion at his hands. This was the first congress after reunion with the Church of England had been formally accepted.

The last census (1930) gave 10,198 as the number of the Dutch Old Catholics, 945 of whom belonged to the " diaspora ". (One of the greatest practical difficulties in all Old Catholic churches is the pastoral care of the " diaspora ", the scattered members living out of reach of any church.) There were twenty-seven Old Catholic parishes in Holland, two of which were modern; not one congregation had been lost since Dr. Neale wrote ninety years ago. Three parishes had no resident priest. There was one congregation in France under the Archbishop of Utrecht. The clergy had all been trained at Amersfoort.[1]

On February 10, 1937, after a long and painful illness, Archbishop Kenninck passed to his rest. It was he who appointed the commission which led to the recognition of Anglican orders, who went himself to the Lambeth Conference, and who carried through the restoration of intercommunion with the Church of England. Under him compulsory clerical celibacy was abolished (1922), and the constitution of the Church of Utrecht made more democratic.

He was succeeded by Professor Andreas Rinkel, parish priest of Amersfoort, who was consecrated at St. Gertrude's Cathedral, Utrecht, June 15, 1937, by the Bishop of Deventer, assisted by the

[1] *Die Altkatholische Kirchen*, pp. 60 ff.

Bishop of Haarlem, the Old Catholic bishops in Germany, Switzerland, and Czechoslovakia, and the Anglican Bishops of Gloucester and Fulham.

In Switzerland, according to Bishop Küry, there were about 30,000 Old Catholics with forty-two priests (1935), and forty congregations.[1] Here there is a very large " diaspora ". Geneva and six other congregations are French-speaking, the rest are German-speaking. The clergy are trained in the Old Catholic Theological Faculty at Berne. Not many are converts from the Roman Communion.

In Germany the number of Old Catholics increased considerably after the war.[2] Several new congregations were established, but a section of the church disapproved strongly of the spirit of the forward movement.

At the end of 1934 Bishop Moog died, and was succeeded by Bishop Erwin Kreuzer, who had been a strong candidate when Bishop Moog was elected, and who had afterwards been parish priest at Freiburg-in-Breisgau. He was consecrated at Mannheim on May 8, 1935, by Bishop Küry, assisted by the Bishops of Haarlem and Deventer. The total number of Old Catholics in Germany was said by Bishop Kreuzer (1935) to be between 25,000 and 30,000.[3] There were seventy-nine parishes (Gemeinden), and eighteen other places where services were held. Three were in Poland, in what was formerly part of Prussia. Old Catholics are found chiefly in the west and south, the Catholic districts, though there are parishes in Berlin and Hamburg. In 1947 Otto Steinwachs was consecrated assistant bishop for Germany at Utrecht by the three Dutch bishops. In 1951 John Joseph Demmel was consecrated at Essen by the Archbishop of Utrecht with Old Catholic and Anglican assistants, as coadjutor for Germany. (I was present at this consecration.) He became diocesan bishop when Bishop Kreuzer died in 1953.

At present (1961) there are 40,000 Old Catholics in Germany, in 77 parishes and 147 out-stations. They have 116 churches and chapels. The great majority of the Old Catholics of Cechoslovakia, being German-speaking, were expelled after the overthrow of Hitler's government; they took refuge in Germany, and founded many new congregations especially in Bavaria, Hanover, and Upper Franconia. Most of the Old Catholic churches in

---

[1] *Die Altkatholische Kirchen.* p. 74.                    [2] *De Voil, op. cit.*
[3] *Die Altkatholische Kirchen.* p. 77.

Germany were destroyed during the war, but they have all been rebuilt, and many new churches and other buildings have been added to them. The seminary at Bonn was renewed in 1960, and a great project for social work in Bielefeld—Krefeld—Hamburg has been begun.

In Czechoslovakia there was slow but steady growth. Bishop Paschek, who lived at Warnsdorf, was a scholar who spoke several languages, and a wise ruler who was universally respected. His people, mostly working men engaged in the glass industry and other trades, were very hard hit by the financial depression. The number of Old Catholics was about 25,000; there were eleven parishes, with many out-stations, fifteen priests, and twelve churches, with two smaller chapels. Old Catholics were forbidden by their synod to dabble in politics. There was one Czech-speaking congregation at Prague; the rest were German-speaking.[1] In Austria the growth of the Old Catholic Church was rapid, but not entirely satisfactory. Many artisans who had become Socialists and left the Roman Communion joined the Old Catholics when the Socialist rule in Vienna was overthrown. Others joined because the Old Catholics permitted divorce and cremation. In spite of the unfriendliness of the government, the Old Catholic Church continued to increase, until it numbered over 45,000. There were six main centres, with perhaps forty-five places where services were held, and about eighteen priests. The training of the clergy was a great difficulty; many of them, like the Bishop, had been ordained in the Roman Communion.

The total number of Old Catholics in Europe was about 170,000. It may be asked why a movement with such great traditions had not made more progress. Possibly it began too late. By 1870 popular interest in Europe had turned away from religion to politics and economics. Nor did it produce any great popular leader: it was mainly led by scholars, and they had no successors. Again, political motives were too much emphasized at the beginning. Old Catholics admit that the " Kulturkampf " and the support of Bismarck did the movement much harm. Nevertheless, the Old Catholics have an importance out of proportion to their small numbers. They are a true " bridge-church " (more so than the Anglican Communion to which the name has been applied). They bear witness that it is possible to be Latin or " Western " Catholics without being Ultramontane;

[1] De Voil, *op. cit.*

they resemble the Roman Communion in their liturgy and law, the Orthodox Communion in their creed, the Anglican Communion in their theological position, and the Continental Protestants in their Teutonic mentality. And the union with the Church of England which they have achieved may be a model for a wider union hereafter.

# CHAPTER XXVI

# THE OLD CATHOLIC LITURGIES [1]

I⊤ is impossible to give here a full account of all the Old Catholic rites. Readers are referred to *Old Catholic Eucharistic Worship*, by Dr. de Voil and Dr. Wynne-Bennett.

There are three independent Old Catholic liturgies: the Dutch, the German, and the Swiss. They are all based on the Roman rite. The Dutch is the latest, and the most conservative; the Swiss the oldest, and the most radical. The German rite is used, with slight changes, in Austria and Czechoslovakia. The Yugoslav and Polish Old Catholics use the Roman rite, translated into the vernacular, with the Filioque clause omitted from the Creed. The Poles in America may use English except for the Mass, which must be in Polish.

The following features are common to the Dutch, German, and Swiss rites. They are all in the language of the country. They all omit the Filioque from the Creed. All of them are recited aloud, and the congregation is expected to join; though in Germany and Switzerland it is common for part of the rite to be said silently while the congregation is singing hymns. In all of them what is regarded as papal or Ultramontane is omitted. The Pope is not prayed for by name; the feast of the Conception of our Lady (December 8) is nowhere observed. The appearance of the churches and the character of the services are similar to those in the Roman Communion, but simpler: how much simpler, varies in different countries.

In Switzerland several unofficial vernacular rites were used, and liturgical confusion prevailed, until 1880, when Bishop Herzog succeeded in getting his proposals for a liturgy, in German and French, accepted. In 1910 the French version of it was revised officially, but the new one is not much used. The following are the most prominent features peculiar to the Swiss liturgy.

---

[1] The following sources have been used: *Misboek* (Dutch Old Catholic Missal); *Liturgisches Gebetbuch* (German: several editions); *Gebetbuch fuer die christkatholische Kirche in der Schweiz*; *Liturgie et Cantiques en usage dans l'Église Catholique Chretienne de la Suisse*; W. H. de Voil and H. D. Wynne-Bennett, *Old Catholic Eucharistic Worship*; *Old Catholic Missal and Ritual* (Mathewite).

The prayer " Oramus Te ", with its reference to relics, is omitted. The " Kyries " are replaced by a series of biddings for prayer for the Church, for the country, and for those in trouble. The reply to each of these is " Lord, have mercy upon us ". The " Gloria in excelsis " may be sung in a metrical form. The prayer " Deus qui humanæ substantiæ " is replaced by one which begins, " O God, Who hast wonderfully created the dignity of man, and still more wonderfully hast renewed it ". The prayer " Suscipiat Dominus " becomes " Sanctify our hearts, O Lord, and let our sacrifice be to the honour of Thy name and for the welfare of all Thy holy Church ". It is said by the congregation, and the priest replies " Amen ".

There are seven Proper Prefaces, besides the ferial Preface, which is abbreviated from the Roman one. The Proper Preface for Whit Sunday contains no reference to the gift of divers languages.

The Canon differs considerably from the Roman one. There is an Epiclesis, which precedes the Words of Institution (as in the First Prayer Book of Edward VI). Both the Epiclesis and the Words of Institution are printed with special letters. The " Unde et memores " has been rewritten. The Commemoration of the Saints mentions only " Mary, the holy Mother of our Saviour, the Patriarchs, Prophets, Apostles, Evangelists, and all the Saints ". The Supplication for the Dead is followed by the Supplication for the Living, which has also been rewritten.

When the priest holds up the Host, he says, not " Behold the Lamb of God . . . ", but " Words of our Saviour: Come unto Me, all ye that labour", etc. Communion is usually given in both kinds. (This practice was introduced through the influence of Bishop Cotterill of Edinburgh, who assisted Bishop Herzog by administering the Chalice, on August 10, 1879, at Berne.)

There are " Propers " for the following days: every Sunday in the year, Christmas Day (three), St. Stephen, St. John, Holy Innocents, " Name-Giving of Jesus " (January 1), New Year (either may be used), Epiphany, Ash Wednesday (with office for the blessing of ashes), weekdays in Lent (one for each day of the week), each separate day in Passion Week and Holy Week (there are special rites for Good Friday and Easter Eve, on which, of course, there is no Mass), and Easter Week; Rogation Days, Ascension Day; each day in Whitsun Week, Corpus Christi, and the following Holy Days; the Presentation of Jesus in the Temple

(February 2), St. Peter and St. Paul, the Assumption of St. Mary, the Day of Prayer for the Swiss Federation (third Sunday in September), All Saints' Day, and the Dedication Festival. There are Masses for any feast of St. Mary, feast of an Apostle or Evangelist, feast of one Saint; and Masses of Thanksgiving, for a Marriage, and for the Dead.

The Swiss Prayer Book contains forms for the administration of all the seven sacraments. The Office of Baptism differs very considerably from the Roman rite, and closely resembles the form used at Stuttgart in 1833, under the influence of Wessenberg. The various ceremonies, breathing, placing salt on the lips, etc., are retained, but all reference to the exorcism of evil spirits is omitted.

The Office of Unction of the Sick is directed to the recovery of the sick person and the forgiveness of his sins, rather than to his preparation for death. There is, however, a prayer to be used if he is not expected to recover.

The forms for the other sacraments call for no special comment, except the Ordinal, which is the same for all Old Catholic churches, and is issued by the authority of the Bishops' Conference. It is almost an exact translation from the Roman Pontifical. There is naturally no reference to celibacy, and the second imposition of the stole at the ordination of priests is omitted. I was present at the consecration of Bishop Schindelaar, and I noticed two remarkable features: the words " Receive the Holy Ghost " were said in Latin (the only instance of the liturgical use of Latin by the Old Catholics), and the bishops did not lay their hands on the candidate's head all together, as Anglican bishops do, but each one stepped out from his place, laid on his hands separately, said the words, and returned. The effect was extraordinarily dignified.

The official French-Swiss liturgy, which is supposed to be used in French-speaking congregations, is slightly different from the German-Swiss rite. There are more detailed rubrical directions. The prayers " Suscipe sancte Pater " and " Deus qui humanæ substantiæ " are translated (except that there is no mention of the Holy Ghost in the latter). There are two extra Proper Prefaces, for Advent and for Saints' Days. There is a prayer for the blessing of incense immediately after the words of consecration. The " Nobis quoque peccatoribus " is somewhat shortened. The 15th of August is called simply " Mort de Marie (death of Mary), and there is no Proper for festivals of the Blessed Virgin other than February 2 and August 15.

The Swiss Prayer Book also contains a short form of Vespers, with three psalms, one lesson, and the Magnificat, which is sung on Sundays and festivals, and in town parishes more often, especially in Advent and Lent. The Swiss liturgical reforms were influenced to some extent by the Prayer Book of the American Episcopal Church. This is probably the source of the Epiclesis, though in the Swiss rite it is not in the usual place.

The liturgy of the German Old Catholic Church was drawn up by Dr. Adolf Thürlings, parish priest at Kempten, and afterwards Professor of Dogmatics and Liturgies in the Old Catholic Theological Faculty at Berne University. It was issued in 1888. A revision was made in 1924 by Dr. Otto Steinwachs of Mannheim.

This liturgy has two alternative forms: one which keeps close to its Roman original, and another which is more modern in expression; in the latter there is an Epiclesis, in the same position as in the Swiss rite. The Gloria in Excelsis is only used on days when the " Kyries " are not used; it is broken up into versicles and responses, instead of being all recited by the priest and the congregation. The lists of saints in the Roman Canon are omitted. Communion is given in one kind only in Germany; in Austria and Czechoslovakia in both kinds, by intinction, the host being dipped into the chalice.

The Proper Prefaces, and the Masses for Sundays and Holy Days, are very much the same as in the Swiss rite. The offices for the administration of the other sacraments are, I understand, simply translated from the Roman rites.

The Dutch Old Catholic Liturgy dates only from 1909: until then the Roman rite was used, in Latin, but it was always audible, and all the people had both Latin and Dutch before them. The following changes have been made in the liturgy:—

(1) In the prayer before the Introit, the words " by the merits of Thy saints whose relics are here, and of all the saints " are replaced by the words " in fellowship with Thy saints ".

(2) Except on days when there is a Sequence, there is no Gradual.

(3) After the Gospel the prayer " Per evangelica dicta " is omitted.

(4) The Filioque clause, as in all the Old Catholic liturgies, is omitted.

(5) There is no Offertory anthem, and the words " Let us pray " precede the " Suscipe, sancte Pater ".

(6) The prayer at the blessing of incense is simplified.

(7) In the " Te igitur ", the words " with Thy servant N. our Pope and N. our Bishop " are replaced by " with our bishops ".

(8) In " Communicantes " the words " semper Virginis Mariæ " are replaced by " maagd Maria " (Virgin Mary). The list of the Apostles, without St. Matthias, follows; but the Roman saints, Linus, Cletus, Clement, etc., are replaced by " the holy Basil and Chrysostom, Ambrose and Augustine, Willibrord and Boniface, Gregory, Martin, Bavo, Lebuinus, and all the saints ". (This Gregory is the Dutch St. Gregory, the third Bishop of Utrecht: S.S. Martin, Bavo, and Lebuinus are the patrons of the bishoprics of Utrecht, Haarlem, and Deventer.) There is nothing corresponding to the " quorum meritis " in the Latin.

(9) The list of saints in " Nobis quoque peccatoribus " is omitted: so is the prayer " Hæc commixtio " (but not the ceremony of the commixture), and the Communion anthem.

(10) " Ite, missa est " is replaced by " Praise and thank the Lord ".

There are fourteen Proper Prefaces, and Proper Masses for every Sunday in the year, and for forty-five Holy Days; also for each separate Ember Day, each Wednesday and Friday in Lent, Monday and Tuesday in Easter Week and Whitsun Week; also the usual " Commons of Saints ", and Masses for various special occasions. Besides the forty-five Holy Days for which there are proper Epistles and Gospels, there are thirty-two others, many of which have proper Introits and Collects. Of the forty-five days with Proper Masses, thirty-five are in the Kalendar of the English Prayer Book (including all the " Red Letter Days "), and three more—St. Ignatius, St. Athanasius, and All Souls—in the revised Kalendar of 1928. Of the thirty-two other days, ten are in the English Kalendar, and five others among those added in 1928; many of the others are Dutch and Flemish saints. Among the more interesting feasts are St. Boniface's Day, which was transferred from June 5 to July 5 by Archbishop Rovenius, apparently on his own authority, because it so often fell within the octave of

Corpus Christi; and the Martyrs of Gorcum, July 9, Dutch priests murdered during the Reformation. St. Ignatius is commemorated on February 1; St. Benedict on July 11 instead of March 21; St. Gregory the Great on September 3, instead of March 12. The office for St. Mary Magdalene's Day (she is joint patron of one of the churches at Rotterdam) does not identify her in any way with Mary of Bethany. August 15 is called " Assumption or Blessed Death of the Virgin Mary " (The Epistle is Ecclesiasticus 24. 8–20, omitting v. 14, and the Gospel is St. Luke 10. 38–42). St. Willibrord and St. Boniface, as apostles of the Netherlands, are given the rank of Apostles.

The Breviary of the Dutch Old Catholic Church is based on the old Utrecht Breviary. The other offices are translations from the Roman books. The usual evening service is Vespers and simple Benediction; the priest takes the ciborium which contains the Host out of the tabernacle or aumbry, and blesses the people with it, but without any hymn or other ceremony.

In Holland twenty-five of the twenty-seven parishes are older than the Reformation; the churches, none of which is older than the seventeenth century,[1] retain the ancient dedications, and a new altar always contains relics. In the other Old Catholic churches new churches are commonly, but not always, given such titles as Church of the Resurrection (Cologne), Church of the Redeemer, Church of the Cross. In some places, as at Rheinfelden and Möhlin in Switzerland and several villages in the Black Forest, the Old Catholics, having been in a majority at the time of the schism, retain the old parish church. In many places, especially in Germany, the Old Catholics have to hire a room, or a Protestant church, for their services.

Two other liturgies ought to be mentioned. The liturgy used by Hyacinthe Loyson in his church at Paris was a free translation and adaptation of the Roman Mass, revised by Dr. Eden, Bishop of Moray and Primus of the Scottish Episcopal Church. It contained a remarkable and probably unique intercession for " the Pope of Rome, the Patriarch of Constantinople, and the Archbishop of Canterbury, all bishops, priests, and deacons, and all who profess the Catholic and Apostolic Faith ". But Loyson's position was anomalous: he was not under any Old Catholic bishop, but received general superintendence from various Anglican bishops (see p. 283).

[1] Except the old St. Gertrude's, Utrecht, now a museum.

*The Old Catholic Missal and Ritual* in English, published by Cope and Fenwick, with an imprimatur by Archbishop Gul, was intended to be used by the short-lived English Old Catholic church under Bishop Mathew; but it was so full of mistakes that it was never actually in use. It is therefore no more than a liturgical curiosity, and in no way represents the practice of any Old Catholic church to-day.

In 1960 the Dutch Church introduced a new Missal. On days when *Gloria in Excelsis* is not used, there is a third lesson from the Old Testament. The "Last Gospel" is now entirely omitted, and the service ends with the Blessing, and in High Mass there is a hymn of thanksgiving. Several Dutch saints have been added, and the new (Old Catholic) translation of the Bible is used. In Germany the alternative form has been revised to bring it nearer to its Roman original.

# CHAPTER XXVII

# THE OLD CATHOLICS AND OTHER CHRISTIANS

ATTEMPTS have been made to show that the difference between the Old Catholics and Rome is not very great, after all; that it is confined to the dogmas of the Vatican Council, and that the Old Catholics hope, if these dogmas can be explained or modified, to return some day to the Roman obedience.[1] Nothing could be further from the truth. The Old Catholics reject, not only the dogmas of the Vatican Council, but the authority of the Council of Trent, and the Papal Supremacy, with all that follows from it. They do not regard the Pope as their patriarch; they do not pray for him by name in any of their rites. They differ from Rome in ethics and discipline, as well as in dogma: and they regard the special Roman dogmas as "unchristian, uncatholic, impossible, and mischievous".[2] There are, of course, different opinions among them on the subject, but there is no Romanizing party, and no one, as far as I know, who thinks that reunion with Rome is practicable.

The relations of the Old Catholics with their Protestant neighbours have always been friendly, but distant. In many places, especially in Germany and Austria, the Old Catholics have to hire Protestant churches for their services. In the early days of the movement many Protestants thought that they would become Protestant. This hope has not been fulfilled. The Old Catholics have really little in common with Continental Protestantism. I understand that very few Old Catholics have become Protestant; nor have many Protestants become Old Catholic. The High Church movement in Germany and Switzerland has shown some interest in the Old Catholics; but its members feel themselves obliged to remain within the Protestant organization (which they could not do if they became Old Catholics), and one of its leaders, Dr. Heiler, has obtained irregular episcopal consecration from a successor of Vilatte.

It was natural that after the breach with Rome the Old Catholic

[1] Pamphlet by S. H. Scott.
[2] Max Kopp, *Die Altkatholische Bewegung der Gegenwart*, pp. 11 ff.

leaders should turn first to the Orthodox Eastern Communion. There have been three periods during which attempts were made to bring about reunion in this direction. The first was the period of the Bonn Conferences, described in Chapter 19. It resulted in an informal agreement on the " Filioque " clause and other subjects. But it came to an end because the Balkan crisis of 1877–78 turned the attention of the Orthodox churches in other directions, while the Old Catholics were fully occupied with their own internal affairs.

The second period began with the Declaration of Utrecht in 1889. The complete agreement between the Church of Utrecht and the other Old Catholic churches gave them a firm basis, and led their friends in Russia, of whom General Kiréev was the leader, to hope for closer relations. Kiréev read a paper at the Old Catholic Congress of Lucerne in 1892; and a commission, appointed by the Holy Synod of Russia, sent to the Eastern patriarchs and the Old Catholic bishops a report on the position of Orthodoxy with regard to Old Catholicism. A similar commission on the Old Catholic side was appointed by the Congress of Rotterdam (1894). The discussions between the two communions went on for years, but never reached any conclusion: the chief points discussed were the " Filioque " clause, the Eucharist, and the Dutch ordinations. In 1902 the Œcumenical Patriarch, Joachim III, asked all the self-governing Orthodox churches to send him their views about the different communions of the West. The Holy Synod of Russia, in the section of its answer dealing with the Old Catholics, declared explicitly that the Old Catholics must recognize that the Orthodox Church of the East was now alone the Œcumenical Church, and must be asked whether they were willing to believe that it was necessary to salvation to belong to the true Church, and would enter into union with it. The Old Catholics were naturally unwilling to accept reunion on these terms; but they found that most of the Greek theologians agreed with the Russians. Though the Russian commission did not actually take up this attitude, the discussions became obviously futile, and came to an end with the outbreak of war in 1914.[1] Still, there was always Orthodox interest in the Old Catholics: the Œcumenical Patriarch Constantine V sent as his last message to his Anglican friends, " Don't forget the Old Catholics ".

[1] Bishop Küry, in *Die Altkatholische Kirche*, pp. 109–111.

The third period began in 1920, with the preparations for the World Conference on Faith and Order; the great changes which had taken place in the Orthodox Communion had brought with them a new spirit, of which the Metropolitan Germanos, Exarch of the Œcumenical Patriarchate in Western Europe, took advantage: he represented the Patriarch at the Congress of Berne in 1925. Close contact was established between the representatives of the two communions at the World Conference on Faith and Order at Lausanne, 1927, and during the Lambeth Conference of 1930 a discussion took place between the three Dutch Old Catholic bishops and the Orthodox delegation headed by the Patriarch Meletius of Alexandria. (I was the only Anglican present on this occasion.) The result of this was that on October 27–28 a joint commission representing both communions met at Bonn. Much information was given on both sides; but no decision has been reached, because the Orthodox Churches have not yet succeeded in holding the proposed Pro-Synod. The present situation of the Russian Church and of the Œcumenical Patriarchate makes it difficult for the Orthodox Churches to come to a formal agreement on any subject with anyone.

The difference between the Old Catholic and the Orthodox Communions is a difference not of dogma, but of outlook and of discipline. The Old Catholics take the teaching of the undivided Church and the Rule of St. Vincent of Lérins as their basis. The Orthodox deny that the Church was ever divided: according to them, what happened in 1054 was that the Latins fell into heresy and schism.

The Orthodox have an unbroken tradition, while the Old Catholics are the heirs of a revolt. Therefore the psychological difference between them is very great. The Orthodox surround the Faith with a great mass of immemorial tradition; the Old Catholics have had to break with tradition, and are inclined to minimize traditional beliefs. For instance, the invocation of the Blessed Virgin and the Saints, which forms so large a part of Orthodox teaching, worship, and piety, has among the Old Catholics been reduced almost to nothing.

There are also important differences in discipline. The Orthodox rule, dating from the Quinisext Council, which is regarded as having œcumenical authority, forbids the marriage of the clergy after ordination, and also the consecration of married men as bishops; consequently the bishops are chosen from the monks only. The Old Catholics give complete freedom to bishops, priests, and deacons to marry before or after ordination or consecration. The Old Catholics have no religious orders: even the conservative Dutch have a prejudice against monasticism, which is associated in their minds with the " storm troops " of the Papacy. Another difference is that confession to a priest is (in theory) compulsory among the Orthodox, but voluntary among the Old Catholics, and not much used outside Holland. The Old Catholics have a somewhat rationalistic mentality; they are stronger on the intellectual than on the mystical side; their piety is of quite a different type from that of the Orthodox. Therefore, although, as the Dutch Old Catholic bishops told the Lambeth Conference of 1930, there is no dogmatic difference between the two communions,[1] and Old Catholic congresses have usually been attended by Orthodox ecclesiastics, the restoration of inter-communion between Constantinople and Utrecht is not easy.

It is with the Anglican Communion that the Old Catholic churches have the closest affinity, and with which their efforts for unity have been most successful.

There have been five periods in the history of the relations between the Anglican and the Old Catholic churches.

The first is the period of John Mason Neale. The earliest English account of the Church of Utrecht known to me is a passage in William Palmer's *Treatise of the Church*, which is part of the learned Tractarian author's polemic against Rome.[2] In 1851 Dr. S. P. Tregelles wrote a small book called *The Jansenists, their Rise, Persecutions by the Jesuits, and Existing Remnant*. This was followed in 1858 by Dr. J. M. Neale's great book, *The History of the So-called Jansenist Church of Holland*. Dr. Neale visited Utrecht in the spring of 1851, and called on Canon van Werckhoven, Archdeacon of Utrecht.[3] This priest sent him to Archbishop van Santen, with whom he had a long conversation. On October 5, 1854, he went to Utrecht again, and spent a week there. He examined the archives, heard Mass at St. Gertrude's Cathedral (of which he was rather critical), and visited the seminary at Amersfoort. He was shown every kindness by the archbishop,

[1] Report of the Commission of the Anglican and Old Catholic Churches, p. 32.
[2] William Palmer, *Treatise of the Church*, vol. i, p. 259.
[3] Eleanor A. Towle, *Memoir of J. M. Neale*, p. 219.

Canon Mulder, and Karsten, the President of the Seminary, and it was on this occasion that he collected the material for his book, which has been the standard English authority on the subject ever since, and which is considered by some to be his greatest work.[1] He ended it with the following prophecy: "It is impossible to close my task without wishing for the knowledge of a prophet as to the future fate of that communion. . . . It seems to me that the little remnant of this afflicted Church are reserved for happier days. Wherever and whenever that Œcumenical Council may be, or whatever other means God shall employ to restore the lost unity of Christendom, the labours, and trials, and sufferings of this communion will not be forgotten. . . . She can scarcely have been held up, from her protest against the 'Unigenitus', till she has also protested against the more dangerous 'Ineffabilis', that after these struggles for the truth she may be permitted to fall. . . . Surely not for this has the steadfast piety that has distinguished this communion for a century and a half, sent up so many earnest prayers to the Supreme Judge to vindicate its innocence, and make known the righteousness of its cause ".[2]

These words were published in 1858. The first German Old Catholic bishop was consecrated only sixteen years later.

The second period may be called the period of Christopher Wordsworth, Bishop of Lincoln. On June 16, 1871, the Convocation of Canterbury, on the motion of Christopher Wordsworth, formally repudiated the authority of the Vatican Council, and sent a message of sympathy to Archbishop Loos of Utrecht. On September 20 the Lincoln Diocesan Synod (the first diocesan synod held in England in modern times) sent an official letter of sympathy to the first Old Catholic Congress at Munich.[3] The following year Bishop Wordsworth was invited to attend the Old Catholic Congress at Cologne, and with the consent of his chapter, and of the Archbishop of Canterbury, did so; it was he who urged the Old Catholics not to retain the Creed of Pius IV, but to appeal to Scripture as interpreted by antiquity, a policy afterwards carried out by the Declaration of Utrecht. Bishop Wordsworth addressed the congress in Latin, and entertained

[1] Letters of J. M. Neale, p. 228.
[2] J. M. Neale, History of the So-Called Jansenist Church of Utrecht, p. 380.
[3] J. H. Overton and E. Wordsworth, Life of Bishop Christopher Wordsworth, pp. 234.

the Archbishop of Utrecht at dinner; the Bishops of Ely (Harold Browne) and Maryland were also present.

This was the beginning of a close connexion between the English and American Churches and the German and Swiss Old Catholics. We have seen (Chapter 19) how prominent a part the Anglican members took in the Bonn Conferences. In 1878 the Lambeth Conference passed a resolution of sympathy with the Old Catholic churches. Shortly afterwards Bishop Harold Browne, who had been translated from Ely to Winchester, invited Bishop Herzog and Hyacinthe Loyson to stay with him at Farnham Castle. An arrangement was made, with the approval of the Archbishop of Canterbury, by which Loyson's congregation in Paris, which for different reasons could not be under the jurisdiction of any of the Old Catholic bishops (see Chapter 22), was placed under the Primus of the Scottish Church, Dr. Eden, Bishop of Moray, who commissioned Bishop Herzog to give confirmation for him at Paris. On August 10, 1879, Bishops Reinkens and Herzog, Bishop Cotterill of Edinburgh, and Loyson communicated together in the Old Catholic Church of St. Peter and St. Paul at Berne; Bishop Herzog celebrated, and Bishop Cotterill assisted with the chalice (see Chapter 26). The incident caused a storm in the Scottish Church (since there was not yet any formal agreement on intercommunion).[1]

In 1880 Bishop Herzog, accompanied by Bishop Cotterill, attended the General Convention of the American Episcopal Church. He communicated at the opening service, and assisted in administering the chalice. He also preached and gave confirmation in America, where he was welcomed by all parties in the Episcopal Church. The American bishops unanimously passed a resolution repudiating the decrees of Trent and the Vatican and the dogma of the Immaculate Conception, and declaring that the Old Catholic consecrations by a single bishop were lawful in the circumstances.

In the autumn of 1881 Bishops Reinkens and Herzog visited England as the guests of Bishop Harold Browne. They were received at Cambridge by the Bishops of Winchester (Browne), Ely (Woodford), and Lichfield (Maclagan), and by the Vice-Chancellor. They stayed with the Archbishop of Canterbury (Tait) at Addington, with the Bishop of Winchester at Farnham, and with the Bishop of Lincoln at Riseholme; they attended a

[1] W. H. de Voil, *Origin and Development of the Old Catholic Churches*, p. 374.

meeting at the Lincoln Theological College (Bishop's Hostel). On his return to Germany, Bishop Reinkens issued a pastoral, in which he expressed his joy in the services which he had attended in Ely, Lincoln, and St. Paul's Cathedrals, and King's College Chapel, Cambridge, and said: " Every Catholic who is not so unhistorically narrow as to recognize only his own Mass, must feel himself at home also in the Anglican celebration of the Holy Communion—must feel borne along by the Catholic spirit ".[1]

In 1879 the Swiss Old Catholic Synod had formally granted permission to members of the Anglican Communion to communicate at its altars. The German Old Catholic Synod passed a similar canon in 1883 specially granting Anglican visitors the right to communicate in both kinds.

From all this the Dutch Old Catholics held aloof. They were as yet unwilling either to give up the authority of Trent, or to recognize the validity of Anglican ordinations; the German and Swiss Old Catholics had done both. There was, however, at least one English Churchman who was admitted to Communion at Utrecht during this period. In 1875 the Rev. F. W. Puller, on his way to the Bonn Conference, called on the Dean of Utrecht. The see was vacant, and the archbishop-elect, Johannes Heykamp, was not in the city. Father Puller's account of what followed is this:—

" I said to him, ' To-morrow is my sister's birthday: would you kindly remember her when saying Mass? ' He said, ' I will insert the Collect *pro quadam amica* '. I answered to that, ' If I had known that you were ready to put a liturgical addition into the Mass for my sister, I would have enlarged the petition and asked if you would communicate me '. He replied, ' Before I can do that, I must catechize you on your belief in the Holy Eucharist '. I replied that I believed that after the Consecration in the Canon, the bread and wine become respectively the Body and Blood of our Lord. But if you press me farther and ask me whether I believe this change is effected by transubstantiation, I have no opinion on that subject either positive or negative. He replied, ' The question of transubstantiation is a philosophical question and not a theological one: it ought never, therefore, to have been made an article of faith '. Accordingly, on the following morning I was present at his Mass and at the proper time I went up to the altar rail and he communicated me. I have a distinct recollection

[1] C. B. Moss, *Church Quarterly Review*, July, 1931, p. 256.

that I have been told that some other member of the Anglican Communion had been allowed to communicate at Utrecht by the Old Catholics." [1]

This is the earliest case of the admission of an Anglican churchman to Communion at an Old Catholic altar of which there is certain evidence. It shows that as early as 1875 the Dean of Utrecht did not regard transubstantiation, though it was a dogma defined by Trent (and indeed by the Fourth Lateran Council), as necessarily binding.

Bishop Christopher Wordsworth died on March 21, 1885. His death may be regarded as the end of the second period, when the Old Catholic institutions were being formed, and when many in the Anglican Communion expected that the majority of German Catholics would join the movement. This expectation was not fulfilled; the leaders on both sides died, and the next generation was not so much interested. The Anglican churches were not yet ready for reunion: the Catholic Revival had not made sufficient progress, and the conception of the English Church as merely the religious aspect of the nation was still too widespread for reunion with foreign churches to be understood.

In the third period the conduct of the Anglican side of the *entente* passed to Bishop John Wordsworth, son of Bishop Christopher Wordsworth, who was consecrated Bishop of Salisbury a few months after his father's death. He had been present, with his father and brother, at the Old Catholic Congress at Cologne in 1872, and had learned German (and most other European languages). In 1886 he was sent, as we have seen, by Archbishop Benson to inquire into the Old Catholic movement in Italy, and empowered to give letters of communion, but he was not satisfied, and did not use his power (see p. 285). In 1887 he visited the chief Old Catholic centres, in order to be able to report to the Lambeth Conference which was to meet in 1888. He had the written sanction of Archbishop Benson. Bishop Maclagan of Lichfield (afterwards Archbishop of York) went with him, and each of them took a chaplain. They went to Bonn, where they held a conference with Bishop Reinkens and Professor von Schulte, to Freiburg-in-Breisgau, and to Olten, where they met Bishop Herzog and other Swiss Old Catholic leaders; they visited Döllinger at Munich and Czech at Vienna. At the conference held at Bonn the German Old Catholics explained that they did

---

[1] Letter from the Rev. F. W. Puller to the author.

not recognize the Council of Trent as œcumenical; that they accepted its dogmatic decrees only so far as they agreed with Holy Scripture, the teaching of the Fathers, and the belief of the Universal Church, and that they held themselves free to alter its disciplinary decrees when they chose. They regarded Six Œcumenical Councils as undisputed. Marriage with unbaptized persons and with divorced persons whose partners were still alive was strictly forbidden in their Church; but marriage within certain degrees prohibited by the English Church (as with a deceased wife's sister) was allowed, and it would be difficult to prohibit it, since it was permitted by both Romanists and Lutherans. Communion was still given in one kind only, but not on principle. On all other matters there was complete agreement.

On June 14, 1888, Bishop Wordsworth and Bishop Ernest Wilberforce of Newcastle-on-Tyne (a son of Bishop Samuel Wilberforce of Oxford, and grandson of William Wilberforce the liberator of the slaves), each with a chaplain, held a conference with Archbishop Heykamp at Utrecht. They were told that the Church of Utrecht repudiated the name " Jansenist " and accepted the dogmatic decrees of Trent, but not its canons of discipline. The Council's teaching was interpreted in accordance with the minimizing commentary of a certain Portuguese divine, Antonio Pereira de Figueiredo, and the priests were not required to sign the Creed of Pope Pius IV. Confession was voluntary, and the laity were encouraged to read the Bible freely (according to the teaching of Quesnel, condemned by the Bull " Unigenitus ", see p. 67). The only difference between the Church of Utrecht and the Church of England on the marriage law was that the former might give a man a dispensation to marry his deceased wife's niece.[1]

The third Lambeth Conference was held that summer, and in consequence of Bishop Wordsworth's report it passed unanimously the following resolution:—

" 15 A. That this Conference recognizes with thankfulness the dignified and independent position of the Old Catholic Church of Holland, and looks forward to more frequent brotherly intercourse to remove many of the barriers which at present separate us.

" 15 B. That we regard it as a duty to promote friendly relations with the Old Catholic Community in Germany, and with the ' Christian Catholic Church ' in Switzerland, not only out of

[1] E. W. Watson, *Bishop John Wordsworth*, pp. 317 ff.

sympathy with them, but also in thankfulness to God, Who has strengthened them to suffer for the truth under great discouragements, difficulties, and temptations; and that we offer them the privileges recommended by the Committee under the conditions specified in its Report.

"15 C. That the sacrifices made by the Old Catholics in Austria deserve our sympathy, and that we hope that, when their organization is sufficiently tried and complete, a more formal relation may be found possible."

(The conditions referred to in the second resolution, as laid down by the committee of the conference dealing with this subject, which consisted of the Bishop of Winchester, the Archbishop of Dublin (Plunket), and the Bishops of Albany, Cashel, Central Africa (Smythies), Cork, Derry, Dunedin, Gibraltar, Iowa, Lichfield, Lincoln, North Carolina, Salisbury, and Western New York, were these: "We see no reason why we should not admit their clergy and faithful laity to Holy Communion on the same conditions as our own communicants, and we also acknowledge the readiness which they have shown to offer spiritual privileges to members of our own Church. We regret that differences in our marriage laws, which we believe to be of great importance, compel us to state that we are obliged to debar from Holy Communion any person who may have contracted a marriage not sanctioned by the laws and canons of the Anglican Church. Nor could we, in justice to the Old Catholics, admit anyone who would be debarred from Communion among themselves." These sentences refer to the German Old Catholics, but not to the Austrian or Italian Old Catholics, with whom it expressed great sympathy, but whom it considered not yet sufficiently tested for more formal relations to be justified. All this was based on a statement welcoming the return of the Old Catholics to the standards of the undivided Church, and denying that their position was schismatic, because to say it was "would be to concede the lawfulness of the imposition of new terms of communion, and of the extravagant assertions by the Papacy of ordinary and immediate jurisdiction in every diocese ".)[2]

These resolutions of the Lambeth Conference of 1888 were the first formal sanction given to intercommunion from the Anglican side. The Swiss Old Catholics had sanctioned it nine years

[1] *Lambeth Conferences of* 1867, 1878 *and* 1888, ed. R. T. Davidson, p. 282.
[2] *Lambeth Conferences, op. cit.,* p. 342.

earlier, and the German Old Catholics five years earlier. It was they who took the first steps; this should not be forgotten. Moreover, the German and Swiss Old Catholic Synods had given to Anglican visitors a right to receive Communion, by canon. The Anglican procedure was more informal. The Lambeth Conference is not a synod: its resolutions bind no one. Hence the intercommunion established by the third Lambeth Conference was informal and provisional: similar to the intercommunion with the Church of Sweden sanctioned by the Lambeth Conference of 1920. It was a privilege, not a right (sometimes called " economic " intercommunion, an unfortunate word, because it seems to imply the Orthodox theory of " economy ", which is unknown to either Anglican or Old Catholic discipline). This agreement, limited as it was, did not apply to the Old Catholic Church of Holland. There were two main difficulties here. The Dutch Old Catholics still adhered (though in a minimizing way) to the dogmas of Trent; and they had not recognized the validity of Anglican Orders, as the German and Swiss Old Catholics had. The former difficulty was removed the next year, by the Declaration of Utrecht; the latter remained for thirty-seven years longer. It is impossible not to admire the firmness of the Dutch Old Catholics. They would not, for any possible advantage, assent to anything of the truth of which they were not sure; though they had closed the gate behind them by throwing over Trent, and though their German and Swiss allies had long since accepted Anglican ordinations as valid. Their firmness made their acceptance all the more valuable when it was finally given.

On August 3, 1888, after the Lambeth Conference, Bishop Wordsworth gathered some Anglican and Old Catholic leaders at his palace at Salisbury. Among those present were Bishop Herzog, Pastoor van Santen from Holland, Amandus Czech, the administrator of the Austrian diocese, and Count Campello from Italy: Lord Plunket, Archbishop of Dublin, and American, West Indian, and South African bishops. All these received the Holy Communion together.[1] In 1889 Bishop Wordsworth went to Warnsdorf for the Synod of the Austrian Old Catholics. He received Holy Communion with their clergy, and spoke in the highest terms of the congregation at Warnsdorf. " I have seldom or never seen," he said, " a more attractive body of people." On

[1] E. W. Watson, *op. cit.*, p. 321. See above, p. 285.

his way home he went to Krefeld to meet Bishops Reinkens and Herzog, who were just starting for the conference at Utrecht which was to result in the issue of the famous Declaration.[1] Unfortunately, the friendship between the two communions now began to suffer a certain coolness. Bishop Wordsworth could not understand why the Dutch Old Catholics were unwilling to accept the validity of Anglican Orders. He wrote two " Epistolæ ad Batavos " (Letters to the Dutchmen) in Latin, to try to convince them, but he only succeeded in irritating them. Archbishop Gul appointed a commission to decide the question, but its report was indecisive,[2] and the distribution of this report to the members of the International Old Catholic Congress of Rotterdam in 1894, the first held in Holland, was not tactful. For fifteen years after this no progress was made. Anglican visitors continued to attend Old Catholic congresses, and there was no setback; but Anglican interest was diverted to the unsuccessful attempt of Lord Halifax to induce Pope Leo XIII to recognize Anglican ordinations (which would not have had any practical result if it had been successful), and the formal condemnation of Anglican ordinations by the Bull " Apostolicæ Curæ " seems to have made a bad impression in Holland.

The fourth period is connected with the name of the Rev. George E. Barber, who in 1908 founded the Society of St. Willibrord, to bring about closer relations between the Anglican and Old Catholic communions. The first committee meeting was held on January 7, 1909; the Bishop of Gibraltar (Dr. W. E. Collins) was the first Anglican President, and the Bishop of Haarlem (Mgr. Prins) the first Old Catholic President; Archbishop Gul accepted the position of Patron. The work of the Society was made very difficult by the refusal of Bishop Mathew, consecrated the year before, to co-operate with it (he first joined it and then left it), and by the bad repute which his strange conduct brought on the Old Catholic name. But it had " corresponding secretaries " in most of the chief Old Catholic centres, and many Anglican bishops and dignitaries joined it, among them Bishop Wordsworth (who soon resigned because of Bishop Mathew's attacks on the English Church) and Bishop Gore. In 1913 Bishop Prins visited England, and he was present at the Holy Eucharist in All Saints', Margaret Street, London, and St.

---

[1] E. W. Watson, *op. cit.*, p. 322.
[2] Not on the historical, but on the doctrinal issue.

Margaret's, Oxford. He was the first Dutch Old Catholic bishop to visit England. The Old Catholic Congress at Cologne, September 9—12, 1913, was attended by the Bishop of Willesden and eight Anglican priests. Greetings were received from the Archbishop of Canterbury, the Primus of the Scottish Church, the Presiding Bishop of the American Episcopal Church, and twenty English, four Irish, two Scottish, and two American diocesan bishops, the Bishop of Gibraltar and the Bishop in North and Central Europe. Mr. Barber died in 1914, and the outbreak of war just afterwards brought the work of the society temporarily to an end. Nothing could be done but wait till better times. The Bishop of Willesden (Dr. Perrin), who had become Anglican President on the death of Bishop Collins, took charge of the books.

The fifth period began after the war. Mgr. Kenninck, the new Archbishop of Utrecht, appointed a fresh commission to examine the question of the validity of Anglican orders. The commission reported favourably, and on June 2, 1925, the Archbishop of Utrecht wrote to the Archbishop of Canterbury announcing that his Church formally accepted Anglican ordinations as valid. This decision was ratified by the Bishops' Conference at Berne in the same year. Thus the last great barrier between the two communions was removed. But they had had little contact with one another for many years, and their mutual ignorance was great. On March 20, 1928, the Bishop of Willesden called a meeting of the surviving members of the Society of St. Willibrord and revived the Society. The Bishop of Fulham went to the Old Catholic Congress of Utrecht, 1928, as the official representative of the Archbishop of Canterbury, and was received with acclamation, the whole Congress rising and cheering when he entered. The Bishop of Haarlem came to the enthronement of Dr. Lang as Archbishop of Canterbury, as the official representative of the Old Catholic Church of Holland—an event without precedent. The way was now clear for negotiations for reunion; the remarkable feature of this period is, that it was with the Church of Utrecht, which had before been inclined to stand aloof, that Anglican relations were most intimate.

# CHAPTER XXVIII

## THE AGREEMENT OF BONN [1]

THE seventh Lambeth Conference of the Anglican bishops was held in 1930. For the first time an official delegation from the Old Catholic churches came to London to discuss the possibility of reunion. It consisted of the Archbishop of Utrecht (Mgr. Kenninck), the Bishop of Haarlem (Mgr. van Vlijmen), and the Bishop of Deventer (Mgr. Berends): this was the first time that an Archbishop of Utrecht had visited England. Bishop Küry would have come too, but he was prevented by illness.

Their first discussion with a committee of the Lambeth Conference was held on July 16, 1930. The committee consisted of the Bishop of Gloucester (chairman), the Archbishop of Dublin, the Bishops of Fulham (Secretary), Western Michigan, Gibraltar, Egypt and the Sudan, Montreal, and Northern Indiana.

The Bishop of Deventer read a short memorandum on the position of the Church of Utrecht, which was a daughter of the English Church, and stood for a Catholicism which was not Roman. The Declaration of Utrecht was discussed clause by clause: the Bishop of Gloucester said that the statement on the Holy Eucharist in that declaration (" The character of the Holy Eucharist . . . communion with one another ") exactly represented the teaching of the English Church. The Archbishop of Utrecht answered questions about the Old Catholic practice as to admission to Communion, and about the Old Catholics in America. He said that as they had recognized Anglican orders as valid, they also accepted the Anglican baptism, confirmation, and Eucharist as valid. English Church people might communicate in the Dutch Old Catholic Church, if they gave notice beforehand, and if they satisfied the priest that they were orthodox. Old Catholics wishing to communicate in Anglican churches might do so at their own discretion. There was no difference in doctrine between the Old Catholics and the Orthodox Church; the Patriarch of Alexandria had said to him, " We are the same

---

[1] Based on the Report of the Meeting of the Commission of the Anglican Communion and the Old Catholic Churches held at Bonn, on Thursday, July 2, 1931, and the Report of the Lambeth Conference, 1930.

and we ought to belong to each other ". The Bishop of Gloucester handed to the archbishop a copy of " Terms of Intercommunion suggested between the Anglican Communion and the Eastern Orthodox Church ", and asked him to study it.

The second meeting was held on July 19. The Bishop in Egypt was not present, but the Bishops of Guildford, Atlanta, Nassau, and Rhode Island were there, as well as those who had been present before. On this occasion Canon J. A. Douglas the Rev. Chauncey Emhardt of the Board of Missions of the American Episcopal Church, and I, were present in the room.

After a short discussion about the relation of Scripture and tradition, and about the Filioque clause, the Archbishop of Utrecht raised the question of the relations of the Anglican Communion to those who did not accept the Apostolic Succession, especially in South India. The Bishop of Gloucester explained that the scheme proposed for South India was an " interim arrangement " : it was not proposed that any of those who would be united should be allowed to celebrate the Sacraments in the Church of England, or the Anglican Communion, but only in those communions to which they already belonged. He hoped that the Old Catholics would become missionaries of Christian Union throughout the continent of Europe : they would never be asked to accept the orders of anyone who had not received episcopal ordination or consecration. The Archbishop of Utrecht observed that a united Christian front in South India was impossible, as the Roman Catholics would never agree to it.

Some discussion then followed about the Old Catholics in America. The Bishop of Haarlem said that he advised Old Catholics emigrating to America to go to the Episcopal Church. The relations between the Old Catholics and the Orthodox churches were discussed. The Archbishop of Utrecht said that they would agree with the words in section 13 of the " Terms of Intercommunion ". They accepted the teaching of the Church in the first thousand years, but they made a difference between the first four Councils and those which followed. In answer to the Archbishop of Dublin, he said that the Declaration of Utrecht could be altered by the Bishops' Conference alone. With this the conference ended : the Archbishop of Utrecht said that a great step had been made towards reunion.

The Lambeth Conference passed the following resolutions, in consequence of this visit and the above discussion :—

" 35 (*a*) The Conference heartily thanks the Archbishop of Utrecht and the Bishops of the Old Catholic Church associated with him for coming to consult with its members on the development of closer relations between their churches and the Anglican Communion, and expresses its sense of the importance of the step taken.

" (*b*) The Conference requests the Archbishop of Canterbury to appoint representatives of the Anglican Communion, and to invite the Archbishop of Utrecht to appoint representatives of the Old Catholic Churches, to a Doctrinal Commission to discuss points of agreement and difference between them.

" (*c*) The Conference agrees that there is nothing in the Declaration of Utrecht inconsistent with the teaching of the Church of England."

The last statement was of first-class importance. It was based on the explanations which the Dutch bishops had given. The Declaration of Utrecht itself was published in full in the Report of the Lambeth Conference. This was probably the first time that most English Church people had heard of it; and in some quarters the statement of the Lambeth resolution was not welcome, because of the clause dealing with the Eucharist, and because the Declaration did not expressly ascribe supreme authority to Holy Scripture.

The report of the Lambeth Conference brought the question of reunion with the Old Catholics clearly before the Anglican public. It was necessary also to explain to the Old Catholic laity the nature and history of the Anglican Communion. With this object I wrote a pamphlet called *The Anglican Churches*, which was translated into German by my friend Pfarrer Hugo Flury, of Möhlin, Canton Aargau, and was published in serial form in the leading Old Catholic papers, including the *Oud Katholiek* (Holland), for which it was translated into Dutch by Professor A. J. van den Bergh; the German version was also published in a separate form by a Berne publisher. (It was also translated into Roumanian and published in *Misionarul*.)

The following year a commission appointed by the Archbishop of Canterbury to enter into formal negotiations with a similar commission representing the Old Catholic churches.

The Anglican commission (which was confined to members of the Church of England) consisted of the Bishop of Gloucester (Dr. Headlam), who was chairman, the Bishop of Fulham (Dr.

Batty), the Dean of Chichester (Very Rev. A. S. Duncan-Jones), the Rev. N. P. Williams, D.D. (Lady Margaret Professor of Divinity at Oxford), the Rev. Canon J. A. Douglas, the Rev. G. F. Graham-Brown (Principal of Wycliffe Hall, Oxford, later Bishop in Jerusalem), the Rev. Philip Usher, the Rev. C. L. Gage-Brown, and myself. Mr. Gage-Brown, who was the interpreter, and I were the secretaries. Mr. Usher was unable to be present at the meeting.

The Old Catholic commission consisted of the Bishop of Deventer (Mgr. Berends), Bishop Küry, Bishop Moog, Professor Gaugler of Berne (who was unable to be present) and Professor Rinkel of Amersfoort Seminary (now Archbishop of Utrecht).

The meeting was held at the Königshof, Bonn, on July 2, 1931. It lasted only one day, and complete agreement was reached. A full report was afterwards published. It is only necessary to give a summary of what happened, with a few personal recollections.

It was clear from the first that the only serious difficulty was the reconciliation of the Old Catholics and the Evangelical party in the Church of England. But for the Evangelicals, the proceedings could have been finished in half an hour or less; for there were no real differences at all. But the Evangelicals had misunderstood what the Old Catholics stood for, and were opposing reunion with them; I had been present at an Evangelical Conference at Oxford a few months earlier, the main purpose of which was to protest against reunion with the Old Catholic and the Orthodox churches. Their objections appeared to me to be partly based on misunderstandings, for they were certainly badly informed (they thought, for instance, that the Old Catholics were bound by the decrees of Trent), and partly by the fear that any such proposals, if carried out, would prevent closer relations with the Nonconformists at home. It was therefore absolutely necessary that whatever the conference at Bonn agreed to should be accepted by the Evangelicals; and the greatest credit is due to Mr. Graham-Brown (as he was then), who was the only representative of that party in the conference, for bringing about this result.

The Bishop of Gloucester was elected chairman of the joint conference, on the motion of the Bishop of Deventer. He said in his reply that the Anglican commission came with authority from the Lambeth Conference and the Archbishop of Canterbury.

The Old Catholics had sent in four sets of questions, and these were taken first.

The first set were concerned with the Lambeth Conference. Did the bishops there pronounce the faith of their dioceses? If so, why did the Evangelicals protest against certain of the resolutions of the Lambeth Conference? With whom lay the final decision as to reunion? Would the consent of Parliament have to be given?

The second set of questions were concerned with the parties in the Anglican Communion. What did the Protestant party hold, as distinct from the Catholic party? Was the Protestant party officially recognized as accepting the teaching of the Church? Would the Old Catholics have to unite with it? How numerous was it?

The third set of questions dealt with the doctrine of the Anglican Communion. Was the Catholic interpretation of the Thirty-Nine Articles, expressed in the Prayer Book, the true one? Why was the Revised Prayer Book of 1928 rejected, and by whom? " Is it universally believed that ordination and consecration can only be given because it is the Church that calls her ministers, and that the holders of office derive their office and their apostolic character only from the will of the Church, so that the apostolic succession cannot be thought of apart from the catholicity of the Church, but has its sole basis therein? " (This question implies a view of the succession different from that of Bishop Mathew and his adherents.) " Is there any part of the Anglican Communion where the intention to carry on the apostolic succession in ordination is purposely omitted, and the intention is merely to appoint a man to a particular office? "

The fourth set of questions dealt with the relations of the Anglican Communion to other churches. " With which churches is the Anglican Communion already in communion? And would the Old Catholics be committed to intercommunion with those churches, if they had intercommunion with the Church of England? "

The Bishop of Gloucester had already, before the conference, sent a statement replying to these questions. He now gave answers to them, in which the following points are the most important.

The Lambeth Conference was not a synod, and its resolutions had no binding force until they were accepted by the Provincial

Synods. The final authority therefore was the Provincial Synods, in England called Convocations. Reunion was a purely spiritual matter, requiring no change either in the civil or the canon law; so that there was no need for the assent of either Crown or Parliament. But the Convocations had no power to enforce their decisions.

He then explained the relations of church parties to the Church, and the relations of the Articles to the Prayer Book. (On this point Mr. Graham-Brown did not entirely agree with the other members of the commission; he held that the Articles were above the Prayer Book.) The Revised Prayer Book was rejected by the House of Commons, but the reasons were not easy to explain. The English Church had always intended to continue the three orders of bishops, priests, and deacons, but the words " propitiatory sacrifices " were omitted from the Ordinal.

The Bishop of Deventer said that they did not want those words.

Mr. Graham-Brown said that Evangelicals did not believe that ordination was merely the appointment of a man to a particular post: they all believed that the Holy Spirit was given in ordination for the work of the ministry.

The Bishop of Gloucester read a list of the Anglican churches. As to the Swedish Church, the Old Catholics would be entirely free to deal with it as they pleased. Canon Douglas added that intercommunion with the Swedish Church was not quite formal.

A statement on the Evangelical view of intercommunion was then read, though the Bishop of Fulham said that they could not guarantee that it was accurate, or that it represented the views of all Evangelicals. According to this statement, Evangelicals denied that it was possible to bring about union on the basis of doctrine. The doctrine of the Church of England (that is, in the opinion of Evangelicals) was not reconcilable with that of the Old Catholics. But no such identity should be insisted upon as necessary for intercommunion. A common allegiance to our Lord should be enough for that; and then Evangelicals might be prepared to agree that there was nothing in the Declaration of Utrecht which might be an impediment to intercommunion (not, as stated, union). (The statement always used the term " Church of England ", not " Anglican Communion ".)

Then followed the first crisis of the conference. The Bishop of

Deventer asked whether Anglican Evangelicals held the Church of England to be identical with the pre-Reformation Church. Mr. Graham-Brown answered, " Certainly ". The Bishop of Deventer then pointed out that the Protestants of Holland and Germany made no such claim for themselves. Did the Anglican Evangelicals regard Dutch and German Protestants as having continuity with the medieval Church? Canon Douglas said that the Evangelicals would accept these bodies' view of themselves, and Mr. Graham-Brown agreed. This cleared the air at once. The Old Catholics were satisfied that all members of the Anglican Communion regarded their Church as continuous from the pre-Reformation Church, and therefore different from communions which had no history beyond the sixteenth century; and this was what they had wanted to know.

Then the Anglican questions were put. They were as follows:—

(1) What is the belief of the Old Catholics as to the authority of Scripture?

(2) Will they accept the position of St. Vincent himself, in the second chapter of the Commonitorium, as interpreting his Canon?

(3) Do they mean to imply acceptance of Transubstantiation?

(4) What is their attitude towards the fourth Lateran Council and the Council of Trent?

(5) Do they consider that the Catholic Faith includes more than the contents of the Creeds and the Christological decisions of the Œcumenical Councils?

(6) Do they allow divorce, or admit divorced persons who have been re-married to Communion? (This question was put by me.)

(7) How far is confession obligatory?

The Bishop of Gloucester asked what was the Old Catholic view of Scripture: the Bishop of Deventer read a statement made at the Bonn Conference of 1874.

Then came the second crisis of the conference. The Old Catholics were asked whether they would agree to Articles 6 and 20. The Bishop of Deventer asked that they might be read; and when this had been done, he announced that this was exactly their teaching.

When this answer had been given, we felt sure that the conference would be successful. The uniqueness of Holy Scripture, which " containeth all things necessary to salvation ", is a Catholic dogma, upon which the Anglican Communion has been compelled to lay special emphasis. If the Old Catholics had differed from us on this (as they would have, if they had still accepted the authority of Trent), reunion would have been impossible, and the Conference would have failed. But it was only Mr. Graham-Brown and his friends who were suspicious: the rest of us knew that the Old Catholics did not differ from us about this, though their history had not forced them to emphasize it as ours had forced us.

The remainder of the questions were then answered. Professor Rinkel said that they accepted the whole Commonitorium of St. Vincent, but emphasized specially the second chapter, on Scripture and tradition.

The Bishop of Deventer said that the first four councils were the most important: the seventh council was less important, and dealt with matters of discipline rather than of doctrine. The Declaration of Utrecht was intended to exclude Transubstantiation in its medieval sense, and the word was no longer used in their teaching.

The Bishop of Gloucester asked how the statement on the Eucharistic Sacrifice in the Declaration of Utrecht could be reconciled with the words " propitiatory sacrifice " (*Versöhnungsopfer*) in the blessing given to newly ordained priests.

Bishop Moog replied that *Versöhnung* did not mean propitiatory.

The Bishop of Deventer said that they did not accept the Fourth Lateran Council or the Council of Trent as binding. The doctrine of the Eucharist had not been formulated, though the Eucharist itself was always there. They did not allow divorce or permit Communion to be given to the divorced, but it sometimes happened. Confession was not obligatory, but every priest must hear confessions if asked.

The second session, held in the evening of the same day, was entirely occupied with drawing up the formal terms in which intercommunion should be recommended. The first draft of the formula was written by Mr. Graham-Brown, and contained five sections. Bishop Küry thought the first two would be enough: it would not do to draw up a new confession of faith. It was decided that the right to receive Communion implied the right to all other ministrations of the Church. At last the following statement was agreed to, and signed by all the members of both communions who were present.

(1) Each communion recognizes the catholicity and independence of the other, and maintains its own.

(2) Each communion agrees to admit members of the other communion to participate in the sacraments.

(3) Intercommunion does not require from either communion the acceptance of all doctrinal opinion, sacramental devotion, or liturgical practice characteristic of the other, but implies that each believes the other to hold all the essentials of the Christian Faith.

The third clause is entirely taken from Mr. Graham-Brown's third section, with some unnecessary words left out.

The Agreement of Bonn was accepted at once by all the Old Catholic churches of Europe. In 1946 it was also accepted by the National Polish Church in America. It was brought before the Convocations of Canterbury and York, and was passed unanimously in all four Houses. One incident is worth recording. During the debate in the Upper House of Canterbury, in answer to a bishop who had said that what was proposed was intercommunion but not union, the Bishop of Lincoln (Dr. Swayne) said that intercommunion was union, the only sort of union that they wanted, the only sort of union that was possible.

Other Anglican churches soon followed. The first was the Episcopal Church of Scotland. By the end of 1932 the Indian and West Indian provinces had also accepted the Agreement of Bonn. The Church of England in Canada and the American Episcopal Church accepted it in the autumn of 1934; the South African Church in 1935; the Church in Wales in September 1936. The Province of New South Wales in Australia has also accepted it. In each case the Synod, General Convention, or Governing Body passed the resolution unanimously, and sent notice that it had done so to the Archbishop of Utrecht.

During the discussion at Lambeth the Archbishop of Utrecht had said that intercommunion would naturally be followed by mutual assistance in the consecration of bishops. The Bishop of Haarlem took part in the consecration by the Archbishop of Canterbury of Mr. Graham-Brown as Bishop in Jerusalem, and of the Rev. B. F. Simpson as Bishop of Kensington, in St. Paul's

Cathedral. On February 24, 1933, the Bishop of Deventer took part in the consecration of the Rev. Harold Buxton as Bishop of Gibraltar and of the Rev. A. M. Gelsthorpe as Assistant Bishop on the Niger. In January 1947 the Bishop of Haarlem took part in the consecration of the Bishop of Edinburgh and the Bishop in Egypt. Care was taken that the Old Catholic bishop should lay his hands on the head of the candidate and pronounce the words of consecration.

(We must not, however, assume that bishops consecrated in this way would be regarded by Rome as validly consecrated. It is not a matter of practical importance, since the dogmatic differences between the Roman and Anglican Communions must be settled before the question of the validity of Anglican ordinations arises; and there is no non-Roman Church which rejects Anglican Orders.)[1]

The Archbishop of Canterbury was invited to send a bishop to take part in the consecration of Bishop Kreuzer, May 8, 1935, but because of the Silver Jubilee of King George V two days before no one was found who could go. But the Bishops of Gloucester (Dr. Headlam) and Fulham (Dr. Batty) took part in the consecration of the Archbishop of Utrecht, June 15, 1937.

Mutual intercommunion has been made very much use of. On July 3, 1932, Bishop Küry celebrated according to the Old Catholic rite, in the English church at Lausanne, assisted by the English chaplain and by an Old Catholic priest, and there were seventy communicants. He also made reunion with the Anglican churches the subject of his Lenten Pastoral Letter.

On September 15 in the same year the Bishop of Deventer and eight Dutch Old Catholic priests came to England to see the English Church for themselves. They were entertained at Canterbury and Oxford, and on Sunday, September 18, they all communicated at the Sung Eucharist in St. Paul's Cathedral, as a public testimony to the establishment of reunion.

Since then an Old Catholic priest has celebrated, according to the English rite, in the English church at Haarlem, in the presence of the Bishop of Haarlem; and an Anglican priest has taken full Sunday duty, celebrating according to the Old Catholic rite, in German, and given Communion to a large number of Old Catholics, at Witten in Germany. A German Old Catholic priest has

[1] The suggestion that any Anglicans think that their ordinations require the Old Catholic succession to make them valid is, of course, absurd.

celebrated according to his own rite in several cathedrals and churches in England. These are only the most remarkable instances of many that might be mentioned.

The Archbishop of Utrecht and the Bishops in Germany and Switzerland attended the International Christian Conference on Faith and Order at Edinburgh, 1937, and on August 8, the first Sunday of the Conference, when a Solemn Eucharist was sung at St. Mary's Cathedral by the Archbishop of York, Chairman of the Conference, the three Old Catholic bishops walked in the procession with the representatives of the Eastern churches, and were the first of the congregation to receive Communion.

The Agreement of Bonn, which made all this possible, is based on three principles: Dogmatic Unity; Mutual Recognition; Independent Co-operation. The reunion of Christendom can only be based on these principles. There must be dogmatic unity—that is, agreement on all those things which anyone on either side regards as essential to the Christian religion. An union which is not unanimously accepted is useless. It is important to distinguish between dogmas which are universally necessary, and which must be proved by Scripture, and doctrines which may be true and valuable, but are not absolutely necessary. There must be mutual recognition, acceptance of one another's belief as orthodox, and sacraments as valid; and this cannot be brought about in a moment. It was only after fifty years of mutual knowledge and growing together that the Anglican and Old Catholic Communions, although they were so near one another in outlook and in practice, were able fully to recognize one another as Catholic.

There must be independent co-operation; no local church has any permanent right to domination or jurisdiction over any other church. There is no " mother and mistress of all churches ". Unity is achieved by mutual love and service, not by subjection to one centre. "" Be not ye called master, for one is your master, even the Christ " (St. Matt. 23. 10).

The Agreement of Bonn is unique in at least two ways. It is the only complete union yet achieved by the Anglican churches since the Reformation. Though but on a small scale, it ends our Anglican isolation. The ecclesiastical Straits of Dover no longer exist. The development foreshadowed in that most valuable statement of principles, the first section of the report of the Committee on the Anglican Communion to the Lambeth Conference of 1930, has already begun. The next Lambeth Conference, at any rate the greater part of it, will be in full communion, for the first time, with churches which are not Anglican.

Also the Agreement of Bonn has bridged the Reformation. The Church of Colet and More and the Church of Erasmus are once again in full communion. This is the only instance of union between a church which has passed through the Reformation and a church which has not; and it shows that the popular contrast between " reformed " and " unreformed " Churches is mistaken. Almost every part of Christendom has been reformed at some time. The real contrast is between reform which gives liberty and truth, and reform which takes them away. The greatest obstacle to reunion is the Counter-Reformation, and the spirit of autocracy and infallibility which embodied itself in the decrees of Trent. As the report quoted above says: " There are two prevailing types of ecclesiastical organization: that of centralized government and that of regional autonomy within one fellowship. . . . The Anglican Communion is constituted upon this latter principle ". So are the Old Catholic churches; so are the Eastern churches; so must every church be, with which reunion is possible.

Thus the Agreement of Bonn is a model for the wider reunion of the future. It is not directed against any other church; but it presents a method by which other churches may hereafter be united, on the three principles of Dogmatic Unity, Mutual Recognition, and Independent Co-operation, and a story of two communions, very different in their history and their outward circumstances, which have learned to love one another, and through love " to speak the same thing, and to be perfected together in the same mind and in the same judgment ".

# THE OLD CATHOLIC CHURCHES
# DURING AND AFTER HITLER'S WAR

DURING the German occupation of Holland, Austria, and Czecho-slovakia, the Old Catholic churches suffered great hardships, but maintained their position. When Rotterdam was bombed in 1940, the historic church of St. Lawrence and St. Mary Magdalene, where Bishop Reinkens had been consecrated, was completely destroyed, with the rectory; and the priest, Canon Gouard, who had also been in charge of the congregation at Paris, perished. The church and rectory of the Helder were also destroyed by the Germans. The congregations were much dispersed, and church buildings in other places much damaged, but the spiritual care of the scattered people was carefully organized. When Holland was liberated, the Anglican chaplains were given the full use of the Old Catholic churches, and the closest relations with the English Church were at once restored.

Bishop Berends died in 1940, and was succeeded by Mgr. Engelbert Lagerwey, who was consecrated by the Archbishop of Utrecht, assisted by the Bishops of Haarlem and Bonn. Bishop van Vlijmen resigned in 1945, and was succeeded by Mgr. Jacobus van der Oord.

During the war the Old Catholic Church in Holland took its full share, in co-operation with the other denominations, in resistance to the invader. The Seminary at Amersfoort was used as a rest centre where thousands who were driven from their homes stayed a night. Many Jewish children were saved, especially those with one Anglican parent, who by a sixteenth century law are regarded as Anglicans.

In Switzerland no Anglican bishop could visit the English churches during the German occupation of France. All the Anglican confirmations were taken by Bishop Küry, at the request of the Bishop of Fulham.

In Germany the Old Catholics were forbidden to have any formal relations with the Church of England, but they undertook the care of scattered Anglican communicants. At the end of the war there were still 120 Old Catholic centres in Germany. But the Allies' bombs destroyed all the Old Catholic churches in towns: not, however, those in the country.

In Czechoslovakia the Old Catholic Church continued to increase until the end of the war. But then a difficult situation arose. The majority, both of the Church as a whole and of most congregations, was German-speaking; and the government of the Republic decided to deport all the Germans. However, the bishop was a Czech, and in every congregation there were some Czechs; it was therefore decided that the congregations were of mixed nationality, and they were allowed to keep their churches and rectories. Bishop Paschek died in 1946. Nine-tenths of the Old Catholics were German-speaking, and were expelled from the country; most of them went to Germany (see p. 317). There are still 17 communities with 5,000 Czech-speaking members: no bishop has been consecrated, and the position is difficult.

In Austria there were considerable difficulties, and some buildings were destroyed. Bishop Tüchler resigned in 1942, and Dr. Stephen Török was consecrated in Vienna in 1948 by the Archbishop of Utrecht, assisted by the Bishop of Deventer, and Bishop Küry. The destroyed buildings have all been restored. At present (1961) there are 40,000 Old Catholics in 13 parishes and 27 out-stations.

In Holland the Church is growing steadily: the last census (1947) reported 13,500 members. The churches destroyed at Rotterdam and the Helder have been replaced by new ones. A new parish has been established at Alkmaar, and there are several out-stations. In 1957 the new Seminary at Amersfoort replaced the historic building. The chapel was consecrated in April by the Archbishop, in the presence of the Bishops of Haarlem and Deventer, and representatives of the Government.

In 1959 the Old Catholic Mission of St. Paul began its work of supporting the Anglican diocese of St. John's, Kaffraria, in South Africa. This important new step was the result of the great Old Catholic Congress at Rheinfelden in 1957. In the Rheinfelden district the Old Catholics are the majority of the population, and possess the old parish churches: and this congress, in which Anglicans as well as Old Catholics took part, was the most notable held for many years. In 1960 the German Old Catholics also decided to support the Mission of St. Paul.

The international Old Catholic and Anglican youth conferences have been held at Saalbach in Austria (1959), Woudschoten in Holland, and Bretaze in Switzerland. At Woudschoten there were 200 persons from 12 countries present.

In 1955 Bishop Küry of Switzerland retired, and died the next year. His son, Dr. Urs Küry, was elected to succeed him, and was consecrated at Olten by the Archbishop of Utrecht. In 1959 Bishop Lagerwey of Deventer died, and was succeeded by Professor Peter John Jans, President of the Amersfoort Seminary, who was consecrated by the Archbishop, assisted by the Bishop of Haarlem, the Bishops in Germany, Switzerland, and Poland, and the Anglican Bishop of Fulham.

It appears that though the Old Catholic churches have suffered heavy losses, they have maintained their organization intact, except in countries from which most of their members have been deported for being Germans: and there is no evidence that they have lost ground for any other reason.

## SINCE VATICAN TWO

In any survey of events in the life of the Churches of the Union of Utrecht since the last edition of this book in 1964, pride of place must be given to the progress made in relations with the Roman Catholic Church. In 1966 the Roman Catholic Bishop of Lausanne, Geneva, and Fribourg, Monsignor F. Charrierre, asked Dr. Urs Küry to begin a dialogue between their respective theologians on the results of the Second Vatican Council, and in the following year the Archbishop of Utrecht received a warm letter from the Vatican which led to the opening of theological dialogue between Roman Catholics and Old Catholics without conditions. The way for this had been paved by the growth of a close relationship between Cardinal Alfrink of Holland and Dr. Rinkel (who has since been succeeded as Archbishop of Utrecht by Monsignor Marinus Kok). This step was marked by a united service in St. Gertrudis' (Old Catholic) Cathedral in Utrecht, which was filled to capacity by a congregation representing both Churches. The letter from the Vatican was read out during the service and both archbishops jointly gave the blessing at the end. It was a most moving occasion and spontaneous clapping broke out as they left the cathedral. In October of that year the Roman Catholic Bishop of Haarlem was present at the consecration of Bishop van Kleef.

The first positive result of the dialogue which ensued was the *Züricher Nota* of 1969 which authorized restricted communion on pastoral grounds for Roman Catholics and Old Catholics in Holland, Germany, and Switzerland. It was intended to extend this to Austria when the new Old Catholic bishop had been consecrated. It was, of course, the first real move towards intercommunion at the official level. Meanwhile the dialogue continues. In Rotterdam both Roman and Old Catholics share the Old Catholic church of SS. Peter and Paul, and are present at the same Mass each Sunday. Their clergy share the same house. The decision to share in this way was brought about by economic reasons but is proving an interesting experiment in ecumenical relations at parish level. At Easter 1975 Pope Paul VI sent personal greetings to the Old Catholic Church of Utrecht through Monsignor Kok, with a special medallion struck for Holy Year.

As we have learnt from chapter XXVII, there have been several attempts at bringing about reunion with the Orthodox Church. After many years of preparation the first official Pan-Orthodox and Old Catholic Dialogue Commission met at Penteli near Athens in July 1973 and this was followed by a second at Chambésy near Geneva in August 1975, the subjects under discussion being the Trinity, tradition and its transmission, the canon of scripture, and certain aspects of Christology. It was planned that the next full session of the Commission should take place in 1977. Contacts with the Orthodox at a more local level also take place from time to time.

In 1965 the Union of Utrecht entered into communion with the Spanish Reformed Episcopal Church, the Lusitanian Church of Portugal, and the Independent Church of the Philippines. Ten years later, in July 1975, at the International Bishops' Conference, the Union of Utrecht as a whole recognized the Croatian Church as the continuation of the Croatian Old Catholic Church which had belonged to the Union of Utrecht. At this same conference negotiations with the Old Catholic Church of the Mariavites in Poland with regard to admission to the Union were discussed further. Some years earlier, Pastoor (now Bishop) van Kleef had spent a fortnight in Poland with the object of clarifying and improving relations between the Mariavites and Utrecht.

At an unofficial level, contacts with the high church movement in the Danish Lutheran Church have been made by the Old Catholic parish priest of Nordstrand in Germany and an annual gathering of clergy is held at Corpus Christi-tide.

The Old Catholic Churches have not been slow in moving into a post-Vatican II era, as a glance at the agendas of the International Bishops' Conferences and Old Catholic Congresses will reveal. Both these events have been held at regular intervals, the last Congress being at Lucerne in September 1974 when the theme was "Life". Some 700 delegates attended, members of both the Anglican and Orthodox Communions also being invited. Life was considered in all its aspects, personal and social, political and economic, scientific and theological, clearly indicating that Old Catholics are concerned with the business of being a Christian in the 1970s. A distinctive contribution was made by young people at this conference and on one evening they conducted an act of worship for delegates.

The liturgical movement has made quite an impact in most Churches of the Union of Utrecht, and new and alternative liturgies have been produced and authorized. On the whole, though, the presentation of the liturgy tends to be rather more conservative than that of the Roman Catholic Church on the continent.

It is a matter of some regret that since the 1960s it has not been possible to organize International Youth Conferences for Old Catholics and Anglicans, largely owing to the changes that have taken place in young people's holiday patterns. Several of these, arranged by both sections of the Society of St. Willibrord, have been held since the one at Saalbach in 1959, viz. at Bretaye in the Swiss mountains (1960), at Bacharach in Germany (1963), at Canterbury (1966), and at St. Pölten in Austria (1969). At Canterbury the theme was: "The Church Looks Forward" and the Conference was visited by Archbishop Ramsey, as he then was. The title of the St. Pölten gathering was: "Old Church in a New Age" and it was held in the fine modern retreat and conference house of the Roman Catholic diocese, where the Rector was extremely welcoming. There was a particularly large contingent from Great Britain and the papers were of an exceptionally high standard, dealing amongst other things with what has come to be called "The New Reformation", and discussing questions such as "Is belief possible?" This was probably the best conference since Woudschoten in 1957.

The Old Catholic Churches have continued to give their support to the Mission of St. Paul in the Transkei. The German Old Catholic Church has taken on All Saints' Hospital as its particular project and now works independently of the Mission. Considerable help has been given to the Grahamstown Area Distress Relief Association, enabling 8,000 children to be fed every school day in the year. Assistance continues also to the Anglican Franciscans in their work at Fiwila, Zambia, and in particular they have been helped with transport and educational materials.

At least two of the Old Catholic Churches have societies concerned with both prayer and action. In Switzerland there is the Brotherhood of St. John the Baptist and in Holland the Brotherhood of St. Willibrord, whose members have a rule of life and organize retreats from time to time. The rule of the Dutch Brotherhood extends to undertaking a project of social concern within or outside the Church, and its motto is "*Ora et Labora*".

During the years under review, regular meetings of the Anglican-Old Catholic Theological Committee have taken place at Oxford, Trier, Berne, Lucerne, and Chichester. At Lucerne, where the theme was "On the Way to Unity of Churches", the Committee looked afresh at such topics as catholicity and apostolicity as they appear in the Bonn Agreement of 1931. Old Catholics were concerned about their relations with Anglicans since the South India Scheme and also since the ordination of three women to the priesthood in the diocese of Hong Kong. The subject of the ordination of women was the main topic discussed at the most recent conference held at Chichester in April 1977. This had now become a matter of urgency owing to the action of both the Episcopal Church of the United States and the Anglican Church in Canada in ordaining several women to the priesthood. As a result, the National Polish Catholic Church in America had terminated sacramental intercommunion with the Episcopalians. At the end of 1976 the International Bishops' Conference had issued the following declaration:

The International Old-Catholic Bishops Conference of the Union of Utrecht in accordance with the ancient undivided Church does not agree with a sacramental ordination of women to the catholic-apostolic ministry of deacon, presbyter and bishop.

The Lord of the Church, Jesus Christ, through the Holy Spirit called twelve men to be his Apostles, in order to perpetuate his work of the salvation of mankind.

The catholic churches of the East and West have called men only to the sacramental apostolic ministry.

The question of ordination of women touches the basic order and mystery of the Church.

The churches which have preserved continuity with the ancient undivided Church and its sacramental ministerial order should jointly discuss this question of sacramental ordination of women, being fully aware of eventual consequences resulting from unilateral decisions.

This has been accepted by all bishops of the Conference with one exception and is considered to be the only official view of the I.B.C. The statement issued by delegates at the end of their Chichester meeting revealed that although the majority of bishops are strongly opposed to the ordination of women, there is a sizeable body of opinion within the other orders of the Church which is not. Nevertheless, the statement did say: "the recent events in the United States and Canada show that such independent action may provoke reaction leading to a suspension of communion on the part of individual Churches, and this could cause a wider disruption of our relationships and hinder further progress towards Christian unity."

Relations between Anglicans and Old Catholics at a parish level continue to be promoted by the Society of St. Willibrord. Holiday exchanges have continued and tend to be more popular nowadays with older people than with the younger generation. The Society's Anglican section is aware that it still has much to do in educating lay people about the Old Catholic Churches and the Bonn Agreement. Since Vatican II and the vast changes that have taken place on the ecumenical front, it realizes that it has new work to do also.

As with most Churches in the West, the Old Catholics have suffered a reduction in the number of men coming forward for ordination. For theological and ecumenical reasons, training for the priesthood in Holland is now done at the State University of Utrecht, students attending lectures at the Reformed Faculty, the Roman Catholic Theological University, and given by their own professors. Previously this training was given in the seminary at Amersfoort. In 1975 the Old Catholic Theological Faculty in Berne celebrated its centenary and during its celebrations made

Dr. Johannes Karmiris of Athens University an honorary doctor for his efforts to improve ecumenical relations between the Orthodox and Old Catholic Churches.

In the field of medico-moral problems, so much exercising Christians today, Archbishop Kok has himself made a statement about abortion. He rejects abortion in all cases except those in which pregnancy could prove fatal for mother or child or both. Even if abortion becomes legal in Holland, he has reminded members of his Church that Christians are personally responsible to God for the protection of human life. At an important conference on pastoral matters in 1975, the German Old Catholic Church discussed the vexed question of the re-marriage of divorcees, and it was suggested that a marriage law centre be established to help with such matters.

No Church has been left untouched by the turmoil of the last one and a half decades or so, and the Old Catholic Churches have probably weathered the storm as well as any other. Since Great Britain entered the European Economic Community contacts between Anglicans and Old Catholics ought to be closer than ever, and in some places Anglican chaplains on the continent work very closely with their Old Catholic neighbours. Language is still the big barrier. Preaching at a recent festival of the Society of St. Willibrord in London, the Bishop of Fulham and Gibraltar, the Rt. Rev. John Satterthwaite, had this to say: "It is obvious that our respective Churches need to find afresh the essentials of catholicism—we need to see what is necessary for the *wholeness* of the Church in the twentieth century. Together we have much to learn, and much to give. The signposts of a full catholicism to which we looked 30–40 years ago have been swept aside. But our pilgrimage has not ended. New signposts will appear, as the way gets rough and the going difficult."

The Rev. Michael J. Woodgate,
Secretary of the Society of St.
Willibrord.

APPENDIX D:—SUCCESSION OF OLD CATHOLIC BISHOPS

*Archbishops of Utrecht*[1]

1. Frederick Schenck . . . . . 1559–1580
2. Sasbold Vosmeer . . . . . 1602–1614
3. Philip Rovenius . . . . . 1620–1651
4. Jacobus de la Torre . . . . . 1651–1661
5. Johannes van Neercassel . . . . 1661–1686
6. Petrus Codde . . . . . . 1688–1710
7. Cornelius van Steenoven . . . . 1724–1725
8. Cornelius Johannes Barchman Wuytiers . 1725–1733
9. Theodorus van der Croon . . . . 1734–1739
10. Petrus Johannes Meindaerts . . . 1739–1767
11. Walter van Nieuwenhuisen . . . . 1768–1797
12. Johannes Jacobus van Rhijn . . . 1797–1808
13. Willibrord van Os . . . . . 1814–1825
14. Johannes van Santen . . . . . 1825–1858
15. Henricus Loos . . . . . . 1858–1873
16. Johannes Heykamp . . . . . 1875–1892
17. Gerardus Gul . . . . . . 1892–1920
18. Franciscus Kenninck . . . . . 1920–1937
19. Andreas Rinkel . . . . . . 1937–1970
20. Marinus Kok . . . . . . 1970–

*Bishops of Haarlem*

1. Nicolas van Nieuwland . . . . 1560–1569
2. Godfrey van Mierlo . . . . . 1569–1578
3. Hieronymus de Bock . . . . . 1742–1744
4. Johannes van Stiphout . . . . 1745–1777
5. Adrianus Johannes Broekman . . . 1778–1800
6. Johannes Nieuwenhuis . . . . 1801–1810
7. Johannes Bon . . . . . . 1819–1841
8. Henricus Johannes van Buul . . . 1843–1862
9. Lambertus de Jong . . . . . 1865–1867
10. Gaspardus Johannes Rinkel . . . 1873–1906
11. Johannes Jacobus van Thiel . . . 1906–1912
12. Nicolas Prins . . . . . . 1912–1916
13. Henricus Johannes Theodorus van Vlijmen . 1916–1945

[1] There were sixty Bishops of Utrecht before Frederick Schenck, the first Archbishop.

*Bishops of Haarlem*—contd.

14. Jacobus van der Oord . . . . 1945–1967
15. Gerhardus van Kleef . . . . 1967–

*Bishops of Deventer*

1. Johannes Mahusius . . . . . 1560–1570
2. Egidius van den Berge (de Monte) . . 1570–1577
3. Bartholomaeus Johannes Byeveld . . 1758–1778
4. Nicolas Nellemans . . . . . 1778–1805
5. Gisbertus de Jong . . . . . 1805–1824
6. William Vet . . . . . . 1825–1853
7. Hermannus Heykamp . . . . 1853–1874
8. Cornelius Diependaal . . . . 1875–1893
9. Nicolas Bartholomaeus Petrus Spit . . 1894–1929
10. Johannes Hermannus Berends . . . 1929–1940
11. Engelbert Lagerwey . . . . . 1940–1959
12. Petrus Josephus Jans . . . . 1959–

*Bishops in Germany (Bonn)*

1. Josef Hubert Reinkens . . . . 1873–1896
2. Theodor Weber . . . . . 1896–1906
3. Josef Demmel . . . . . . 1906–1913
4. Georg Moog . . . . . . 1913–1934
5. Erwin Kreuzer . . . . . . 1935–1953
6. Johan Josef Demmel . . . . . 1953–1966
7. Josef Brinkhues . . . . . 1966–
   Otto Steinwachs Suffragan. . . . 1947–

*Bishops in Switzerland (Berne)*

1. Edward Herzog . . . . . . 1876–1924
2. Adolf Küry . . . . . . 1924–1955
3. Urs Küry . . . . . . 1955–1972
4. Léon Gauthier . . . . . . 1972–

*Bishops in Czechoslovakia (Warnsdorf)*

Amandus Czech, Administrator, never consecrated
1. Alois Paschek . . . . . . 1924–1946
2. Augustin Podolak . . . . . 1968–

### Bishops in Austria (*Vienna*)

1. Adalbert Schindelaar . . . . 1925-1926
2. Robert Tüchler . . . . . 1928-1942
3. Stefan Török . . . . . 1948-1972
4. Nicholas Hummel . . . . . 1975-

### Bishops in Yugoslavia (*Zagreb*)

1. Marko Kalogjera . . . . . 1924-1933
2. Vladimir Kos . . . . Died 1959
3. Vilim Huzjak . . . . . 1961-1974
No successor yet appointed

(see Chapter 25)

### Bishops of the Polish National Catholic Church in America

1. Stanislas Kozlowski (Chicago) . . . 1897-1907
2. Francis Hodur (Scranton, Pa.) . . . 1907-1953
also
Vladimir Gawrychowski (Chicopee, Mass.) . 1921-1934
Francis Bonczak (Poland) . . . . 1921
Leon Grochowski (Scranton) . . . 1921
J. Grittenas (Scranton) . . . . 1921-1928
John Zenon Jasinski (Buffalo) . . . 1928-1951
Walter Martin Faron . . . . . 1930
John Misiaszck (Suffragan at Scranton) . . 1936
Joseph Padewski (Cracow, Poland) . . 1936-1951
Joseph Lesniak . . . . . . 1937
Joseph Soltysiak (Manchester, N.H.) . . 1952
Thaddeüs F. Zielinski (Buffalo) . . . 1954
Joseph Kardas (Chicago) . . . . 1954
Francis Carl Rowinski (Chicago) . . . 1957
Maximilian Rode (Poland) . . . . 1959
Joachim Pekala (Suffragan, Poland) . . 1961
E. W. Magyar (Slovak-speaking churches in
U.S.A.) . . . . . . 1963

SUCCESSION OF THE OLD CATHOLIC BISHOPS

Dominique Marie Varlet . (Babylon)
|
Petrus Johannes Meindaerts . (Utrecht)
|
Johannes van Stiphout . . (Haarlem)
|
Walter van Nieuwenhuisen . (Utrecht)
|
Adrian Broekman . . (Haarlem)
|
Johannes Jacobus van Rhijn . (Utrecht)
|
Gisbert de Jong . . . (Deventer)
|
Willibrord van Os . . (Utrecht)
|
Johannes Bon . . . (Haarlem)
|
Johannes van Santen . . (Utrecht)
|
Herman Heykamp . . (Deventer)
|
Gaspard Johannes Rinkel . (Haarlem)
|
Gerardus Gul . . . (Utrecht)
|
Henricus Johannes Theodorus van Vlijmen (Haarlem)
|         |
|    Francis Hodur . (U.S.A.)
|
Franciscus Kenninck . . (Utrecht)
|
Alois Paschek . . (Czechoslovakia)
|       |
|   Adolf Küry (Switzerland)
|       |
|     J. H. Berends (Deventer)
|       |
Robert Tüchler (Austria)  Andreas Rinkel (Utrecht)
|       |
Erwin Kreuzer (Germany)  |

Tüchler (Austria)  Demmel (Germany)  Urs Küry (Switzerland)

Lagerwey (Deventer)  Van Der Oord (Haarlem)  Jans (Deventer)

APPENDIX E:—INTERNATIONAL OLD CATHOLIC CONGRESSES

| | | |
|---|---|---|
| 1. Cologne | . . . | 1890 |
| 2. Lucerne | . . . | 1892 |
| 3. Rotterdam | . . | 1894 |
| 4. Vienna | . . | 1897 |
| 5. Bonn | . . . | 1902 |
| 6. Olten | . . . | 1904 |
| 7. The Hague | . . | 1907 |
| 8. Vienna | . . . | 1909 |
| 9. Cologne | . . . | 1913 |
| 10. Berne | . . . | 1925 |
| 11. Utrecht | . . . | 1928 |
| 12. Vienna | . . . | 1931 |
| 13. Constance | . . . | 1934 |
| 14. Zürich | . . . | 1938 |
| 15. Hilversum | . . . | 1948 |
| 16. Munich | . . . | 1953 |
| 17. Rheinfelden | . . | 1957 |
| 18. Haarlem | . . . | 1961 |
| 19. Vienna | . . . | 1965 |
| 20. Bonn | . . . | 1970 |
| 21. Lucerne | . . . | 1974 |

In 1959 the Old Catholic International Information Service was established.

# INDEX

ACTON, LORD, 191*n.*, 194, 216; never accepted Vatican dogmas, 224
Aglipay, Gregory, pseudo-bishop, 286
Alfonso Liguori, 115, 176
Amersfoort, Seminary at, 129, 353
*Amor Poenitens*, 103
Angélique, Mère, *see* Arnauld.
Anglican Bishops at Old Catholic Consecration, 348–349
Anglicanism, 1, 330–351; Jansenism and, 87–89
Anglican succession, recognized, 339
Arnauld family, 35–50, 103
Auctorem Fidei, Bull, 147–149, 281
Audu, Chaldean Patriarch, rebuked by Pius IX, 201, 225
Augustine, St., 33, 36, 39; on original guilt, 173, 180
*Augustinus*, by Jansen, 34, 36, 101; van Santen on, 164–165
Austria, Old Catholics in, 280, 285, 294–296, 312–313, 319, 353

Barber, Rev. G. E., 154, 338–339
Barchman Wuytiers, Cornelius John, Archbishop of Utrecht, 125–130
Barrow, Isaac, 78
Basle, Council of, 19–20; Bishop of, 245–250
*Batavia Sacra*, 106
Beauvoir, William, Anglican chaplain, 70
Bekkens, André Henri, Abbé, 284
Bellarmine, Cardinal, on papal infallibility, 191–192
Berends, J. H., Bishop of Deventer, 340–341, 347, 349, 352
Bernard, St., 146*n.*, 174
Berruyer, errors of, 134
Birgitta, St., 176
Bock, Jerome de, Bishop of Haarlem, 132
Bon, John, Bishop of Haarlem, 156, 162, 166
Boniface, St., 90–91; feast of, 101, 237
Bonn, Reunion Conferences at (1874–5), 259–270; (1931), 342–348; See of, 276, 289
Bossuet, Jacques Benigne, Bishop of Meaux, 54, 57, 287
Breviary, Roman, introduced into France, 170; Old Catholic, 325
British Embassy Church, Paris, 284
Brothers of the Common Life, 92
Browne, Harold, Bishop of Winchester, 234, 261, 332
Butler, Dom Cuthbert, 190–205, 215–225, 229; mistakes of, 242, 279
Byeveld, Bartholomew John, Bishop of Deventer, 133, 139

Byevelt, John, vicar-apostolic, banished from Holland, 118

Cabrera, Juan, Bishop in Spain, 285, 286
Campello, Count Enrico de, Italian Old Catholic leader, 284
Capaccini, papal nuncio, and Archbishop van Santen, 163–166
*Case of Conscience*, 61
Catherine of Siena, St., 14, 176
Catz, Baldwin, vicar-apostolic, 102
Catz, Jacob, vicar-general, 111–112, 116
Celibacy, clerical, abolished, 255, 257, 274–276, 295
Chrysostom, St. John, 67, 173
Clement IX, Pope, and "Peace of the Church", 50
Clement XI, Pope, and Bull "Vineam Domini Sabaoth", 62; suppresses Port Royal, 63, and Bull "Unigenitus", 65; and Archbishop Codde, 107; death of, 121
Cock, Theodore de, pro-vicar-apostolic, 106–108
Codde, Peter, Archbishop of Utrecht, 105–113
Coffin, Charles, hymn-writer, 78
Cologne, Old Catholic Congresses at, 238, 339; Archbishop of, 150
Conry, Florence, titular Archbishop of Tuam, 87
Constance, Council of, 17–19; Wessenberg at, 158–160; congress at, 257, 316
"Constitutional Bishops", 153
Conti, Armand, Prince de, conversion of, 58
Contrition, necessity of, 37, 103
Cornet, Nicolas, and the Five Propositions, 44
Councils, General, 14–22; infallibility of, 27, 215–217
Cremation in Austria, 296
Croon, Theodore van der, Archbishop of Utrecht, 131
Czech Amandus, Administrator in Austria, 280, 285, 295, 312
Czechoslovakia, 296, 312, 318, 352–353

Daemen, Adam, vicar-apostolic, 112–113
Damen, Hermann, on the consecration of Steenoven, 127–128
Darboy, Georges, Archbishop of Paris, 194, 199, 215, 233
Denmark, 261, 266
Deventer, Bishopric of, 93–95; revived, 133

365

CPSIA information can be obtained at www.ICGtesting.com
Printed in the USA
BVOW04s1848150816

459109BV00001B/16/P